# Landscape in Sight

# Landscape in Sight

## Looking at America

**John Brinckerhoff Jackson**

Edited by Helen Lefkowitz Horowitz

**Yale University Press**   **New Haven and London**

Published with assistance from the Charles A. Coffin Fund.

Permissions for use of texts appear on page 370.

Designed by Rebecca Gibb. Set in types by Adobe Garamond and Nobel by The Marathon Group, Inc., Durham, North Carolina. Printed in the United States of America by

*Library of Congress Cataloging-in-Publication Data*
Jackson, John Brinckerhoff, 1909–1996
Landscape in sight : looking at America / John Brinckerhoff Jackson ;
edited by Helen Lefkowitz Horowitz.
p. cm.
Includes bibliographical references and index.
ISBN 0-300-07116-7 (alk. paper)
1. Landscape assessment—United States. 2. Human geography—United States. 3. Architecture—United States. 4. United States—Description and travel. I. Horowitz, Helen Lefkowitz. II. Title.
GF91.U6J317 1997
304.2—DC21
96-48728 CIP

A catalogue record for this book is available from the British Library. The paper in this book meets the guidelines for permanence and durability of the Committee on Production Guidelines for Book Longevity of the Council on Library Resources.

10   9   8   7   6   5

# Contents

# J. B. Jackson and the Discovery
# of the American Landscape

Helen Lefkowitz Horowitz

When I found the writings of J. B. Jackson a quarter-century ago, it was an answer to a deeply felt need. As a novice historian with an amateur's interest in architecture, I was exploring areas close to home, armed with the new architectural guides to neighborhoods. I had become aware that the surrounding world was not simply a given but was a historically created artifact. Yet I had no way to read it. The guides at hand were too technical, too focused on decorative motifs and facades. I wanted to understand how people lived in the houses and prayed in the churches, how they imagined and used the spaces they had made.

My husband, Daniel Horowitz, and I saw an advertisement for a new book—*American Space: The Centennial Years* by John Brinckerhoff Jackson. Sight unseen, we agreed to review it for a historical journal. The book was delightful, and, with all the presumption of youth, we assumed that such fresh prose and engaging ideas came from a young man at the outset of his career. Just to check, however, we looked up the author in the card catalogue of the Library of Congress. To our surprise, we learned that from 1951 to 1968 he had edited and published *Landscape,* a magazine with which we were unfamiliar, and that he was then teaching at Harvard and at the University of California at Berkeley.

I began to read *Landscape,* starting with its first issue, and it was a revelation. Here was everything about which I wanted to know—houses, fields, roads, front yards, garages—all vividly described and interpreted. Jackson wrote many of the magazine's most important articles. His essays link the common everyday elements of the landscape to broad themes of history and culture. He establishes that the way we build our cities and countryside reveals our society and culture. Implicitly, he states what he later explicitly proclaimed: "Landscape is history made visible."[1] He demonstrates how landscape makes manifest our strivings, how the basic human motive for creating landscape, especially the domestic landscape, is "the recreation of heaven on earth."[2] As I sat in the stacks of the Library of Congress pulling down the volumes, this way of seeing the physical world converged with my own thinking. At one level, my desire to see this anthology come into being began at that moment.

There have been, of course, other collections of J. B. Jackson's work. Since 1970, seven books—edited either by him or by others—have offered selections of his writing. Each of these books has opened to a widening public Jackson's insights and images. *Landscape in Sight,* however, attempts something that the others did not: it offers in a single volume Jackson's most highly regarded writing on the American landscape. It ranges from the first issue of *Landscape* in 1951 to his last book, *A Sense of Place, a Sense of Time,* which won the 1995 PEN prize for essays, and includes a new piece written for this anthology shortly before his death in August 1996.

J. B. Jackson was an artist as well as a writer. His sketches and photographs of the American scene illustrate this anthology. Although the first essay on the American landscape comes from mid-century, the sketches provide a record of his imaginative recreation of landscapes that reaches back to his days as a Harvard undergraduate in the early 1930s.[3] Drawing continued to be an important part of Jackson's creative life. The sketches and photographs give us another way to experience and learn from the power of his eye.

In 1951, when Jackson began to publish his writings and drawings in *Landscape,* he brought talents that had been carefully nurtured in his youth and broadened in the 1930s and 1940s by travel, drawing, and writing in Europe, ranching in New Mexico, and military service in World War II. He was born in 1909 in Dinard, France, of American parents.[4] The household settled for a time outside of Washington, D.C., but returned to Europe when he was four. It was in Switzerland in these early years that Jackson gained his first clear sense of a landscape. Several years ago he recalled its meadows bordered by mountains and forests. He particularly delighted in the openness of the Swiss meadow and lawn, with flowers that a child could pick. This remembered view remained for him a vision of a civilized world.[5]

Jackson's formal education gave him a fine classical training. After an interlude in America during World War I, during which he attended public school in a Washington suburb, he went in 1921 to an international boarding school in Switzerland. There he learned French and German. A third year of exposure to French in a school in Paris nourished his deep attachment to French culture and the French point of view. He later reflected that it was his skill at a young age in speaking French that shaped the distinction he ultimately would make between the cultures of the establishment and the vernacular world. Through this youthful experience in France, he had developed an awareness of two quite different languages.

At age eleven he discovered the works of Charles Dickens. "Whoever admires Dickens will eventually develop a deep sympathy for vernacular culture," he wrote later.[6] *Eventually* is a key word: his childhood years as student and tourist instilled in Jackson a deep knowledge of and admiration for European high culture.[7]

Jackson returned to the United States and continued his education in several New England preparatory schools. He spent summers on the New Mexico ranch of an uncle and learned to ride. Although he came to enjoy the New Mexico landscape and Spanish culture, his first reaction was characteristic of his eastern and European upbringing. He disliked what he saw, finding the southwestern earth too dry. He missed green lawns.

In the fall of 1928, encouraged by his headmaster to make an unconventional college choice because of his artistic abilities, Jackson enrolled in the Experimental College of the University of Wisconsin in Madison. Except for the New Mexico summers, it was his first trip west of Albany. The brainchild of Alexander Meiklejohn, the former president of Amherst College, the Experimental College was in its second year. Students resided in a common dormitory, ate in a common dining room, and took all their classes together on a common theme, what Jackson recalled as a broad and stimulating survey of art, literature, and society. In his freshman year they studied Athens in the fifth century B.C.

The year at Wisconsin was a momentous one intellectually, but less because of the formal curriculum than because of Jackson's exposure to two contemporary social critics. Lewis Mumford's writings on American architecture and planning were eagerly read by the students. And during Jackson's freshman year the first volume of Oswald Spengler's *Decline of the West* was published to great acclaim in the United States. "I got a copy of it and it transformed me," he said. "It is a fascinating, obsessive book." Spengler argued that civilizations rose and fell by biological rules, going through the seasons of the year. The West, which Spengler defined as a restless, Faustian civilization propelled toward a goal, had its springtime in the Gothic, its high summer from the Renaissance to the eighteenth century, and began its autumn with the Romantics. Spengler urged his contemporaries to forget about current art and music and look at engineering and technology to understand the present.

Spengler's ideas appealed to Jackson on many levels. He recalled the message the philosopher delivered at the end of the book: "He who knows what his fate is will accept it. He who doesn't know will be dragged by his fate." Jackson felt the power of Spengler's vision of the twentieth century and compared it to the Fritz Lang film *Metropolis:* the city with its purring machinery sucking the countryside dry, technology robbing people of jobs, and a powerful engineering elite controlling the subject masses.

What entranced the young Jackson, however, was the way Spengler put together elements of a culture. He recalled that he had been delighted by the way Spengler used similes and made comparisons. He remembered how Spengler had stressed that the appeal of the Greek statue came from its corporeality, its nakedness, and led the reader to make an analogy between it and the Greek column. He recollected Spengler's definition of the Faustian spirit of Western culture and its demonstration in the ferocity of Gothic architecture, music, and mysticism. In addition to Spengler's images, it was the linkages he made among different aspects of the culture—poetry, art, architecture, religion, and music—that Jackson found compelling.

In the summer of 1929, Jackson went back to Europe in search of Gothic cathedrals and Baroque churches. Spengler had given him a new way to see the world. Though Jackson made it clear that as a youth he was still focused on the traditional tourist pursuits of high culture, Spengler opened his eyes to the landscape. *The Decline of the West* gave him a fresh concept of landscape as a key to interpreting cultural history. One of Spengler's chapters was on landscape; it treated the "range of the environment . . . mostly, of course, rural . . . saying how landscapes reflected the culture of the people that were living there. . . . That's what I've been talking about for thirty years, but in that time . . . what a revelation!"

When he returned from abroad at the end of the summer, Jackson transferred to Harvard, where he enjoyed his three years thoroughly. He lived in

JBJ, sketch, Dunster House, Harvard University, 1931

Eliot House in the early years of the house system under President A. Lawrence Lowell. He majored in history and literature, concentrating on America in the first half of the nineteenth century. His tutor was F. O. Matthiessen, who was then an assistant professor of English. Jackson also studied German, French, and English. He wrote for the *Harvard Advocate,* the undergraduate literary magazine, and served on its editorial board.[8]

In the light of his later interests, Jackson remembers distinctly "Principles of Geography," the two half-courses taught by Derwent Whittlesey: "The Geography of Manufacturing and Transportation" and "The Geography of Agriculture and Extractive Industries." Whittlesey was a broad-gauged and well-published scholar. A man who held no higher degrees, he was writing on human geography during Jackson's years at Harvard. Jackson took the courses to fulfill a requirement. He recalls Whittlesey as "a very attractive man" who "gave very entertaining lectures. The subject was fascinating, and I was delighted with it. It did not occur to me to go into it any further, but I did like it."[9] Whittlesey, "full of wit and fascinating insights," had a way "of drawing conclusions from obscure and unimportant facts" that his pupil enjoyed.[10] Whittlesey's lectures may have helped shape Jackson's distinctive style.

An important influence on Jackson at Harvard was Irving Babbitt, a leading conservative literary critic whose course on Rousseau he took. The class read Rousseau's *Confessions* in French, and Babbitt read passages aloud. Jackson recalled that as an undergraduate he idolized Babbitt. In listening to Babbitt's lectures, what particularly delighted the student was the way the teacher lambasted Rousseau's romanticism by pointing out its individualism, selfishness, and lack of discipline. Babbitt's words resonated with him.

One of Jackson's contributions to the *Harvard Advocate,* "Our Architects Discover Rousseau," published in May 1931, clearly states an aesthetic that is echoed in his later reaction to the American scene. Jackson faulted architectural critics of the day for lauding the modern movement as the natural expression of the machine. His objections took several forms. He joined those who opposed modernism as a celebration of twentieth-century business culture, perceiving it as ruthless, selfish, and no proper guide to taste. More important, he linked this justification of modernism to the spirit of Rousseau as being one with the romantic insistence on nakedness. "Perhaps we are too remote from Nature," Jackson wrote, "but it is hard to understand what is so vile about pretense as long as it represents a sincere effort to be better, and even harder to understand what is so edifying about nakedness."

While proponents of modernism rejected style and history, the young Jackson had a firm appreciation of the Baroque. "Baroque was a magnificent style because it typified a magnificent age." It was to him the "last vital style which fulfilled its function of interpreting an age," a style that depended "on man for its growth, and not material or method." The Baroque era was a time "when man allowed no factors of environment or primitive peculiarities to deter him from becoming what he considered cultured."

In 1931, high culture was what Jackson valued. "Our attempts to glorify our prosaic edifices may not always be happy, but anything is better than revealing their true nature. Such frankness means that a home is an animal's den, that a railroad station is the assembly place for dirty engines and hurried people, that a dinner is stuffing food into the mouth; whereas it has been the constant endeavor of humanity to dignify itself by dignifying its functions and habitats, making a home the image of the owner's taste, a station a public monument, a dinner a ceremony."[11] Throughout his life, Jackson revered the Baroque; his awareness of culture and aspiration as the critical link between humankind and nature was the foundation of his understanding of the American landscape.

After graduation from Harvard in 1932, Jackson entered the School of Architecture at the Massachusetts Institute of Technology. Located at the time in an old building on Boylston Street in Boston, it was a small program of about ten students. He withdrew at the end of the academic year. Next he tried writing as a reporter for the *New Bedford Mercury,* a daily paper. After six months he left and went to Europe, enrolling in a commercial drawing school in Vienna. Older than most of the students and less focused on vocation, he nonetheless respected the serious atmosphere of the school and the technical

JBJ, sketch, Austrian dwelling, 1934 (courtesy F. Douglas Adams)

precision that it fostered. Austrian politics, however, soon came to dominate his interests. Hitler had risen to power in Germany and nazism was spreading throughout central Europe. Jackson recalled that many art students in their late teens and early twenties were drawn to the movement.

He quit art school, bought a motorcycle, and set out to explore the Baroque architecture of central Europe. It was a time of personal freedom. He traveled to Munich and later to a small town on the Austrian frontier. It was probably during this period that he went to Liechtenstein and observed at close hand the rise of fascism. Then he returned to Vienna.

His *Wanderjahr* stretched into two, from 1934 to 1935. Although Jackson himself did not say so, the published record suggests that in these years in Europe he was, at some level, thinking of himself as a writer and reporter. As eastern Europe tilted toward national socialism, he was listening, observing, interviewing, and writing. Under the name Brinckerhoff Jackson, he published "Prussianism or Hitlerism" in the *American Review* in 1934, largely inspired by Spengler. He also published a work of fiction: "A Führer Comes to Liechtenstein," which appeared in *Harper's Magazine* in 1935, describes how nazism invaded a small rural community. Later he expanded on the theme in *Saints in Summertime,* a novel of ideas published by Norton in 1938. These works represent intelligent efforts to understand, but not condone, political currents in eastern Europe.[12] The fictional pieces allow the reader to feel the attraction that belonging to a paramilitary group held for young men. Although some of Jackson's social class were drawn to fascism's energy and anti-Semitism, he seems to have completely resisted its hatreds and calls to action. *Saints in Summertime* received positive reviews—the *New York Times* called it "a remarkable piece of work, crafty, witty and original."[13] Although Jackson wrote other works of fiction, they did not find their way into print.

In 1936 Jackson returned to the United States and took a job in the president's office at Harvard serving on the Harvard Tercentenary Committee. He helped coordinate conferences held to celebrate "the significance to the people of the United States of three hundred years of academic history."[14] During this period of uncertainty about his future, his uncle advised him to study art history in graduate school at Yale, but Jackson resisted.

Jackson later characterized himself as restless and rebellious. Thinking back to the 1930s, he recollected that he did not want to work in an office or hold a white-collar job. He wanted to go west at a time when it still appeared to him to be a place where a person could start life anew. And so he left Boston for New Mexico—not to become a gentleman rancher, like his uncle, but to work as a cowboy. He found a job on a large ranch in Cimarron, in northeastern New Mexico, near the Colorado border. It was his first experience working with ordinary Americans, and he responded to it enthusiastically. He later recalled that he loved his work, the riding, and the companionship of the bunkhouse. He reflected that he responded as he did to ranch life not because he was tolerant but because he had in him a streak of commonness.

In 1940, along with other men from New Mexico, he enlisted in the army, serving initially in the First Cavalry Division based at Fort Bliss, Texas. He learned what it meant to be an ordinary soldier, not allowed to speak to an officer without permission and barred from certain bars and restaurants. Civilians mocked him as he boarded an airplane. It was a common practice for people to make gestures about the bad smell of cavalry men. Yet Jackson savored this escape from respectability when he spoke to Bob Calo in 1988 about his experiences as an enlisted man: "I was happy in the army. This is something you better not say in polite society, but I loved the army."[15]

The value of his education and his knowledge of languages became apparent to the army only after he entered the service. At Fort Bliss he took a correspondence course to enable him to become an officer. On passing it, he became a second lieutenant and was reassigned to Fort Riley, Kansas, to train enlisted men for the cavalry. The Japanese attack on Pearl Harbor and the United States' declaration of war made the cavalry obsolete and other military needs immediate. Because of his knowledge of French and German, Jackson was reassigned to Washington. Working in the Munitions Building, he read overnight dispatches from Europe and edited them for the generals who gathered each morning. From Washington he went for six months to the Military Intelligence Training Center at Camp Richie, Maryland, to prepare for service with combat troops as an intelligence officer. He studied map reading and the composition of the German army.

He was assigned to the Ninth Infantry Division during the Tunisian campaign. Traveling by way of Brazil and the coast of North Africa, Jackson arrived in Algiers in 1943. He first saw war and death in the field at El Guettar. From there he went to Oran, where he was assigned to the combat unit. Later he was wounded during the invasion of Sicily. After hospitalization, he rejoined the Ninth Division and as an assistant G-2 was stationed in England to prepare for the invasion of Normandy.

On D-Day plus two he landed on the beaches of Normandy. He moved through the Arden and saw combat as a staff officer at the Battle of the Bulge. The war correspondent Ernie Pyle wrote of him in *Brave Men:*

> Captain John Jackson was an unusual fellow with an unusual job. It fell to his lot to be the guy who went in and brought out German generals who thought maybe they would like to surrender. This happened because he spoke German. . . . Captain Jackson was a short dark man with a thin face. He wore a long trench coat with pack harness, and his helmet came down over his ears, giving him the appearance of a Russian soldier rather than an American. He spoke perfect French, but he said his German was only so-so. It was actually better in his job not to speak German too flawlessly, for then the captured officers might have thought he was a German turned American and been so contemptuous they wouldn't have talked to him.[16]

Jackson has written that when he advanced with the invading troops "across a dry and relatively empty landscape" in Tunisia and Sicily, maps were a reliable guide.[17] In the more complex landscape of Normandy, however, more than maps were needed. "It was when the division headquarters was billeted in a Norman chateau that I discovered a sizable library devoted to the bocage country—something I had never heard of before, though we were in the midst of it and having trouble getting out of it."

Jackson spent the long winter of 1944–45 in the Huertgen Forest with the Ninth Infantry Division. To understand his surroundings, he bought guidebooks, postcards, maps, and elementary-school geography texts, and through them he began to learn about the landscape. His immediate goal was military: to find out what the Germans were doing. "If the farmers raised wheat (as some of them did), would our half-tracks bog down in the naked winter fields? Were there roads in the valleys, where there was a problem of bridges, or on the hilltops, where there was a problem of visibility? And the house types had to be identified, so I thought, because I wanted to know if the barns were large enough to accommodate trucks and whether there were orchards where guns could be concealed." He interrogated German prisoners to get more information about the land. He learned to read and interpret aerial photographs.

As he awaited the collapse of the German army that did not come, he read the French cultural geographers—Pierre Deffontaines, Vidal de La Blache, and Albert Demangeon—and absorbed their understanding of human geography, of man the inhabitant shaping the land. He found, as he put it, "these [geography] books lying around, little paperbacks that cost about $1.00 or so, written by distinguished people on subjects that dealt with the landscape, whether it was man and domestic animals, man and the soil, man and the wind, man and the sea. And [they were] charmingly written . . . they were marvelous." The books were part of a Gallimard series edited by Deffontaines in the 1930s, a systematic effort to set forth the field of human geography.[18] It was a perspective to which Jackson had been introduced at Harvard by Derwent Whittlesey, but only now was he able to appreciate it fully.

Jackson also read during that winter a popular book about Frederick the Great. As an old man, Frederick had traveled in the countryside asking peasants about the prices they paid and the crops they were planting. Jackson saw Frederick collecting "intelligence of an almost Classical sort: What men did was what mattered, not what they thought or felt; what the countryside provided in the way of food and shelter was what interested him, not its beauty or its barrenness."

During the day, as Jackson saw the growing destruction, he realized that the saturation bombing preceding the advance of the Allied troops would totally transform the land. At night, as he worked on his G-2 report, he began to form "a private image of the world" ahead of him: "I was transported into an entirely different landscape—a Classical landscape of well-defined places and well-defined inhabitants, all animated by that one collective purpose."

JBJ, sketch, road with telegraph wires, 1947

The military landscape and the eighteenth-century European landscape converged. In his "mind's eye" he began to see "a place where men and environment were in harmony with one another and where an overall design was
manifest in every detail." He was recalling the lessons that Spengler had taught
him many years before.

In February 1945, the American army broke out of the Huertgen Forest
and crossed the Rhine, and the world that Jackson had imagined as he was billeted in French manor houses disintegrated. Remaining for a time in France
at the war's close, he wrote guidebooks for the use of American soldiers in
Europe.

Returning to the United States, he waited, still in uniform, in the East
for his papers. Discharged from the Army in January 1946 with the rank of
major, he bought a jeep and drove to New Mexico, a trip that he recalled
with relish. He was seeing the American countryside with fresh eyes. He
began to take notes, jotting down information on the types of trees he en-
countered and the roads on which he was traveling. As he wrote, he felt
something crystallizing in his mind: he began to link his new fascination
with the American scene to what he had learned during the war about the
French countryside.

Once again he tried his hand at ranching, leasing with a partner a ten-thousand-acre ranch in Clines Corners, about fifty-five miles east of Albuquerque. But a riding accident put an abrupt end to his work. Recovery took eighteen months and surgery in New York. During the long convalescence in New Mexico, Jackson returned to the plan that he had begun to develop at the war's close: to found a magazine of geography comparable to the French publications he admired.

The appearance in 1948 of the *Revue de géographie humaine et d'ethnologie*, edited by Deffontaines, gave additional stimulus. In his interview with Bob Calo, Jackson recalled writing to Deffontaines to ask, "If I tried to put out a magazine, could I borrow, or translate some of the things you had? And he said, 'Certainly, you can take anything you want,' which was the case."[19]

Jackson began *Landscape* in the spring of 1951. In the previous year he had published two articles in the *Southwest Review*, both suggestive of his approach. "The Spanish Pueblo Fallacy" decried the popular confusion of Pueblo Indian and Spanish-American building, two quite distinct traditions, that had led to what Jackson called "Santa Fake" architecture. "The Pueblo as a Farm" explored the Indian settlement not as a precursor of modern urbanism but as a collective agricultural settlement shaped by the economic system, technology, and religion of its inhabitants. Jackson was obviously situating himself in New Mexico.[20]

When it first appeared, *Landscape* reflected that orientation, beginning as a journal of the human geography of the Southwest and rural places. Human geography was a new concept for Americans. Toward the back of the first issue, Jackson included a statement by the French geographer Maurice le Lannou. Human geography, le Lannou wrote, is the "straightforward study, one as little systematized as possible, of the settlements of human groups on the face of the earth. We have before us a picture, constantly being retouched, that is vigorously composed of spots of light and zones of shadow, of remarkable convergences of lines of forces at certain points, of road networks sometimes loose, sometimes extremely closely knit, and testifying all of them to the heterogeneous and complex organization of the world." These settlements are "human creations," expressing "the current methods by which man-the-inhabitant organizes the world."[21]

In *Landscape*'s opening essay, "The Need of Being Versed in Country Things," Jackson introduced by example the field that le Lannou offered by definition. Perhaps moved by translating the French geographer's image, Jackson began by positing that the distances of the Southwest meant that its residents were likely to travel by air: "It is from the air that the true relationship between the natural and the human landscape is first clearly revealed. The peaks and canyons lose much of their impressiveness when seen from above. . . . What catches our eye and arouses our interest is not the sandy washes and the naked rocks, but the evidences of man." He describes fences, fields, farms, houses, and roads. The image from the airplane window "stirs us not only because of its beauty and vastness but because of its meaning." As one seeks to penetrate that meaning, one must ask about the natural setting, forces in the economy, and historical factors. What matters is less the answer than the question and the curiosity underlying it. The human geographer's eye makes the whole world fascinating. "To the naturalist the whole world of beasts and plants is worth studying. The common and familiar specimens are no less instructive than the rare. How much more rewarding is the world which we ourselves have helped to make!" The city is a part of the design, "but beyond the last street light, out where the familiar asphalt ends, a whole country waits to be discovered: villages, farmsteads and highways, half-hidden valleys of irrigated gardens, and wide landscapes reaching to the horizon. A rich and beautiful book is always open before us. We have but to learn to read it."[22]

Jackson began to read that book in "Chihuahua as We Might Have Been," the first substantive piece in *Landscape*. As Jackson looks at the border of Mexico and the United States in the southwestern desert, he sees not nature but the force of human history: in a land unified by climate, topography, and vegetation, "an abstraction, a Euclidean line drawn across the desert, has created two distinct human landscapes where there was only one before." He makes it clear that in reading the book of landscape, culture has a preeminent place. In describing Chihuahua, Jackson establishes two enduring themes of his life work: the discovery of the American landscape, and its contrast to Europe. He insists on looking—as a naturalist, with an unflinching eye—at the American scene: Indian pueblos, the grid of towns, Spanish villages, and the filling stations and tourist courts of the highway. But he sees these in relation to the classical world of European culture and design. His youth, education, and wartime service in Europe have shaped his perceptions. Understanding Europe, he can use Chihuahua as a foil for understanding the American Southwest. His love of the Baroque and his questioning of the romantic roots of much of contemporary culture enable him to perceive what is hidden to others.

In these essays, it is not only the novelty of the subject that appeals, it is also the manner in which it is written. "Ghosts at the Door," first published in 1951, begins with a descriptive evocation worthy of a novelist:

> The house stands by itself, lost somewhere in the enormous plain. Next to it is a windmill, to the rear a scattering of barns and shelters and sheds. In every direction, range and empty field reach to a horizon unbroken by a hill or the roof of another dwelling or even a tree. The wind blows incessantly; it raises a spiral of dust in the corral. The sun beats down on the house day after day. Straight as a die the road stretches out of sight between a perspective of fence and light poles. The only sound is the clangor of the windmill, the only movement the wind brushing over the grass and wheat, and the afternoon thunderheads boiling up in the western sky.

At this point the reader anticipates that the author is about to introduce his main character. Indeed he does; only instead of a person, Jackson introduces the American front yard. To his discussion of the American landscape, Jackson brings his gifts as a writer of fiction.

By the second year of publication, Jackson announced that *Landscape* had outgrown its distinctly regional focus and had a new perspective. His editorial "Human, All Too Human, Geography" redefines the subject of inquiry as "man the creator of dwellings and landscapes; the creator of his own habitat, his own microcosm." Jackson issues a call for the study of the house, not just as the naturalist's shelter or as the economic determinist's tool but as "the prime example of Man the Inhabitant's effort to recreate heaven on earth." The house serves as "the most reliable indication of man's essential identity." "The Westward-Moving House," published in the next issue, demonstrates these propositions. Jackson continued to think creatively about the house and its associated structures in essays such as "The Domestication of the Garage," originally published in 1976, and in his more recent studies of the trailer.

Jackson took on a wider field, adding articles on highways and cities to those on farms and small towns. While other commentators were proudly asserting that American grain elevators and barns were the forerunners of modernism, pure expressions of function, Jackson proclaimed them expressions of culture with deep historical roots. Twenty years after he had linked Rousseau with the modern movement, Jackson insisted on the cultural foundation of typically American forms. The lawn expresses a memory of the British pastoral landscape first imagined by landscape painters. The house is reshaped by religion and attitudes toward environment. The grid plan is a spatial representation of eighteenth-century classicism.

Having no formal training as a geographer beyond a college course, Jackson has been criticized for what others have called his intuitive method. Yet it was the very freedom from academic training that gave him the ability to see what has been invisible to others. "The Stranger's Path" conveys his approach and its power. Jackson describes what a male tourist experiences in a small American city. Arriving by bus, train, or automobile, the traveler is "welcomed to the city by a smiling landscape of parking lots, warehouses, pot-holed and weed-grown streets, where isolated filling stations and quick-lunch counters are scattered among cinders like survivals of a bombing raid." In this essay, Jackson the traveler is the Jackson who went west to be an ordinary cowhand and who entered the army as a G.I. He sees not the city of elite neighborhoods and expensive hotels but the one that reveals itself on the solitary walk from the bus depot to skid row, the financial district, and city hall. The Stranger's Path is both tawdry and vital, keeping alive the city's essential function as a place of exchange. Yet, even here, the Jackson schooled in Switzerland and summers abroad returns, enabling him to compare the path to the Rambla in Barcelona and the Cannebière in Marseilles. It is this understanding of both the ordinary and the extraordinary that underlay the questions Jackson raised about contemporary American urban planning. As Paul Groth has suggested, Jackson studied the landscape "with categories that address workplace and home, rich and poor, insider and outsider."[23]

"The Almost Perfect Town" gives us a different perspective, linked more to the world of the reader than to that of the writer. It starts with the way that many Americans experience a small town: traveling by car, reading a guidebook, seeing the blur of motels as one stops for gas. "What is there to see? Not a great deal, yet more than you would at first suspect." As Jackson describes the fictional town of Optimo—moving past its warehouses, railroad depot, factory, slum, fashionable houses on the hill, shopping street, ordinary residential area bordering on the countryside, and courthouse square—he establishes the archetypal plan of the American town and links it to its economic and political origins. Jackson's seemingly effortless description is, in fact, both an insightful reading of the evidence before the eyes that few are able to see and a vivid distillation of the work of academic geographers.

When pressed by others to define himself and what he did, Jackson often stated what he was not, emphasizing his lack of professional training or position. Once, however, after the usual disclaimers, he declared: "I *see* things very clearly, and I rely on what I see. . . . And I see things that other people don't see, and I call their attention to it."[24] Sometimes, as in "Looking at New Mexico," what he saw was provoked by photographs. Sometimes, as in "The Accessible Landscape," it was through his car window. But always, seeing was accompanied by reading, hard thought, and the discipline of words.

In its first issues, *Landscape* was largely written by Jackson, under his own name, anonymously, or using various pseudonyms, such as A. W. C., A. W. Conway, and Ajax.[25] Pseudonyms allowed him to try out many voices, and under their cover he could raise significant philosophical, religious, and aesthetic questions. Intelligent and wide-ranging book reviews, especially in the personae of H. G. West or P. G. Anson, raised provocative issues and formulated a critique of the international style.[26] The reviews suggest that in the early 1950s, as well as reading geographers and architectural critics, Jackson was immersing himself in Freud and Jung. It is possible that his reading of Jung deepened his understanding of symbol and myth in ways that interacted creatively with the earlier influence of Spengler to encourage Jackson to make the bold statements that enliven his essays.[27]

In addition to book reviews and essays, the journal contained short descriptive studies, interesting quotations from the past, and discussions of such common geographic phenomena as maps and place names. Jackson regarded as one of his most important contributions his translations of excerpts from Continental writers and summaries of their recent work. In an interview with Bob Calo, Jackson noted that a virtue of *Landscape* was that "it gave an insight into foreign writers," and "foreign ideas were introduced. . . . I did know French and German, and I could struggle along in Italian and Spanish . . . just a few little articles from those things would open up a European scene."[28]

Jackson created a "Notes and Comments" section for his editorials on the American landscape. From the outset it was clear that he had a point of view at odds with many of his contemporaries. Jackson's mistrust of the philosophical roots and central premises of liberalism often led him to question contemporary wisdom and social and environmental planning.[29] He was open to change. His delight in older cities abroad made him see texture where others saw disorder. In a Southwest enshrouded by the myths of tourism, he insisted that his neighbors, especially the neglected Spanish Americans, were real. He questioned matters as simple as grocery-store layout. He doubted whether the results of experiments on animals could be applied to human beings. He appreciated the automobile's freedom of movement and the experience of speed offered by the motorcycle. He did not, however, shield his eyes from potholes in the streets. Many of his judgments were laced with individualism; some suggested an anarchism not far below the surface.

Although Jackson could take the moral highroad, he was also given to wit and whimsy. In *Landscape* he signed his most irreverent pieces with the pseudonym "Ajax." Two grace this anthology. "Living Outdoors with Mrs. Panther" pokes fun at magazine presentations of the contemporary house. "The Tale of a House" discusses approaches to planning through the imaginary search by a landlord for a caretaker of his property. It is noteworthy that the landlord finds business approaches, preservation, and social planning to be inadequate; only the practical, visually messy, and socially anarchistic caretaker will do. If any voice speaks that of J. B. Jackson himself, it is the caretaker Ecos: "Think of me as a gardener, one who prepares and maintains a place where plants can grow and flourish and eventually bear fruit. . . . If he [the gardener] knows his business, the plants will do better in his garden than in the wilderness outside. But he does not try to prescribe the kind of fruit they will bear: indeed, he cannot always be sure that they will bear any fruit at all. That is out of his hands."

Jackson's opposition to modernism and his love of the Baroque also made him attuned to important developments that other observers were trying to block from consciousness. In "Other-Directed Houses," Jackson celebrated the highway strip. He took on its critics by reminding readers that driving is a recreation and that the highway strip offers diversion, meets important economic needs, and provides aesthetic pleasure. Jackson determined that a salient characteristic of a building on the strip is that it must catch the eye and please the automobile driver moving at forty miles an hour. Jackson's witty delineation of the characteristics of strip architecture predated *Learning from Las Vegas,* the clarion call to postmodernism, by sixteen years.[30]

Jackson's enjoyment of the car and motorcycle gave him an understanding of the meaning of speed. "The Abstract World of the Hot-Rodder" presents sympathetically the youthful driver of souped-up cars, who, like the skier or the yachtsman—enjoys the sensation of "abstract travel": "One feature of the familiar world after another is left behind, and the sportsman enters a world of his own, new and at the same time intensely personal; a world of flowing movement, blurred lights, rushing wind or water; he feels the surface beneath him, hears the sound of his progress, and has a tense rapport with his vehicle." Jackson returned to pondering these sensations in his last essay, "Places for Fun and Games."

JBJ, sketch, Berkeley, California, 1968

Although the number of subscriptions remained very small, *Landscape* began to attract good writers and exciting minds, such as Edgar Anderson, Edward T. Hall, and Lewis Mumford.[31] It shifted its focus from the American Southwest to the world beyond and began to probe urban life as seriously as it did rural. The growth happened by several stages. Anderson, a botanist and the assistant director of the Missouri Botanical Garden, not only subscribed but sent essays to *Landscape* that were published beginning in 1953. In a 1963 appreciation, Jackson wrote, "We see with some astonishment that we have assimilated a great deal of what Edgar Anderson wrote for us; in a sense, it is chiefly he who has helped determine the way in which *Landscape* has grown."[32]

More recently, Jackson suggested that what moved a journal of personal expression to a different plane was its connection to the geographers at the University of California at Berkeley. Anderson interested his friend Carl O. Sauer, the chairman of Berkeley's Department of Geography, in the magazine, and Sauer wrote appreciatively to Jackson. In 1956, when Jackson visited the Bay Area, he telephoned Sauer, who immediately invited him to a party of the department. This provided Jackson with an instant introduction to the many talented geographers who began to write for *Landscape:* Clarence Glacken, Erhard Rostlund, and Carl Sauer at Berkeley; and geographers who taught elsewhere, such as John Fraser Hart and Cotton Mather.[33] In addition to geographers, Jackson added a brilliant group of writers—such as Jean Gottman, Lawrence Halprin, Herbert Gans, Lewis Mumford, Christopher Tunnard, Kevin Lynch, and Paul Shepard—who tried out their ideas in *Landscape* prior to the publication of their own influential books.

In the years that followed, Jackson began to teach as adjunct professor in the College of Environmental Design and the Department of Geography at Berkeley. He recalled the invitation in this way: "There was a sort of informal sitting around on the grass. 'Would you talk to us about something?' And then they'd say, 'Well, how about a three week's extension of it?'" Beginning in 1967, he taught for a term each year, developing courses on the history of the European and the American landscapes. He recalled the intellectually stimulating atmosphere of Berkeley's Geography Department, to which he no doubt contributed, if only to dissent: "Most informal geography discussions involved a wide variety of nongeographical points of view: conservation, Marxism, Zen Buddhism, Freud and Jung and Alan Watts, landscape architecture and backpacking and organic farming."[34] In the fall of 1969 he also began teaching at Harvard, serving simultaneously as lecturer in the Department of Visual and Environmental Studies and as visiting professor in the Department of Landscape Architecture.

Teaching changed his life markedly. For about a decade he divided his life between a Cambridge autumn, a Berkeley winter, and a New Mexico spring and summer. He moved to a house of his own devising in La Cienega, a village to the southwest of Santa Fe.[35] In 1968 Blair Boyd succeeded him as publisher of *Landscape*, and the magazine continued to be a constructive publication until the mid-1990s. Jackson wrote for it and for many other journals in the years that followed.

As Jackson developed popular courses on the history of the American and European landscapes, he broadened and deepened his inquiry, and this was reflected in his writing. Early pieces, such as "High Plains," originally published in *Landscape* in 1954, demonstrate Jackson's fascination with history and the land. His 1972 book *American Space* gave him a broader canvas on which to describe the American continent in the decade following the Civil War. "Expansion" and "Environments," two sections of its first chapter, are included in this anthology. One of the most memorable images in *American Space* is that of the automatic turnstile, first used at the entrances to the 1876 exposition in Philadelphia. A visible demonstration of the "steady uninter-rupted flow" that became the "universal American requirement, not merely in industry but in every field of production of goods and wealth," the turnstile embodies the spirit of the centennial years.[36]

In "By Way of Conclusion: How to Study the Landscape," first pub-lished in 1980, Jackson distills his approach to teaching the landscape. He clar-ifies how he progressed in the classroom from the appealing presentation of slides and analysis of familiar themes to consider the fundamental question of landscape: "how space is organized by the community." Although most of Jackson's lectures at Harvard and Berkeley and some of his writing on the American landscape remain unpublished, several essays in this collection con-vey their style and content: "The Virginia Heritage: Fencing, Farming, and Cattle Raising" and "The Nineteenth-Century Rural Landscape: The Court-house, the Small College, the Mineral Springs, and the Country Store" were initially occasioned by lectures on the southern landscape heritage in Texas. "From Monument to Place" examines how the living have memorialized the dead. "Places for Fun and Games," written in 1995–96 and published here for the first time, combines elements of Jackson's earlier lectures on the history of American sports with themes drawn from his recent reading and thinking.

Yet, with all his interest in history, Jackson never lost sight of the pres-ent. He had an uncanny eye for change on the land. Many short anonymous pieces, news reprints, and excerpts in *Landscape* document Jackson's concern with evolving landscapes. In "An Engineered Environment," which originally appeared in *Landscape* in 1966, Jackson set forth the ways in which farmers were redesigning fields and barns in a mechanized agricultural world.[37]

After he stopped teaching in the late 1970s, Jackson began to lecture widely. Design periodicals invited him to publish in their pages, provoking some of his most engaging work. One of those pièces d'occasion, "The Ver-nacular City," an essay exploring urban issues, is an excellent example of Jack-son's thinking about a common subject—in this case, Lubbock, Texas. In good American studies fashion, he links the sunbelt city to Babbitt's Zenith as imagined by Sinclair Lewis. Weaving back and forth from past to pres-ent, Jackson treats suburban development, cars, roads, and parking as serious subjects.

In the last decade of his life, though retired from the lecture circuit, Jackson continued to write and publish. He became increasingly aware of the power of religion in shaping the landscape. He returned to manual labor, spending his mornings as a man of work who lived as well as wrote the principles of the caretaker Ecos. Some of his most important essays came from this time of quieter reflection.

Increasingly, Jackson saw the importance of roads, not just as lines between two points but as a landscape in themselves, "the scene of work and leisure and social intercourse and excitement." "Roads Belong in the Landscape," excerpted here, alerts us to a new science of roads and the importance that traffic control plays in it. Today's highway, Jackson asserts, is "a managed authoritarian system of steady, uninterrupted flow for economic benefits," and we have lost much of the freedom we once had. "Truck City" opens our eyes to a critical change in the contemporary landscape, one we have been trying not to see: the growing importance of commercial vehicles with their loading docks, vast parking lots, and warehouses; and the mobile workshops of small service vans and trucks—both working to create a more fluid, expansive city.

In one critical way Jackson was at odds with contemporary thinking. He always insisted that human beings belong in the landscape and that they are linked not only to the natural world but to society and culture. During his *Landscape* years, he addressed many of his "Notes and Comments" editorials to this issue; several of his most powerful statements are reprinted in this volume. His position put him in opposition to much of the conservation movement and many environmentalists. Jackson contended that the romantic approach to the landscape as wilderness destroys the appropriate balance between nature and human beings essential to a healthy urbanism and a wholesome agrarianism. Jackson found his American exemplar of romanticism in Thoreau, "the most eloquent American spokesman of an attitude toward the environment first expressed many years earlier by Rousseau and his followers." Whereas Jefferson advocated agrarian life to foster a democratic citizenry, Thoreau sought isolation in wilderness. Jackson judged that Thoreau's approach had impoverished planning for American cities and countryside. "Jefferson, Thoreau, and After," initially published in 1965–66, is an eloquent statement of his position.

It is wrong to see the landscape as raw nature. It is wrong to see it as a work of art: "We are *not* spectators; all human landscape is *not* a work of art," Jackson insisted. As much as he appreciated the loveliness of cities and countryside, he insisted that the purpose of landscape is to provide a place for living and working and leisure. A few of his "Notes and Comments" statements are excerpted here, as well as the entire editorial "To Pity the Plumage and Forget the Dying Bird," regarded by some as his most memorable testament. Not nature, not beauty, and finally, not history: Jackson insisted that landscapes must be shaped by present needs. As intrigued as he was by history, he never believed that landscapes ought to remain frozen in time to preserve historical memory. "'Sterile' Restorations Cannot Replace a Sense of the Stream of Time," a 1976 letter to the editor of *Landscape Architecture,* states this position most clearly.

Jackson always asserted that to interpret landscapes accurately we must turn to the common places of ordinary people rather than to the rarefied designs of architects and planners. As Marc Treib has put it, Jackson's writing "turns our perceptions on edge while showing that it is endemic ideology and attitude, rather than designers concerned with formal ideas, that shape America and its cultural landscape."[38] Jackson's understanding of these American landscapes changed, however. In 1951 he emphasized the historic and cultural roots of the American front yard. Looking at the lawns of farmers and middle-class suburbanites, he traced their origins back to the early European clearing of meadows from forest land, the "protolandscape" that Americans hold in their collective memory. With its layers of association, the common front lawn could be allied to Jackson's 1931 defense of the Baroque against modernist functionalism: it represented culture and civility, not nakedness and use.

In his more recent writing on the workaday world and ordinary building, Jackson turned to the trailer park, the yard filled with car parts, and the road. The side of him that recognized his own "commonness" insisted the landscape shaped by the needs and tastes of average working people was more important than that created by architects and planners. In this vein, he argued that we should consider the houses and places of work of the poor as well as the rich, of those on the margin as well as those at the center. In essays that others have criticized as being too accepting of contemporary blight, Jackson insisted that we not reject the common landscape but seek to understand and love it. "The Movable Dwelling and How It Came to America" exemplifies his approach.

The essay also clarifies the degree to which the shift in the object of his attention involved a rethinking—or, more precisely, a reevaluation—of earlier categories. As Jackson attempted to describe and interpret the dwellings of the working class, especially in the West, he replaced history and culture with economic pressures and habits of life as factors that shape the landscape. In his recent writing he gave much thought to the meaning of the word *vernacular.* Deriving as it does from the Latin word for house slave, vernacular connotes immediate and temporary use, in contrast to the elite's need of status and permanence. Jackson's mind delighted in dualisms. His new understanding of the vernacular dwelling suggested that he had returned to his earlier distinction between utility and civilization with a new appreciation of use.

It also demonstrated an intellectual strategy that proved fruitful to Jackson's study of the landscape: inquiry into the derivation of words. As Jackson explores the meaning of *landscape* in "The Word Itself," he distills much of what he has come to understand through his long and arduous search. In 1972 it may have been possible to read and hear the voice of a young man. The depth of learning and the wisdom of Jackson's recent, more theoretical writing unmistakably reveal the voice of an older seer.

In all of his writing, J. B. Jackson demonstrated not only a penetrating vision but also a philosophical turn of mind. He was not content with description but looked at the values that underlie landscapes. He was never afraid to speculate on the meaning of what he saw. In his study of American space, he came to look for "the image of our common humanity." As his own life took an increasingly religious direction, he injected into his inquiry on landscapes a moral point of view. To the study of space, he sought to restore the presence of humankind. As creatures of God, men and women, not wilderness, should be the focus of human inquiry. "The older I grow and the longer I look at landscapes and seek to understand them," Jackson wrote, "the more convinced I am that their beauty is not simply an aspect but their very essence and that that beauty derives from the human presence."[39]

## Editor's Note

I chose essays for the anthology according to three criteria. The first was importance. Here I let the collective wisdom of scholars in geography and history guide me. The second was J. B. Jackson's own wishes. After receiving this list, he picked additional essays that he particularly wanted to see included in this volume. Finally, having made these selections, I let my own, more idiosyncratic judgments prevail, choosing from among the vast number of works those essays that broadened the range of Jackson's voices and demonstrated additional facets of his complex point of view. With the essays in mind, I turned to Jackson's drawings and photographs, looking for images that either gave visual form to his ideas or served as their counterpoint. To these I added a few of the symbols he had chosen for sections of *Landscape* magazine when he was its editor.

Jackson began publishing essays on the American landscape in 1951, after two decades of writing in other veins. By this point he had developed clear notions of language and style. The essays are published as they appeared, without any attempt to adapt them to the present. The 1950s figures for money have not been adjusted for inflation, references have not been changed to sound more up to date, and Jackson's use of "man" and the male pronoun has been allowed to stand. To aid contemporary readers, Harry Haskell of Yale University Press and I have silently added first names and occasional words of clarification. Trying to be as sparing as possible, especially with his best-known essays, we have made minor changes to correct obvious mistakes. We have adapted punctuation to conform to contemporary usage. Lovers of Jackson's use of the colon will find fewer: we hope we have left enough to satisfy them.

## Editor's Acknowledgments

Common appreciation and knowledge of J. B. Jackson's writing has made this volume possible. Daniel Horowitz, my mainstay in all things personal and professional, shared my early enthusiasm for Jackson's writing and experienced with me Jackson's hospitality and conversation. In this project Dan has offered advice and encouragement at every turn. Early in the development of the anthology I began working with Paul Groth of the University of California at Berkeley. With unstinting generosity Paul has assisted in innumerable ways to guide this project. He has offered his annotated bibliography, suggested names to consult, read drafts, provided interview material, and made available Jackson's slide collection in his possession for illustrations.

Bob Calo has helped in many ways. He has provided encouragement, let me quote the informative transcripts of his interviews with J. B. Jackson, and suggested the title of this book. Francis Douglas Adams allowed me to select from Jackson's sketches in his possession and generously provided selected copies for review and publication. His interest and good will have been sustaining.

Colleagues of Jackson and scholars offered advice about which essays to include and assistance with the Bibliography. I am grateful to Kurtis Fuellhart, Dan Gregory, Paul Groth, Thomas Harvey, David Hooson, Pierce Lewis, Donald Meinig, Richard Schein, David Schulyer, Michael Steiner, Marc

Treib, Robert Weyenreth, and Chris Wilson. It was Donald Meinig's suggestion that led me to excerpt materials from "Notes and Comments." Thomas Harvey went beyond the call of duty to aid me in the Bibliography and to send to me xeroxes of materials not originally listed. The fresh readings of Kurtis Fuellhart, a graduate student in geography at Penn State, help me rethink selections.

This volume would not have been possible without the generosity of the publishers of Jackson's work, who have allowed reprinting of these essays.

I am grateful to Smith College for funds supporting travel and research assistance. Able undergraduates have contributed their skills and intelligence: I am especially indebted to Sara Fisher, Abby Rupp, Burd Schlessinger, Patricia Brand, Ellen Weiss, and Mildred Joyce for their careful work.

Judy Metro, Jackson's editor for *A Sense of Place, a Sense of Time*, which won the 1995 PEN International award for the best book of essays, has offered consistent encouragement and support. Harry Haskell has contributed his careful thought and wordcraft.

The warm enthusiasm of Betsy and Ted Rogers for the man and his work brightened Jackson's last year and helped to ease my deep loss at his death. It is to them that I dedicate my contributions to these pages.

**Landscape in Sight**

JBJ, photo, playground

## Places for Fun and Games

We find ourselves driving down a street in a poor section of town. The uniform frame houses, each with a front porch and a patch of grass, are separated by narrow alleyways leading to the garages. In places the street is bordered by vacant lots and billboards, but along both curbs cars are closely parked.

Traffic proceeds by fits and starts. A dozen or more small children are running along the sidewalks; when they suddenly decide to cross the street and dart out from between the parked cars, some of them stoop to recover a cap or a glove or a baseball they might have dropped. Cars and trucks come to an abrupt halt, but the children show no alarm. They playfully slap the fenders of cars and pluck the car aerials. They call out some kind of greeting or defiance, and skip out of sight.

The vacant lots, ugly with trash and bottles and cans, slope down to a small stagnant puddle overgrown by weeds. What charm there is in the scene comes from the running children in their bright-colored parkas—blue and purple and green and pink.

When we have worked our way through the street congestion and halt to get our bearings, we watch them as they run and skip. We say what all drivers say on such an occasion: it is a public scandal for children to have to play in so dirty and hazardous a place. Why have they chosen it when they might have been playing in their familiar brick-paved schoolyard? But the street has undeniable attractions: there is a noisy construction site where great trucks come and go; the dark alleyways with their rows of trash barrels invite exploration, and each parked car offers a hideaway. For most of the children home is in one or another of the frame houses, and though they are old enough (so they think) to take care of themselves, they are happy to feel the eye of a parent or of an older brother or sister watching from an upstairs window. Lastly, the proprietor of the small corner convenience store has sworn undying hostility to them. If a ball so much as bounces—or even rolls—on his portion of the sidewalk, he runs out and yells that the police are on their way. The children respond with jeers and name calling and a chorus of forbidden words. Then they take flight to the vacant lot beyond the billboards.

We who watch are curious to know what game it is that they are playing. It has features which all of us recognize from our own childhood: the children vaguely establish boundaries which they are not to cross, and choose home bases. Other, smaller children hope to be included, but they are told to go away; they don't belong. Then, by the familiar process of counting out ("eeny, meeny, miney, moe"), they choose two team captains. The group disperses: all race through the scarred, vacant lots looking for places to hide. The more adventurous deliberately ("accidentally on purpose" is their phrase) splash through the oily puddle and emerge wet and muddy and triumphant.

The game, whatever it is, involves running and being caught, and proceeds with screams of delight. Then someone discovers a small garter snake moving in the grass, and it becomes the center of attention. With a long stick a child turns it over and exposes its pale underside. Others dare to pick it up and watch it writhe. Laughing and shouting obscenities, they throw it into the air, hit it, and before they know what they are doing, they have killed it. Then they fail silent; play has suddenly ceased to be play.

Those of use still watching from the sidewalk are revolted. Dirty, cruel little brats! And what language! Why is there no one to supervise their play? Those less harshly critical try to interpret the misbehavior as a temporary act of rebellion against adults—parents and policemen and teachers with their rules and restrictions. All agree that there ought to be a better place for play: one with a fence or a wall where there would be no intrusion, no dirt.

A fence, if it were high and strong enough, would be an excellent solution. It would keep out blowing trash and prevent shortcuts by strangers (so our speculations go). A fence would allow us to take care of the grounds, plant trees and grass; a place where all children, whatever their size, would be safe and have an equal chance; lawsuits would be unknown. Having a fence with a gate would mean that we could control how and when the playground was used and by whom; it would allow for special hours and special groups, and do away with quarrels. We could discourage troublesome gangs. This would, of course, entail constant supervision: a caretaker or a groundskeeper who could also serve as a program director. He should have training in play or recreation supervision. That would give the playground a special identity and even create a sense of group identity among the children. The smooth, accident-proof surface would allow for a variety of games. More important, a fenced, well-kept playground would encourage efficiently organized activity, with records and scores and a kind of membership badge or uniform. Thus we visualize the ideal playground.

These are amenities we already have in many playgrounds. We find them in tennis courts and basketball courts and hockey rinks: all have man-made surfaces and limited access, and all are permanent. They cost money. But that, after all, is what makes a playground valuable: children learn to respect timetables and rules and the authority of the coach, and learn to respect the immediate environment. In short, a playground—fenced and well kept—allows children to develop skills, learn cooperation, and be valuable citizens. So what we must have (it is agreed) is more such playgrounds: efficiently designed and administered. Each one is an essential element in any urban or rural landscape.

But play and playground are different, and play is not an easy thing to define, especially when we include adults, as we are learning to do. The *Oxford Dictionary* lists no fewer than thirty current meanings, from "play" the guitar, "play" the stock market, "play" tennis, "play" house, and "play" the role of Hamlet to play in the sense of "to move or operate freely within a bounded space, as machine parts do."

The most common definition is that play is a way of spending our leisure time in games and sports; play is an agreeable pastime. That is hardly precise, but it reminds us of an important characteristic which we sometimes overlook: play is essential, for any existence would otherwise be divided between work and idleness. It is something we freely and gladly choose.

The man who first studied the concept of play—especially adult play—was the Dutch historian Johan Huizinga. In 1935 he published his most influential work, *Homo Ludens* (Man the Player). It has been criticized by anthropologists and sociologists for being what we now call Eurocentric; but it is widely recognized as the first serious attempt to analyze play as a cultural, not a biological or psychological, trait. Huizinga's thesis was that play is a basic, innate human urge; not only predating the religious impulse and cultural institutions but actually influencing their emergence and evolution. Play has had an impact on the practice of law, the performing arts, and even international policy because it emphasizes and codifies procedures and produces dialogue, and also (according to Huizinga) because it requires certain distinct, consecrated spaces, such as "the arena, the card table, the screen, the tennis court . . . forbidden spaces, isolated, hedged around, hallowed, within which special rules pertain. Play creates order, and *is* order."

Huizinga sums up play as being "a free activity standing quite consciously outside 'ordinary' life as being 'not serious' but at the same time absorbing the player intensely and utterly. It is an activity connected with no material interest, and no profit can be gained from it. It proceeds within its own proper boundaries of time and space according to fixed rules and in an orderly manner. It promotes the formation of social groupings which tend to surround themselves with secrecy." Throughout the book, he underscores the physical and emotional benefits of play: a sense of bodily well-being and an awareness of our kinship with fellow participants. For to him play is essentially a group or interpersonal activity. The solitary play experience—that of the mountain climber, the hunter, the explorer—is of little cultural consequence. The truly unforgettable manifestations of play—the procession, the dance, the ritual reenactment of myths, above all competition in games and sports—what he calls the element of *agon*, from the Greek word for contest—are what matter. And since children rarely respond to play in this coherent manner, Huizinga has little to say about the rowdy or spontaneous aspects of play, or play as the pursuit of "fun."

What were the sources of this theory? In the years between the world wars, Huizinga was identified with a group of eminent central European intellectuals and scholars who shared a vision of the future that was profoundly pessimistic. In their search for a good society, they turned (as their predecessors had turned) to the classic past. They sought to revive the values implicit in the culture of pre-Socratic Greece, and in particular its philosophy of education and character formation. Like other critics, Huizinga was inspired by Homer and Hesiod and Xenophon. What they had to say about the upbringing of young Athenians and Spartans confirmed his theory that play produced not only healthy bodies but also sound minds and sound morals. Parents did not merely instruct the young in the martial arts and social graces, they impressed on them the cardinal importance of acting with justice and honor when dealing with others, and the importance of knowing how to compete.

"From childhood until the onset of the supreme attributes of culture," Huizinga wrote, "the urge to be praised and honored for one's superior qualities provides a powerful incentive to reach individual or collective perfection. . . . Virtue, honor, nobility and glory are to be found in the earliest kind of competition, that is to say, in games."

Here is one of the few references in *Homo Ludens* to the play of children, and the context suggests that Huizinga means adolescents who are already trained in the martial arts and in the rules of fair competition in sports. Instruction thus taking place in the youths' earlier years would have been a private family affair, involving competition between equals or associates, a kind of restrained competition that might be called "playful" in that it entailed no reward.

In his discussion of what was essentially an aristocratic definition of play as "fair" competition in manly sports, Huizinga refers to the terrain of the ancient Olympic Games as a *gymnasium*. He thereby calls our attention to a link between landscape design and education: the gymnasium or play space as the locus of moral and physical development for an aristocratic society. The Academy in Athens (which we usually associate with Plato and his teachings) was in fact the most celebrated gymnasium in the city, a designed park with flowing water, groves of trees, and spaces for play. The man-made landscape in the form of garden or park or collection of buildings and spaces became a part of the Renaissance revival of aristocratic sports, and in a debased form it flourishes today. Agon is part of the modern setup: all that is now missing is the moral or ethical ingredient.

In 1801, an Englishman named Joseph Strutt published a book entitled *Sports and Pastimes of the People of England*. By profession he was an engraver; an early job had been the producing of illustrations for a book on antiques. He became interested in what we now know as popular culture, and before he died he had written several volumes on the subject. His unfinished novel about medieval England came to the attention of Walter Scott, who later acknowledged that without the wealth of historical material provided by Strutt's manuscript, the Waverly novels could never have been completed.

*Sports and Pastimes,* Strutt's last work, proved to be very popular. For its period it was a model of research into obscure chronicles and ancient texts. It was reprinted several times up to 1903, when it was carefully edited and brought up to date. An American edition appeared in 1968. It deserves to be better known. It tells in detail how English men and women enjoyed themselves during a period of some seven hundred years. It does not pretend to be a sociological treatise, merely a vivid account of some of the more carefree aspects of everyday life in all classes of society.

"War, policy, and other contingent circumstances," Strutt writes, "may eventually place men at different times in different points of view, but when we follow them into their retirements, where no disguise is necessary, we are most likely to see them in their true state and may best judge of their natural dispositions." By "retirements" Strutt must have meant leisure, for what he describes are the pastimes, the diversions and pleasures of public life, chiefly in London. These were surprisingly numerous and varied. Quoting from Robert Burton's *Anatomy of Melancholy*, he notes how Londoners "take pleasure to see some pageant or sight go by, as at a coronation, wedding and such like solemnities, to see an ambassador or a prince received and entertained with masks, shows, and fireworks." But Londoners also created their own entertainments. "Dancing, singing, masking, mumming and state plays," to quote again from Burton, "are reasonable recreations in season. . . . Let them play at ball and barley brakes and afterwards, plays, masks, jesters, gladiators, tumblers, and jugglers are to be winked at, lest the people should do worse than attend them."

The public street, well into the eighteenth century, was the favorite place for adult play: football, wrestling, ninepins, shovel board, bear and bull baitings, cockfighting, and meeting friends took place in crowded streets and alleys and open places. Strutt conscientiously describes them and tells when they were likely to be seen on holidays and which group, young or old, poor or rich, took part. He writes about ceremonial costumes and banquets, and about how the facades of houses were occasionally decorated for celebration. He has much to say about fireworks—how Handel wrote music for them at Vauxhall Gardens and Ranelagh, both popular pleasure gardens.

Diversions of this sort were not confined to London. Just as in ancient Greece, many smaller games were played elsewhere, other than at the main Olympic gymnasium; rural England saw a number of annual celebrations of sports in the provinces. For several days on end, thousands of country people gathered in small towns to take part in traditional games and sports or to witness displays of strength and agility and grace. There were trained dogs and trained bears and trained horses, acrobats and slight-of-hand artists and tightrope walkers. Musicians played and people danced. Charles II, on his way to Spain, stopped to watch such a rural meet in Cornwall, a region known for its wrestlers and boxers, and found the event so enthralling that he stayed all day and "became a brother of the jovial society."

"Persons of rank" seldom participated in these countrified celebrations, preferring their own pastimes and their own company. As they understood the concept, play meant certain traditional sports such as hunting, hawking, horse racing, or archery, or perhaps a version of handball or tennis. These called for expertise and knowing how to behave. It is true that until the nineteenth century "persons of rank," when indoors at home, played games which we now associate with children: puss-in-the-corner, blind man's bluff, and musical chairs. But outdoors, when they engaged in other competitive games, they were usually in a more concentrated frame of mind: they wanted to excel. They had been brought up to believe that sports made them braver and stronger, more respectful of rules and (socially speaking) more acceptable; if they won, they expected to be praised.

When common people played, however, the tone was informal and spontaneous and full of expectations of a good time. Often there were players who knew nothing about the game and had to be taught. While they played, they had no time to think about the workaday world to which they would soon return; "fun" was what they were after. Both kinds of play brought excitement and pleasure, but in intention they were very different, and their modern equivalents still are.

One important difference (at least in landscape terms) was this: with groups of working people—families or neighbors or fellow workers—play began wherever would-be players happened to be. In town the street was the logical place; in the country it might be the village green, the churchyard, or the field where they had been working. In any case, it was not a terrain especially prepared or set aside; merely one which was available and accessible. But when the gentry decided to play their various games of agon, the play space was familiar and well prepared. It was free of obstacles and uncertainties: a "level playing field," as the saying goes. That was probably what Huizinga had in mind when he stipulated that play should occur in spaces that were "hedged around, hallowed, within which special rules pertain."

Throughout Western history there has always been a class requiring, and able to produce, such areas dedicated to athletic performance and moral training. Those spaces not only multiplied throughout our landscape but have persisted up to the present: spaces designed to suit the tastes of a class of citizen who thinks of play as an effective way of teaching the young how to conduct themselves and how to develop certain physical skills. Even our comparatively new American landscape contains innumerable examples, some inherited, some recently designed: the college campus, the country club, the sports arena, not to mention the many once private parks and estates now open to all. What more can we ask for than well-kept, enclosed areas of greenery where we can (if we want to) develop our social talents and at the same time acquire strong bodies? Only one need is neglected: the inner need to be part of a non-human cosmic order: that we have to satisfy as best we can by ourselves.

Historically speaking, the hunting forest is the earliest and the most familiar of these "consecrated" spaces for play. We tend at present to perceive the forest as an unspoiled and beautiful fragment of nature; if it has any moral function at all, it is to encourage a kind of nature mysticism. But beginning more than a thousand years ago, when it was already legally defined and protected against intruders, the forest was identified with skill and bravery and a rigid social hierarchy. It is in the forest that we glimpse an attitude toward the natural environment that we have long ignored: nature was to be *used* and modified and even occasionally destroyed, in order to produce an environment to promote a certain kind of behavior. In the medieval forest, undesirable types of game and objectionable vegetation were done away with, and desirable specimens introduced. Forests were logged and, as we have seen in many European forests, long, straight avenues or drives were often cut for the convenience of hunters.

On a smaller scale, other agon sports demanded a similar remodeling of the environment. Horse racing, as well as bowling and archery, required a small version of the "level playing field"—usually a smooth stretch of lawn surrounded by a hedge or fence. Tennis, when it was introduced in a refined and regulated form from France, was particularly demanding. As a kind of handball, it had long been played by schoolchildren on any convenient open field, but when it became popular among the English gentry in the fifteenth century, it required the smoothest of surfaces and walls, along with protective gloves and eventually racquets. The only suitable setting was at first the exterior of a church, and for a brief time tennis was played *inside* St. Paul's Cathedral in London. An indignant clergy put an end to this desecration, and the totally man-made artificial environment in the form of a measured court soon evolved.

An unusually elaborate example of space for agon in the late Middle Ages was one for tournaments; strictly speaking, the space devoted to combat between knights was called the lists. A medieval chronicler defined the tournament in what could be called terms of make-believe or play: "a military exercise carried out not in the spirit of hostility but solely for practice and the display of prowess." Surprisingly, Huizinga treated tournaments with scorn. In the *Waning of the Middle Ages* he dismissed them as essentially shallow pageants without deep meaning. "Overloaded with pompous decorations, full of heroic fancy, they serve to express romantic needs too strong for mere literature to satisfy." Strutt, by contrast, wrote enthusiastically about the tournament as theater. "Such a show of pomp, where wealth, beauty, and grandeur were concentrated, as it were, in one focus must altogether have formed a wonderful spectacle."

To this day, agon sports are the ones we take most seriously. They are the ones with their own permanent terrain, not accessible to everyone; the ones with established historical records and their roster of heroes; the ones with their own uniforms and logos, their own hierarchies. Huizinga was not entirely accurate when he declared that agon games provided no material rewards or social advantages. Thus it is that even in the modern commercial city, with its monuments and spaces dedicated to government, crown, or church, there are those, often architecturally impressive, that celebrate a certain kind of play and certain players. In time we may learn to include other, more vernacular kinds of play: many communities in America are learning to provide permanent, designed spaces for skateboards, and many resorts, of course, focus on ambitious and expensive ski and toboggan runs. On the whole, however, we still identify agon sports with the secluded "level playing field" of grass (or Astroturf) in its own protected terrain: ornamental areas, identified with traditional notions of sportsmanship, and as such worth preserving. It was only a few years ago that the International Olympic Committee consented to include a number of sports that placed less emphasis on person-to-person competition and more on awareness of the natural environment: scuba diving, hang gliding, alpinism, and surfing.

There has never been a time when agon was the only game in town, nor when there was not a vernacular or working-class version of collective play. They first confronted each other in our Western landscape about four hundred years ago, when cities grew in size and brought together in one place many elements of the population. The impact of archery—essentially an aristocratic agon sport—on vernacular sports is an instance.

The use of the bow and arrow in fighting, hunting, and target practice was probably the favorite sport of all classes in fifteenth-century England. The average archer was a working man, but his leader and commander was usually a person of rank. To the nobility archery symbolized manly virtues: strength, bravery, skill, and patriotism. English bowmen were widely respected for their effectiveness in warfare, and the fact that gunpowder (and ultimately artillery) threatened to make archery obsolete by the sixteenth century merely served as a reason for cherishing the long bow and arrow as signs of England's past military prowess. Englishmen of every class were obliged to have a bow in their dwelling, and to practice their skill in leisure hours. Indeed, many English cities retained spacious fields in the center of town, even when open spaces were becoming rare, where archers could practice.

But working-class Englishmen, like working-class men and women throughout the world in the Renaissance, had discovered newer, more profitable ways of spending their leisure: in gambling. We think we have learned to exploit all forms of gambling in our bingo parlors, casinos, slot machines, lotteries, and other venues: but as long ago as the eleventh century an English authority listed no fewer than ten ways of gambling with dice, and even chess, checkers, and backgammon were considered games of chance. When small coins and decks of playing cards became common, gambling was almost irresistible: not simply as a way of making money but as a way of demonstrating skill and judgment, and of foretelling the future. Tarot became immensely popular in the sixteenth century.

England's conservative establishment reacted to this competition with a vigor which anticipated by several centuries that of the National Rifle Association. A lobbying group composed of "bowers, fletchers, stringers and arrow-head makers of the realm" petitioned the crown in the fifteenth century to repress the spread of gambling, and the crown obliged by forbidding all "artificers, apprentices, labourers, mariners, fishermen, watermen or any serving man" from playing any of the following games, except on Christmas: "football, quoits, putting the stone, kails, tennis, bowls, clash legating, half bowl, slide thrifts, or shore groat or backgammon." (Gambling had previously been banned.) What these various games with Gothic or Celtic names might have been, I cannot discover, but they were presumably popular, and their outlawing must have had its effect on the public play. A list, compiled at a later date, of locations in the city where all public games were forbidden gives us a picture of how scattered and how modest those places of vernacular diversion must have been: "public houses, bars, archways, small plots of wasteland, bootmakers' stands and even the large umbrellas of bookmakers."

This campaign against gambling may not have had the intended effect—to return working-class men to the practice of archery—but it undoubtedly discouraged much informal play in crowded parts of town. Gambling moved out to the racetracks or into clubs, and street lotteries became popular; but the increasing shortage of space did the most damage. Strutt and other chroniclers of sports often note that because of the heavy traffic in city streets, one game or another went out of existence. Football, in its vernacular form, was always a violent and dangerous sport, played only by the roughest element and constantly condemned by the authorities. It disappeared from the streets in the sixteenth century and took refuge in graveyards—specifically, those on the north sides of churches, where few bodies were buried. Even in the countryside, space for casual play became hard to find: the introduction of cattle raising fostered the planting of hedges; new kinds of crops produced land unsuited to games. In sixteenth-century France, changes in cultivation forced such rural games as bowling and ninepins and horseshoe pitching to seek space in the village, and the players had to pay for using private land. In brief, much traditional play, popular with working-class citizens, located in the center of town where the players lived and worked, was driven out, either by the shortage of space or by police decisions to improve traffic circulation and promote order.

Archery long held out in the city, thanks to powerful protectors. But Strutt reports that in 1780, when a last ceremonial unit of archers went to what was later for Huizinga its consecrated space, "hedged around, hallowed, within which special rules pertain," it discovered that its field had been enclosed by a brick wall. A determined group of "toxophiles" (amateurs of archery) sought to keep the sport alive in the nineteenth century by promoting it as a suitable recreation for ladies and gentlemen. The same process of gentrification, led by Thomas Arnold of Rugby, kept football alive in the 1850s, much regulated and refined. Cricket was also rescued—and subject to "agonization" and the rule of white flannels—at much the same time.

Historians are in general agreement that sometime in the second half of the eighteenth century, what we call popular or vernacular culture began to lose its vitality and charm. Until about that date, almost all classes of society shared the same tastes in dress and music and play and speech; what differences there were came from different ways of life and never implied a different culture. But the nineteenth and twentieth centuries were hard on the vernacular. The cult of agon, with all its rites and restrictions and ethical hangups, drove much innocent public life from the streets and quite unintentionally fostered the mania for gambling by emphasizing the role of money. Gambling brought hardships of its own: it produced economic instability and discouraged both work and play in favor of low-spirited idleness. In the cities of the United

States in the first years of our independence, there was joblessness and much bad behavior. "The great number of idle boys who frequented the wharves on Sunday," the historian McMaster wrote, "playing pitch and toss and other games destructive of morals, and who during the week spent their time in pilfering goods landed on the wharves from ships, was an evil as serious as any which received public attention." In town after town, therefore, the citizens formed committees to improve the economy and the moral tone. The poor were given food and fuel and shelter, and among the first resolutions passed by the various societies for moral and economic improvement were those which proposed schools for the training of youths and the production of healthy and useful citizens.

The usual agon response was to create new and specialized spaces in the landscape. Early in the nineteenth century, middle-class America started to think about parks in our towns and cities, carefully designed cemeteries and college campuses, and promenades along the waterfronts. In keeping with the ancient Greek idea of agon and the importance of healthy bodies and healthy minds, we created a space, distinct from the street, where gymnastics could be taught and practiced.

The idea came from Germany. In that country a young theology student named F. L. Jahn, much distressed by the despondent moral tone among young Germans occasioned by their defeat by Napoleon in 1809, resolved to remedy the situation by offering vigorous outdoor gymnastic exercises to all young Germans; to the space where this training was to take place, he gave the classic name of gymnasium. The students were required to wear uniforms and to receive political indoctrination as well as bodily exercises. The gymnasium experience proved highly popular.

In 1819 Jahn fell out of favor with his Prussian superiors and the experiment came to an abrupt end. Three of his assistants, Karl Beck, Francis Lieber, and Charles Follen, young theology students, fled to the United States. Beck created the first gymnasium class in a small school in Northampton, Massachusetts. Lieber started a public outdoor gymnasium on Tremont Street in Boston. He later became the first professor of German at Columbia University, and it was he who translated de Tocqueville into English. Follen established the first course in gymnastics at Harvard and was also the first to teach German there.

Much of the enthusiasm for the new kind of sport called gymnastics derived from the physical well-being it produced: its moral and patriotic teachings left most young Americans unimpressed, and yet one is struck by the numerous references in early gymnastic writing to the influence of religion, beginning in Germany and continuing throughout the nineteenth century in New England. Edward Hitchcock, son of the clergyman and geologist who presided over Amherst College, was the head of the first comprehensive program in gymnastics in Amherst College, held in one of the first college buildings to be labeled a gymnasium. He described his program as designed "not with exclusive attention to the muscular system, but to keep bodily health up to the normal standards so that the mind may accomplish the most work, and to preserve the bodily powers in full activity for both the daily duties of college and the promised labor of a long life." The body, in other words, was a machine, and play represented occasional maintenance.

The plight of young men working in factories or ships or offices in unfamiliar cities far from their homes was of prime importance to reformers in nineteenth-century industrial cities. The Young Men's Christian Association evolved into centers for social contact and religious instruction. After the Civil War, when the larger YMCAs included a gymnasium and often a swimming pool, they became responsible for the sports and leisure of a whole generation. It became the duty of several of the urban YMCAs to invent suitable games for playing in gymnasiums; and it is to the YMCA college in Springfield, Massachusetts, that we owe the formulation of two of America's most popular games: basketball and volleyball. It was also in the Y that competitive swimming, together with its rules and procedures, was first instituted. But the remarkable aspect of these invented games was the considerations given to the limitations and needs of the players. The principles of agon promoting fairness in competition, simplicity of action, and a regard for justice and goodwill among the players, previously not a matter of regulation, were made basic features.

It was at the end of the nineteenth century that the influence of the theological student was replaced by that of the professional coach and athletic director. The clergymen had tried to respect the identity of the individual amateur player and normal human limitations in sports. In contrast, at the close of the century, John Hoberman writes in *Mortal Engines: The Science of Performance and the Dehumanization of Sport*, "physiological thinking began to be applied to athletic performance. . . . Anthropological and physiological assessments of the human organism during this period were cultural symptoms of an Age of Calibration—a mania for measurement that continues unabated to this day."

Yet, concurrently with the development of performance-oriented sport, with its dependence on drugs and medicine, there has emerged a new concept of sports, reminiscent in many ways of vernacular attitudes. It requires us to reexamine our definition of play and its significance.

A generation ago, in an essay entitled "Games of Dizziness and Fear," the French psychologist Jean Caseneuve wrote: "There is a kind of game or sport which can be designated by the term *Helix,* the Greek word for whirlwind or an evolving spiral, to which is related a word which can be translated as vertigo or the dizziness of intoxication." How can dizziness be experienced as a sport? "By an effect both physical and psychological. The organs of balance, particularly in the inner ear, are momentarily disturbed by unusual movements and the result is a modification of the way we perceive our surroundings. Our relation to the world around us takes on a strange quality, and our self-awareness undergoes change. Even in harmless cases, as on a swing or merry-go-round, there is a certain shift in perception that is part of the pleasure children get from this kind of play. The definition of helix games and sports should include all activities involving . . . loss of physical balance and all the means we use to modify our self-perception." Caseneuve noted that in those sports the spatial dimension is not always well defined, but that the dimension of time remains precise; for only by consciously controlling the length of time we undergo this experience can we continue to maintain our freedom; the sport is still a game, still a kind of make-believe.

Helix sports are what we in America have called sports of mobility: skiing, gliding, soaring, sailing, snowboarding, skateboarding, as well as car and motorcycle racing, surfing, and mountain climbing. Most were inspired by the automobile. Most of them got their start in the Depression years and became more widespread after World War II. Some arose among the unemployed youth of central Europe, some among the prosperous younger generation of postwar California; still others are contemporary civilian adaptations of military performances. All seem to have certain characteristics in common.

In all of them we see an instinctive avoidance of the "beaten track": the familiar itinerary, the rails, the surfaced highway, the track, the lawn, even the gymnasium. We can see a revolt against the timetable, the schedule, the planned journey. It is as if a whole generation had taken off cross-country to explore the unfamiliar, nonhuman aspect of an environment where tradition offered no guidance or warning.

Another characteristic is the rejection of traditional equipment and techniques. No matter how a sport may have originated—as Hawaiian ritual games in the case of surfing, or as Norwegian peasant transportation in the case of skiing—sooner or later the prototype is discarded or modified. The new sports of solitary mobility are no longer willing to follow established procedures.

A third characteristic is that these sports are not highly competitive. It is true that in many respects skiing has been assimilated into the world of commercialized competitive sports, but few skiers—and surely fewer surfers and hang gliders and mountain climbers—are primarily concerned with achieving "victory" or breaking records. Possibly related to this lack of competitiveness is the fact that few of the sports are inspired by an ulterior practical motive, or are practiced because they are body building or character forming or socially acceptable. The ski bum, the surf bum, the motorcycle bum are typical products of such sports of mobility.

Finally, a most important characteristic of helix sports is the terrain itself, especially where there is an apparent absence of design or structure. I say "apparent" because many resorts design and engineer their ski runs, and surf-producing beaches have been built in California—to say nothing of the totally artificial surfing beaches in Phoenix. Yet, compared with the terrain of traditional competitive sports, the terrain of helix sports usually bears few visible signs of its function: a few marks in the snow, a strip in the desert, a buoy, a light. Weather, which plays so important a role in most helix sports, is of course unpredictable. What the participant sets out to do is not to follow a well-defined course; he simply heads toward some remote destination: a new experience, a new environment, a dehumanized, abstract world of snow or water or sky or desert, where there are no familiar guidelines. With this goes a sense of uncertainty and of being totally alone. We note how we tend to revive an intuitive awareness of our surroundings, reacting to textures, currents, tides, temperatures, slopes, lights, and clouds and winds, even directions. The essential value of these sports seems to lie in a fresh contact with the environment and a new sense of our identity. Even if briefly, there ensues a temporary reshaping of our being.

The pursuit of many helix sports is unfortunately now confined to the few who can afford to go into the wilderness or to ski resorts. But their experience is one that many aspire to—of an unexplored world of great spaces: desert and mountain and sky and open water—and it is there that we can formulate a new relationship to the natural environment, or revive an old one. The helix movement involves something much more than a belated return to nature. I think it derives from a basic impulse is to search for a fresh identity (or, more accurately, to search for a way of changing the identity we have). To quote Caseneuve: "This kind of sport finally results in diverting our consciousness, in creating the illusion of abandoning our everyday personality by modifying the relationship between the individual being and his environment. . . . It is not speed in itself that we seek . . . but the intoxication it produces. . . . There would be no helix sports if there were not a profound urge in all of us to escape from ourselves, and if there did not come to every living being a time to turn away from mundane existence."

# 1 Landscape Explorations

JBJ, photo, "Rex Club"

## The Stranger's Path

As one who is by way of being a professional tourist with a certain painfully acquired knowledge of how to appraise strange cities, I often find myself brought up short by citizens remarking that I can't really hope to *know* a town until I have seen the inside of one of its homes. I usually agree, expecting that there will then ensue an invitation to their house and a chance to admire one of these shrines of local culture, these epitomes of whatever it is the town or city has to offer. All that follows is an urgent suggestion that I investigate on my own the residential quarter before I presume to form a final opinion. "Ours is a city of homes," they add. "The downtown section is like that anywhere else, but our Country Club Heights"—or Snob Hill or West End or European Section or Villa Quarter, depending on where I am—"is considered unique."

I have accordingly set out to explore that part of the city, and many are the hours I have spent wandering through carefully labyrinthine suburbs, seeking to discover the *essential* city, as distinguished from that of the tourist or transient. In retrospect, these districts all seem indistinguishable: tree- and garden-lined avenues and lanes, curving about a landscape of hills with pretty views over other hills; the traffic becomes sparser, the houses retreat further behind tall trees and expensive flowers; every prospect is green, most prosperous and beautiful. The latest-model cars wait on the carefully raked driveway or at the immaculate curb, and there comes the sound of tennis being played. When evening falls, the softest, most domestic lights shine from upstairs windows; the only reminder of the nearby city is that dusty pink glow in the sky which in any case the trees all but conceal.

Yet why have I always been glad to leave? Was it a painful realization that I was excluded from these rows and rows of (presumably) happy and comfortable homes that has always ended by making me beat a retreat to the city proper? Or was it a conviction that I had actually seen this, experienced it, relished it after a fashion countless times and could no longer derive the slightest spark of inspiration from it? Ascribe it if you like to a kind of sour grapes, but in the course of years of travel I have come to believe that the home, the domestic establishment, far from being a unique symbol of the local way of life, is essentially the same wherever you go. The lovely higher-income residential zone of Spokane is, I suspect, hardly to be distinguished (except for a few interesting but not very significant architectural variations) from the corresponding zone of Oslo or Naples or Rio de Janeiro. Granted the sanctity of the home, its social, cultural, biological importance, is it necessarily the truest index of a society? Offhand, I would say the stranger could derive just as revealing an insight into a foreign way of life by listening to a country sermon or reading the classified ads in a popular newspaper or watching the behavior of a crowd during a street altercation—or, for that matter, by deciphering the graffiti on public walls.

At all events, the home is not everything. The residential quarter, despite its undeniable charms, is not the entire city, and if we poor lonely travelers are ignorant of the joys of existence on Monte Vista Terrace and Queen Alexandra Lane, we are on the other hand apt to know much more about some other aspects of the city than the lifelong resident does. I am thinking in particular of that part of the city devoted to the outsider, the transient, devoted to receiving him and satisfying his immediate needs. I am possibly prone to overemphasize this function of the city, for it is naturally the one I see most of; but who is it, I'd like to know, who keeps the city going, who makes it important to the outside world: the permanent resident with his predictable tastes and habits, or the stranger who brings money and business and new ideas? Both groups, of course, are vital to the community; their efforts are complementary; but there is a peculiar tendency among us to think of the city as a self-contained and even a sort of defensive unit forever struggling to keep its individuality intact. "Town" in English comes from a Teutonic word meaning hedge or enclosure; strange that this concept, obsolete a thousand years and more, should somehow have managed to stow away and cross the Atlantic, so that even in America we are reluctant to think of our cities as places where strangers come; with us the resident is always given preference. I gather it was quite the opposite in ancient Egypt; there the suffix corresponding to "town" or "ton" meant "the place one arrives at"—a notion I much prefer.

Anyhow, regardless of our hesitation to think of our cities as "places one arrives at" in pursuit of business or pleasure or new ideas, that is actually what most of them are. Every sizable community exists partly to satisfy the outsider who visits it. Not only that; there always evolves a special part of town devoted to this purpose. What name to give this zone of transients is something of a problem, for unlike the other subdivisions of the city, this one, I think, must be thought of in terms of movement along a pretty well defined axis. For the stranger progresses up a reasonably predictable route from his point of arrival to his final destination—and then, of course, he is likely to retrace his steps. Call it a path, in the sense that it is a way not deliberately constructed or planned for that purpose. Actually, the Strangers' Path is, in most cities, easily recognizable, once a few of its landmarks are known, and particularly (so I have found) in American cities of between, say, twenty and fifty thousand. Larger cities naturally possess a Strangers' Path of their own, but often it is so extensive and complex that it is exceedingly hard to define. As for towns of less than twenty thousand, the Path here is rarely fully developed, so that it is equally difficult to trace. Thus the Path I am most familiar with is the one in the smaller American city.

Where it begins is easy enough to establish, for it is the place where the stranger first disembarks. You may object that this can be almost anywhere, but the average stranger still arrives by bus or train or truck, and even if he arrives in his own car, he is likely to try to park somewhere outside the more congested downtown area. Arrival therefore signifies a change in the means of transportation: from train or truck or bus or car to something else, and this transfer is likely to take place either at the train station or the bus depot. Near these establishments (and for a variety of obvious reasons) you will also find the truck centers, the larger parking lots, and even a taxi stand or two.

So the beginning of the Path is marked by the abandoned means of transportation and the area near the railroad tracks. We are welcomed to the city by a smiling landscape of parking lots, warehouses, pot-holed and weed-grown streets, where isolated filling stations and quick-lunch counters are scattered among cinders like survivals of a bombing raid. But where does the Path lead from here? Directly to the center of town? To the hotels or the civic center or the main street? Not necessarily, and I believe we can only begin to follow the strangers' progress into the city when we have found out who these strangers are and what they are after. There are cities, to be sure, where most transients are well-heeled tourists and pleasure seekers: Las Vegas is one, and Monte Carlo is another; so are countless other resort towns all over the globe. The Path in such places usually leads directly to a hotel. But "stranger" does not always mean "tourist," and by and large the strangers who come to town for a day or two belong to a more modest class: not very prosperous, often with no money at all. They are men looking for a job or on their way to a job; men come to buy or sell one item in their line of business, men on a brief holiday. In terms of cash outlay in the local stores, no very brilliant public; in terms of labor and potential skills, in terms of experience of other ways of doing things, of other ways of thinking, a very valuable influx indeed. Besides, is it not one of the chief functions of the city to exchange as well as to receive? Furthermore, the greater part of these strangers would seem to be unattached men from some smaller town or from the country. These characteristics are worth bearing in mind, for they make the Path in the average small city what it now is: loud, tawdry, down-at-the-heel, full of dives and small catchpenny businesses, and (in the eyes of the uptown residential white-collar element) more than a little shady and dangerous.

Some urban geographer will be able to explain why the Strangers' Path becomes more respectable the further it gets from its point of origin; why the flophouses and brothels and the poorest among the second-hand shops (now euphemistically called loan establishments—the three golden balls are a thing of the past), the dirtiest and steamiest of greasy spoons tend to cluster around those first raffish streets near the depot and bus and truck terminals, and why the city's finest hotel, its most luxurious night club, its largest restaurant with a French name and illustrated menus are all at the other end. But so it is; one terminus of the Path is Skid Row, the other is the local Great White Way, and remote though they seem from each other, they are still organically and geographically linked. The moral is clear: the Path caters to every pocketbook, every taste, and what gives it its unifying quality and sets it off from the rest of the city is its eagerness to satisfy the unattached man from out of town, here either for a brief bout of pleasure or on some business errand.

Still, it would be foolish to maintain that the Path is everywhere identical; somewhere between its extremes, one of squalor, the other of opulence, it achieves its most characteristic and vigorous aspect, and it is in this middle region of the Path that the town seems to display all that it has to offer the outsider, though in a crude form. The City as Place of Exchange: such a definition in the residential section, even in the section devoted to public institutions, would seem incongruous, but here you learn its validity. Nearby on a converging street or in a square you find the local produce market. It is not so handsome and prosperous as it once was, for except in the more varied farming regions of the United States it has dwindled to a weekly display of potted plants and fryers and a few seasonal vegetables; Lancaster, Pennsylvania, has a noteworthy exception. But still the market, even in its reduced state, survives in most of the small cities I have visited, and it continues to serve as a center for a group of feed and grain stores, hardware stores, and an occasional tractor and farm implements agency. Here in fact is another one of those transshipment points; the streets surrounding the market are crowded with farm trucks, and with farmers setting out to explore the Path. Exchange is taking place everywhere you look: exchange of goods for cash, exchange of labor for cash (or the promise of cash) in the employment agencies, with their opportunities scrawled in chalk on blackboards; exchange of talk and drink and opinion in a dozen bars and beer parlors and lunch counters; exchange of mandolins and foreign pistols and diamond rings against cash—to be exchanged in turn against an hour or so with a girl. The Path bursts into a luxuriance of colored and lighted signs: *Chiliburgers. Red Hots. Unborn Calf Oxfords: They're New! They're Smart! They're Ivy! Double Feature: Bride of the Gorilla—Monster from Outer Space. Gospel Evangelical Mission. Checks Cashed. Snooker Parlor. The Best Shine in Town! Dr. Logan and His Amazing Europathic Method. Coney Islands. Fortunes Told: Madame LaFay.* And Army surplus stores, tattoo parlors, barbershops, poolrooms lined with pinball and slot machines, gift shops with Chinese embroidered coats and tea sets. Along one Path after another—in Paducah and Vicksburg and Poplar Bluff and Quincy —I have run across, to my amazement, strange little establishments (wedged in, perhaps, between a hotel with only a dark flight of steps on the street and a luggage store going out of business) where they sell joke books and party favors and comic masks—worthy reminders that the Path, for all its stench of beer and burning grease, its bleary eyes and uncertain clutching of doorjams, its bedlam of jukeboxes and radios and barkers, is still dedicated to good times. And in fact the Path is at its gayest and noisiest and most popular from Saturday noon until midnight.

You may call this part of town what you like: Skid Row, the Jungle, the Tenderloin, Hell's Kitchen, or (in the loftier parlance of sociology) a depressed or obsolescent area; but you cannot accurately call it a slum. It is, as I have said, primarily a district for unattached men from out of town. This implies a minority of unattached women, but it does not imply that any families live here. No children are brought up here, no home has to struggle against the atmosphere of anarchy. That is why you find no grocery or household furniture or women's and children's clothing stores, though stores with gifts for women are numerous enough. Not being an urban morphologist, I have no inkling of *why* there are no slum dwellings here, nor, for that matter, of where in the city makeup slums are likely to occur; but I have yet to find anywhere even the remotest connection between an extensive slum area and the Strangers' Path.

But then there is much in the whole matter that mystifies me. I cannot understand why loan establishments always exist cheek by jowl with the large and pretentious small city bank buildings; why the Path merges almost without transition into the financial section of the city. Yet I have observed this too often to be entirely mistaken. Scollay Square in Boston is not far from State Street, New York's Bowery is not far (in metropolitan terms) from Wall Street, and Chicago's Skid Row, the classic of them all, is only a few blocks from the center of the financial district: and nowhere is there a slum between the two extremes. I imagine the connection here is one easily explained in terms of the nineteenth-century American city and its exchange function; perhaps the Path was originally a link between warehouse and counting house, between depot and Main Street. And there are other traits I find equally hard to fathom: why the Path rarely if ever touches on the fashionable retail district or the culturally conscious civic center with its monument and museum and library and welfare organizations housed in remodeled old mansions. These two parts of town are of course the favorite haunts of the residents of the city: is that why the Path avoids all contact with them?

When the Path has reached the region of banks and hotels—usually grouped around one or two intersections in the average small city—it has lost much of its loud proletarian quality, and about all that is left is a newsstand with out-of-town papers, a travel agency, and an airline office on the ground floor of the dressy hotel. Here at one of the busiest corners it seems to pause and hesitate: Main Street leads to the substantial older residential district, and eventually (if you're persistent and ambitious enough) to beautiful, restricted Country Club Heights. Broadway is the beginning of the retail shopping district. The Path finally makes its way to City Hall; and here it is, among the surrounding decrepit brick office buildings dating from the last century, that it touches upon another and final aspect of the city: the politico-legal. Lawyers, the legal aid society, bonding companies, insurance agents, a new (but no less rapacious) breed of finance establishments proliferate among dark, wainscoted corridors and behind transoms in high-ceilinged rooms. With a kind of artistic appropriateness, the initial hangdog atmosphere of the depot and flophouse reasserts itself around the last landmark on the Path, the City Hall. Groups of hastily sobered-up faces gather forlornly outside the traffic court and the police court, or on the steps of the City Hall itself, while grimy documents are passed about. From across the street, the YMCA, the Salvation Army, and the Guild of Temperance Women look on benevolently, wanting to make friends but never quite succeeding. The Red Cross, on the other hand, dwells in proud seclusion in the basement of the Federal Building, several blocks away.

Is it in this manner that the Strangers' Path comes to an end? If so, how sad, and how pointed the moral: Start your career in brothels and saloons and you wind up, hat in hand, before the police magistrate. But this is not invariably the case, and for all I have been able to discover the Path (or some portion of it) may go on to other, happier goals. Yet it is here that it ceases to be a distinct feature of the urban landscape; from now on it is dispersed among all the other currents of city life. And the simile which inevitably comes to mind is that of a river, a stream; a powerful, muddy, untidy, but immensely fertile stream which, after being joined by its tributaries, briefly cuts its own characteristic channel in the gaudy middle section of its course, then, arrived at the center of town, fans out to deposit its waters and their burden, and vanishes.

There are two reasons for my trying to describe this part of the average American city that I have called the Stranger's Path. First, I wanted to show the people of that city that while they may know the residential section and be immensely proud of it, there is probably something about the downtown section (something very valuable in its way) that they have never recognized. My second reason is that I have derived much pleasure from exploring the Path and learning a few of its landmarks; hours in unknown cities that might otherwise have been dull thereby became enjoyable. And indeed *every* city has such a section; there are remains of it among the ruins of Pompeii; it was an integral part of every medieval town, and I have run across it in its clearest form in Mexico and in the Balkans.

But what many people will ask is, how important is the Strangers' Path to the modern city? What sort of a future does it have? To such questions I can give no educated answer. When I likened it to a river, I was using no very original simile, yet a simile having the virtue of aptness and of suggesting two characteristics. The Path, as I see it, has the prime function of introducing new life to the city, of bringing the city into touch with the outside world. (That it also has the no less valuable function of bringing the villager, the lonely field worker or traveling salesman or trucker, or the inhabitant of a de-humanized commercial farming landscape into touch with urban culture goes without saying.) Granted that these contacts are not always on a very exalted or even worthwhile scale, and that they are increasingly confined to the low-est class of citizen; nevertheless, they are what keep an infinite number of busi-nesses and arts and crafts alive, and they represent what is after all one of the chief purposes of the city: to serve as a place of general exchange. For my part, I cannot conceive of any large community surviving without this ceaseless in-flux of new wants, new ideas, new manners, new strength, and so I cannot conceive of a city without some section corresponding to the Path.

The simile was further that of a stream which empties into no basin or lake, merely evaporating into the city or perhaps rising to the surface once more outside of town along some highway strip; and it is this lack of a final, well-defined objective that prevents the Path from serving an even more im-portant role in the community and that tends to make it a poor-man's district. For when the stranger, the transient, has finished his business, something in the layout of the city should invite him to linger and become part of the town, should impel him to pay his respects, as it were. In other words, the Path should open into the center of civic leisure, into a square or plaza where citi-zens gather.

"Well," says the city planner, "we have given that matter some thought. We have decided to demolish the depressed area of the city (including your so-called Path where the financial return is low, the sanitation bad, and the traf-fic hopeless) and erect a wonderful series of apartment houses for moderate-income white-collar workers, who are the backbone of our country. We will landscape the development with wading pools, flagstone walks, and groves of Chinese elms, and we are also putting in a series of neighborhood shopping centers. And that is not all," he continues enthusiastically. "The City Hall is being removed, a handsome park will take its place, with parking facilities for five hundred cars underneath, and *more* shops, as high-class as possible, will be built around the square." He then goes on to talk about the pedestrian traffic-free center, with frequent references to the Piazza San Marco in Venice.

All well and good; freedom from traffic is what we want, and no one can object to a pretty square where none existed before. But I am growing a little weary of the Piazza San Marco. I yield to no one in my admiration of its beauty and social utility, but it seems to me that those who hold it up as the prototype of all civic (traffic-free) centers are not always aware of what makes it what it is. The piazza is not an area carved out of a residential district; its animation comes not from the art monuments which surround it; on the contrary, it is enclosed on three sides by a maze of streets and alleys whose function is almost exactly that of the Path; moreover, the Piazza San Marco has a landing-place where farmers, fishermen, sailors, merchants, and travelers all first disembark—or used to disembark—in the city. These prosaic characteristics are what give life to it. And then, how about the *universal* absence of wheeled traffic in Venice? The Mediterranean plaza is a charming and healthy institution, which American cities would be wise to adopt, but the plaza is organically connected with the workaday life of the city. It has never served, it was never intended to serve, as a place of business. It is the center of group leisure; it is the civic parlor and it therefore adjoins the civic workroom or place of exchange. The notion of a pedestrian plaza in the center of every small American city is a good one, but if it is merely to serve as a focal point for smart shops and "culture," then I still do not see in it any substitute for the Path.

There are others who try to persuade us that the suburban or residential shopping center is the civic center of the future. Victor Gruen, who is justifiably happy over his enormous (and enormously successful) shopping centers in Detroit and Minneapolis, tells us that these establishments (or rather their handsomely landscaped surroundings) are already serving more and more as the scene of holiday festivities, art shows, and pageants, as well as of general sociability and of supervised play for children. I have no doubt of it; but the shopping center, no matter how big, how modern, how beautiful, is the *exact* opposite of the Path. Its public is almost exclusively composed of housewives and children, it imposes a uniformity of taste and income and interests, and its strenuous efforts to be self-contained mean that it automatically rejects anything from outside. And compared to any traditional civic center—market place, bazaar, agora—what bloodless places these shopping centers are! I cannot see a roustabout fresh from the oil fields, or (at the other extreme) a student of manners willingly passing an hour in one of them; though both could spend a day and a night in the Path with pleasure and a certain amount of profit. Art shows indeed! It strikes me that some of our planners need to acquire a more robust idea of city life. Perhaps I do them an injustice, but I often have the feeling that their emphasis on convenience, cleanliness, and safety, their distrust of everything vulgar and small and poor, is symptomatic of a very lopsided view of urban culture.

Possibly this is the price we have to pay for planning becoming respectable, but it would be well if a wider and more humane understanding of the city and its problems soon evolved in this country. There is much to be done, and planners are the only ones who can do it. No one, I suppose, would wish to see the Stranger's Path remain as it is: garish and dirty and decaying, forced to expend its vitality in mean and neglected streets, cheated of a final merger with the broader life of the city. Yet even in its present sad state it has the power to suggest the avenue it might become, given imaginative treatment. Among the famous and best-loved streets of the world, how many of them are simply glorifications of the Strangers' Path! The Rambla in Barcelona, more than a mile of tree-lined boulevard with more trees and a promenade down the center, is such a one; and the Cannebière in Marseilles is another. They both link the harbor (the point of arrival) with the uptown area; neither of them is a show street in terms of architecture, and they are not bordered by expensive or fashionable shops. The public which frequents them at every hour of the day and night is not a "class" public: it is composed of a large cross-section of the population of the city—men, women, and children, rich and poor, strangers and natives. It happens that the residential section of both of these cities contains architectural wonders which must be visited—Gaudi's church in Barcelona, Le Corbusier's Cité Radieuse in Marseilles—and here (as in so many other places) I have done my duty, only to return as fast as possible to the center of town and those marvelous avenues.

There are few greater delights than to walk up and down them in the evening along with thousands of other people; up and down, relishing the lights coming through the trees or shining from the facades, listening to the sounds of music and foreign voices and traffic, enjoying the smell of flowers and good food and the air from the nearby sea. The sidewalks are lined with small shops, bars, stalls, dance halls, movies, booths lighted by acetylene lamps; and everywhere are strange faces, strange costumes, strange and delightful impressions. To walk up such a street into the quieter, more formal part of town is to be part of a procession, part of a ceaseless ceremony of being initiated into the city and of rededicating the city itself. And that is how our first progress through even the smallest city and town should be: a succession of gay and beautiful streets and squares, all of them extending a universal welcome.

Unlike so many visions of the city of the future, this one has a firm basis in reality. The Stranger's Path exists in one form or another in every large community, either (as in most American cities) ignored, or, as in the case of Marseilles and Barcelona and many other cities in the Old World, preserved and cherished. Everywhere it is the direct product of our economic and social evolution. If we seek to dam or bury this ancient river, we will live to regret it.

"The Stranger's Path," *Landscape* 7, no. 1 (Autumn 1957): 11–15.

JBJ, drawing of Optimo, *Landscape* 2, no. 1 (Spring 1952): 2

## The Almost Perfect Town

OPTIMO CITY (pop. 10,783; alt. 2,100 ft.), situated on a small rise over-looking the N. branch of the Apache River, is a farm and ranch center served by a spur of the S.P. County seat of Sheridan Co. Optimo City (originally established in 1803 as Ft. Gaffney) was the scene of a bloody encounter with a party of marauding Indians in 1857. (See marker on courthouse lawn.) It is the location of a state Insane Asylum, a sorghum processing plant, and an overalls factory. Annual County Fair and Cowboy Roundup Sept. 4. The highway now passes through a rolling countryside devoted to grain crops and cattle raising.

Thus would the state guide dispose of Optimo City and hasten on to a more spirited topic—if Optimo City as such existed. Optimo City, however, is not one town, it is a hundred or more towns, all very much alike, scattered across the United States from the Alleghenies to the Pacific, most numerous west of the Mississippi and south of the Platte. When, for instance, you travel through Texas and Oklahoma and New Mexico and even parts of Kansas and Missouri, Optimo City is the blur of filling stations and motels you occasionally pass; the solitary traffic light, the glimpse up a side street of an elephantine courthouse surrounded by elms and sycamores, the brief congestion of mud-spattered pickup trucks that slows you down before you hit the open road once more. And fifty miles farther on, Optimo City's identical twin appears on the horizon, and a half-dozen more Optimos beyond that, until at last, with some relief, you reach the metropolis with its new housing developments and factories and the cluster of downtown skyscrapers.

Optimo City, then, is actually a very familiar feature of the western American landscape. But since you have never stopped there except to buy gas, it might be well to know it a little better. What is there to see? Not a great deal, yet more than you would at first suspect.

Optimo, being after all an imaginary average small town, has to have had an average small-town history, or at least a western version of that average. The original Fort Gaffney (named after some inconspicuous worthy in the U.S. Army) was really little more than a stockade on a bluff overlooking a ford in the river; a few roads or trails in the old days straggled out into the plain (or desert, as they called it then), lost heart, and disappeared two or three miles from town. Occasionally even today someone digs up a fragment of the palisade or a bit of rust-eaten hardware in the backyards of the houses near the center of town, and the Historical Society possesses what it claims is the key to the principal gate. But on the whole, Optimo City is not much interested in its martial past. The fort as a military installation ceased to exist during the Civil War, and the last of the pioneers died a half-century ago, before anyone had the historical sense to take down his story. And when the county seat was located in the town, the name was changed from Ft. Gaffney, with its frontier connotation, to Optimo, which means (so the townspeople will tell you) "I hope for the best" in Latin.

What Optimo is really proud of even now is its identity as county seat. Sheridan County (and you will do well to remember that it was NOT named after the notorious Union general but after Horace Sheridan, an early member of the territorial legislature; Optimo still feels strongly about what it calls the War between the States) was organized in the 1870s, and there ensued a brief but lively competition for the possession of the courthouse between Optimo and the next largest settlement, Apache Center, twenty miles away. Optimo City won, and Apache Center, a cowtown with one paved street, is not allowed to forget the fact. The football and basketball games between the Optimo Cougars and the Apache Braves are still characterized by a very special sort of rivalry. No matter how badly beaten Optimo City often is, it consoles itself by remembering that it is still the county seat, and that Apache Center, in spite of the brute cunning of its team, has still only one street paved. We shall presently come back to the meaning of that boast.

To get on with the history of Optimo.

JBJ, sketch, courthouse, Pueblo, Colorado, 1975 (courtesy F. Douglas Adams)

### The Inflexible Gridiron

Aided by the state and Army engineers, the city fathers, back in the 1870s, surveyed and laid out the new metropolis. As a matter of course, they located a
square or public place in the center of the town, and eventually they built
their courthouse in the middle of the square, such having been the layout of
every county seat these western Americans had ever seen. Streets led from the
center of each side of the square, being named Main Street North and South,
and Sheridan Street East and West. Eventually these four streets and the square
were surrounded by a gridiron pattern of streets and avenues—all numbered
or lettered, and all of them totally oblivious of the topography of the town.
Some streets charge up impossibly steep slopes, straight as an arrow; others
lead off into the tangle of alders and cottonwoods near the river and get lost.

Strangely enough, this inflexibility in the plan has had some very pleasant results. South Main Street, which leads from the square down to the river,
was too steep in the old days for heavily laden wagons to climb in wet weather,
so at the foot of it on the flats near the river, those merchants who dealt in
farm produce and farm equipment built their stores and warehouses. The
blacksmith and welder, the hay and grain supply, and finally the auction ring
and the farmers' market found South Main the best location in town for their
purpose—primarily dealing with out-of-town farmers and ranchers. And

when, after considerable pressure on the legislature and much resistance from Apache Center (which already had a railroad), the Southern Pacific built a spur to Optimo, the depot was naturally built at the foot of South Main. And of course the grain elevator and the stockyards were built near the railroad. The railroad spur was intended to make Optimo into a manufacturing city, but it never did; all that ever came was a small overalls factory and a plant for processing sorghum, with a combined payroll of about 150. Most of the workers in the two establishments are Mexicans from south of the border—locally referred to in polite circles as "Latinos" or "Hispanos." They have built for themselves flimsy little houses under the cottonwoods and next to the river. "If ever we have an epidemic in Optimo," the men at the courthouse remark, "it will break out first of all in those Latino shacks." But they have done nothing as yet about providing the workers with better houses, and probably never will.

### Downtown and Uptown

Depot, market, factories, warehouses, slum—these features, combined with the fascination of the river bank and stockyards and the assorted public of railroaders and Latinos and occasional ranch hands—have all given South Main a very definite character: easygoing, loud, colorful, and perhaps, during Fair Week or at shipping time, a little disreputable. Boys on the Cougar football squad have specific orders to stay away from South Main, but they don't. Actually, the whole of Optimo looks on the section with indulgence and pride; it makes the townspeople feel that they understand metropolitan problems when they can compare South Main with the New York waterfront.

North Main, up on the heights beyond Courthouse Square and past the two or three blocks of retail stores, is (on the other hand) the very finest part of Optimo. The northwestern section of town, with its tree-shaded streets, its view over the river and the prairie, its summer breezes, has always been identified with wealth and fashion as Optimo understands them. Colonel Ephraim Powell (Confederate Army ret'd., owner of some of the best ranch country in the region) built his bride a handsome limestone house with a slate roof and a tower, and Walter Slymaker, proprietor of Slymaker's Mercantile and of the grain elevator, not to be outdone, built an even larger house farther up Main; so did Hooperson, first president of the bank. There are a dozen such houses in all, stone or Milwaukee brick with piazzas (or galleries, as the oldtimers still call them) and large, untidy gardens around them. It is worth noting, by the way, that the brightest claim to aristocratic heritage is this: grandfather came out west for his health. New England may have its "Mayflower" and "Arabella," East Texas its Three Hundred Founding Families, New Mexico its Conquistadores; but Optimo is loyal to the image of the delicate young college graduate who arrived by train with his law books, his set of Dickens, his taste for wine, and the custom of dressing for dinner. This legendary figure has about seen his day in the small talk of Optimo society, and the younger generation frankly doubts his having ever existed; but he (or his ghost) had a definite effect on local manners and ways of living. At all events, because of this memory Optimo looks down on those western mining towns where Sarah Bernhardt and Jean de Reszke and Oscar Wilde seem to have played so many one-night stands in now-vanished opera houses.

## A World in Itself

Wickedness—or the suggestion of wickedness—at one end of Main, affluence and respectability at the other. How about Sheridan Street running East and West? That is where you'll find most of the stores, in the first four or five blocks on either side of Courthouse Square. They form a rampart: narrow brick houses, most of them two stories high with elaborate cornices and long narrow windows, all of them devoid of modern commercial graces of chromium and black glass and artful window display, all of them ugly, but all of them pretty uniform. And so you have on Sheridan Street something rarely seen in urban America: a harmonious and restful and dignified business section. Only eight or ten blocks of it in all, to be sure; turn any corner and you are at once in a residential area.

Here are block after block of one-story frame houses with trees in front and picket fences or hedges; no sidewalk after the first block or so; a hideous church (without a cemetery, of course); a small-time auto repair shop in someone's backyard dirt roadway, and if you follow the road a few blocks more— say, to Tenth Street (after that there are no more signs)—you are likely to see a tractor turn into someone's drive with wisps of freshly cut alfalfa clinging to the vertical sickle bar. The countryside is that close to the heart of Optimo City, farmers are that much part of the town. And the glimpse of the tractor (like the glimpse of a deer or a fox driven down out of the hills by a heavy winter) restores for a moment a feeling for an old kinship that seemed to have been destroyed forever. But this is what makes Optimo, the hundreds of Optimos throughout America, so valuable: the ties between country and town have not yet been broken. Limited though it may well be in many ways, the world of Optimo City is still complete.

The center of this world is Courthouse Square, with the courthouse, ponderous, barbaric, and imposing, in the center of that. The building and its woebegone little park not only interrupt the vistas of Main and Sheridan—they were intended to do this—they also interrupt the flow of traffic coming and going in all four directions. A sluggish eddy of vehicles and pedestrians is the result. Optimo's animate existence slowed and intensified. The houses on the four sides of the square are of the same vintage (and the same general architecture) as the monument in their midst: mid-nineteenth century brick or stone; cornices like the brims of hats, fancy dripstones over the arched windows like eyebrows; painted blood-red or mustard-yellow or white; identical except for the six-story Gaffney Hotel and the classicism of the First National Bank.

Every house has a tin-roofed porch extending over the sidewalk, a sort of permanent awning which protects passersby and incidentally conceals the motley of store windows and signs. To walk around the square and down Sheridan Street under a succession of these galleries or metal awnings, crossing the strips of bright sunlight between the roofs of different height, is one of the delights of Optimo—one of its amenities, in the English sense of that word. You begin to understand why Courthouse Square is such a popular part of town.

### Saturday Nights–Bright Lights

Saturday, of course, is the best day for seeing the full tide of human existence in Sheridan County. The rows of parked pickups are like cattle in a feed lot; the sidewalks in front of Slymakers, the Mercantile, the Ranch Cafe, Sears, the drugstore resound to the mincing steps of cowboy boots; farmers and ranchers, thumbs in their pants pockets, gather in groups to lament the drought (there is always a drought) and those men in Washington, while their wives go from store to movie house to store. Radios, jukeboxes, the bell in the courthouse tower; teenagers doing "shave-and-a-haircut; bay rum" on the horns of their parents' cars as they drive round and round the square. The smell of hot coffee, beer, popcorn, exhaust, alfalfa, cow manure. A man is trying to sell a truckload of grapefruit so that he can buy a truckload of cinderblocks to sell somewhere else. Dogs; ten-year-old cowboys firing cap pistols at each other. The air is full of pigeons, floating candy wrappers, the flat strong accent erroneously called Texan.

All these people are here in the center of Optimo for many reasons—for sociability first of all, for news, for the spending and making of money, for relaxation. "Jim Guthrie and wife were in town last week, visiting friends and transacting business," is the way the Sheridan *Sentinel* describes it, and almost all of Jim Guthrie's business takes place in the square. That is one of the peculiarities of Optimo and one of the reasons why the square as an institution is so important. For it is around the square that the oldest and most essential urban (or county) services are established. Here are the firms under local control and ownership, those devoted almost exclusively to the interests of the surrounding countryside. Upstairs are the lawyers, doctors, dentists, insurance firms, the public stenographer, the Farm Bureau. Downstairs are the bank, the prescription drugstore, the newspaper office, and of course Slymaker's Mercantile and the Ranch Cafe.

### Influence of the Courthouse

Why have the chain stores not invaded this part of town in greater force? Some have already got a foothold, but most of them are at the far end of Sheridan, or even out on the Federal Highway. The presence of the courthouse is partly responsible. The traditional services want to be as near the courthouse as they can, and real estate values are high. The courthouse itself attracts so many out-of-town visitors that the problem of parking is acute. The only solution that occurs to the enlightened minds of the Chamber of Commerce is to tear the courthouse down, use the place for parking, and build a new one somewhere else. They have already had an architect draw a sketch of a new courthouse to go at the far end of Main Street; a chaste concrete cube with vertical motives between the windows—a fine specimen of Bureaucrat Modernism. But the trouble is, where to get the money for a new courthouse when the old one is still quite evidently adequate and in constant use?

If you enter the courthouse, you will be amazed by two things: the horrifying architecture of the place, and the variety of functions it fills. Courthouse means of course courtrooms, and there are two of those. Then there is the office of the county treasurer, the road commissioner, the School Board, the agricultural agent, the extension agent, the sanitary inspector, and usually a group of federal agencies as well—PMA, Soil Conservation, FHA, and so on. Finally, there are the Red Cross, the Boy Scouts, and the district nurse. No doubt many of these offices are tiresome examples of government interference in private matters; just the same, they are, for better or worse, part of almost every farmer's and rancher's business, and the courthouse, in spite of all the talk about county consolidation, is a more important place than ever.

As it is, the ugly old building has conferred upon Optimo a blessing which many larger and richer American towns can envy: a center for civic activity and a symbol for civic pride—something as different from the modern civic center as day is from night. Contrast the array of classical edifices, lost in the midst of waste space, the meaningless pomp of flagpoles and war memorials and dribbling fountains in any American city from San Francisco to Washington, with the animation and harmony and the almost domestic intimacy of Optimo's Courthouse Square, and you have a pretty good measure of what is wrong with much American city planning; civic consciousness has been divorced from everyday life, put in a special zone all by itself. Optimo City has its zones, but they are organically related to one another.

Doubtless the time will never come when the square is studied as a work of art. Why should it be? The craftsmanship in the details, the architecture of the building, the notions of urbanism in the layout of the square itself are all on a very countrified level. Still, such a square as this has dignity and even charm. The charm is perhaps antiquarian—a bit of rural America of seventy-five years ago; the dignity is something else again. It derives from the function of the courthouse and the square, and from their peculiarly national character.

## Communal Center

The practice of erecting a public building in the center of an open place is in fact pretty well confined to America—more specifically, to nineteenth-century America. The vast open areas favored by eighteenth-century European planners were usually kept free of construction, and public buildings—churches and palaces and law courts—were located to face these squares; to command them, as it were. But they were not allowed to interfere with the original open effect. Even the plans of eighteenth-century American cities, such as Philadelphia and Reading and Savannah and Washington, always left the square or public place intact. Spanish America, of course, provides the best illustrations of all: nine times out of ten, the plaza is surrounded by public buildings, but it is left free. Yet almost every American town laid out after, say, 1820 deliberately planted a public building in the center of its square. Sometimes it was a school, sometimes a city hall, more often a courthouse, and it was always approachable from all four sides and always as conspicuous as possible.

Why? Why did these pioneer city fathers go counter to the taste of the past in this matter? One guess is as good as another. Perhaps they were so proud of their representative institutions that they wanted to give their public buildings the best location available. Perhaps frontier America was following an esthetic movement, already at that date strong in Europe, that held that an open space was improved when it contained some prominent freestanding object—an obelisk or a statue or a triumphal arch. However that may have been, the pioneer Americans went Europe one better and put the largest building in town right in the center of the square.

Thus the square ceased to be thought of in nineteenth-century America as a vacant space; it became a container or (if you prefer) a frame. A frame, so it happened, not merely for the courthouse but for all activity of a communal sort. Few esthetic experiments have ever produced such brilliantly practical results. A society which had long since ceased to rally around the individual leader and his residence and which was rapidly tiring of rallying around the meeting house or church all at once formed a new symbol: local representative government as embodied in the courthouse. A good deal of flag waving resulted—as European travelers have always told us—and a good deal of very poor "representational" architecture; but Optimo acquired something to be proud of, something to moderate that American tendency to think of every town as existing entirely for money-making purposes.

**Symbol of Independence**

At this juncture, the protesting voice of the Chamber of Commerce is heard: "One moment. Before you finish with our courthouse, you had better hear the other side of the question. If the courthouse were torn down, we would not only have more parking space—sorely needed in Optimo—we would also get funds for widening Main Street into a four-lane highway. If Main Street were widened, Optimo could attract many new businesses catering to tourists and other transients—restaurants and motels and garages and all sorts of drive-in establishments. In the last ten years," continues the Chamber of Commerce, "Optimo has grown by twelve hundred. *Twelve hundred!* At that rate we'll still be a small town of less than twenty thousand in 1999. But if we had new businesses, we'd grow fast and have better schools and a new hospital, and the young people wouldn't move to the cities. Or do you expect Optimo to go on depending on a few hundred tightfisted farmers and ranchers for its livelihood?" The voice, now shaking with emotion, adds something about "eliminating" South Main by means of an embankment and a cloverleaf and picnic grounds for tourists under the cottonwoods where the Latinos still reside.

These suggestions are very sensible ones on the whole. Translate them into more general terms and what they amount to is this: If we want to get ahead, the best thing to do is break with our own past, become as independent as possible of our *immediate* environment, and at the same time become al-most completely dependent for our well-being on some remote outside re-source. Whatever you may think of such a program, you cannot very well deny that it has been successful for a large number of American towns. Think of the hayseed communities which have suddenly found themselves next to an oil field or a large factory or an army installation, and which have cashed in on their good fortune by transforming themselves overnight, turning their backs on their former sources of income, and tripling their population in a few years! It is true that these towns put all their eggs in one basket, that they are totally at the mercy of some large enterprise quite beyond their control. But think of the freedom from local environment; think of the excitement and the money! Given the same circumstances—and the Southwest is full of surprises still—why should Optimo not do the same?

**A Common Destiny**

Because there are many different kinds of towns, just as there are many dif-ferent kinds of men; a development which is good for one kind can be death on another. Apache Center (to use that abject community as an ex-ample), with its stockyards and its one paved street and its very limited re-sponsibility to the county as a community, might well become a boomtown and no one would be worse off. Optimo seems to have a different destiny. For almost a hundred years—a long time in this part of the world—it has been identified with the surrounding landscape and been an essential part of it. Whatever wealth it possesses has come from the farms and ranches, not from the overalls factory or from tourists. The bankers and merchants will tell you, of course, that without their ceaseless efforts and their vision the countryside could never have existed; the farmers and ranchers consider Optimo's prosperity and importance entirely their own creation. Both par-ties are right to the extent that the town is part of the landscape—one might even say part of every farm, since much farm business takes place in the town itself.

Now, if Optimo suddenly became a year-round tourist resort, or the Overalls Capital of the Southwest, what would happen to that relationship, do you suppose? It would vanish. The farmers and ranchers would soon find themselves crowded out and would go elsewhere for those services and benefits which they now enjoy in Optimo. And as for Optimo itself, it would soon achieve the flow of traffic, the new store fronts, the housing developments, the payrolls, and bank accounts it cannot help dreaming about; and in the same process it would achieve a total social and physical dislocation, and a loss of a sense of its own identity. County seat of Sheridan County? Yes. But, much more important, southwestern branch of the American Cloak and Garment Corporation, or the "Little Town with the Big Welcome," boasting three hundred tourist beds which, when empty for one night out of three, threaten bankruptcy to half the town.

As of the present, Optimo remains pretty much as it has been for the last generation. The Federal Highway still bypasses the center (what a roadblock, symbolical as well as actual, that courthouse is!), so if you want to see Optimo, you had better turn off at the top of the hill near the watertower of the Lunatic Asylum—now called Fairview State Rest Home, the hideous high fence around it having been torn down. The dirt road eventually becomes North Main. The old Slymaker place is still intact. The Powell mansion, galleries and all, belongs to the American Legion, and a funeral home has taken over the Hooperson house. Then comes downtown Optimo; and then the courthouse, huge and graceless, in detail and proportion more like a monstrous birdhouse than a monument. Stop here. You'll find nothing of interest in the stores, and no architectural gems down a side street. Even if there were, no one would be able to point them out. The Historical Society, largely in the hands of ladies, thinks of antiquity in terms of antiques and art as anything that looks pretty on the mantelpiece.

The weather is likely to be scorching hot and dry, with a wild, ineffectual breeze in the elms and sycamores. You'll find no restaurant in town with atmosphere—no chandeliers made out of wagonwheels, no wall decorations of famous brands, no bar disguised as the Hitching Rail or the Old Corral. Under a high ceiling with a two-bladed fan in the middle, you'll eat ham hock and beans, hot bread, iced tea without lemon, and like it or go without. But, as compensation of sorts, at the next table there will be two ranchers eating with their hats on and discussing the affairs, public and private, of Optimo City. To hear them talk, you'd think they owned the town.

That's about all. There's the market at the foot of South Main, the Latino shacks around the overalls factory, a grove of cottonwoods, and the Apache River (north branch) trickling down a bed ten times too big; and then the open country. You may be glad to have left Optimo behind.

Or you may have liked it, and found it pleasantly old-fashioned. Perhaps it is; but it is in no danger of dying out quite yet. As I said to begin with, there is another Optimo City fifty miles farther on. The country is covered with them. Indeed, they are so numerous that it sometimes seems as if Optimo and rural America were one and indivisible.

"The Almost Perfect Town," *Landscape* 2, no. 1 (Spring 1952): 2–8.

## Chihuahua as We Might Have Been

There have not been many frontiers like this one, I imagine. An abstraction, a Euclidean line drawn across the desert, has created two distinct human landscapes where there was only one before. Much of the frontier is river, and rivers are meant to bring men together, not to keep them apart. The rest of it is a straight scientific line inscribed in sand, no more related to the terrain, no more part of the view than are those groups of letters which maps show to the north and south of it: Chihuahua and Texas and New Mexico.

Line and river, idea and unifying force, they have been made to divide an entity which the earth created and men accepted for some three hundred years—the Spanish Southwest. Speaking in terms of a relatively lengthy past and its physical setting, New Mexico and that western wedge of Texas and Chihuahua all belong to the same high, mountainous, semi-arid region which was once called New Biscay. Or should I say that New Mexico and a fragment of Texas are the northward extensions of Chihuahua? Politically, they certainly were. All three areas were not only discovered, explored, and taken possession of in the same northwestward movement of the Spaniards out of Mexico, but were eventually settled by the same breed of colonists: miners and hunters and ranchmen. And Santa Barbara, the southernmost (and the oldest) town in Chihuahua, to this day likes to think of Santa Fe far to the north as a sort of daughter city. The Romeros, Trujillos, and Martinezes who abound in both places must then be cousins, I suppose, many miles and generations removed. One language, one law, one kind of economy—a predatory one—and one prevailing set of manners and values; all these things the line has destroyed.

But it is of course the physical make-up of this old Southwest that gives it its fundamental unity, and a whole network of Euclidean lines could not destroy that. Topography, climate, vegetation, the very quality of the sunlight and distance and solitude are the same north of the border and south. Though it may change its name from Rio Grande to Rio Bravo, its course from due south to southeast, the one great river with its tributaries dominates the region, just as its articulations, its valleys and passes, have always determined the location of roads and farms and villages. As for mountains, who can say in the Southwest what range or system any of them belongs to? Only the Sangre de Cristo, we are told, are part of the Rockies; all the others have origins of their own. Still, I think that most of them, aside from their differences of altitude and bulk, share a certain local southwestern character and are unlike mountains elsewhere. They tend for the most part north and south, and are isolated from one another by great wide valleys and plains. They leap up out of the range or desert like dark red spiny-backed monsters at play in the sea, and sink abruptly. Their steep flanks are barren except for cascades of sand and gravel and rock, cascades which seem only now to have stopped streaming, as if yesterday the mass had suddenly heaved out of the flatness. No horizon to the south but is alive with extravagant peaks: dark orange, dark blue, pale blue and pink and violet, the color of clinkers. And yet for all their omnipresence the mountains here and in Chihuahua are almost totally useless, producing no gold, no rain, no permanent streams, no forests, and scarcely any pasture. They are background, essential for esthetic purposes, dignifying or dwarfing the activities of man, whichever you prefer.

Mountains are the same, weather is the same; a little dryer to the south, a little hotter, but not without bleak winds to whip across the treeless expanses. Vegetation likewise much the same. Chamiso is absent, and so are piñon trees, but their places are taken by creosote and mesquite. After one of the rare showers in the Chihuahua desert, the dampened leaves of the creosote make the air smell of witch hazel, just as it does in southern New Mexico. And while the moisture lasts, the short, sparse grass becomes green, wildflowers cover the hollows of the range with sheets of yellow and silver, and there is a profusion of meadowlarks singing. The same limpid air, the same overpowering sun. And the same intense blue sky, immaculate day after day except for one long thin cloud the tone of aluminum.

So they were made to be one and the same, Chihuahua and west Texas and New Mexico, and they were thought of as one by the people who lived north and south—until the line was drawn. Now there are two Southwests, or rather a Mexican Northwest and our own Southwest, related but no longer identical. For what has happened is not merely that a homogeneous region has been divided between two nations—that could always be undone—but that two distinct human landscapes, each the expression of a different kind of society, have been created; and such a distinction is likely to last forever.

Our own we know, or think we know. But what is the most marked characteristic of the human landscape immediately to the south of us? To the North American traveler, in search of that color and variety usually associated with Mexico, Chihuahua is bitterly disappointing, and its most striking feature, exhilarating at first, then depressing, is its emptiness. Our own Southwest has its lonely prospects, but none so lonely, I should think, as those in Chihuahua. Vast enough to contain the history and monuments of a whole race, its wide valleys seem to be as devoid of humanity as was the world on the eve of the sixth day. No matter where you look in New Mexico or west Texas —provided the view is of normal extent—you are likely to see some evidence of man's work; a far-off ranch house with a windmill, a wire fence, a telephone or light pole, a roadside store, sometimes the green of a patch of irrigated land down in a wash. In Chihuahua there is little of the sort; nothing for twenty or thirty or forty miles at a stretch to reassure you that men have lived here and probably live here still. The miles go by, the mountains slowly revolve out of sight and new ones appear; and at last you see a file of mottle-faced, long-limbed, wild-eyed cows, of the sort we still derisively call Chihuahuas, wandering across the range. Strictly speaking, even these are not evidence of human occupancy of the landscape, though they would certainly be elsewhere greener and better watered were it not for human interference.

There are towns and even cities to the south, quite true; and whole countrysides where the soil is cultivated with an intensity we scarcely know; but these are merely interruptions of the prevailing solitude; they do not constitute a continuous pattern and do little to alter that first impression. It happens to be a very correct impression, I believe. It is another and more immediate way of sensing that the human landscape is only feebly developed. I do not mean merely that the population is small for so large an area (it is, though it is actually more dense than that of New Mexico); nor that there is anything primitive about the social setup in Chihuahua. On the contrary. But whatever the society, it has only sketched the broad outline of its pattern on the face of the earth. It has built towns and cities in considerable number, but it has only begun to formulate its own characteristic countryside. Our own Southwest, on the other hand, has been almost completely transformed in the image of our own way of life. It is as if two different sets of laws, two distinct psychologies, were at work.

Now, the explanation for this underdevelopment—or at least one explanation—is not hard to discover. It is undoubtedly true that much of Chihuahua is rangeland, if not worse, and could at best support a very small number of ranchers. But the thing is, during most of the four centuries since the arrival of the Spaniards, it has supported no one at all. The Apache and Comanche raids, beginning as soon as those tribes had acquired horses from the invaders, made the region an unhealthy one not only for would-be settlers but for military and commercial traffic passing through to New Mexico in the north. Garrisons were established at strategic points, especially in the open country where the Apaches preferred to operate, and expeditions against the Indians were almost constant. With little success. Toward the middle of the eighteenth century, security, at least for travelers, was achieved, but then the Jesuit missionaries in the mountains to the west were withdrawn on orders from Spain, and Spanish authority was weakened as a result. The Apaches once more became aggressive, and when Mexico declared its independence of the mother country, the greatest concern of Chihuahua was not the drawing up of a suitably republican state constitution but how to defend itself against the Indian raids. These in fact had become so effective that the settlers in the open country had retreated altogether to the garrison towns or to the mountains or to the larger centers like Chihuahua city and Parral. The chronicles of these communities make for sorry reading: settled in the seventeenth or eighteenth century and given a resounding name, abandoned a few decades later (and often once again) because of the depredations of the Indians, the "Naturales."

Such a state of affairs was more or less paralleled in our own part of the continent, but here it never resulted in the complete depopulation of a desirable stretch of land, nor did it ever last for long. In Chihuahua it lasted until about the middle of the 1880s. It was only then that the vast cattle country in the northern and eastern part of the state was finally safe for settlement. And again a political situation intervened. If ranching had long been delayed by the inability of the government to maintain order, ranching on a prosperous basis was handicapped under the regime of President Porfirio Díaz by a government policy of encouraging monster cattle empires. The largest ranch in

Chihuahua (and incidentally in all of Mexico) contained no less than six and a half million acres—about the size of Belgium. There were until not many years ago five other ranches with more than a million acres apiece, and altogether more than a third of the entire state, which is not much smaller than Arizona, was owned by seventeen men. Much of this land was to be sure of very limited worth, but some of it was extremely valuable. A ranch of almost a million acres west of Chihuahua city, once the property of a family who ran a few thousand head of cattle on it and eventually went bankrupt, now supports ten thousand prosperous Mennonite farmers, with room for many more.

I see no reason, I confess, why a large ranch cannot exploit the land just as well as a medium-size or small one. But in practice these enormous holdings were totally inefficient. At a time when the Anglo-Saxon world was beginning to discover the romance of ranching in the Wild West, and when British and American capital was pouring into the cattle industry, the ranchers of northern Mexico had an altogether different point of view. Disdaining to live in the primitive solitude of their estates, they built palaces in town and furnished them with boatloads of finery from Italy and France. Their lavish spending was the admiration of Europe, but they begrudged money for nails, and so the ranch buildings were held together with rawhide. One of these ranches is said to have branded 140,000 steers in one year. But no equipment was bought for farming, no wells were drilled, no good stock was ever bred, and no range conservation even of the most rudimentary sort was dreamed of. Nor were any fences to divide the range into pastures ever erected, though stone walls, miles in extent and still a conspicuous feature of the otherwise bleak landscape, were sometimes built. The enforced self-sufficiency of these ranches, to say nothing of the low pay of the workers, discouraged the growth of any rural retail centers in the neighborhood. All in all, it would be hard to conceive of a more benighted economy than this, or a more picturesque one. The florid mansions and the legends of high living are only part of its legacy, however. Rangeland remote from the natural waterholes is still largely untouched, villages are still practically nonexistent, and, except for the overgrazed areas near water and the tumbled remains of those massive walls, the whole countryside is today much as it must have been four hundred years ago.

Would efficiency have overtaken these holdings in time? Quite possibly. The American market for beef has always been the largest one for Chihuahua, and in the course of organizing to exploit it, the landowners in spite of themselves might have incidentally created a more articulate landscape—retail villages, small farms, roads and windbreaks and water tanks and small pastures.

In any case, such was the development in the United States. But a generation ago the era of large ranches in northern Mexico came to an end—not, as we are fond of supposing in parallel cases, because they were uneconomical or obsolete, but because of a revolution. The revolutionary wars started in the first decade of the century and lasted until well after 1920, causing almost as much damage of every description as did the far better known First World War in Europe. The large ranches were naturally objects of special attention from the revolutionists, but the whole region, indeed the whole nation, suffered to a degree that we in this country have never appreciated. Before the revolution Chihuahua had two and a half million head of cattle; twenty years later it had little more than a quarter of that amount. The Mexican Northwest has always been the land of horsemen; Chihuahua had 730,000 horses before the revolution and lost four-fifths of them. Nor was this the result of any shift in the economy; it was entirely the work of a prolonged and ruinous war which leveled villages, destroyed railroads, uprooted the population, and brought every agricultural enterprise to a standstill.

Actually, it was not so much the violent aspect of the revolution that did away with the big ranches as it was the social revolution which came after; and the first real change in the human landscape—a change more evident on paper than in the scenery itself, but still a change—came when the large holdings were divided up for the benefit of the less prosperous. Socially and economically speaking, the Land Reform Laws were epochal, I have no doubt, but their total effect on the pattern of settlement has been far less marked than one might suppose. For unhappily it is not enough to give a man a few thousand acres of land; he needs not only cattle but money for wells and fences and corrals and feed, and the average rancher south of the Rio Grande has never had money or credit of that kind. And then finally, two more factors (not political this time) have militated against a full development of the rural areas: the hoof-and-mouth disease and the local drought. The disease never prevailed in Chihuahua, but the United States embargo on Mexican meat nevertheless killed the best outlet for beef. The prolonged drought, still not everywhere broken, affected the grass on the range less than it affected the supply of surface water; but the results were the same. As for the underground water supply, it is largely intact, because who has the money to drill wells and put in windmills and tanks? Plaintive and frequent requests have been made to the government, but to no avail. The chief concern at the moment is not the rancher and his plight—a perennial topic—but the small farmers, the colonists on the large and costly irrigation projects.

So the ranchers, obliged to shift for themselves, have been able to do little or nothing. The countryside, however equitably subdivided, remains much as it has always been, and the development of a full-fledged pattern of settlement remains a very nebulous prospect.

Here then is an environment in every important respect like our own rangeland—in climate, vegetation, water supply, topography—where nevertheless a totally different kind of human landscape prevails. And how are we to account for this dissimilarity? Chiefly, I think, by considering some of those imponderable factors which go to make every landscape what it is, and of these the psychological is not the least influential. There has in fact evolved to the south of us a landscape of towns and cities, a surprisingly rich and numerous constellation of communities, located as it were in a void. Chihuahua has more towns of over ten thousand inhabitants than New Mexico and Arizona, and they are not sleepy market towns, either. That is one reason why they are not visited by tourists; they are almost completely lacking in beauty and charm. The air does not smell of cinnamon and chocolate and lime, no wild birds call out in the laurel trees of the plaza, and there is little of the public gaiety of a more genial climate. The antiquities of Chihuahua are neither numerous nor impressive (though they would loom large in New Mexico or Arizona), and they are usually hidden in the welter of neon signs and telegraph poles and dwarf skyscrapers and neo-Aztec architecture of the business streets. The smaller towns are a gridiron of low houses bordering dusty and windswept streets, streets too broad and too long, and with the harsh mountains or the desert at the end of all of them, no matter what their length. You begin to suspect in these drab surroundings that Texas cannot be very far away, and that Yankee imperialism is doing its fell work in even the remotest places.

But actually these towns are all bona fide Chihuahuan—which is to say they have a character very much their own: detached from the countryside, self-contained, and, within limits, remarkably urban. Chihuahua city, neither particularly rich nor blessed with many monuments, has nevertheless a dignity and a scale which would put many North American cities to shame. What should not be forgotten is that these towns were none of them originally rural marketplaces; they are all artificial and carefully designed communities which have not yet attained their full metropolitan growth, and perhaps never will.

There are several very good reasons for this concentration in towns and for the urban character of the towns themselves. The largest and oldest settlements in Chihuahua are after all mining centers, possessing many features of cities far larger and more industrialized than they: a small class of very rich

JBJ, sketch, Pancho Villa's tomb, Chihuahua, Mexico, 1973 (courtesy F. Douglas Adams)

men, a large proletariat, and little if any traditional connection with the nearby farmers and ranchers. All past efforts to expand into the open country have been roughly discouraged, and finally a large community in the midst of semidesert country has to be self-sufficient if it is to survive.

But still, I cannot believe that such explanations, practical though they are, really account for the concentration in towns; I cannot believe that there is not some national or racial trait also at work: in brief, a partiality for city life. The kind of architecture a group prefers—when it has any choice in the matter—can be very revealing of the group's temperament. The poor in Chihuahua, even in the large cities, build as best they can, which is to say they build as the farmers do: out of adobe. But the more prosperous citizens like their houses to be more elegant, and so in northern Mexico the rural architectural tradition is one of the first things to be discarded when social respectability arrives. As for the very rich, the ranchers or mine owners or office holders or generals, their houses are likely to repudiate every local tradition of plan and material and ornamentation. Not deliberately, I suppose, but nonetheless completely. In the old days of Porfirism, as they call the regime of Díaz, the ideal home seems to have been something ornate, formal, and reminiscent of a European social order—Paris or Madrid at two removes. What is the ideal now? Something not easy to define, but easy enough to recognize: a blend of Hollywood and Tel Aviv and Frank Lloyd Wright; wrought iron and plate glass and tapestry brick and bougainvillea and Kublai Khan's pleasure dome, conspicuously, not to say defiantly, located in the midst of an English lawn. If, as someone once incautiously remarked, architecture is frozen music, this is Spike Jones straight from the deep freeze. But more than that, it is a very definite rejection of the whole rural background.

It may be objected that Chihuahua has no rural tradition except of having to flee from the Apaches and that, unlike other parts of Mexico (and New Mexico), it never had a sedentary Indian population to establish an indigenous architectural style. True; but what it *does* possess is a vast amount of that kind of building which we in the Southwest call the Spanish Pueblo style. Without going into the touchy problem of where this style originated, I think most will agree that Chihuahua, however scantily populated, has an infinitely greater number and variety of those squat adobe constructions than we in the Southwest ever had. But here is where one of those imponderables comes in: Chihuahua, the rich and official Chihuahua, the Chihuahua which builds churches and public buildings and hundred-thousand-dollar residences, will have none of this adobe style. It wants something more elaborate, even if synthetic. It wants an architecture which reflects what may be called the southwestern dream, a dream which was (and in Mexico still is) compounded of wealth based on mining and ranching, Spanish background, and the amenities of city life: a culture which has unconsciously retained the original dual meaning of urbanity.

As to what the racial origins of the population of Chihuahua are, I have no idea. They may well all be descendants of the Spanish conquistadores, and again they may be a mixture of every Indian group in Mexico. But what matters is how they think and act, and to me one of the charms of northern Mexico is that its people think not as Indians but as Latins. More than a century ago, Alexander von Humboldt was much impressed by the vigor and clarity of thought among a group which at that time was still a rough pioneer community for the rest of Mexico, and he predicted that this northern region—in which I suppose he meant to include Arizona and New Mexico, for he wrote before they were annexed to the United States—would in time be distinguished for its mathematicians and scientists. Was it Los Alamos that he foresaw?

Latin rationalism, however, has assumed a different form—a taste for politics and political theory—and it is that taste which has to a surprising extent formed the human landscape. *If* the missionaries had not been withdrawn in the eighteenth century, there would have been a peaceful Indian population to contribute to the welfare of the country. *If* the Apache had been prevented by a strong government from going on the warpath in the nineteenth century, there would have been more ranches, more farms, more country villages. *If* there had been no revolution in the early decades of this century, there would have been a more even distribution of the population. And if in the past political events have so determined the demographic aspects of the world, or at least of Chihuahua, why can they not continue to do so in the future? Divide the estates by law, build highways and new towns and irrigation projects according to a plan, create a new party to execute the plan, and the political process goes on with unabated vigor. And no doubt it will. Much Mexican political activity must forever bewilder the foreigner, but some of it becomes intelligible, I find, when it is understood that to the south of the Rio Grande the world of Man is thought of as created in the likeness of a social theory and not, as with us, in the likeness of an economic force. The elaborate geometrical layout of every modern Mexican community—gridiron or hexagon or concentric figures; the policy of renaming streets after political abstractions when they are not numbered, and even sometimes when they are, and of renaming old towns after contemporary political heroes—these are merely the most obvious manifestations of a determination to impose design and political direction on an unreasoning world. *Gentes de razón* versus *Naturales;* and when the *Naturales* vanish, then versus Nature itself.

This theoretical conquest of the region has already been accomplished. On paper, and in the conviction of its citizens, the Mexican earth, amorphous as much of it must seem to us, is divided and subdivided a dozen different ways, classified and surveyed. In this manner, even the uninhabited desert has been tamed. The steepest hill, the poorest village in Chihuahua can always somehow be benefited by an application of geometry and politics.

Something of the same belief persists among the Spanish population of New Mexico and Arizona. It would do us no harm, I think, if we had more of it, if more of the Latin faith in reason rather than in power had spread northward into our country before the line was drawn. But it was drawn a hundred years ago, and now there are two nations, two landscapes, two ways of looking at the world and of living in it. In time the Southwest will lose its identity, but the aspects of it that we value and try to keep alive hark back to that large, undivided region; it is Chihuahua which represents the original even now. What is alike in New Mexico and the old is the heritage of Chihuahua. Chihuahua is what we once were: a sun-struck landscape full of bright plans for the future.

"Chihuahua as We Might Have Been," *Landscape* 1, no. 1 (Spring 1951): 16–24.

JBJ, photo, edge of High Plains between Las Vegas and Tucumcari, New Mexico

## Looking at New Mexico

We learn about history by reading it in school; we learn to see it when we travel, and for Americans the place where we see most clearly the impact of time on a landscape is New Mexico.

Our history is more complicated than most, and it is far more visible. In regions to the east of us, more prosperous and blessed with more abundant rainfall, the past, even the recent past, soon vanishes from sight: bulldozed out of existence in favor of something new and larger and more costly, it is also often quickly hidden by exuberant vegetation. Even the rubble of abandoned tenements in the Bronx soon acquires a covering of weeds and vines, and sometimes wildflowers; trees conceal the abandoned farms of Appalachia. But here in New Mexico history remains exposed to the sun for all to see. Our landscape is everywhere spotted with ruins—ruins of ancient towns, ruins of sheepherders' shelters built a decade ago. It is as if we had been struck by a neutron bomb, eliminating people while leaving their dwellings intact, at the mercy of wind and sun. It is to see our past that thousands of tourists come to New Mexico: archaeologists, geologists, antiquarians, lovers of whatever is old or out-of-date or mysterious because of its age. Our history invites the photographer.

The best time for seeing history is the summer. That is when the remoter country can be explored; it is when schools and colleges all over America are closed, and teachers and students and scholars are free to wander. It follows, therefore, that awareness of southwestern history is a seasonal phenomenon determined by the academic calendar, much as a certain kind of piety is determined by phases of the moon. Summer is the time for looking back and recording what we see. Family reunions, two-hundred strong, gather in the shade of a cottonwood grove, in a dance hall, in a half-forgotten village once an ancestral stronghold. Veterans' organizations parade down Main Street, and Santa Fe and Wagon Mound and Arroyo Seco deck themselves out in Indian or Spanish-American or cowboy or counterculture costume, celebrating the Old Days. The sun shines out of a deep blue sky; it is hot, but not too hot, and history is transformed into a photographic pageant, an ideal subject for color slides.

Yet it is hard not to be fleetingly aware of a background suggestive of a kind of history with a different dimension, no matter where we are in New Mexico. We glimpse it in a dark face in the crowd; we catch an echo of it in the voices and the music coming from a corner bar. We see and never quite forget the horizon of range after range of mountains of diminishing blue. In every background there lurks another kind of past, far more ancient, far less easy to comprehend than the strictly human history on display.

There is one region of New Mexico where we can come closer to a time measured not by events or seasons but by millennia, a landscape with a history of its own that is perhaps not history at all, merely the unending repetition of cosmic cycles, a landscape where by a paradox the still photograph records all we can ever know of its past.

The Colorado Plateau is the name given by geographers and geologists to an immense region covering most of Utah, western Colorado, eastern Arizona, and northwestern New Mexico. When you drive due west out of Albuquerque toward Grants and the uranium country, you catch a glimpse of a small portion of it—a horizon like a long, pale-blue rampart extending beyond sight to the north and south. It is deceptively unspectacular, almost a continuation, one would say, of the pleasantly humanized landscape of the Rio Grande country. But this is actually only the eastern edge of a province distinguished by its great elevation (reaching in places to eleven thousand feet), its hundreds of remarkable canyons (including the Grand Canyon), and its overall horizontality. Every mesa, every canyon, every freestanding mountain seems composed of layer upon layer of a red and brown and yellow and dead-white rock.

Only a small fragment of this spectacular landscape lies in New Mexico, but it is a fragment containing some of the largest prehistoric ruins in the United States, as well as areas with occasional stands of trees and small streams meandering through canyons. There are expanses of pale grass and sagebrush, and piñon and juniper trees in groves on the slopes of the valleys. It seems to be empty of life, but in summer it sometimes has a strangely pastoral, almost arcadian quality. Navajos graze their flocks of goats and sheep on the grass among the miniature forests of sagebrush, bells tinkling. In the middle of the day they rest in the dense black shade of the piñons. The air is fragrant, the light on the perpendicular dark red canyon walls is golden. Small clusters of ragged Navajo dwellings, with a peach tree or two nearby, stand under the piñon trees, and a saddle horse sleepily hangs his head. Turn elsewhere and the view is perhaps a little too vast for comfort: a panorama of endless range country with a rim of violet mesas and dark mountains where there must be forests and streams of water, though very far away. The days are all alike; the summer is long and immobile. In the late afternoon immense black clouds boil up to the zenith, and then some small portion of the hot and thirsty landscape is suddenly blessed with a brief, violent downpour which makes every rock, every patch of earth glisten. The storm comes to an abrupt end like a duty routinely performed and is followed by not one but two perfect rainbows. It is as if some rite has been reenacted, some myth made visible for the millionth time, antiphony to a ceremonial dance in a nearby Indian village.

Which comes first: the blessing or the prayer? It is not easy in this landscape to separate the role of man from the role of nature. The plateau country has been lived in for centuries, but the human presence is disguised even from the camera's eye. There are ruins like geological formations, disorders of tumbled stone. There are immense arrays of slowly crumbling rocks that look like ruins. The nomenclature we Americans have imposed on much of the landscape testifies to our uncertainty: the ruins have unpronounceable Navajo names; the natural formations are called Gothic Mesa or Monument Valley or Chimney Rock.

It is the sort of landscape which (before the creation of the bomb) we associated with the world after history had come to an end: sheep grazing among long-abandoned ruins, the lesson of Ozymandias driven home by enormous red arches leading nowhere, lofty red obelisks or needles commemorating events no one had ever heard of, symbols of the vanity of human endeavor waiting to be photographed. But is that really the message of the plateau country? There was a time, several generations ago, toward the end of the last century when photographers, masters of their art, had a clearer vision:

they wanted to leave history, even human beings, out of their pictures. Per- haps there were technical reasons for wishing to exclude all movement, or per- haps it was a matter of belief, a way of responding to the concept of time in the Colorado Plateau. For what makes the landscape so impressive and so beautiful is that it teaches no copybook moral, no ecological or social lesson. It tells us that there is another way of measuring time, and that the present is, in fact, an enormous interval in which even the newest of man-made structures are contemporary with the primaeval. That is why it is possible to see that the dams on the Colorado and San Juan Rivers, the deep pits of the Santa Rita copper mines, and the terraced mountains near Laguna where uranium has been extracted are all as old or as young as the canyons and mesas and the un- dulating plains of sagebrush.

Not far from Quemado (which is not far from the Arizona line) there is a field of innumerable lightning rods, geometrically planted in an expanse of range grass. As an example of contemporary environmental art, it is a source of infinite curiosity and bewilderment. Some day, centuries hence, the field of lightning rods will have been forgotten by tourists and entirely assimilated into the landscape. Navajos grazing their sheep among them will know that these rods derive from the same cosmic occurrence that balanced liver-colored rocks on pedestals of yellow mud in the Chaco region: objects identified with an Emergence myth, easily explained, provided our small-scale microhistory is left out of the picture.

The school of "timeless" photography flourished at a period when all of New Mexico was described by outsiders, and even admiringly described, in terms of its peculiar notions of time. It was "the land of poco tiempo," "the land of mañana," "the land where time stood still." What was meant was not Indian or prehistoric New Mexico but Spanish-American New Mexico.

By and large this is the New Mexico associated with the upper Rio Grande Valley and the mountains containing it. For it was here that the first colonists settled in the late sixteenth century, and it was here that the province (or state) acquired its identity. What attracted settlement was the mild climate, the apparent abundance of water, the fertile soil, and the forests covering the mountains. In many ways the landscape seemed to resemble that of Spain. Al- most from the time of the first explorations, New Mexico was seen as a kind of promised land: not a paradise of ease and abundance, to be sure, but a land of grass and forests and flowing water where the efforts of working men and women would be duly rewarded. For it so happens, even today, that no matter whether you come to New Mexico from the immediate east, the High Plains, the arid south, or the canyon landscape in the west, the region always seems, by comparison with the country you have been traveling through, something like a land flowing with milk and honey. What shatters the illusion is the long, dry summer that afflicts the greater part of the state.

How long it took the earlier generations of Spanish-speaking colonists to learn that lesson is a complicated question: the presence of hostile Indians in the plains of the eastern part of New Mexico acted to discourage their settlement and even exploration until the mid-eighteenth century. In any event, Spanish settlement was long confined to the Rio Grande region, which to this day remains the heartland of Spanish-American culture. The small lateral valleys of the Rio Grande, as well as the valley of the Rio Grande itself, provided the colonists with an environment suited to their kind of agriculture and their kind of living—in small villages where old established customs and relationships could be continued. Settlement in colonial New Mexico was in effect a transplantation, a new version of the order that had prevailed in colonial Mexico and in Spain. It was the work not of footloose individuals in search of adventures or wealth but of small, homogeneous groups of simple people who brought with them their religion, their family ties, their ways of building and working and farming.

Farming meant irrigation; to that extent they were aware of the climatic limitations of the region, and they knew that the only places where that kind of farming was possible were along the few permanent water courses in the foothills and valleys. Each village devised its own communal irrigation system—an accomplishment deserving of more recognition than it has so far received; and each village gradually created its own miniature landscape of gardens and orchards and fields and pastures, a landscape distinct from the surrounding wilderness. Farmers introduced not only new kinds of vegetation—crops and grasses and fruit trees—but also another climate, for their irrigation system made them relatively independent of the unpredictable local rains.

The history of these villages is largely unrecorded; all we usually know about them is roughly the decade of their settlement, the date of the first church, and the place of origin of the first settlers. Indian raids, feuds with neighboring villages, the building of a road to the outside world—important events in their time—remain matters of legend or hearsay. The destruction of the irrigation system by a cloudburst, the erosion of fields, the gradual destruction of the nearby forest, and the gradual desertion of the village itself—

JBJ, drawing and watercolor, Spanish-type cattle ranch, northern New Mexico, 1952

these are confirmed by visual evidence. But what is lacking is any picture of the villages in their prime. Those of us who are old enough can remember places in the foothills of the Sangre de Cristos or in the valleys of the Rio Puerco, the Pecos, the Rio Grande as they were a half-century ago. They had already begun to decline, and signs of increasing poverty and depopulation were painfully clear, yet there were still cultivated fields and well-kept irrigation ditches; there was a general store, there was a school, there was a freshly painted church and a neat graveyard. On Sunday afternoons the young men of the village and from the nearby ranches, dressed in finery, galloped up and down the only street. There were still men and women in those days who could identify the village which a stranger came from by his accent, who knew the local name for every field, every hill, every wild plant. They knew their landscape by heart.

One after another, over the decades, the villages died, but, like all other small farm communities, not without a struggle. A flood buried gardens and fields under gravel or sand; a local resource—wood or game or a special crop —lost its market; a railroad ceased operation; the school was closed. Rather than abandon their home, the villagers became ranchers and raised cattle or sheep. But in the end it died, and others died: first the remote villages on the margin of the plains, where there were no other jobs, and then the villages where the rangeland had deteriorated and the cedars and junipers were coming back into the abandoned fields. Now all that is left of that traditional farming landscape are the villages in the mountain heartland and in the Rio Grande Valley.

Time in those secluded places has a special flavor—a resigned, slow, autumnal beat. The colors linger into the early winter, in the brown and orange leaves on the cottonwoods along the streams and irrigation ditches, in the strings of red chili on the fronts of houses, and in the groves of lemon-yellow aspens far up in the mountains. Then a winter wind sends all their leaves to the ground in a shower of gold, and the chamisa turns grey.

Snow that lasts comes in later November and remains on the higher slopes of the Sangre de Cristos and the Jemez until well into the spring. In the valley and in the foothills it slowly melts, leaving patches hiding under the piñon trees, but in the heights and in places the sun reaches only for a few hours a day, winter is a season to be taken seriously. It transforms the smaller dirt roads into lanes of bottomless mud. The rancher stays close to headquarters, and villagers think twice before driving their mud-splattered pickups into the forest after firewood; even in town we are careful to stay on the paved surfaces. What was recently a landscape of coming and going and outdoor work —a landscape of gardens and orchards and small farms—almost overnight has turned into a scattering of isolated villages and hamlets. The cold and the wretched roads make every community, every family shrink into itself, and the silence is rarely broken.

In the old days the clanking of tire chains was part of winter in the country, but in the mountains of northern New Mexico, as elsewhere, we no longer hear it, and the almost perfect soundlessness is what visitors notice first of all. Find out for yourself what this means: stand on a hillside overlooking a village of tin-roofed houses on the edge of the forest in the Sangre de Cristos or in some part of the Pecos Valley; if it is a bright day in January or February, you will hear the screaming of flickers in the groves of piñon. Then in a backyard, perhaps a half-mile away, someone is slowly chopping wood. Go down into the village where there are the familiar sounds of melting snow coming off the tin roofs or out of the *canales*. Not a voice is heard; life has withdrawn into the houses behind closed doors, and the windows, with their displays of geraniums in tin cans, are half obscured by frost. Someone tries to start a car but soon gives up. In the cold, starry night the lights are few and dim, and you can barely make out the landscape of black forest and small, snow-covered fields. If you are lucky you may hear, very late at night, the yelp of a coyote. It sets the village dogs into a brief frenzy of barking.

It is hard to remember, despite all we have read about the history of this landscape, that as the crow flies (or as the car travels) Mexico, once the motherland, is not distant. But it is separated from us by more than barriers of mountains and desert. Snow and total darkness have imposed a kind of environmental Calvinism on northern New Mexico that all but obliterates the historic ties with that talkative and gregarious nation south of the Rio Grande, and not even the happiness of summer can entirely dispel it. Climate, no less than an ingrained sense of what is fitting, clears the plazas and the lanes of the last summer idlers, one leg propped against the wall, talking in grave voices. Climate, coupled with loyalty to family, keeps us home, where we sit in silence, pondering old grievances and searching our souls. Outside, the clear bright air smells of snow and piñon smoke; inside, it smells of coffee and roasting chili and wet clothes drying near the stove.

Climate, sooner or later, makes us return to origins, makes the tourists and environmentalists and students of folklore and handicrafts scurry back to Berkeley or New York or Dallas to show their brightly colored slides of the Land of Enchantment, and to dream of owning an adobe house of their own, with hollyhocks in the front yard, and a loom or a potter's wheel or a dulcimer in the cool, dark room within. Climate tells us to stay where we belong and to do what we have always done. On Sunday (in remoter, smaller villages, every other Sunday), the cracked church bell sounds of with an unmelodious Bang! Bang! Bang! A stove in the corner crackles and shines but fails to heat. After the service there are brief greetings on the church doorstep, yet nothing in winter can keep us together for long. That is the virtue and even the beauty of this time of year in northern New Mexico: it isolates and intensifies existence, it creates a landscape and then preserves it by freezing it.

Decay can be halted, but only briefly, and then it resumes. It is the negative image of history, and its presence throughout northern New Mexico has long fascinated the wandering photographer, hunting for the essence of Spanish-American rural culture. The relentless progress of ruin and abandonment was interpreted as a kind of romantic growth, something to be recorded and perpetuated before it is too late. There was, in fact, a period after World War II when the landscape of the Sangre de Cristo villages and the upper Rio Grande Valley was seen exclusively as a panorama of crumbling adobe walls, sagging roofs, doorways without doors, abandoned roads bordered by rusty barbed wire, leading uncertainly to overgrown fields and resurgent forest. There was never a face except the old and defeated, never a sign of continuing life, but many sad pictures of deserted graveyards. This vision, repeated by artists in many other parts of the country, seems in retrospect to have been less a reflection of reality than a way of expressing a nostalgic version of history: a desperate, last-minute recording of old and once-cherished values, the New Mexico chapter in that once-popular chronicling of "vanishing America," the old America of small farms and small villages and small hillside fields. We captured on film the ghosts of places not yet entirely dead.

As long as those remnants of an old, nineteenth-century New Mexico survive as more or less recognizable human artifacts, they will remind us of the old order—and of an older photographic approach to the rural world. But it is increasingly evident, I think, that Americans, especially young Americans, are beginning to discover the new landscape that is evolving, demanding our attention and interpretation, if not necessarily our critical acceptance. History has started a new chapter, and our vision expands to include the newer landscape.

Actually, it is not a new landscape; it is an aspect of the essential New Mexico landscape—hitherto empty and forbidding—that has been explored, invaded, and occupied. In the last generation we have, for the first time, ventured out beyond the familiar, protective landscape of watered valleys and forested mountains, beyond the green landscape of rain and snow and the traditional succession of seasons, and have undertaken the settlement of the semi-arid plains, the naked mountains, and the deserts of the Southwest.

*Desert* is not a word people in New Mexico like to hear carelessly used. It hurts us deeply to read in eastern papers references to the "desert" around Santa Fe, or the "desert" climate of Albuquerque. No offense is intended, of course. The term conjures up a pleasant image of silence and mystery and strange beauty, and its use is a carry-over from the writings of early nineteenth-century explorers who believed that desert began somewhere in eastern Kansas. To them any region without trees and not adapted to traditional eastern methods of farming was desert. Much of New Mexico, in fact, can be called arid or semi-arid—an immense, rolling, underpopulated country covered by short, wiry grass, which in the early summer turns the color of straw.

Geologically speaking, much of eastern New Mexico is an extension of the High Plains—of the Texas Panhandle and Oklahoma. But what distinguishes it from that impressively monotonous region is its variety of landforms—innumerable, widely scattered, dark, steep-sided mesas, floating on the sea of pale-yellow grass like a fleet of flat-tops riding at anchor; the cones of extinct volcanoes; the many canyons. These last are remote and hidden from view, and those who formerly explored the rangeland on horseback rather than from the air came upon them with frightening suddenness. All that betrays their existence is a scanty fringe of piñon and juniper on their rim. You find yourself gazing down into a long, deep, narrow valley with almost vertical walls of red or brown rock, and below where you halt there are the tops of cottonwood growing hundreds of feet along some meandering river.

These enormous landforms are about the only variety the arid (or semi-arid) landscape of New Mexico provides. In the spring, long after the winter snows have melted and left pools of clear water in the hollows of the rangeland, the grass is a brilliant green, and the expanses of wildflowers—there are said to be more than six thousand varieties in the state—are spectacular. But much depends on when you see the eastern region. If in April it seems to be potentially ideal farming country, in July it is a sun-baked emptiness, to be avoided whenever possible. Those of us who live here the year round are well aware of the seasonal change. Our lives, like all lives, revolve around the man-made elements in the landscape. We shuttle between people and places—specific people and the specific places where they live and work and relax, and the expressionless solitudes of the open road between, let us say, Vaughn and Roswell, or Tucumcari and Hobbs or Logan occupy—or used to occupy—little of our thought. We learned to welcome almost every trace, every sign, no matter how incongruous or unsightly, that reminded us of the human presence: the lonely, two-pump gas station, the gate-and-cattleguard entrance to some far-off, invisible ranch, the tattered billboard out in the middle of nowhere. We were (and perhaps still are) attracted to ruins, no matter what their size or age. Their shabbiness served to bring something like a time scale to a landscape, which for all its solemn beauty failed to register the passage of time.

The story of the dying of small rural communities in every part of the world has become familiar to us all over the last century and a half. It is most impressive, most regrettable when it tells of the decay of a well-known and well-loved landscape, like that of New England or New Mexico, but the moral of the story is in almost every case the same: existence for people in the country became more and more difficult, more and more joyless and without reward. Low pay, monotonous work, a sense of being isolated and forgotten, a sense of diminishing hope for the future afflicted one village, one farmstead after another. For more than a century, here in America, we have seen it happening, so perhaps it is not too early for us to look elsewhere in the countryside to become aware of the new communities, the new installations that are evolving in that rural landscape. If much of the migration from that landscape has found its way to large cities, much of it, perhaps most of it, has swelled the population of small towns and even created entirely new types of settlement—still rural in location but essentially industrial or commercial in economy, dependent not on a stream or river or a climate of familiar seasons but on a highway, a dam, a mine, a tourist attraction. The movement away from the countryside is everywhere, but in our relatively empty landscape, the fluidity is more easily discerned, and in New Mexico we can, when we look, see more than the decline and death of the traditional order. We can see the emergence, all over the state, of a new kind of community—new in that it represents a different relationship with the environment, a deliberate confrontation with elements in the landscape that earlier generations sought to avoid.

Like many such revolutions, this radical change in settlement patterns was inspired more by hope than despair: hope that a better way of life would come when the steady job was seen as preferable to the exploitation of land, particularly the modest-sized holding of land. The shift got under way in earnest at the time of the depression and the drought of the 1930s. It was then that small farmers and ranchers and farm laborers gravitated to those towns and centers where there was a prospect of work or of some sort of welfare. County seats usually offered some promise of help, and the advent of the unemployed produced a ring of small, inconspicuous shanty towns or Hoovervilles—crude and presumably temporary dwellings which represented the first visible rejection of the traditional, land-oriented adobe house. These emergency settlements, usually located near the railroad tracks or on vacant lots in the Spanish-speaking neighborhoods, have long since disappeared, replaced by more permanent structures or deserted in favor of other, more suitable public housing projects. Survivals, scarcely recognizable, can still be found on the outskirts of Albuquerque and Santa Fe and Grants, and in other smaller towns. But even if they were short-lived, these emergency communities testified to the existence of a new relationship with the landscape: the dwelling, and even the community, moved to be near the source of employment, in contrast to the traditional relationship where employment centered on the dwelling and the land.

Another reason for the proliferation of new settlement types was the advent, after the Depression and beginning with the war, of new industries, new construction projects, and numerous military installations throughout New Mexico—oil in the southeastern quadrant of the state, gas in the Farmington area, increased mining in the Gila region. The airfields and army posts attracted a working population to parts of New Mexico that had hitherto been little settled, and when we look back over the last decades, we are struck by the manner in which the emptier and less inviting areas have become integrated into the new landscape. It was not merely a matter of discovering and exploiting natural resources of a kind earlier generations had ignored; it was also a discovery of a new way of living, a new environmental relationship. How else are we to account for the new popularity of the snow-bound, wintry landscape of the northern mountains, the attraction of the desert for resort or retirement living? It is true that technological advances have helped to make the remoter regions livable: air-conditioning, new, rapid, and relatively inexpensive forms of housing—notably the mobile home—and the building of gas lines, airports, and highways have all encouraged the new kind of pioneering, but there have been other forces at work. It is significant that the average prosperous New Mexico suburb has forsaken the familiar valley environment, with its cottonwoods and fields of corn and alfalfa, for the rocky and treeless heights and mountain slopes: the desirable environment no longer involves the exploitation of land; it is an environment of isolation and extensive views, with few reminders of the traditional community based on agriculture.

The same invasion of the arid or desert environment has taken place in Arizona and California. Wherever we can, we seek out a fresh, untried, unknown setting and impose a new technology upon it, a new awareness of environmental factors, and permanence. Local attachments and identification are not always what we are after: resources can and probably will be exhausted; tastes will change; and better jobs will lure us to another part of the desert or the mountains, or even back to the city. What New Mexico seems to offer is what it has always offered: the dramatic confrontation between the new and mobile and optimistic human installation on the one hand, and the overpowering "timelessness" of an ancient landscape with its visible cosmic chronology on the other—Los Alamos on the flanks of an extinct volcano, the array of lightning rods near Quemado, the clocklike precision of modern irrigation techniques in a region where seasons scarcely exist.

The uranium country near Laguna and Grants can be seen as a sample—and not a very happy one—of the new landscape. It is now idle and without movement; perhaps it never will be active again. But it is here that the photographer, seeking to record the new relationship with the environment, can find the most revealing evidence. Mountains have been carved into stepped pyramids and in places planted with bright green grass; the vast piles of waste and slag are, in fact, more natural in appearance than the natural landforms themselves. Model workers' villages, strikingly Mediterranean in style, alternate with villages of mud and rock. Both kinds of community are languishing, each in its way evolving into ruins. The fine paved roads are empty of traffic. The immediate background of this enforced still life is the old grazing landscape of sheep and cattle raising, of half-dead Spanish villages and the deceptively classical, piñon-covered hills and sun-baked rock. Beyond that is the horizon of dark blue mountains. All New Mexico can be seen, superimposed and blending.

The photographer who explores the last landscape—whether in the Four Corners region or in the farmlands of Clovis and Hobbs, or even in the lower Rio Grande Valley—will record in a fresh and direct manner the immensely significant change in environmental relationships, typical of much of the Western world. It is by no means the first such change, nor the last. The prehistoric Indian migrants produced on a modest scale the same juxtaposition of the primordial and the human; the Spanish farmers and ranchers produced their own traditional European version. The drama of New Mexico's attraction and conquest is being continued, and we are in the fortunate position of being able to observe and record that wave of optimistic expansion and discovery. It is no less a fact of history than the compromise and defeat that ultimately overtake our endeavors to live in a region which continues to fascinate us, allure us, and teach us the hard lessons of the passage of time.

1983. From *The Essential Landscape: The New Mexico Photographic Survey, with Essays by J. B. Jackson,* ed. Steven A. Yates (Albuquerque: University of New Mexico Press, 1985)

## The Accessible Landscape

About fifty years ago Americans of my generation had the kind of experience that comes once in a lifetime and, overnight, changes the way we view the world. What happened was that with the coming of commercial aviation we were all able to take to the air and fly across America. We thereby discovered a new way of seeing and interpreting the landscape.

To the present generation this is an old story. But until some time in the 1930s we had always seen our country on foot or when we rode in a car or a train. We had seen it as an evolving sequence of views. To cross the continent in those days was a serious undertaking, and we said harsh things about the monotony of Kansas and the emptiness and dust of Texas. Then, in the course of a few years, we learned to see America from twenty or thirty thousand feet in the air.

We saw it first of all as a marvelous multicolored map, a vast, rectangular pattern: fields, orderly towns, white farmsteads strung out along straight white roads. In the background was a river winding through wooded hills. It took time for us to perceive the national grid system, which few of us had heard about. But eventually we recognized that it was the product of a national land policy whereby millions of Americans became landowners and farmers. This meant that we could interpret the enormous panorama of stripes and squares and rectangles reaching out of sight in every direction as being composed entirely of small, individual properties. Even the close-packed blocks of houses in towns could be seen as clusters of independent domains. Confronted, as we were for hours at a time, with the monotony of the grid beneath us, we sought some variation in the pattern, some individual feature to focus on. It was a relief to single out the freestanding, lonely farm house in the countryside. It was only when we could divide and subdivide it into a million small private spaces, each clearly bounded and protected by fences and hedges and rows of trees, that the monolithic landscape acquired a human scale. Thus the aerial perspective reinforced our modern tendency to analyze and reduce phenomena to their smallest components. The more extensive our view, the more we concentrate on details, and for many Americans, especially those involved in environmental studies, the landscape as a composition has almost ceased to exist. Fragments of the whole—studies of microecosystems, isolated structures and spaces of little significance—are all that matters.

There is nothing wrong in concentrating on small-scale variations in the landscape. Variety is essential not only as a source of delight and inspiration; biologically and socially, it is essential to our well-being. No one questions that. What we *can* question is how these highly specialized structures and spaces relate to their wider workaday setting. Should the wilderness area, the traditional farming landscape, the historic urban district be preserved forever, fenced off and protected from change? Should they be assimilated? We can only give an answer when we have defined their function.

Several years ago a book called *The Territorial Imperative,* by Robert Ardrey, enjoyed wide popularity. Ardrey was not a scientist, but he wrote extremely well and persuasively. His thesis was that the impulse, which all human beings and all animals have, to organize their own private space or territory was based on a universal, biologically determined need to establish boundaries and defend them against all intruders. "The territorial principle," Ardrey wrote, "has been evolution's most effective implement in the distribution of animal space. And if Man is a being biologically equipped with territorial patterns then at least we have a premise to work from. Urbanization is deterritorialization in the classic sense of denial of land. But perhaps there may be conceptual substitutes or symbolic channels that will preserve our biological sanity. We may be sure, however, that we must somehow preserve NO TRESPASSING signs."

Ardrey had no special ideological axe to grind. All that he wanted to prove was that human behavior is determined more by biological than by cultural factors, and that the territorial instinct was to be taken into account in every aspect of our life, from family relationships to relationships between nations.

But the reader is likely to be repelled by his persistent references to defense and privacy and the sanctity of boundary lines. The world he depicts is just as fragmented as the one so many scholars now see, and more secretive. My own reaction is that the territorial imperative he describes is by no means as universal or as innate as he claims. Indeed, I believe it is a relatively modern development, not more than two or three hundred years old, and, as I see it, already on its way out.

Another explanation of that impulse to create exclusive defensible spaces was recently proposed by an American geographer, Robert Sack. He rejected the biological basis of territoriality and suggested that it was a political or economic device. "Territoriality," he said, "is the attempt by an individual or a group to affect, influence, or control people, phenomena, and relationships by delimiting and asserting control of a geographical area. . . . [It] is a strategy to establish different degrees of access to people, things, and relationships." There is in consequence a history of human territoriality—and indeed that is the title of his book. He illustrated his thesis by describing the political divisions within the United States, the bureaucratic divisions within the Catholic church, and the architectural divisions within a modern factory as various ways of acquiring political or economic power and control.

Both Ardrey's and Sack's books give us an informed way of looking at the landscape. When we glance down from the plane, we can interpret what we see either as a composition of private, jealously defended territories, protected by laws and topographical barriers, or else as the diagram of a long-range plan for economic or political exploitation by a powerful minority.

I was an early advocate of studying landscapes from the air. At one time I had a large collection of aerial views. But when flying became increasingly unpredictable I gave it up, and I recently drove from New Mexico to Illinois and Iowa in my pickup truck. It was a long trip with many monotonous hours, but I do not regret it. It broke the spell cast by the air-view of the grid system and reminded me that there is still much to be learned at ground level. What goes on *within* those beautifully abstract rectangles is also worth observing.

Almost everything I saw on my way east was familiar. I was glad to refresh my memory of the midwestern landscape and at the same time to note the changes which had taken place over the past decade. In retrospect, all the towns I passed through seem to merge into one image of an archetypal American town or small city. Main Street has lost much of its earlier vitality and has become, particularly in the center of town, a kind of skid row minus the drunks and tattoo parlors; a shabby corridor between decaying buildings with empty store windows, cars parked every which way in the vacant lots. But where it extends out into the new part of town it recaptures its style. It is bordered by used-car lots decorated with pennants and flags, motels and ethnic restaurants, and it passes a vast shopping mall with a skating rink. There are rows and rows of parked cars and beyond the mall is a new low-cost housing development. It too has pennants and flags, and pickups are already parked on some of the new driveways. In the past I had been attracted by the strip. It seemed new and full of promise, and not yet integrated into the fabric of the town. Now I discovered that its drive-in facilities, once so novel, had become commonplace throughout the city, at least along the wider commercial streets. The houses had been taken over by small businesses catering to daily needs, and each, from the doctor's office to the beauty parlor and laundromat, had its miniature front parking lot and its own conspicuous sign. A great deal of writing and photography is currently being produced about the strip and its architecture: it has become a favorite topic with many students of American vernacular culture, but I suspect they run the risk of already being out of date. The strip is in disarray, and the relationship it once established between business and street, and its once distinctive jumble of signs and drive-ins and parking facilities and commercial facades, are now best seen in the downtown section.

Downtown has sprouted a half-dozen medium-size glass high-rise office buildings with underground parking garages and stylish lobbies. The oldest and once the best hotel in town, with an ornate ballroom and a uniformed doorman, now accommodates a modest population of senior citizens. The railroad station, long since abandoned, has been restored, painted in bright colors, and converted to a popular eating place, "The Chew-Chew Train," and the ornate nineteenth-century city hall has been torn down to make way for a metered parking lot. There is an old-fashioned factory or brick warehouse, once identified with the railroad tracks, made over into apartments and boutiques, and the elegant old mansions on tree-lined streets are occupied by law offices or the offices of insurance companies, the front lawn turned into a tastefully designed parking lot. Abruptly, in the midst of what was formerly a blue-collar neighborhood of bungalows and shabby houses with wide porches, there emerges an ethnic community with spray-can graffiti in an unknown tongue.

There is much to be learned from reading the local newspaper and watching the local "eyewitness" news. That was how I found out that the public library was being invaded every day by street people looking for a place to sleep, and that the art museum had been the scene of a fashionable fundraising dinner followed by dancing. That was how I learned that the mayor and the city council were at odds about the location of a new super-convention center: should four blocks of low-quality downtown housing be razed, or should the site be out where there was an important interchange on the interstate highway?

I made notes of these random sights and events because each of them, in one way or another, seemed to indicate that a number of changes under way in the city could tell me more about the contemporary American scene. Many were of an almost predictable kind: age and decay meant that some buildings had outlived their usefulness and had to be replaced; growth and prosperity demanded large spaces, and more of them. A common spectacle across the country are the cars, three abreast and ten deep, waiting at an intersection and watching the intricate choreography of the traffic lights overhead—then surging away to travel miles across open country between billboards and auto junkyards, to some satellite industrial suburb. Automobiles, in fact, account for more changes than anything else, and denouncing automobile culture is one way of denouncing the American city. But I admit that I was unable to pass coherent judgment on the city as a landscape. Was it handsome? Was it healthy? Was it a good place to live? Was all that growth and change headed in the right direction—was it in fact headed in any direction at all? The scattered observations I collected were vivid enough, but added up to very little. I was suffering (like many other commentators on the landscape) from that myopic vision, the environmentalist's inability to see the forest for the ecosystems, the inability to see the city as an entity. Much writing on the American city tells of its fragmentation, but often that writing comes from our predilection to *see* fragmentation; to see territories isolated from their setting, and to lament their disappearance.

There is clearly such a thing as a middle- or upper-class American way of perceiving and creating a landscape. It comprises those spaces and structures and relationships which people of those classes are familiar with and find pleasant as a setting for their way of life. It is a spacious rural (or semirural) landscape of woods and green fields (plowed fields are suspect, hinting at mechanization or, worse yet, commercialized farming). It is a landscape of private territories, admission to which is by invitation only. The houses, substantial and usually architect-designed, are self-sufficient and somewhat with-drawn from too close a contact with their neighbors, and are surrounded by a buffer zone of lawns and shrubbery and trees. Not far away is a small forest or miniature wilderness area, tacitly recognized as the exclusive playground of the local families. Life proceeds according to a fixed schedule from one terri-tory to another: from private house to private tennis club to parish church and private school. To pass through a gate, a portal, or a front door, or to park in a private driveway is more than merely entering: it affirms membership in a well-established group. As in a Jane Austen novel, nothing of significance hap-pens in the public realm, and with little traffic and no sidewalks, the streets are like country roads all eventually leading to privacy and home.

The urban version of this middle-class landscape has seen its best days. We do what we can to preserve and even restore its few remnants: the Victo-rian mansion, the early factory or mill, the romantic Olmsted park and the old-style neighborhood of row houses, however impoverished and dilapidated it may be. By holding on to these landmarks and giving them a special status, we are underscoring their isolation, their out-of-date territoriality, but we are preserving some of the variety of the urban landscape.

Whenever I could, I made a detour (as I passed through towns) to visit these so-called historic areas, and I enjoyed seeing them. But inevitably I found myself returning to the more active part of town and the through streets, leaving behind those quiet residential streets, similar in atmosphere to the streets in small towns—little used and almost rural in their profusion of trees and lawns. I could sense that the nearby urban streets were beginning to take over; streets which were like turbulent streams flooding their banks and drowning what was left of the old boundaries, the old privacy and autonomy. In the end the driver's perspective saw all those changes and adaptations, all that destruction and leveling as elements in a battlefield. Two concepts of how to organize and use space were meeting head-on: privacy and security and per-manence as symbolized by those established territories or domains versus a vernacular impulse toward accessibility and freedom of movement.

The traveler who, like myself, rarely gets out of his car is more likely to be more aware of the roadway ahead of him than of the spaces and buildings on either margin. But if you have had, as I have had, the experience of driving fifty or more years ago, you cannot fail to be struck by how the street in the average American town or city has been transformed, how it dominates its immediate environment, how complex it is in design, how many functions it now serves, and how it constantly creates new ancillary spaces and structures:

parking garages, underground parking, parking lots, drive-in facilities and skyways and overpasses and interchanges and strange little slices and islands of greenery. In its most inclusive sense, the street has taken over the role of making landscapes, changing them and destroying them. In the old days, roads were cautiously planned and built solely to reach a specific destination. Now we build highways hundreds of miles in length to open a whole region to development, and even a new street cut across a vacant suburban area promptly produces house after house along its margin, the way the branch of a tree produces leaves in spring. In the hands of a skilled planner or traffic engineer, a street becomes a versatile tool: outlawed parking, limited speed, one-way traffic, and a succession of traffic lights can either ruin the social and economic life of a neighborhood or cause it to flourish.

Sometimes, it is true, the scale and complexity of this highway environment can make a driver break out in a cold sweat. In town after town I have found myself enmeshed in a tangle of interchanges and overpasses and ramps, and have been reduced to total helplessness, timidly seeking to follow signs and numbers and arrows, and to obey the commands and warnings painted on the surface of the road in front of me.

Still, it is easy to exaggerate how sensitive we are to the modern highway environment. Without our always admitting it, we are at home, we know what to expect, when we drive for block after block between a succession of drive-ins, parking lots, used-car lots, garages, and gas stations. We are not simply in a commonplace, often unsightly part of town, we are in a new organization of urban space, one designed for work, for accessibility, and for the satisfaction of short-term essential needs—all based on the presence of the automobile.

Automobile culture is a topic far too complicated for me to discuss. Let me merely say that I think we can begin to understand it when we overcome two deep-rooted middle-class prejudices. The first is that "automobile" means passenger car; not truck or van or pickup, but the automobiles that we see advertised and buy. The second prejudice is that the automobile, thus defined, is a vehicle used for going to work in the morning, parked during the work hours, then used for going home, for paying visits, and over the weekend for driving in the country, as remote as possible from other automobiles. I would hazard a guess that for three-quarters of the American public the automobile (in its widest definition) is seen primarily as essential to the process of making a living. It not only takes us to work, it is part of work itself: it collects, hauls, distributes; it carries people and equipment and materials. It is part of every

JBJ, photo, road with signs

industrial enterprise, every service, every job, and it intrudes on every work site. That is why the working automobile demands accessibility even in the private realm, and that in turn is why its impact on the older and more densely built-up parts of town has been so destructive. The harmonious street per-spective, the homogeneous neighborhood of spacious private territories, the last traces of established boundaries, have all been destroyed by the piecemeal and unplanned introduction of a new ordering of space.

Yet one reason the auto-oriented street is so intrusive is that the nine-teenth century, unlike previous centuries, failed to provide any transitional zone between the private realm and the street. The territorial imperative of the period refused to admit any dependence on the outside mobile world—hence the forbidding facades, the awe-inspiring doorways, locked and bolted, hence the "no trespassing" signs which Ardrey considered essential. The city was not always so exclusive, so determined to defend its boundaries. In earlier times the landscape, rural as well as urban, always contained a variety of spaces and structures which the public, no matter how humble, could occupy and use on a strictly temporary basis. The origin of these common spaces and of the right to use them is obscure, but their effect on the social order was good. They brought classes together and allowed people to work and come together without competitiveness and suspicion. This tradition of common spaces and structures directly contradicts Ardrey's theory that the basic spatial division is one of defensible private territories. But it is also at variance with the theory proposed by Sack: that territoriality is a means of establishing control over people and things.

The nineteenth century helped do away with most of those customary rights and spaces, but our own century has seen the beginning of their return. A social historian could establish within a decade or two when a reaction set in against autonomy and toward greater accessibility—accessibility not only *to* work and the public realm but also *from* the street to the house.

I am tempted to dwell on the importance of the parking lot. I enjoy it as an austere but beautiful and exciting aspect of the landscape. I find it easy to compare it with such traditional vernacular spaces as the common: both are undifferentiated in form, empty, with no significant topographical features to determine use, both easily accessible and essential to our daily existence. But on another level, the parking lot symbolizes a closer, more immediate relationship between various elements in our society: consumer and producer, public and private, the street and the dwelling.

I am very much aware of the excesses of accessibility, of the confusion and squalor of the environment often created by the rejection of the traditional private organization and use of space. I wish there were fewer cars. I wish distances were not so great. I wish the pursuit of accessibility, the constant striving for the attention and good will of the mobile consumer did not often mean lack of dignity and individuality. And I have dark moments when I foresee that the American city will in the future come to resemble those immense and formless cities of the third world.

That may be what happens. In the meantime, we should perhaps remind ourselves that behind this new way of building and planning and incessantly moving about is a basic universal urge: not to withdraw into a private domain of our own but to participate in the world and to share it with others. Ours is a society where vernacular values are taken seriously. However extravagant and unsightly much of the contemporary urban scene may be, it is essentially vernacular in that it offers the public, and particularly the working public, an easy and presumably attractive way of satisfying the needs of everyday existence.

Ardrey and his followers taught us how to distinguish one space from another and how each had its own unique character. What Sack, in his book *Human Territoriality*, taught us was how these various spaces were related to one another and how they often compete. Perhaps we can go one step further and see how in the vernacular world we are learning to *share* spaces, learning how to use them in a temporary way in order to overcome both the old-fashioned biological exclusiveness and the more modern overemphasis on competition and control.

"The Accessible Landscape," *Whole Earth Review* 58 (March 8, 1988): 4–9.

2 First Comes the House:
  The Evolving Domestic Landscape

JBJ, photo, house detail

# The Westward-Moving House

## Nehemiah's Ark

Three hundred years ago one Nehemiah Tinkham, with wife Submit Tinkham and six children, landed on the shores of New England to establish a home in the wilderness.

Like his forefathers, Tinkham had been a small farmer. He brought with him in addition to a few household goods those "needful things" which a catalogue for "prospective New England planters" had suggested several years before: two hoes, two saws, two axes, hammer, shovel, spade, augers, chisels, piercers, gimlet, and hatchet. These were all he had, these and a knowledge of certain traditional skills, necessary not only for building a house but for clearing and farming new land. There were no nails on the list—nails being expensive—and no equipment for livestock.

Nehemiah soon acquired some sixty acres of virgin land at Jerusha, a new settlement a day's journey from Boston. He did not buy the land from a private owner, white man or Indian, still less appropriate a likely corner of the New England forest for himself. He bought it from the Jerusha town authorities who had obtained it from the crown, and the town assigned him his land without giving him any choice of location.

Nevertheless, his farm was as good as his neighbors'. It comprised three kinds of land: the smallest (and most valuable) section was the home lot, of about ten acres, that faced the green or common and was near not only other houses but the site of the future meetinghouse. The Massachusetts General Court had recently ruled that no dwelling was to be built farther from the meetinghouse than half a mile. The two other subdivisions of the farm were meadow and woodland. The meadow, located in the well-watered and protected valley, was gradually cleared of trees and planted to wheat and oats and corn, though some of it was left untilled for the cows which Nehemiah hoped to acquire. The woodlands on the rocky hills served to provide building materials and fuel.

The broad axe which he had brought with him from England stood him in good stead; for though he and his neighbors had originally staked out their settlement in a thick forest, they cleared the land so rapidly of its trees that within a decade they had to go elsewhere for wood. While this cutting of trees lasted, it concerned all men. Neighbors helped Nehemiah fell the largest trees—the oak and pine he intended to use for his house—and he in turn helped them. All joined forces to clear the common, to build a fence around it to prevent livestock from straying, to build a meetinghouse and a home for the minister. The Tinkhams had to live in a temporary half-underground shelter during the first winter, and all that Nehemiah could do was plant two acres of wheat—never a successful crop in New England and from the beginning overrun by barberry—plant some of the unfamiliar Indian corn, and set out a small apple orchard on the home lot.

Until he died, Nehemiah never grew nor tasted a tomato, an Irish potato, or a sweet potato. He never tasted either tea or coffee, and seldom tasted fresh beef or pork or lamb. The farm eventually provided the family with flour, a few fruits and vegetables, milk, butter, cheese, and eggs. These, together with game, made up most of their diet.

Nor did the Tinkhams possess a yoke of oxen or a workhorse until many years after they arrived in the New World. The fields which Nehemiah cultivated in spite of the many stumps were plowed for him by the one man in Jerusha who owned a plow. He harvested his wheat with a sickle, threshed it with a flail. He was fortunate to possess a crude two-wheeled cart for hauling loads, though whatever traveling he and his family did (it was little enough) was done on horseback. The few roads in the center of the village were rough and narrow; between villages there were no roads at all, merely trails through the woods.

### Family and Superfamily

Had Nehemiah wanted to expand his farming activities, had he been interested in greater yields and in selling to city markets and buying city goods in return, he would have resented these restrictions on movement and sought to improve his agricultural methods. But he was concerned first with keeping himself and his family alive, and then with maintaining an established way of life. It was a monotonous one, perhaps, but it provided him with food and clothes and shelter, and with the kind of sociability he wanted.

Poor communications with the outside world, a large degree of self-sufficiency, the pioneer custom of all men working together on certain undertakings, and lastly the grouping of all houses around the "Place for Sabbath Assembly" made for a very compact village. In our more charitable appraisals of early New England, we speak of its democracy. Actually, its guiding principle was something else. There was nothing particularly democratic about the social setup of proprietors, yeomen, and latecomers in descending order of importance and privilege. There was nothing democratic about the law which forbade those having less than a certain amount of money to wear expensive clothes. Nor were these latter-day backslidings from an earlier democracy; as early as 1623 it had been proposed that New England be settled by "Three sorts—Gentlemen to bear arms, handicraftsmen of all sorts, and husbandmen for tilling the ground." Likewise, the Puritan church had its hierarchy of elders, deacons, and ministers. In the Jerusha meetinghouse, the higher your social position, the nearer you sat to the pulpit; when Nehemiah acquired a servant, she was obliged to sit in the cold gallery with the children. The right to vote, the right to live within the township, the right to speak one's mind— these were jealously controlled by law.

Yet if Jerusha was not as democratic as a modern American town, it had a quality which the modern town has lost. It was a kind of superfamily, more like the highest stage in a domestic hierarchy than the smallest unit of a nation, as it is now. Nehemiah found Jerusha a good substitute for the rural society he had left behind. He had never traveled much in England, and his father and grandfather had traveled even less. To generations of Tinkhams, *family* and *village* had been almost interchangeable terms. Nehemiah had been related to most of his neighbors in the Old World and had shared customs and traditions with them all. The people who came to Jerusha came, of course, from different places and from different walks of life; but, like the Tinkhams, they were all of them homesick not so much for the safety and comfort of England as for the superfamily they had known. What could take the place of that? Nothing so impersonal as a social contract; what they created instead was the domestic village, with its established hierarchy and its working together on a common task.

Certainly, the most obvious symbols of the urge for a superfamily were God the stern Father; the Jerusha meetinghouse as a sort of superparlor where the family gathered for prayers; and the genealogical enthusiasm which still possesses New England. But the individual house was scarcely less important, and Nehemiah hastened to build his family as good a house as he could in order to reproduce still another aspect of the traditional background. The completed article was naturally reminiscent of the house he had known in England. It was of wood, of course, much of it unseasoned, with a stone foundation, and it was two stories high with a third story or attic under a steeply pitched roof.

*The House*

As Anthony Garvan has pointed out in his *Architecture and Town Planning in Colonial Connecticut*, the early builders (Nehemiah included) used as a basic measurement in their houses the sixteen-foot bay—a span originally adopted in England because it was wide enough to house two teams of oxen. In America this was modified to the extent that almost every dimension in the colonial house was divisible by eight, or half a bay. Another sign of Nehemiah's conservatism was the manner in which he built the house. The frame of oak which he laboriously constructed with the simplest of tools was a heavy and intricate piece of carpentry, unlike anything we see in contemporary construction. To quote Garvan: "Such frames . . . not only carried the whole weight of the building but were also mortised and tenoned together so that they withstood any horizontal thrust of the elements. . . . The task of the frame was to carry the weight of the roof and ridgepole, not just to resist their outward thrust."

Thus Nehemiah's house was built to last, built to be inflexible, built to carry a load, and not built for easy alteration or enlargement. Like his theology, perhaps.

He never painted the house, nor sought to adorn it, but the passage of years has given it softness and beauty, and now we hear persons admire its functionalism. Hugh Morrison remarks in his *Early American Architecture* that the seventeenth-century builder was so far from being functionally minded that he never thought of inserting sheathing between the frame and the outside clapboards; never realized that the huge chimney was inefficient, or that the lighting in the house was atrociously bad. He never realized that the old-fashioned frame he took such pains with was needlessly slow and difficult to make.

The plan of the house was equally nonfunctional as we understand the term. The ground floor had two main rooms: a combination living room-workroom-kitchen with a large fireplace, and a parlor, also with a fireplace. The parlor was reserved for important guests and family religious observances. Between these two a flight of stairs led to the two bedrooms where the family slept, and above these, reached by a ladder, was the attic where slept the servant. There were in addition several outbuildings, including a barn, all near the house. Outside the back door there was a small garden chiefly devoted to vegetables and herbs, but containing a few flowers as well. The lawn, which we always think of as in front of the colonial house, did not exist; a rail fence surrounded the place and kept out cows. The appearance of the house was for long bleak and graceless; its windows were small, the proportion of the rooms ungainly, and the furnishings scanty and of necessity crude. But Nehemiah and his wife, Submit, found little to criticize in it. It was solid, practical, and defensible against Indian assaults. If anyone dared mention its discomforts, Nehemiah quoted Romans 5:3.

*Meetinghouse as Parlor*

We cannot judge the house without knowing what functions it was supposed to serve and what functions it relegated to some other establishment. We are no more entitled to speak of the gloom of the Tinkhams' existence simply because their house lacked facilities for conviviality than a foreigner would be entitled to speak of the idleness of modern American existence because our houses do not contain places of work. Nehemiah's home cannot be understood without some understanding of the importance of the meetinghouse, for the one complemented the other. If the dwelling sheltered the economic and biological functions of domestic life in Jerusha, the social and cultural functions belonged to the meetinghouse. That perhaps is why Nehemiah was almost as attached to the square edifice on the common as he was to his own home: not because he had helped build it with his own hands, not because he thought it beautiful, but because it was an essential part of his life.

It was school and forum for the discussion of civic affairs. It was his barracks and the place where he stored his weapons and ammunition. It was the spot for community gatherings and celebrations. Most important of all, it was the image of the kind of world order that Nehemiah believed in. Here and here alone he felt that he was occupying his ordained place in the scheme of existence, even if that place was humble. He did not enjoy sitting for two hours in a cold building while the Reverend Jethro Tipping expounded the Significance of the Tenth Horn of the Beast, but he believed that all was well while he did so. Dozing off during the exegesis, he saw the world as an enduring and majestic pyramid, an orderly succession of ranks—yeomen, husbandmen, squires; elders, deacons, ministers; heathen, gentile, elect—each one indispensable to the solidity of the structure and helping to bear the weight of the crowning stone. Apt as it was to think in allegories, Nehemiah's fancy saw the same spirit manifest in the landscape around him, in the ascending order of woodland, meadow, and home lot; in unredeemed wilderness, settlement, and meetinghouse on the common.

In this hierarchical view of the world, he was a child of his age. What distinguished him, however, from his cousins in Europe was his conviction that the order could and should be simplified. Some of the steps in the pyramid ought to be eliminated, as it were, for communication between the highest and the lowest to be more direct and certain. If this world was but a preparation for the next (and the Reverend Jethro Tipping assured him that it was), men should organize it simply and efficiently. And in fact Nehemiah and his fellow colonists had already done this so well that in the eyes of their Old World contemporaries they passed for revolutionaries.

### The Hostile Environment

Nevertheless, Jerusha was aware that it was only a small, beleaguered island of holiness in the midst of a hostile country. Almost within gunshot of the meetinghouse was an unredeemed wilderness inhabited by savages. A variety of factors prevented Nehemiah from venturing very far or very often into this hinterland. His farming methods were too primitive. Labor was too scarce for him to exploit all the land he owned—much less acquire more. The absence of roads made settlement difficult in the more remote parts and again prevented him from selling to distant towns. Furthermore, neither he nor his friends were adventurous spirits; they were slow to adopt new ways and new ideas, since the old ones were backed by unimpeachable authority. Remembering the cultivated countryside they had left in England, they were appalled by the lawlessness of the New World environment. Emerson once said that the early settlers "do not appear to have been hardy men. . . . They exaggerate their troubles. Bears and wolves were many, but early they believed there were lions. Monadnoc was burned over to kill them. . . . In the journey of the Reverend Peter Bulkley and his company through the forest from Boston to Concord they fainted from the powerful odor of the sweet fern in the sun."

No doubt much of this fear came from the hardships of pioneer life. A spiritual descendant of Nehemiah, Silas Lapham of Vermont, remarked almost two hundred years later: "I wish some of the people that talk about the landscape and *write* about it, had to bust one of them rocks *out* of the landscape with powder. . . . Let 'em go and live with nature in the *winter* . . . and I guess they'll have enough of her for one while."

But in fact later generations of American pioneers had little or none of this hostility to nature; the sentiment was largely confined to Nehemiah and his time. What helped confirm it and make it almost an article of faith was the habit the early colonists had of comparing themselves to the Children of Israel in the Wilderness. "Thou hast brought a vine out of Egypt. Thou hast cast out the heathen and planted it." Such was the biblical inspiration of the motto of Connecticut and of the state seal adopted in 1644. How great is the contrast between such an emblem and those of the western pioneer states of two centuries later, with their rising suns and optimistic plowmen!

It is possible to interpret the landscape of Jerusha as the expression of pioneer economic conditions. The village centered on the common and meetinghouse, the houses turning their backs on the woodlands, the small fields surrounded by fences and walls—these are certain traits of a subsistence economy and of a society compelled to think in terms of self-defense. Even the nonexistent lions and the soporific ferns, in one form or another, are part of every pioneer environment. But we should not forget that Nehemiah thought of himself not as a pioneer but as an exile, that he strove throughout his life not only for security but for holiness, and that his interests never wandered very far from that font of holiness, the meetinghouse. He never aspired to much more than establishing as firmly as he could a superdomestic order. He closed his eyes on this vale of tears in 1683, satisfied until his latest breath that two things at least were permanent: his own identity (which would rise in the flesh on the Day of Judgment) and the indestructible, unalterable house which he bequeathed to his widow, Submit.

It was lucky he died when he did. Had he lived to see his grandson Noah come of age, he would have witnessed the beginning of the end of the old order. Noah was one of the first in Jerusha to start speculating in land values. He realized that there was no longer room near the common for more houses and that newcomers were not eager to belong to the church community; they were willing to live far away. It was Noah who persuaded the town selectmen

JBJ, photo, New England extended barn

to build roads into the forest five miles distant, and he made a substantial profit selling off some of his grandfather's unused woodland.

His was not so well-behaved a world as Nehemiah's, but it was more extensive. It included the West Indies and Virginia and many new towns and frontier farms off by themselves in distant clearings. It included men who went about on horseback preaching a road to salvation much shorter and simpler than the one Nehemiah had so earnestly followed, and others who talked of a more direct relationship between people and government. Noah built himself a three-story house and furnished the parlor with mahogany and silver. The old house, now grey and in poor repair, was lived in by one of Noah's aunts. She prided herself on being loyal to the old ways, but she complained that the house was cramped and put in larger windows on the ground floor; and she always referred to New England as home.

### Pliny's Homestead

The first time a member of the Tinkham family built a house outside of New England was when Pliny Tinkham moved west a little over a century ago and homesteaded near Illium, Illinois.

Pliny was young to be married and the father of three children, and young (his parents thought) to be going so far from Jerusha. But though he was not rich, he had much more to start with than his ancestors had had two centuries earlier. He needed much more; he intended to farm on a larger and more complicated scale. Aside from money, Pliny and his wife, Matilda, took little with them, having been advised to buy whatever they needed near their destination. When they finally arrived at Illium, they bought (in addition to the same set of tools that Nehemiah had for pioneering) a team of horses, a yoke of oxen, a milch cow, a wagon, a plow, a pitchfork, a scythe—and ten pounds of nails. These were the articles listed as necessary in the *Farmers' and Emigrants' Handbook* which Pliny consulted.

*Pioneering in the Plains*

Nehemiah, it will be remembered, had been assigned land by the township; land comprising three different kinds of terrain. Pliny, though no judge of prairie real estate, was obliged to choose the land he wanted and to bargain for it. He finally bought 120 acres from a man who had acquired it as a speculation, had done nothing to improve it, and now wanted to move even farther west. It was excellent land, gently rolling prairie with very rich soil; it contained a small amount of woodland and was about ten miles north of Illium on what would some day be a road. The nearest neighbor was a mile away.

Like Nehemiah, Pliny built a temporary shelter for the family first of all, only he built it out of logs and thus made it larger and more comfortable than that first underground Tinkham shelter. He did not have to cut down many trees to clear his land, for most of it was clear already, but he did have to cut them down for the log cabin, for a barn for the livestock, and for fences to keep the animals from wandering across the prairie. He soon saw that wood was not to be wasted in southern Illinois; there was too little of it. Again like his ancestor, Pliny hastened to plant the fields he had prepared; but instead of planting for family needs, he planted twenty acres to wheat—in order to have a cash crop as soon as he could.

In many ways his pioneering was easier than that of Nehemiah. Pliny had no "hostiles" to deal with. The land was fertile and open, and he had the tradition of adaptability and self-reliance in a new country. He had a growing market not too far away, and a place where he could always buy to satisfy his needs. And then, finally, he and Matilda were optimistic and adventurous; the very fact that the purchase of the land had been a kind of speculation encouraged them to look at the whole enterprise of homesteading as speculative, for in a pinch they could always sell out and begin again.

On the other hand, life during the first years was often harsh. Matilda had a recipe for bread made of powdered beechwood and another for salad made of young pine needles, both to be used in times of near-famine. She found herself having to practice a variety of domestic skills which the people of Jerusha had either never known or had been able to delegate to specialists within the village—the making of candles and soap and dyes, of sugar from corn and yeast from milk. She had to tend a much larger vegetable garden than Submit Tinkham had ever seen, and preserve vegetables that Submit had never heard of. She had to nurse a family and keep it well according to methods which were scientific if rudimentary, whereas Submit had merely relied on traditional quackery and semimagic formulae, or had turned to any neighbor who had had medical experience. As for Pliny, he was not only farmer, carpenter, mason, engineer, and blacksmith, he was also veterinarian, hunter and trapper, experimental agriculturalist, and merchant.

Moreover, the Tinkhams of Illinois were from the beginning much more on their own than the Tinkhams of Massachusetts. What neighbors they had were friendly, but they were remote and few. The Tinkham dwelling was several miles from Illium (and a good distance across prairie mud from the road leading to Illium), and once Pliny reached the town he discovered that no one there felt any responsibility for his welfare, spiritual or physical. The banker, the storekeeper, the shipper were all eager to do business with him, but they were not much interested in his personal problems. There was not one church in Illium; there were three. One of the ministers came out to see the Tinkhams, led a prayer, left a few tracts, and never came back. The population of Illium was constantly growing and changing. The rumor of a new railroad, of a packing plant, of a new county seat sent half of them scurrying elsewhere. In spite of his spending a good deal of time at the courthouse and in the bank, and attending every fair, Pliny always felt like an outsider in the town.

*Flight from the Village*

To his forefather, such a feeling would have been almost too humiliating to bear, but Pliny was a different person. He needed a different society, a different economy, and a different landscape, and he had left New England because he knew that he needed them. The reasons given by the Tinkham tribe for the young man's defection were that there was more money to be made in farming out west, which was true, and that the old farm was exhausted after two hundred years of cultivation, which was not. They also blamed the railroads, the cheap land, the growth of large cities—everything except themselves. But the fact is, Pliny had rebelled against the old-fashioned farming methods of his father and against the old-fashioned domestic tyranny. The elder Tinkham, obsessed by the ancestral craving for security and solvency, and, like his ancestors, indifferent to the promise of wealth, had steadfastly refused either to enlarge the farm or to improve it in keeping with new ideas. What had been good enough for Nehemiah was good enough for him. Furthermore, he firmly believed that as father, as representative of God in the home, he always knew best, that he was the apex of the established domestic order. He treated Pliny like a child of ten. Thus when Pliny moved west it was not so much in search of easy money as in flight from the Old Testament household, the old self-sufficient economy; in a way, it might be said he was fleeing the New England village: common, meetinghouse, and all.

It was natural that the landscape which he and the other fugitives created in the West should have been in many respects the direct opposite of the landscape they had known as children. Instead of the cluster of farmhouses around the church, there were farmhouses scattered far and wide across the prairie; instead of the land being fairly and equally apportioned by a benevolent authority, it was bought on the open market; and instead of the superfamily life of the New England village, there was no village life at all. It was as if Pliny (like his remote ancestor) had set out in his turn to eliminate a few more steps in the hierarchy, some of the barriers between himself and immediate experience. Parents, clergy, aristocracy, township in the old sense were all abolished. And the chief artificer of the landscape was no longer the community but the individual. The independence that Pliny felt was expressed in a popular song:

> I have lawns, I have bowers
> I have fruits, I have flowers
> The lark is my morning alarmer.
> So jolly boys, now,
> Here's God speed the plow
> Long life and success to the farmer!

### The Functional House—1860

Most significant of all of Pliny's creations was his house, for it incorporated more revolutionary features than had any previous house in America. He placed it on a height in the center of the farm, where the air was fresh and the view wide, though he built at some distance from the highway and out of sight of neighbors. He and Matilda agreed that their house should be built primarily for the use of the family rather than for display or entertaining, and that it should be designed so that if need arose it could be easily sold. This was the advice that every homeowner gave them, and it was in keeping with the speculative attitude they both unconsciously retained from the very first days on the farm. But that was only the beginning. After reading several useful handbooks on building, Pliny and Matilda decided that their home should be a place which could be added to in the future as the family grew and as they put aside more money. They planned for rooms which could be used as bedrooms now and later as storerooms; they planned for sliding doors which could divide a room in two.

A house with a flexible plan, a house designed so sensibly that it could be used by one family and then sold to another—a house, in short that adjusted itself willingly to that outward thrust which Nehemiah's house had resisted so stoutly—was in itself a totally new concept. Equally new was the way Pliny built it. He abandoned the time-honored frame construction of his ancestors—and (significantly enough) the traditional dimensions based on the bay and the half-bay—and used the latest method, the so-called balloon construction. Balloon construction is actually the type of construction we now use in every frame house in this country, but it was invented only a little over a century ago. Its principle, as Siegfried Gideon defines it in *Time, Space and Architecture*, "involves the substitution of thin plates and studs, running the entire height of the building and held together only by nails, for the ancient and expensive method of construction with mortised and tenoned joints. To put together a house, like a box," he adds, "using only nails—this must have seemed utterly revolutionary to carpenters." But to Pliny, who never prided himself on being a radical innovator, it was the logical procedure. It called for cheap and plentiful nails, and these he had.

So the house was inexpensive and fast to build, and it was larger, better lighted, and more convenient than the house in Jerusha. Its rooms were numerous, and whereas Nehemiah had thought chiefly in terms of the social function of each room—one for the family, one for ceremonies, one for the servant, and so on—Pliny thought in terms of domestic or practical function: kitchen, milkroom, pantry, living room, bedrooms, and of course a piazza. Just as he had promised, it was a house designed entirely for family life and not for show. What was the spiritual center of this dwelling? In Jerusha it had been the formal parlor, with its Bible and hearth. But because of the scarcity of wood around Illium, and because of the more sensible arrangement of the rooms, Pliny had only Franklin burners and a cook-stove; two fires sufficed to heat the entire establishment. All that remained of the hearth was an open

Franklin burner in the living room (or sitting room, as Matilda called it). There was a small collection of books for family reading: Whittier and Longfellow and *Household Words* took their places alongside the Bible.

To say that the most important room in the Tinkham house was dedicated to family gatherings rather than to ceremonial occasions is to say that the house was designed for social self-sufficiency. None of the previous Tinkhams ever had so complete and independent a home life as Pliny. This was chiefly because the house had to take the place of the church and meetinghouse and school—and sometimes even the tavern. Weddings, funerals, burials, business deals, holidays gave it an importance that no Tinkham dwelling had ever had before or ever had afterwards. It expanded to include almost every aspect of country living; it represented in its way the golden age of the American home.

*The Functional Farm*

The farm which Pliny operated was not only larger than the one in Jerusha, it was far more efficient. Nehemiah had done everything by hand except haul stone and wood, and plow. On the farm near Illium, every phase of the process of raising corn, except for husking, was done by horse power—and this long before the Civil War. Nehemiah had not owned one piece of farm machinery; Pliny had wagons, plows, cultivators, and harrows, and after ten years, when the roads had been improved, he acquired a buggy. Gail Hamilton, a popular Boston essayist in the 1860s, compared the midwestern farmer with his New England counterpart. The midwestern farmers, she wrote, "do not go on there in the old ways in which their fathers trod for the very good reason they have neither ways nor fathers. . . . They make experiments, for they must make them. Indeed their farming is itself an experiment. Their broad lands necessitate broad vision. They farm with their brains as well as their hands. . . . Instead of taking his hoe and going to work, the [midwestern] farmer harnesses his horse and takes a drive, but his drive does a good deal more hoeing than the Massachusetts man's hoe."

The Massachusetts man—to be specific, Nehemiah—had chiefly sought to satisfy his family needs from the proceeds of the farm, and as long as the family needs remained pretty much the same year after year, he saw no point in increasing the size of the farm or its yield. Pliny, on the contrary, gave up after the first few years any attempt to provide for the family in the traditional way. Why raise sheep and spin wool and weave and dye and sew, when the railroad was bringing in ready-made clothes from the East? So he devoted more and more of his land to a cash crop—corn—which he could easily dispose of for ready money.

Once embarked on commercial farming, Pliny no longer had any reason for limiting the size of his farm; no matter how much he raised, he could always sell it—or so it seemed; and as a result, the farm started to expand. He bought other small farms, leased land, sold land, cleared land until he never quite knew how much he controlled. The expanding farm went hand in hand with the expanding house. Nehemiah had never changed the shape of his fields, bordered as they were with stone walls and each distinct as to soil and slope from the others. But Pliny, using wooden fences, could change his fields at will, and as he acquired large horse-drawn machinery, he consolidated many small fields into a few big ones. Again, the flexible plan of the farm paralleled the flexible plan of the house.

From the beginning Pliny had never seen the wisdom of having a diversity of land; he had naturally wanted as much of the best as he could afford to buy, and a uniform topography was certainly most practical for a uniform crop. He never had any of Nehemiah's feeling that even the worst and least productive patch of land served some inscrutable purpose in an overall scheme. He spent much time and thought trying to modify the farm and increase its yield, thus making it impersonal and efficient, and easier to sell to another corn farmer.

It is unfortunately true that Pliny robbed the farm of variety and human association, and made it look more like a place of work than a traditional landscape; but it would be wrong to say that he did not love it. He probably never had that dim sense which Nehemiah had of being in partnership with a particular piece of earth. Pliny was indeed a strict and arbitrary master. Nevertheless, he and Matilda and the children felt another kind of love which their colonial ancestor had never known. They enjoyed what in those days was called the grandiose spectacle of Nature. Pliny rode and hunted and fished in the remoter parts of the countryside, his children played in the woodlot and in the streams, and around the house Matilda planted a grove of locust trees and a romantic garden of wildflowers and vines. They belonged to a generation which believed that only good could come from close contact with nature; like Thoreau, they regarded Man as "an inhabitant or part and parcel of Nature, rather than a member of society." Never a churchgoer but always inclined to piety, Pliny was fond of saying that God could be worshipped in the great out-of-doors without the assistance of a preacher. As one of the emigrant handbooks put it (no doubt to reassure those pioneers who had always kept up their church attendance at home), "The church-going bell is not heard within his wild domain, nor organ, nor anthem, nor choir. But there is music in the deep silence. . . . He is indeed within a Temple not made with hands."

### The Family as a Natural Society

It is hard to realize that there was ever a time when such sentiments were new. But a century ago they not only represented a fresh approach to the environment, but a greatly simplified religious experience. Pliny loved the world of unspoiled nature for the same reason Nehemiah had dreaded it: it afforded him a direct and unimpeded glimpse of reality. Nehemiah had preferred to retain a hierarchy of scripture and clergy between himself and the source of wisdom. Pliny liked to imagine that God was separated from him by little more than the thin veil of appearances.

The same sentiment inspired his concept of the ideal homelife. Remembering his family in Jerusha, forcibly subordinated to Old Testament law and parental authority, he chose to think of the household on the farm at Illium as a happy group of free individuals held together by common interests and affections, a beautifully natural society, independent of the outside world and unspoiled by artifice.

As he grew older, Pliny had from time to time an uneasy suspicion that the house and the farm were no longer quite in harmony. The old domestic crafts had long since been abandoned, and increased contact with the national economy, increased dependence on hired help and semiprofessional skills, all tended to disrupt the ancient unity and self-sufficiency. But until his death in 1892, Pliny looked upon the homestead as the source of every virtue he admired: frugality and simplicity and independence. The free American farmer was the noblest of men, and to think of leaving the farm was to risk losing his identity. His solution to every problem, domestic or agricultural, was to "add a new room" or "buy some more land." He insisted on a home burial (the last in the county) as a sort of final investment in the land, a final planting. He had no doubt that the proceeds would be profitable to everyone.

He never dreamt that his grandchildren would desert the place as soon as he vanished. They did, however. They could no longer enjoy the kind of life Pliny had arranged for them. They wanted less routine, more excitement; they took no pride in owning a large farm and having little cash, and they were bored with their identity as independent landowners. They rapidly went their several ways and the farm was eventually acquired by a Lithuanian immigrant with fourteen children, who raised onions, acres and acres of onions.

JBJ, photo, Kansas house

Pliny's way of life died with him, but Pliny's ghost and Pliny's home continue to haunt us. To many urban Americans they still embody a national
ideal. Thanksgiving in Pliny's kitchen, fishing in the "ole swimmin' hole" on
Pliny's farm. Pliny himself behind a team of plow horses now advertises beer
and refrigerators and Free Enterprise. But the Tinkham family (who ought to
have known what they were leaving behind, and why they left it) have long
since moved on, and not all the persuasion of advertising copy writers and
politicians can make them return to the farm near Illium.

## Ray's Transformer

The latest Tinkham house is not yet finished. It is being built in Bonniview, Texas, by Ray Tinkham, who hopes to have it completed sometime in the spring of 1953.

Meanwhile, he and Shirley and the two children, Don and Billie-Jean, are still living out on the ranch with the Old Man. The Old Man, though a widower, does not want to leave the story-and-a-half frame house with its broad veranda that he built at the turn of the century. It is set in the midst of the cottonwoods which he and his wife planted, thinking of the grove of locusts around the house in Illinois. So he will stay there until he dies. Ray and he have a written partnership agreement by which the Old Man feeds a certain number of steers, while Ray manages the farm. It used to be a cattle ranch, but, having discovered a vast underground supply of water, Ray now plans to raise large crops of wheat or cotton or sorghum or castor beans, depending on the market. For the last month the bulldozers and earthmovers and caterpillars of a contracting firm have been leveling part of the range, contouring slopes, building irrigation ditches and storage tanks, and installing pumps. "You'd never know the place," the Old Man says as he looks at the brand-new geometrical landscape. He often wonders how the venture is being financed—as well he might, for Ray Tinkham has little cash, and there is hardly a farm credit institution, public or private, that is not somehow involved. But Ray is not worried, and the Old Man has confidence in his son.

Now is the slack time of the year, and every afternoon the two men and Ray's boy Don, and once in a while a neighbor, go to work on Ray's new house. It is being built out of the best-grade cement blocks, brought by truck some two hundred miles, and it is to be absolutely the last word in convenience and modern construction. It is to be flat-roofed and one story high, with no artistic pretensions, but intelligently designed. It is located on a barren and treeless height of land on the outskirts of town. It has city water, of course, as well as city gas. Ray bought four lots on speculation when he came out of the Navy. From the large picture window in the living room there will be a view of prairie and a glimpse of a strange rock formation in the valley below. It will even be possible to see a corner of the ranch twelve miles away; the dust being raised by the caterpillars is very visible when the wind is right.

### Planning the House

Twelve miles is an ideal distance. It means that Ray can get out to the headquarters (as he calls the old ranch house) in less than twenty minutes in his

JBJ, photo, suburban house

pickup, and leave his work far behind him at the end of the day. If the young Tinkhams were to continue to live out on the ranch, the children would have to travel by bus to the new consolidated school in Bonniview, and even then miss the supervised after-school play period. As it is, they will be able to walk the four blocks to school and their mother will be near her friends after the daily trip to the supermarket and the foodlocker. She will be able to drop in on any of them for coffee. Ray approves all these arrangements and is counting the days until he and Shirley and the children have their own home.

He has even put up a rough frame where the picture window will eventually be, and Shirley never tires of looking out of it, over the vacant prairie and the strange rock formation below. Ray, who is a graduate of an agricultural college, pretends that he knows nothing about planning a house and leaves almost every decision to his wife. A very wise move, for she has not only pored over every home decorating magazine available, she has practical ideas of her own. She wants the house to be informal and not too big; easy to take care of, easy to live in, cheerful and comfortable. Styles and periods mean nothing to her, and since the place will be adequately heated by gas, she suggests they save money by doing without a fireplace and chimney. She apparently knows the role the house can be expected to play in the life of the family, regardless of the role it might have played in the past. She knows that once in the new home the children will spend most of their time elsewhere and receive little of their upbringing in the house or from her. She will give them bed and breakfast, send them off to school, and in the late afternoon they will return in time to eat, having learned from their teachers how to sew, how to be polite, how to brush their teeth, how to buy on the installment plan—knowledge which Shirley herself acquired (after a fashion) from her parents. Eventually the two children will leave the house altogether, and their mother has already decided what to do with their bedrooms when that happens.

Ray, as a matter of principle, has never transacted any of his work at home and even leaves the ranch books with an expert accountant in Bonniview. For the new house Shirley plans a small dressing room off the garage where her husband can wash and change his clothes after work. It is not that she feels that the home should be devoted exclusively to her interests, though the family recognizes her as the boss; indeed, she is just as eager as anyone to reduce the functions of the house and to make it a convenience rather than a responsibility.

She wants as many labor-saving devices as they can afford; she wants to buy food which is already half-prepared—canned or frozen or processed—and then entrust it to the automatic time controls of an electric range; she wants to have an electric dishwasher, and a garbage disposal unit and incinerator built into the wall of the kitchen; she wants thermostat heat control and air-conditioning. She wants an automatic washing machine. Confronted with these demands and with Shirley's reluctance to have a lawn or a vegetable garden—"Who would water it?"—or a separate dining room for company—"Just another room to take care of and more people to feed"—Ray is tempted to ask what she expects to do with her leisure. But he knows the answer; actually, she will be lucky to have two free hours a day. He himself thinks leisure—time spent away from routine work—a very desirable thing, though he cannot say precisely why, and he knows that Shirley is not lazy, that the house should not monopolize her time. It is not important enough to any of them for that.

### The Function of the House

He is right. It would be absurd to talk of the new Tinkham house as an institution, in the sense that the house near Illium was an institution, when it represents so little of permanent significance. What connection, for instance, can it possibly have with the process of earning the daily bread when it is twelve miles distant from the place of work? Its educational function will grow slighter every year; even homework has been done away with in the Bonniview public schools, and discipline is largely left to the teachers. Whoever falls sick goes to the hospital, for modern medical practice involves the use of complicated technical equipment. What social prestige is attached to the house that Ray is building? Neither he nor Shirley gave any thought to social or snobbish factors when they chose its site; convenience was all that mattered. They will sooner or later clamor for a paved road in front, but expensive and time-consuming landscaping they both consider superfluous until they know how long they will continue to live there. Although the Tinkhams have social ambitions like everyone else in Bonniview, they instinctively know that their standing depends more on the organizations they belong to, the car they drive, the clothes they wear, than on the house and its furnishings.

They have no illusions as to the permanence of the establishment they are about to set up. It does not occur to them that they will spend their old age in the house, much less that the children will inherit it and live in it after they have gone. As for the kind of family life that the Old Man knew back east in Illinois—reading out loud together, Bible instruction, games, large holiday dinners, winter evenings in the sitting room, and so forth—the very mention of it makes Shirley impatient. The only time *her* family spends its leisure together—except for rapid meals—is when they are out in the car. And when the children *do* stay home, they go to their separate rooms and listen to their favorite programs on their radios. The Tinkham house will have no provision for a permanent library of books, for a common literary heritage; an unending stream of newspapers and magazines, scarcely ever read, will pass through the living room. The Old Man regrets that the children have no religious instruction; has Shirley ever tried reading the Bible to them? "For pity's sake, Dad! Ray and me never go to church, so why should the kids?"

If such is to be the economic and social and cultural status—or lack of status—of the new Tinkham home, what will actually distinguish it from a motel (which indeed it promises to resemble, at least on the outside)? Chiefly this: it is the one place where certain experiences, certain external energies are collected and transformed for the benefit of a group. This is clear in the design of the house itself: it is consciously planned to "capture" the sun, the breezes, the view; to filter the air, the heat, the light—even the distance—through the picture window, transforming them and making them acceptable to everyone. The kitchen is essentially a marvelous electric range which transforms raw or semi-raw materials into food; the living room is the radio (and someday the television set) which transforms electronic impulses into entertainment; the dressing room transforms Ray from a workingman into a different person. The whole house exists not to create something new but to transform four separate individuals into a group—though only for a few hours at a time.

In a word, the Tinkham house is to be a transformer; and the property of transformers is that they neither increase nor decrease the energy in question but merely change its form. There is no use inquiring what this house will retain from the lives of its inhabitants, or what it will contribute to them. It imposes no distinct code of behavior or set of standards; it demands no loyalty which might be in conflict with loyalty to the outside world. No one will be justified in talking about the "tyranny" of the Tinkham home, or of its ingrowing other-worldly qualities. Neither of the children will ever associate it with repression or wax sentimental at the thought of the days back in the Bonniview house. But still, it serves its purposes. It filters the crudities of nature, the lawlessness of society, and produces an atmosphere of temporary well-being where vigor can be renewed for contact with the outside.

### The Function of the Farm

It is no doubt significant that the house should be deliberately located at some distance from the farm and that it should have no connection with the farm setup. There are definite similarities, however, between the farm which Ray is creating and the house still under construction. Both of them, of course, disregard traditional form and layout, and the landscape which Ray will eventually produce will be as functional and as unincumbered as the house he is building. But how does he think of his farm? Does he, like Nehemiah, think of it as a fragment of creation which he is to redeem, to support himself from, and pass on to his progeny? Or, like Pliny, as an expanding organism, the victory of one individual over nature? Does he look upon his produce as God's reward for work well and piously done, or as part of a limitless bounty given by a benevolent Nature to those who understand and obey her laws? Neither; Ray is the first of the Tinkhams to doubt the unending profusion of nature, the first of ten generations to believe that the farm can and should produce much more than it has in the past, that much energy now being wasted can be put to use. Nehemiah, who saved every penny and never contracted a debt without examining his soul beforehand, would deny that Ray has any sense of economy; he would turn in his grave at the thought of the mortgages and pledges and indebtedness, and of the small balance in the Bonniview bank.

But Ray knows something that Nehemiah never knew and Pliny never quite grasped: that work and time and money are interchangeable, and that the farm serves only to transform each of these several kinds of energy into another. What does this knowledge of Ray imply? Nehemiah was aware that his occasional small farm surplus could be converted into shillings and pence, but he never put those shillings back into the farm. Pliny, who disposed of most of his produce on the market, knew that in order to get money out of a farm you had to put money into it. Yet he never calculated the worth of his own labor or that of his sons, never kept account of the milk and eggs and meat the family took. He refused to make a distinction between the family and the farm; they belonged together. Finally, it never occurred to him to expect the cost of certain improvements to be balanced by greater yields or lower overhead. If the price of corn was low, why bother to spend money on fertilizer? The farm, like the family, was not to be treated in terms of dollars and cents.

Ray is organizing his farm along entirely different lines. As he sees it, it is to be an instrument for the prompt and efficient conversion of natural energy in the form of chemical fertilizer or water or tractor fuel or man hours or whatever into energy in the form of cash or further credit—into economic energy, in a word. There are still a few old-fashioned ranchers near Bonniview who accuse young Tinkham of being money-minded. Farming, after all, is a way of life, they say, and science and new ideas can be carried too far. They think that if he had not gone to agricultural college but had served an apprenticeship with his father on the ranch, he would be more respectful of the old order.

### The Identity of House and Farm

Ray dismisses these criticisms as beside the point. He did not invent this kind of farming all by himself; his chief contribution is a willingness to accept certain definite trends. Labor is expensive and hard to get, so he has to mechanize and streamline his operations. Mechanization is expensive on a small irregular farm, so he has to expand and gamble on the results. The market fluctuates, so he must be ready to adjust the farm to more profitable operations, or to sell it at a good price and get out. The farm is not a self-supporting economic unit, it depends on the outside world, so he must be assured of good roads and efficient transportation. Thus the new farm reproduces many of the characteristics of the new house: labor-saving devices, efficient and simplified layout, adaptability to and anticipation of change, and dependence on the proximity of a complex economy; on markets, super- or otherwise. Like every other new house in rural America, the Tinkhams', in materials, method of construction, and location, has no organic relationship to its environment—weather or topography or soil. The Tinkham farm is of course something of a new departure, and its efficiency is yet to be proved. But it, too, is pretty much detached from the semi-arid southwestern landscape which surrounds it. Ray has changed the topography in no uncertain manner; his abundance of water for irrigation amounts to a change in the climate, and the soil—which even his father had always thought to be a constant factor—is being altered and improved in a variety of effective ways. Nothing more need be said of the infinitesimal cultural role which the home plays in the Tinkham family, but it is worth noting that the farm is, if anything, even less productive on that score. In the days when the Old Man ran the ranch and had several families of workers living on the place, there was such a thing as a sense of unity among them all, and there was a distinctive way of life. Ray's few workers are paid well and treated well; but they check in and out like factory hands and think of their boss as an impersonal entity known as the Tinkham Land Development Company. In fact, Ray pays himself a salary as manager.

Two pinto ponies stand in the corral waiting for Don and Billie-Jean to ride them. Once the farm is in operation, they will be ridden on weekends only, and in certain prescribed areas. Ray has made it clear that the farm is no place for Don to play at being farmer or rancher. "If he wants to learn this business, he'll have to go to agricultural college the way I did, and study chemistry and engineering and accounting." Don, however, at present wants to be a jet pilot.

The ranch will not take every one of Ray's working hours. He hopes in time to be able to leave it to look after itself, not merely overnight but for weeks on end, while he and Shirley and the children take winter vacations in California. He even dreams of having a small business in town to keep himself occupied. At present there are only two operations which he will delegate to no one: the preparing of the soil and planting of the seed, and investing the financial proceeds. The harvesting of the crop he has already contracted out to an itinerant crew which has its own machinery, and for several months of the year the Old Man's steers will be turned out into the stubble. In a sense, all that interests Ray are the first process and the last—the energy which goes into the soil in the planting and fertilizing, and the energy which comes out of it in the form of money. How can he and the rest of the family help but think of the new farm as essentially an impersonal and flexible instrument of transformation? How can they help but be indifferent to the traditional aspects of farming? The farm at Bonniview is not and cannot be a way of life. It is not even negotiable property (since Ray can scarcely be said to own it); it is a process, a process by which grass is converted into beef, nitrogen into wheat, dollars into gasoline and back into dollars.

### Ray's Identity

It would probably be fair to say that Ray is not a farmer at all, any more than his house is a farmhouse. Ray would be the first to agree. Nevertheless, there is a bond between him and the land that cannot be entirely overlooked. He himself is subject to the same forces (however defined) which have modified so drastically the concept of the farm. For one thing, Ray's identity, like the identity of the land, has become alarmingly mobile and subject to rapid change. His remote ancestor Nehemiah (of whom he has never even heard) remained true to his identity of yeoman throughout his life—and even died believing he would some day rise again intact in every particular. But for some reason Ray is leery of any kind of permanent label. He will not call himself a farmer, for instance; he says he is engaged in farming. And who knows what he may not be doing ten years hence, when he has made a success or failure of the Bonniview venture? Head of a trucking firm, oil well driller, owner of a farm equipment agency? They all cross his mind. He encourages his employees as well as his children to call him by his first name, as if he were reluctant to have any public status. He would probably explain this aversion of his to a permanent economic or social identity by saying that he merely wants to be himself. But even that identity refuses to be defined, just as it does to a lesser degree with his wife, Shirley. Ray laughs at her incessant attempts to be someone different: now a peroxide blonde, now a redhead with a poodle haircut; following diets and mail-order courses in the Wisdom of the East; dressing up in slacks and cowboy boots and then reverting to femininity—never a dull moment when Shirley is trying to develop a new personality. But at the same time he is not always very sure of himself. Far more intelligent, far more sensitive than the first American Tinkham, he has inherited none of Nehemiah's tough integrity and self-assertiveness. It is easy for him to lose himself, as the phrase goes, and to become a totally different person at a prize fight, or after two or three drinks, or at the scene of a bloody accident. "You should have seen yourself at the movie," Shirley says when they get home. "You sat there in the dark imitating every single expression Humphrey Bogart made on the screen."

Ray does not know the difference between hypnotism and amnesia and "getting religion," but he likes to talk about them; he likes to read in science fiction about brainwashing and thought control and transmuted identities. "It isn't scientifically impossible," he says, and he thinks of how he himself is radically changing the composition of the soil, how he is changing the face of the earth on a small scale. He thinks of the new house, not yet completed, ready to change its form, its owners, its function at a day's notice.

Bonniview is no more immune to the spiritual forces at large than were Illium and Jerusha. Ray is no less moved by an urge to apprehend truth than were Nehemiah and Pliny. If he has unconsciously destroyed the order which his father had established and made his home a very different place—much freer, in many ways much poorer—it is chiefly because he has wanted to eliminate some of the stages between reality and himself as his predecessors tried to do. He sees the relationship in his own characteristic terms: he sees himself not as a child of God wishing to learn the parental command, not as a child of nature heeding the good impulse, but as an efficient and reliable instrument for transforming the invisible power within him into a power adapted to the world as he knows it.

"The Westward-Moving House," *Landscape* 2, no. 3 (Spring 1953): 8–21.

JBJ, sketch, courtyard with cottonwoods, residence, La Cienega, New Mexico

## Ghosts at the Door

The house stands by itself, lost somewhere in the enormous plain. Next to it is a windmill, to the rear a scattering of barns and shelters and sheds. In every direction, range and empty field reach to a horizon unbroken by a hill or the roof of another dwelling or even a tree. The wind blows incessantly; it raises a spiral of dust in the corral. The sun beats down on the house day after day. Straight as a die the road stretches out of sight between a perspective of fence and light poles. The only sound is the clangor of the windmill, the only movement the wind brushing over the grass and wheat, and the afternoon thunderheads boiling up in the western sky.

But in front of the house on the side facing the road there is a small patch of ground surrounded by a fence and a hedge. Here grow a dozen or more small trees—Chinese elms, much whipped and tattered by the prevailing gale. Under them is a short expanse of bright-green lawn.

Trees, lawn, hedge, and flowers—these things, together with much care and a great expenditure of precious water, all go to make up what we call the front yard. Not only here on the western farmstead but on every one of a million farms from California to Maine. All front yards in America are much the same, as if they had been copied from one another, or from a remote prototype.

They are so much part of what is called the American scene that you are not likely to wonder why they exist. Particularly when you see them in the East and Midwest; there they merge into the woodland landscape and into the tidy main street of a village as if they all belonged together. But when you travel west you begin to mark the contrast between the yard and its surroundings. It occurs to you that the yard is sometimes a very artificial thing, the product of much work and thought and care. Whoever tends them so well out here on the lonely flats (you say to yourself) must think them very important.

And so they are. Front yards are a national institution—essential to every home, like a Bible somewhere in the house. It is not their size which makes them so. They are usually so small that from a vertical or horizontal distance of more than a mile they can hardly be seen. Nor are they always remarkable for what they contain. No, but they are pleasant oases of freshness and moving shade in the heat of the monotonous plain. They are cool in the summer and in the winter their hedges and trees do much to break the violence of the weather. The way they moderate the climate justifies their existence.

They serve a social purpose, too. By common consent, the appearance of a front yard, its neatness and luxuriance, is an index of the taste and enterprise of the family who owns it. Weeds and dead limbs are a disgrace, and the man who rakes and waters and clips after work is usually held to be a good citizen.

So this infinitesimal patch of land, only a few hundred square feet, meets two very useful ends: it provides a place for outdoor enjoyment, and it indicates social standing. But in reality, does it always do those things?

Many front yards, and by no means the least attractive, flourish on western ranches and homesteads many miles from neighbors. They waste their sweetness on the desert air. As for any front yard being used for recreation, this seems to be a sort of national myth. Perhaps on Sunday afternoons when friends come out from town to pay a visit, chairs are tentatively placed on the fresh-cut grass. For the rest of the week the yard is out of bounds, just as the now obsolete front parlor always used to be. The family is content to sit on the porch when it wants fresh air. It admires the smooth lawn from a distance.

The true reason why every American house has to have a front yard is probably very simple: it exists to satisfy a love of beauty. Not every beauty, but beauty of a special, familiar kind; one that every American can recognize and enjoy, and even after a fashion recreate for himself.

The front yard, then, is an attempt to reproduce next to the house a certain familiar or traditional setting. In essence, the front yard is a landscape in miniature. It is not a garden; its value is by no means purely esthetic. It is an enclosed space which contains a garden among other things. The patch of grass and Chinese elms and privet stands for something far larger and richer and more beautiful. It is a much reduced version, as if seen through the wrong end of a pair of fieldglasses, of a spacious countryside of woods and hedgerows and meadow.

Such was the countryside of our remote forebears; such was the original, the protolandscape which we continue to remember and cherish, even though for each generation the image becomes fainter and harder to recall.

Loyalty to a traditional idea of how the world should look is something which we do not always take into account when analyzing ourselves or others. Yet it is no more improbable than loyalty to traditional social or economic ideas or to traditional ideas in art. The very fact that we are almost completely unaware of our loyalty to a protolandscape allows us to express that loyalty with freedom. We have not yet been made ashamed of being old-fashioned. But what precisely is that landscape which our memory keeps alive and which an atavistic instinct tries to recreate?

It is not exclusively American. It is not New England or colonial Virginia or Ohio. It is nothing based on pictures and vacation trips to the East. It is northwestern Europe. Whatever the ethnic origin of the individual American, however long his family may have lived in this country, we are all descendants, spiritually speaking, of the peoples of Great Britain and Ireland, of the Low Countries, and to a lesser extent of northern France and western Germany. It was from those countries that the colonists transferred the pattern of living which is still the accepted pattern of living in North America. It may not remain so much longer, but that is something else again. We are all of us exiles from a landscape of streams and hills and forests. We come from a climate of cold dark winters, a few weeks of exuberant spring, and abundant snow and rain. Our inherited literary and popular culture both reflect that far-off environment, and until recently our economy and society reflected it too.

For almost a thousand years after the collapse of the Roman Empire, the history of Europe was the history of a slow and persistent deforestation. When the classical civilization began to die, Europe ceased to be one unit and became two. The region around the Mediterranean preserved a good deal of the Roman heritage; for the most part its population did not greatly change and the land remained under cultivation. But for several reasons the entire northwestern portion of the empire—Great Britain, the Low Countries, northern

France, and western Germany—began to revert to wilderness. Roads, towns, cities, and farms were gradually abandoned, fell into ruin, and in time were hidden by brush and forest. The peoples whom we call the barbarians, who later moved in from the East, had thus to reclaim the land all over again. They were obliged to take back from the forest by main force whatever land they needed for farms and pastures and villages. They were pioneers no less tough than those who settled our own West. Their numbers were so few and their means so primitive that every lengthy war and every epidemic saw much newly cleared land revert to undergrowth once more. It was not until a century ago that the last wastelands on the Continent were put under cultivation. The whole undertaking was an extraordinary phase of European history, one which we know very little about. How well it succeeded is shown by the fact that Holland, now a land of gardens, originally meant "Land of Forests."

Could this incessant warfare with the forest fail to have an effect on the men who engaged in it? Does it not help to explain an attitude toward nature quite unlike that of the peoples farther south? The constant struggle against cold and solitude and darkness, the omnipresent threat of the wilderness and the animals that lived in it, in time produced a conviction that there was no existing on equal terms with nature. Nature had to be subdued, and in order to subdue her, men had to study her and know her strength. We have inherited this philosophy, it sometimes seems, in its entirety: this determination to know every one of nature's secrets and to establish complete mastery over her; to love in order to possess and eventually destroy. It is not a point of view which has worked very well here in the West. If we had thought more in terms of cooperation with a reluctant and sensitive environment, as the Mediterranean people still do, and less in terms of "harnessing" and "taming," we would have not made such a shambles of the southwestern landscape.

That aggressive attitude is, however, only part of what the earliest farmers in northern Europe bequeathed us. Since they created the human landscape themselves and under great difficulties, they had a deep affection for it. They looked upon the combination of farmland and meadow and forest as the direct expression of their way of life. It was a harsh and primitive landscape, just as by all accounts it was a harsh and primitive way of life, but it was not lacking in a sentiment for the surrounding world, nor in an element of poetry. The perpetual challenge of the forest stirred the imagination as did no other feature in the environment. It was the forest where the outlaw went to hide, it was there that adventurous men went to make a new farm and a new and freer life. It teemed with wolves, boars, bears, and wild oxen. It contained in its depths the abandoned clearings and crumbling ruins of an earlier civilization. It was a place of terror to the farmer and at the same time a place of refuge. He was obliged to enter it for wood and game and in search of pasture. For hundreds of years the forest determined the spread of population and represented the largest source of raw materials; it was an outlet for every energy. Its dangers as well as its wealth became part of the daily existence of every man and woman.

When at last it was removed from the landscape, our whole culture began to change and even to disintegrate. A Frenchman has recently written a book to prove that the decline in popular beliefs and traditions (and in popular attitudes toward art and work and society) in his country was the direct outcome of the destruction a century ago of the last areas of untouched woodland. If he is correct, how many of those traditions can be left among us who have denuded half a continent in less than six generations? The urge to cut down trees is stronger than ever. The slightest excuse is enough for us to strip an entire countryside. And yet—there is the front yard with its tenderly cared for Chinese elms, the picnic ground in the shadow of the pines, and a mass of poems and pictures and songs about trees. A Mediterranean would find this sentimentality hard to understand.

The old ambivalence persists. But the reverence for the forest is no longer universal. Our household economy is largely free from dependence on the resources of the nearby forest, and any feeling for the forest itself is a survival from childhood associations. Until the last generation, it might have been said that much of every American (and northern European) childhood was passed in the landscape of traditional forest legends. Time had transformed the reality of the wilderness into myth. The forest outlaw became Robin Hood. The vine-grown ruins became the castle of Sleeping Beauty. The frightened farmer, armed with an axe for cutting firewood, was the hero of Little Red Riding Hood and the father of Hansel and Gretel. In a sense, our youngest years were a reenactment of the formative period of our culture, and the magic of the forest was never entirely forgotten in adult life. Magic, of course, is part of every childhood; yet if a generation grew up on the magic of Superman and Mickey Mouse and Space Cadet instead, if it lived in the empty and inanimate landscape which provides a background for those figures, how long would it continue to feel the charms of the forest? How long would the Chinese elms be watered and cared for?

After the forest came the pasture, and the pasture in time became the lawn. When a Canadian today cuts down trees in order to start a farm, he says he is "making land." He might with equal accuracy say that he is "making lawn," for the two words have the same origin and once had the same meaning. Our lawns are merely the civilized descendants of the medieval pastures cleared among the trees. In the New Forest in England, a "lawn" is still an open space in the woods where cattle are fed.

So the lawn has a very prosaic background, and if lawns seem to be typically northern European—the English secretly believe that there are no true lawns outside of Great Britain—that is simply because the farmers in northern Europe raised more cattle than did the farmers near the Mediterranean, and had to provide more feed.

As cattle and sheep raising increased in importance, the new land wrested from the forest became more and more essential to the farmer: he set the highest value on it. But to recognize the economic worth of a piece of land is one thing; to find beauty in it is quite another. Wheat fields and turnip patches were vital to the European peasant, yet he never, as it were, domesticated them. The lawn was different. It was not only part and parcel of a pastoral economy, it was also part of the farmer's leisure. It was the place for sociability and play; and that is why it was and still is looked upon with affection.

The common grazing land of every village is actually what we mean when we speak of the village common, and it was on the common that most of our favorite group pastimes came into being. Maypole and Morris dances never got a foothold in northern America, and for that we can thank the Puritans. But baseball, like cricket in England, originated on the green. Before cricket the national sport was archery, likewise a product of the common. Rugby, and its American variation, football, are both products of the same pastoral landscape, and golf is the product of the very special pastoral landscape of lowland Scotland. Would it not be possible to establish a bond between national sports and the type of terrain where they developed? Lawn bowling is favored in Holland and near the Mediterranean—both regions of gardens and garden paths. A Continental hunt is still a forest hunt; the English or Irish hunt needs a landscape of open fields and hedgerows. Among the many ways in which men exploit the environment and establish an emotional bond with it, we should not forget sports and games. And the absence among certain peoples of games inspired by the environment is probably no less significant.

In the course of time, the private dwelling took over the lawn. With the exclusion of the general public, a new set of pastimes was devised: croquet, lawn tennis, badminton, and the lawn party. But all of these games and gatherings, whether taking place on the common or on someone's enclosed lawn, were by way of being schools where certain standards of conduct and even certain standards of dress were formed. And in an indefinable way the lawn is still the background for conventionally correct behavior. The poor sport walks off the field; the poor citizen neglects his lawn.

Just as the early forest determined our poetry and legend, that original pasture land, redeemed from the forest for the delectation of cows and sheep, has indirectly determined many of our social attitudes. Both are essential elements of the protolandscape. But in America the lawn is more than essential; it is the very heart and soul of the entire front yard. We may say what we like about the futility of these areas of bright green grass; we may lament the waste of labor and water they represent here in the semi-arid West. Yet to condemn them or justify them on utilitarian or esthetic grounds is to miss the point entirely. The lawn, with its vague but nonetheless real social connotations, is precisely that landscape element which every American values most. Unconsciously, he identifies it with every group event in his life: childhood games, commencement and graduation with white flannels or cap and gown, wedding receptions, "having company," the high school drill field and the big game of the season. Even the cemetery is now landscaped as a lawn to provide an appropriate background for the ultimate social event. How can a citizen be loyal to that tradition without creating and taking care of a lawn of his own? Whoever supposes that Americans are not willing to sacrifice time and money in order to keep a heritage alive regardless of its practical value had better count the number of sweating and panting men and women and children pushing lawnmowers on a summer's day. It is quite possible that the lawn will go out of fashion. But if it does, it will not be because the toiling masses behind the lawnmower have rebelled. It will be because a younger generation has fewer convivial associations with it; has found other places for group functions and other places to play: the gymnasium, the school grounds, the swimming pool, or the ski run. It will be because the feeling of being hedged in by conventional standards of behavior has become objectionable.

To hedge in, to fence in; the language seems to shift in meaning and emphasis almost while we use it. Until not long ago, neither of those words meant "to keep in"; they meant "to keep out." A fence was a de-fence against trespassers and wild animals. The hedge was a coveted symbol of independence and privacy. Coveted, because it was not every farmer who could have one around his land.

Like the lawn and the tree, the hedge is something inherited from an ancient agricultural system and an ancient way of life. The farming of the Middle Ages is usually called the open-field system. Briefly, it was based on community ownership (or community control) of all the land—ownership by a noble amounted to the same thing—with fields apportioned to the individual under certain strict conditions. Among them were rules as to when the land was to lie fallow, what day it was to be plowed, and when the village cattle were to be allowed to graze on it. Much modified by social and economical revolutions, the open-field system still prevails over much of northern Europe. Fences and hedges, as indications of property lines, naturally had no place in such a scheme.

In the course of generations, a more individualistic order came into being, and when for several good reasons it was no longer desirable to have the cattle roaming at will over the countryside, the first thing to appear, the first change in the landscape, was the hedge. With that hedge to protect his land against intruders of every kind, the individual peasant or farmer began for the first time to come into his own, and to feel identified with a particular piece of land. He did not necessarily own it; more often than not he was a tenant. But at least he could operate it as he saw fit, and he could keep out strangers.

Each field and each farm was defined by this impenetrable barrier. It served to provide firewood, now that the forests were gone, shelter for the livestock, and a nesting place for small game. Most important of all, the hedge or fence served as a visible sign that the land was owned by one particular man and not by a group or community. In America we are so accustomed to the fence that we cannot realize how eloquent a symbol it is in other parts of the world. The Communist governments of Europe do realize it, and when they collectivize the farms, they first of all destroy the hedgerows—even when the fields are not to be altered in size.

The free men who first colonized North America were careful to bring the hedge and fence with them, not only to exclude the animals of the forest but to indicate the farmers' independent status. Hedges and fences used to be much more common in the United States than they are now. One traveler in revolutionary New England enumerated five different kinds, ranging from stone walls to rows of upended tree stumps. In Pennsylvania at the same period, fields were often bordered with privet. As new farms were settled in the Midwest, every field as a matter of course had its stone wall or hedge of privet or hawthorn, or permanent wooden fence. And along these walls and fences a small wilderness of brush and vine and trees soon grew, so that every field had its border of shade and movement, and its own wildlife refuge. The practice, however inspired, did much to make the older parts of the nation varied and beautiful, and we have come to identify fences and hedges with the American rural landscape at its most charming.

As a matter of fact, the hedge and wooden fence started to go out of style a good hundred years ago. Mechanized farming, which started then, found the old fields much too small. A threshing machine pulled by several teams of horses had trouble negotiating a ten-acre field, and much good land was wasted in the corners. So the solution was to throw two or more fields together. Then agricultural experts warned the farmers that the hedge and fence rows, in addition to occupying too much land, harbored noxious animals and birds and insects. When a farm was being frequently reorganized, first for one commercial crop then another, depending on the market, permanent fences were a nuisance. Finally, Joseph Glidden invented barbed wire, and at that the last hedgerows began to fall in earnest.

There were thus good practical reasons for ridding the farm of the fences. But there was another reason too: a change in taste. The more sophisticated landscape architects in the midcentury strongly advised homeowners to do away with every fence if possible. A book on suburban gardening, published in 1870, flatly stated: "that kind of fence is best which is least seen, and best seen through." Hedges were viewed with no greater favor. "The practice of hedging one's ground so that the passer-by cannot enjoy its beauty, is one of the barbarisms of old gardening, as absurd and unchristian in our day as the walled courts and barred windows of a Spanish cloister."

Pronouncements of this sort had their effect. Describing the early resistance to the antifence crusade during the last century, a writer on agricultural matters explained it thus: "Persons had come to feel that a fence is as much a part of any place as a walk or a wall is. It had come to be associated with the idea of home. The removal of stock was not sufficient reason for the removal of the fence. At best such a reason was only negative. The positive reason came in the development of what is really the art-idea in the outward character of the home . . . with the feeling that the breadth of setting for the house can be increased by extending the lawn to the actual highway."

Utilitarian considerations led the farmer to suppress the fences between his fields; esthetic considerations led the town and city dwellers to increase the size of their lawns. Neither consideration had any influence on those who had homesteaded the land, lived on it, and therefore clung to the traditional concept of the privacy and individualism of the home. The front yard, however, had already become old-fashioned and countrified fifty years ago; the hedge and picket fence, now thought of as merely quaint, were judged to be in the worst taste. Today, in spite of their antiquarian appeal, they are held in such disrepute that the modern architect and the modern landscapist have no use for either of them; and they are not allowed in any housing development financed by the FHA.

Why? Because they disturb the uniformity of a street vista; because they introduce a dangerous note of individualistic nonconformity; because, in brief, they still have something of their old meaning as symbols of self-sufficiency and independence. No qualities in twentieth-century America are more suspect than these.

It is not social pressure which has made the enclosed front yard obsolescent, or even the ukase of some housing authority, egged on by bright young city planners. We ourselves have passed the verdict. The desire to identify ourselves with the place where we live is no longer strong.

It grows weaker every year. One out of a hundred Americans lives in a trailer; one out of every three American farmers lives in a rented house. Too many changes have occurred for the old relationship between man and the human landscape to persist with any vigor. A few decades ago the farmer's greatest pride was his woodlot, his own private forest and the forest of his children. Electricity and piped-in or bottled gas have eliminated the need for a supply of fuel, and the groves of trees, often fragments of the virgin forest, are now being cut down and the stumps bulldozed away. The small fields have disappeared, the medium-sized fields have disappeared; new procedures in feeding and fattening have caused meadows to be planted to corn, range to be planted to wheat; tractors make huge designs where cattle once grazed. A strand of charged wire, a few inches off the ground, takes the place of the fence, and can be moved to another location by one man in one day. The owner of a modern mechanized farm, and even of a scientific ranch, need no longer be on hand at all hours of the day and night. He can and often does commute to work from a nearby town. His children go to school and spend their leisure there, and the remote and inconvenient house on the farm is allowed to die.

All this means simply one thing: a new human landscape is beginning to emerge in America. It is even now being created by the same combination of forces that created the old one: economic necessity, technological evolution, a change in social outlook and in our outlook on nature. Like the landscape of the present, this new one will in time produce its own symbols and its own beauty. The six-lane highway, the aerial perspective, the clean and spacious countryside of great distances and no detail will in a matter of centuries be invested with magic and myth.

That landscape, however, is not yet here. In the early dawn where we are, we can perhaps discern its rough outlines, but we cannot have any real feeling for it. We cannot possibly love the new, and we have ceased to love the old. The only fraction of the earth for which an American can still feel the traditional kinship is that patch of trees and grass and hedge he calls his yard. Each one is a peak of a sinking world, and all of them grow smaller and fewer as the sea rises around them.

But even the poorest of them, even those which are meager and lonely and without grace, have the power to remind us of a rich common heritage. Each is a part of us, evidence of a vision of the world we have all shared.

"Ghost at the Door," *Landscape* 1, no. 2 (Autumn 1951): 3–9.

# The Domestication of the Garage

To be interested in the popular culture of contemporary America is to be interested in our popular architecture, the architecture of those buildings in which we live or work or enjoy ourselves. They are not only an important part of our everyday environment, they also reveal in their design and evolution much about our values and how we adjust to the surrounding world.

That is why the study of vernacular (as opposed to "polite") architecture is more and more appreciated as a source of fresh insights into the social history of a period or a people. The question is (and always has been), which architectural forms are we to choose? Until about a century ago, little confusion existed; historians and cultural geographers told us that vernacular architecture meant the dwelling and its dependencies, public works such as bridges and mills and fortifications, and even sometimes the church. These were the products of craftsmen, members of a predominantly rural or pretechnological society, using traditional methods and locally available materials and working with practical ends in view. Folk or vernacular architecture was thus largely interpreted in terms of structure, and by extension in terms of the exploitation of local natural resources. At its best it represented a willing acceptance of the environment; the French geographer Albert Demangeon defined the peasant dwelling as an agricultural instrument, a means of exploiting the surrounding land.

But since the nineteenth century there have been many changes; we have learned to see the dwelling as a much more complicated thing, and the architectural scene has immensely expanded. Innumerable new forms have evolved, not only in our public existence—such as the factory, the shopping center, the gas station, and so on—but in our private lives as well. The home has been radically changed by the elimination of certain spaces and the addition of new ones.

The garage is a case in point. How is this particular feature—now almost essential to every family dwelling—to be interpreted in traditional vernacular terms? Is it to be thought of as the product of the craftsman? Is it somehow to be related to the economic function of the dwelling? Are we to try to establish regional or ethnic variations? Or must we reject the garage altogether? On the other hand, should we perhaps work toward a new definition of vernacular architecture that would *include* the garage?

## The Romantic Garage

The word is of French origin, of course, and means, more or less, a storage space. It is related to the English *ware* as in warehouse, and we could easily have devised an appropriate term such as "warage." But our borrowing from the French was an indication of the exotic (not to say expensive) nature of early automobile culture. Current descriptions of the introduction of the automobile, with their exaggerated emphasis on breakneck races and the contributions of small mechanics, do not give us a true idea of the original status of the automobile in this country. To most of its owners at the turn of the century, it was a pleasure vehicle and a toy, costly, exciting, and of extraordinary elegance: gleaming with brass and rich enamel, its form (even then) suggestive of power and speed. For controlling and maintaining this complicated machine it was wise to engage a specialist—who (again) was given a French name: chauffeur, meaning fireman, and who, because of his daring, his mechanical genius, and his style, had a special status. In *Man and Superman,* Henry Straker, Tanner's chauffeur, was the object of respect and uneasy admiration on the part of his employer. Shaw suggests that he represented the male counterpart of the New Woman, someone disdainful of traditional social views and in touch with future realities.

The housing of this valuable plaything, and of the chauffeur as well, was a matter of importance. In town the problem was solved by the availability of livery stables and improvised storage spaces where rentals, even in the first decade of the century, were likely to be as high as fifty dollars a month. But automobile owners who lived in the suburbs or the country depended on the stable or coach house. For sanitary reasons, this was usually isolated at some distance from the dwelling, in the rear of the grounds—an arrangement which seemed suitable for the automobile as well, for who knew what might not happen if the gasoline fumes made contact with the kitchen stove? Part of the stable became what was briefly called the "motor house," and the chauffeur had his lodgings in a room overhead.

Architects were even engaged by the well-to-do to design combination stables, carriage houses, and garages; in 1911 Frank Lloyd Wright produced a monumental example on a suburban Chicago estate. Nevertheless, the solution proved impractical. Acids emanating from the stables repeatedly tarnished the brass trim on the cars and even threatened to damage the paint. Keeping the cars clean and polished called for a special washing area, and no doubt the horses and their attendants were likewise inconvenienced. So at an early date the single-purpose garage emerged as an autonomous, more or less self-sufficient building type, stylishly functional. In 1906 *House Beautiful* published a spread of the more imposing specimens—Colonial, Tudor, Craftsman, as the case might be. Few subsequent designs surpassed them in size and dignity. A second story accommodated the chauffeur; the storage space itself was large, well lighted, and efficiently planned; often with a turntable (to eliminate having to back out), an overhead hoist, and a pit. This last feature disappeared when cars were designed to give access to the motor from above instead of underneath.

There are suggestions in the brief literature on garage design of the period that architects enjoyed the challenge of producing strictly utilitarian interiors, which would serve as settings for the engineered beauty of the automobile and the spit-and-polish work of the chauffeur; there seems to have flourished (not for very long) a kind of Machine Age esthetic of the garage.

But physically as well as psychologically, the garage remained isolated from the dwelling; at the end of a long driveway behind the house, when not hidden by a wall. Only after the chauffeur had cranked the motor into action, tested the sparkplugs and the tension of the leather fan belt, checked the oil, and poured in a gallon or two of gasoline did the car, figuratively speaking, join the family. Outside the front door ensued the ritual of pulling on gauntlets, adjusting veils and goggles and lap robes (while the automobile quivered restlessly), and finally waving good-bye. There was an early tendency—happily long since overcome, but natural enough in those adventurous days—to show off while driving. Various periodicals dealing with country or suburban life urged their readers to behave with dignity on the highway:

"No toes peeping over the body of the tonneau or feet resting on the dashboard or arms or wraps hanging over the sides, smoking limited to one person, preferably not the driver," *House and Garden* cautioned in 1909. "Whistles, bells, quacking novelties and sirens seem out of place in town although in the country they may be used to advantage. . . . Among the purely ornamental novelties of motordom the small gilt figure of an eagle has almost entirely monopolized the place on top of the radiator. . . . This is a very pretty custom if the figure be small, and quite patriotic where the bill holds a narrow ribbon of the national colors."

There exists a body of attractive if ephemeral writing—mostly novels and brief travel accounts—dealing with the early days of the car and the romance of driving. *The Wind in the Willows* is perhaps the only title to have survived.

## The Practical Garage

In the meantime, a much more prosaic automobile culture, and a much more popular one, was emerging among middle-class Americans. Entirely excluded from the wealthy world of imported pleasure cars and know-it-all chauffeurs, the world of automotive sport, hundreds of thousands and eventually millions of car owners learned to value their automobile as an increasingly important element in their everyday existence—for pleasure, of course, but also for the daily domestic routine and for work. The first Americans to see the car in these terms were probably farmers and country doctors; for them it was a vehicle for emergencies. But it was not long before many others whose work called for mobility—traveling salesmen and agents, repairmen and servicemen and deliverymen—used the automobile in their work, made their own repairs, and aspired to nothing more than models which were inexpensive and reliable.

Consequently, a very different garage came into existence. The small portable or prefabricated item, scarcely larger than the car itself, was for many working owners the practical answer. In closely built-up neighborhoods in most American cities, the service alley, beginning at about the time of the First World War, was lined with these boxlike structures. The dimensions of the average American city lot—twenty-five by one hundred feet—precluded building any garage next to the dwelling itself; and as a result the home garage for the freestanding dwelling was relegated to the rear of the lot. Two parallel cement pathways provided a lane from garage door to curb. It was an unsightly arrangement, and it had the effect of completing the ruin of the backyard. This small private area had rarely been attractive: surrounded by a high wooden wall, dominated by the revolving clothesline, a convenient place to put the trashcan and the ashes from the furnace and the doghouse, it had become a source of shame, and the advent of the garage completed its disgrace.

Those days, a half-century ago, after the car became popular but before the garage had been assimilated into the dwelling, can perhaps be thought of as a period of transition, from the concept of the home as the locus of high-minded educational and hygienic endeavor to the present concept of the home as a place for recreation and fun. Yet it is hard to find any evidence that architects or planners recognized the existence of the family automobile or of the problems it created in the years between the wars. It was only in 1916 that city planners began to take the automobile into account even in the discussion of urban transportation. Many well-intentioned designs for moderately priced houses were published during the twenties, and not a few of them received awards; but although a number of them included maids' rooms, scarcely one of them thought of the garage or even of overnight parking space. Radburn, New Jersey, the garden city designed in 1928, is perhaps the first sign we have of awareness of the garage as an essential adjunct to the dwelling—and even there it was segregated and hidden from view.

What one *does* find, however, are occasional examples of relatively expensive architect-designed suburban dwellings—especially in California— where the garage is attached to the house. This innovation became noticeable in the thirties. Yet the purpose seems to have been primarily esthetic: to heighten the interest of the architectural composition, to produce striking or picturesque masses or roof lines. The proof is that the garage rarely if ever communicated directly with the house. It remained functionally isolated from the domestic establishment, as if the vehicle it contained were little more than an occasional convenience having no bearing on the way life was lived. In 1939 a columnist in a magazine devoted to domestic architecture remarked, "You can't have failed to notice how in all the new home plans the family garage is 'tied in' with the house if the architect can possibly manage it. But the old garages, plunked down on one side of the house, halfway back in the garden, their doors yawning to the street, their walls bare, and their angular lines unsoftened by shrubbery—they *are* ugly."

### The Family Garage

Two decades later, after World War II, the whole garage scene had undergone a radical change. Not only was the garage in the average detached dwelling thoroughly integrated into the street facade of the house—to the point where its wide doors served to balance the picture window so popular in the fifties — it was *internally* integrated. A conveniently placed door led either into the kitchen or into what is known among home builders as the "mud room" — a kind of decompression chamber for members of the family returning from work or school. Furthermore, the garage itself had greatly expanded, becoming spacious enough to accommodate not only two cars but a deep freeze, a washer and dryer, and even a hot-water unit and a hobby work bench — to say nothing of broken lawn furniture, skis, tangles of garden hose. In short, it had become thoroughly domesticated, an integral part of home life and the routine of work and play. On its wide concrete apron — often occupying a third of the frontage — the family car is washed and polished every Sunday, and on weekday afternoons the young of the family shoot basketball. What the stork's nest on the chimney of the northern European home traditionally signifies, the basketball backstop over the garage door signifies for the American home: a leisure-oriented domesticity.

How are we to account for this relatively abrupt transformation? We can perhaps enumerate some of the external forces — forces not originating within the family itself — which were at work between the Depression and the end of World War II, though it would be impossible to say which of these was most important in changing the whole form of the middle-class American home. For one thing, cars increased in width and length and outgrew the old backyard garage and the narrow driveway leading to it. Then the boom in suburban and tract-house building produced houselots with a wider frontage in many outlying communities, and this of course allowed for a garage on the street. Families acquired two cars and even three; the decline in public transportation and the growth of urban and suburban distances meant that two cars were a necessity for many families of moderate income — one for work and one for household errands and transporting the children. A decrease in home delivery services had two very different consequences: the dwelling had to become more self-sufficient (acquiring a washer and dryer and deep freeze) and more trips were called for, more loads had to be brought home — and deposited in the garage.

In all of these changes or adjustments in the spatial organization of the American home, the garage has of course played a most important role. And since the garage was provided and designed by the builder, it might be said (and often is said by critics) that the contemporary house is entirely the creation of the housing industry, therefore not vernacular in the accepted meaning of the word.

But this verdict disregards the *internal* changes—the changes which the occupants themselves have produced or inspired. For it is easy to establish that many shifts in domestic values and objectives took place *before* the home-builders altered their designs. Only one of these internal changes can be mentioned here: the advent, some time in the late thirties, of the concept of the home as a place for recreation and entertainment. Long before mass-produced housing recognized this tendency and began to introduce festive elements, American families were transforming the basement (where the oil burner had replaced the coal furnace) into a rumpus room or game room or activities room. Long before colorful kitchens with Mediterranean decor came into vogue, Americans were busily disguising the bleak white antiseptic surface of the scientific kitchen. What the earlier "efficient" house had been like is well described in David Handlin's recent article in the *Architectural Association Quarterly*.[1] The contemporary leisure-oriented home has yet to be defined in detail.

There is in fact scarcely a space in the modern American dwelling that the owners themselves have not transformed in keeping with this new image. Even the backyard, freed of its clothesline and rubbish, and of the obsolete garage, became a recreation area well before homebuilders saw its potential charm. Barbeque pit, plastic wading pool, power lawn mower, all antedate the developers' concept of Holiday Homesteads. And the garage as a family center half outdoors, part work area, part play area, is a family invention, not the invention of designers.

The contribution of the homebuilder to the promotion of the leisure-oriented home has certainly been important, but it has chiefly been a matter of sensing shifts in taste and giving them a salable form. It is only lately, for instance, that the housing industry saw what the garage had come to signify. The *Practical Builder* in 1968 proposed the *three-car* garage. The added massiveness, the magazine suggested, would make for a more impressive house, and the three garage doors would imply three cars and a corresponding larger income. Surely these are very out-of-date concepts, long since abandoned by the prospective homeowner! And the magazine added (as if it had made a startling discovery) that the extra space could be put to use for the storage of pleasure boats, for the pursuit of hobbies, for a play area on rainy days. But in scores of housing developments we had already acted on the suggestions. It is we who design or redesign our homes; the homebuilder merely provides the structure.

**What Is Vernacular?**

Just as the builders were a good decade behind the times in realizing the importance of the garage in the twenties and thirties, they have been behind the times in seeing that the multipurpose garage has become an integral part of the new leisure-oriented dwelling. There is nothing blameworthy in this; the housing industry had not claimed to do more than satisfy well-established needs, though it does not always do this very well. But the mass homebuilder has in a sense come up with a good working definition of vernacular architecture: it is the visible result of a confrontation between the aspirations of the occupying family and the realities of the environment—natural, social, economic. There is no permanent solution to the conflict; there will never be. That is why we will go on evolving new kinds of vernacular architecture; that is why the contemporary American dwelling, with its all-purpose garage and its attempts to be something other than what it has been in the past, is an authentic example of what vernacular means (or should mean) structurally and socially; just as authentic in its complex and restless way as the dwelling of the Pueblo Indian or the Greek peasant.

"The Domestication of the Garage," *Landscape* 20, no. 2 (Winter 1976): 10–19.

# 3 The Unfolding American Past

JBJ, photo, Appalachia

## Virginia Heritage:
## Fencing, Farming, and Cattle Raising

Without having any such intention in mind, the earliest English colonists in North America, almost from the start, created two distinct landscapes: one in New England and the other on the shores of Chesapeake Bay. These two landscapes, together with a landscape created somewhat later in eastern Pennsylvania, for more than a century and a half provided models, as it were, to the American colonies as they grew and to the young republic as it expanded to the west. A hundred and fifty years ago, these three landscapes and their extensions were still more or less distinct in character. It would have been easy for a traveler in the newer parts of the United States in those times to deduce from the appearance of a town or a countryside where its settlers had come from; the methods of farming, the crops raised, the appearance of the villages, of the houses and churches, even the accent of the people and the food they ate would all have suggested the place of origin of the inhabitants. The three landscapes, once so different from one another, have now of course been assimilated into a much larger national landscape; yet the more I travel through the country, the more I am struck by the persistence, even to this day, of the southern landscape heritage. Reminders of the Old South are still strong north of the Ohio and emerge in such unlikely places as Utah and California and New Mexico. They flourish, of course, in eastern Texas. All hail from a small and not very populous region of the Chesapeake country known as Tidewater Virginia.

When the first Englishmen landed near the mouth of the James River in 1607, the land was at its most beautiful. It was spring, the days were mild and sunny, and in the splendid forest reaching to the very edge of the water the trees were in full leaf. Dogwood blossoms gleamed among the tall, straight trunks, and the ground was covered with wildflowers and strawberries four times as large (so the colonists said) as those in England. Immense flocks of birds flew over the bay or floated on its surface, thousands upon thousands of ducks and geese and swans and gulls and herons and even eagles, all making an incessant clamor. They were on their way north. There was a fragrance of vegetation and damp earth, and to the colonists who had been more than four months crossing the ocean, the place seemed a luxuriant park or garden, almost a paradise.

When we remember the tragic events which lay in store, the months, even years of sickness and starvation and despair that awaited the colonists, we are first of all aware of the irony of their lighthearted enthusiasm for that glimpse of the New World. Then we find the extenuating circumstances: every decision, every plan was made by the few men in command; the rest were merely hired laborers, young and inexperienced men—for there were no women among the first two hundred to arrive. Furthermore, most of them came from towns, with little or no knowledge of hunting or farming or how to fend for themselves. But we run the risk of doing them an injustice when we dismiss them as unrealistic, for in fact their response to the Virginia wilderness had roots in an ancient and respected tradition, in a nature philosophy older than our civilization.

Every culture and every period within a culture has its own way of adjusting to a new and unfamiliar environment. Our own response—very effective from our point of view—is to calculate how we can control the environment and turn it to practical uses; we analyze it as best we can in terms of its resources and of our own needs. But three centuries ago the approach was more personal and more instinctive; the quality of a landscape was judged largely by the response of the four senses: sight, smell, taste, and touch. Each of these corresponded to one of the four humors and to one of the four elements, and ultimately to cosmic powers; and when the senses testified to harmony, then it was logical to assume that the environment was favorable to man.

I am not the one to discuss this doctrine and how it was expressed in many fields from agriculture to mining to medicine and philosophy, but one instance of its authority can be seen in the manner in which the first settlers sought to estimate the fertility of the Virginia soil. An early report stated that "the soil was so aromatic that it imparted a spicy flavor to the roots of the herbs, plants, and trees springing from it. In appearance it was a dark, sandy mould, that was sweet to the taste and very slimy to the touch." Touch, sight, smell, and taste all indicated that Virginia was a favorable place for settlement. And this conviction was confirmed by the repeated references in the accounts of early explorers to the marvelous fragrance of America, perceptible even on ships far offshore; in the loving descriptions of plants and flowers and flowing water. No wonder the rich sensory experiences of the Virginia spring elated the settlers and inspired Capt. John Smith to declare that "heaven and earth never agreed better to frame a place for man's habitation."

But at the end of that first summer—a very difficult summer in many respects—the settlers discovered that the Virginia landscape had at least one serious shortcoming. They had brought cows and horses and pigs and sheep and poultry with them, and when they had built a fence across one of the peninsulas, they turned the livestock loose. After all the months at sea, the animals were weak and sickly. They at once started to devour the fresh grass in the woods. They grew fat and sleek; but when cold weather came, and the colonists began to think about putting up hay for the winter, they discovered that the native vegetation made poor hay, rough and coarse, with little nourishment. The fact was, since the Indians had never raised livestock, no good forage plants had ever evolved. The native grasses were annuals; they were eaten before they could reseed, and they could not withstand constant trampling and grazing.

In New England, as well as in New York and Pennsylvania, the early colonists discovered the same thing: during the summer there was plenty of luscious grass, but no grass which made good hay for winter feeding; and the first difference between a northern and a southern landscape appeared in the two solutions to this serious problem.

In the North, where the winters were long and fierce, the first generation of farmers learned to build sheds and barns to protect their livestock—something they had never had to do in England—and eventually they learned to import grass seed from England and plant meadows for hay. It was not the best or purest grass seed, for it contained the seeds of many English wild plants that had never grown in the New World: daisies and dandelions and buttercups and yarrow and plantain. We think of these as part of our American landscape; actually they are illegal aliens, smuggled into the country from overseas. The result was that the northern colonists not only solved the cattle feed problem, they also transformed the natural landscape of a great portion of America. This development is no part of our story; but when you see plants or trees which stay green all winter—like our lawns—you are usually looking at a plant which was imported from Europe.

What was the southern solution? Naturally enough, the colonists in Virginia tried the same procedure; they too sent back to England for supplies of what used to be called English grasses, and they too planted the seeds. But the results were disappointing. The grass failed to take hold; it could not survive the hot summers and the hard, sun-baked soil. English grasses and clover never became a familiar aspect of the colonial southern landscape, though Jefferson and Washington both later experimented successfully with forage crops and improved grazing. As far as we now know, the only foreign grasses imported into the colonial South were brought over from Africa on the slave ships. Bermuda grass was probably one of them.

The southern farmer found a simple answer to the problem: he continued to turn the livestock loose in the woods to fend for themselves; if he wanted the cows to stay near home, he threw out a few ears of corn or corn husks. It was by no means a perfect solution: many of the cows and hogs bogged down in the swamps and marshes. Others were eaten by wolves or hunted by Indians, and some, of course, wandered off and were never seen again. But enough survived to make the experiment profitable, and indeed the hogs learned so well to take care of themselves that they multiplied and became more numerous than the deer. They lived on mast, which is the accumulation of roots and nuts and acorns in the forest, and their flesh acquired so wonderful a flavor that Virginia hams were much sought after in England.

Let me here mention an everyday feature of the southern landscape that came into being in the early years. This was the rail fence, or snake fence. It is still to be seen in many parts of America, and though we find it picturesque, it was long considered unsightly. It was the most practical fence for Tidewater Virginia, where there was no fieldstone but an abundance of wood. Moreover, it could be taken down and moved to another place when a field was abandoned, as it usually was after three or four years.

There is one characteristic of the southern fence that sets it apart from the New England fence or stone wall, a matter perhaps of definition: in the South, fences were built to keep animals out, to exclude them, whereas in New England fences were built to contain animals, to keep them in.

Actually, the distinction is not so much between regions as between a landscape largely devoted to stock raising and one largely devoted to farming. When, as in the North, most of the cleared land in colonial times was given over to corn or wheat or even clover, it was essential to keep cows and horses and hogs penned *in* a pasture to prevent their wandering about and devouring the crops. But in a region of cattle raising—which is usually a frontier region—the role of the fence is to keep the cattle *out* of the new fields that exist. It is largely a question of who has to go to the trouble and expense of building many miles of fence, the farmer or the stockman? And in regions of agricultural transition, a serious conflict often develops between them. The conflict was in fact very much part of the history of the American landscape throughout the nineteenth century, and one of the final and most dramatic episodes took place in the Texas Panhandle about one hundred years ago.

We usually think of the colonial Virginians as tobacco planters, making their living by raising and exporting tobacco to England. But they were also stockmen, with herds of cows, as well as hogs and sheep and horses, and to many of the smaller landowners, cattle were the chief source of income. Cattle, in fact, did well in early Virginia; they found food not only in the surrounding forest but in the many abandoned clearings where the Indians had once planted their gardens. But it was inevitable that many domestic animals, left unattended as they were, went wild and multiplied in the back country. They proved to be a nuisance; they invaded the fields of the farmers and led the domestic cattle astray, and to handle the problem the settlers developed a procedure for separating the domestic cattle from the wild, for marking the cattle of the individual owners, and for regulating grazing in the forest. All this was new to the Virginians. In the old country, cattle raising was part of farming: the cows and hogs and horses and sheep were kept in pastures or on the village common, and never allowed out of sight. But in the New World, especially in the South, an entirely different way of raising cattle had to be found.

A historian once wrote that "cattle raising in the United States began in Virginia, rather than in Texas, as is commonly supposed." By that he meant that as early as the mid-seventeenth century farmers and planters learned to organize to round up all the cattle, brand them, and cut out those they intended to sell. The expression "open range" was first used in Virginia; the range was originally a frontier district to the west of the settled Tidewater region, and rangers were the mounted soldiers who patrolled this range to protect it against Indian incursions. But it was also the region where the colonists' livestock wandered, a region where there was good grass, good water, and shelter. The Tidewater farmers periodically came together to round up their stray cows. For days on end they rode through the forest and the open grasslands looking for cows and calves, slowly pushing them to a central collecting place which in those days was called a cowpen, but which we now of course call a corral. There the cows were sorted out and branded. The brands were registered at the courthouse, and the first record we have of the use of the word *cowboy* dates from the mid-1600s in Maryland.

In time, settlement invaded the wilderness rangeland, and the open-range cattle industry shifted into the foothills in the west, and south into North Carolina, where the climate was mild and there was much grassland. And it was perhaps in that part of the South—extending from Virginia all the way to Georgia and Florida—that the first great commercial herds and full-time cattlemen or herdsmen were found. There were men who owned as many as six thousand head and who controlled many thousand acres of rangeland. Until the Revolution they flourished throughout the hilly back country of the South, and the term "Georgia cracker" is said to have come from the long whips used by the herdsmen of Georgia. The great herds were driven to the seaports to be shipped overseas, or to such large towns as Philadelphia or even New York, and several of the first long-distance roads or trails were the creation of these cattle drives along the eastern foothills of the Blue Ridge Mountains. As might be expected, some of the less admirable features of the cattle business came to the surface. There were frequent cases of changing brands and of cattle rustling, and in 1630 no less a person than a former governor of Virginia was found guilty of stealing cattle. A hundred years later the offense had become so widespread that South Carolina passed a law stating that rustlers were to be hanged without benefit of clergy.

Who were these early ranchers or stockmen? Some historians believe that they were small farmers and tobacco planters who failed and then moved out to a remoter, wilder part of the colony, driving their few head of cattle with them. These men often homesteaded in the back country or in North Carolina. Many prosperous plantation owners also took part because they enjoyed the sport and adventure of the roundups and were enthusiastic horsemen.

But there is reason for believing that many of the early stockmen and cowboys hailed from Scotland and northern Ireland (or Ulster). Throughout the colonial period, many young people came from those countries to Virginia as indentured servants. In their homelands they had often taken part in village cattle roundups. Every household in Scotch villages was allowed to graze its hogs and cows on the common lands, and every fall there was a roundup of the animals, with each household cutting out its own livestock. It was an ancient and carefully organized custom, and it may well have been introduced to the farmers of Virginia by the young immigrants from Scotland and Ireland. I say young immigrants advisedly. Before the use of black slaves became general in Virginia, the ideal farmhand was a youth of fifteen years or over. At that age he was easy to train and discipline, strong and with many years of hard work ahead of him. Boys of this age were often problems in the villages and towns of Great Britain; they drifted to the cities, and as a result a flourishing kidnapping business developed in English and Irish ports. Ships going to America for tobacco, having space on their westbound voyage, often called at an Irish port and took on a cargo of kidnapped boys to dispose of as indentured servants (or field hands) in Virginia. It was this practice which incidentally contributed what must be one of the most popular terms in American English: the word *kid*—short for kidnapped—to indicate a young person, usually male. A historian of colonial Virginia writes that "the sea captains hunted Protestant 'kids' preferentially because they brought a higher price in the Colonies," and he mentions a local tradition which traced the ancestry of a distinguished Tidewater family to "a 'kid' from Wales."

This colonial ranching tradition eventually moved further south, spread along the grasslands of the Gulf region of Georgia and Alabama and Mississippi, and joined with the cattle-raising traditions of French Louisiana and Mexico to appear after the Civil War as a new and very picturesque way of life: open-range ranching. It lasted until about a century ago; but the Virginia heritage lingered until the end: the classic cowboy of American literature is still known as "the Virginian."

It is time to return to colonial times and the colonial landscape. Although the invention of ranching in early Virginia is an interesting link between that part of America and Texas and the West, its significance is much more than economic. How can we understand a landscape until we understand the emotional and psychic bond between that landscape and the people who live in it and helped to create it?

I suggested that the very first settlers in Tidewater Virginia responded primarily in a sensory way to the new environment. I am inclined to believe that this response persisted for many generations, particularly among simple people and those living in the remoter areas, white people as well as black. It was, historically speaking, already an old-fashioned response, pretty well abandoned by the more educated English men and women. That perhaps is why the sensory response was less common in New England than in the South. We have only to compare the Virginian response to that of the Puritans. The Puritans had a far more intellectual way of judging the New World environment. They were not looking for easy living in a land of abundance; they were looking for a place where they could establish a Christian social order.

It would certainly not be accurate to say that the southern colonists were exclusively interested in finding an earthly paradise; they were eager to make money and prosper. But I believe that their initial reaction to the beauties of the natural landscape and to its atmosphere of physical well-being was never entirely forgotten. I believe that they continued to remain loyal to that obsolete but very attractive natural philosophy of the four elements.

In fact, they were constantly reminded that they had come to an environment very different from the one they had left behind. The absence of good grass was one instance; another was the bewildering variety and distribution of the soils of Virginia. In New England the soil, as well as the climate, were similar to those in England; but in Virginia the quality of the soils, which were preglacial, and the variations of the climate had to be learned through sometimes harsh experience. Even the search for good pasturage for the cattle—to say nothing of the search for the cattle themselves—obliged the Virginia farmers to become explorers and keen observers of their surroundings. As they rode through the forests and clearings, looking for good grass, good soil, good water, learning to read the signs of the weather, they inevitably developed those talents which in time made them the first pioneers in America.

It was quite possible that this search for water—and for deposits of salt for the cattle—led to the discovery of the mineral springs which abound in northern Virginia. In any case, in the first decades of the eighteenth century many of the springs became popular with the more prosperous planters, and the custom was established of spending two or three weeks at a spring, partly for sociability and relaxation, but primarily for health. The belief in the therapeutic value of mineral waters, taken either internally or externally, is an essential part of the classical doctrine of nature: the restoration of the balance among the four humors by means of absorbing one of the elements. The village of Bath in Virginia, later known as Berkeley Springs, was patronized by young George Washington and was a fashionable resort. The practice became widespread, and mineral springs throughout the mountains remained popular until the beginning of this century. They are still more frequented by Southerners than by other Americans. It is strange to see how completely the contemporary discussion of medicine ignores these springs. Whereas the *Encyclopedia Britannica* of 1910 devotes several thousand words to what it calls "balneotherapeutics" (from the Latin *balneum,* meaning bath), the contemporary *Encyclopedia,* largely American, does not even mention them—a good indication of how we have forgotten the old theories of medicine and nature.

Let me give one final example of the southern devotion to the doctrine of the four elements: the raising of tobacco. Tobacco was, of course, in use long before Virginia was colonized. Its popularity and prestige in Europe came from the fact that it was first introduced as snuff—in other words, as an enjoyable smell. But it was soon observed that the herb had medicinal properties which made it an invaluable medium for balancing the four humors: the inhaling of tobacco smoke stimulated and soothed, and healed all respiratory ailments, so it was believed. "Tobacco," one writer exclaimed, "divine, rare, super-excellent tobacco, which goes far beyond all their panaceas, potable gold, and philosophers' stones, a sovereign remedy for all diseases!" Another seventeenth-century writer described how it operated: "It drives out all ill-vapors but itself, draws down all bad humors by the mouth, which in time might breed a scab over the whole body." A third writer explained that "the smoke of tobacco filleth the membranes of the brain, and astonisheth and filleth many persons with such joy and pleasure, and sweet loss of senses, that they can by no means be without it."

Tobacco has another characteristic which identified it with the doctrine of the four elements: it adapts itself to almost every soil and climate and grows well in almost every part of the world, but it takes its flavor from the soil in which it grows. The Virginia planters quickly discovered this. Tobacco grown in one part of the colony would be mild and sweet, while tobacco grown from the same kind of seed, but in another kind of soil, would be harsh and unpalatable. Scientifically, this is easy to explain; but it can also be explained in terms of classical nature philosophy. It is quite true that the Virginians raised tobacco because it was a profitable crop, but we must remember that they first raised tobacco for their own consumption, and that Virginians, and indeed most Southerners, have long been great users of tobacco; early travelers were amazed to see women and eight-year-old children smoking as they waited on Sundays to enter the church.

Unfortunately, this colonial devotion to the sensory aspects of the environment did not mean that they treated the environment intelligently. On the contrary, tobacco exhausted the soil after three years, and much of Virginia was ruined by the growth of the crop. Forests were ruthlessly destroyed to clear more land for tobacco, the soil eroded and turned the once clear streams blood-red.

Overgrazing and the plowing of hillside land reduced wide areas to naked hills and gullies. After little more than a century, Tidewater Virginia was a landscape of abandoned fields, taken over by second growth, of houses fallen into ruin, with an impoverished and undernourished population. It was part of that early southern attitude toward nature that they had complete confidence in the inexhaustible richness and recuperative power of the environment and never developed a real sense of caution or responsibility. They ruined one region only to move on and repeat the process elsewhere.

The moral is very clear to us; we are paying the price of this attitude now. But responsibility and love do not always go together, and sometimes it seems that our renewed sense of responsibility toward the environment is producing an overwhelming sense of guilt. It would do us no harm to look back to a time when people turned to nature to solve every problem, like children turning to their mother.

"The Virginia Heritage: Fencing, Farming, and Cattle Raising," from *The Southern Landscape Tradition in Texas* (Fort Worth: Amon Carter Museum, 1980), 1–10.

## The Nineteenth-Century Rural Landscape:
## The Courthouse, the Small College,
## the Mineral Springs, and the Country Store

We should try to visualize that landscape of colonial Virginia as a vast forest. Here and there along the banks of the many rivers were open fields and scattered houses surrounded by barns and sheds with gardens and orchards, and older farms had their own private graveyards. Many fields had been abandoned and were reverting to second growth. But forest covered most of the flatland near Chesapeake Bay and covered the foothills to the west. Villages were small and few; and aside from Williamsburg (which was never very large) and Jamestown (an unhappy place, always on the verge of extinction), there were no real towns in Virginia.

And yet, as we all know, the early Virginians were sociable men and women, and liked nothing better than parties and games and sports and opportunities for coming together. Even though the stockmen and woodsmen could be thought of as the first Americans to go native, to spend many days and even weeks away from home, they too looked forward to sociability.

Without towns or lively villages, where did those early colonists go for pleasure and company? Houses and plantations were far apart and often isolated by rivers hard to cross, but the well-to-do planters had house parties, and even the small farmers celebrated weddings and christenings in dances and feasts which lasted for days on end. There were horse races and hunts; there was church to go to every Sunday.

We read about the young indentured servants spending their Sundays visiting the nearby Indian settlements and frequently getting into trouble there, and other young men so desperate for amusement that they rode cross-country all day long paying calls. Along the few roads and trails that crossed the forest, there were taverns where men gathered and argued and watched cockfights and listened to traveling musicians.

But for the rank and file of Virginians, I think we can say that the most popular meeting place was the county courthouse. It was an institution which played a unique role in the lives of country people in the South, and it continues to play an important role in every community where southern influence has been strong. That is to say, it is a familiar feature of that part of the American landscape everywhere south of the Ohio River and more or less south of the Red River; it is even part of the landscape called Little Texas in New Mexico—the region where there is oil and where farmers raise cotton. On the other hand, the courthouse does not amount to much, socially speaking, in the East and the North and throughout the High Plains.

The South could hardly have survived without that gathering place, that center of sociability. Very early in its history Virginia was divided into counties. By the early 1700s there were twenty-two of them, all very small; and every county had its courthouse. But in a landscape still thinly populated, with very few villages, where was the courthouse to be placed? It became the practice to build it on a spot near the center of the county, even if that was deep in the wilderness. Sometimes the courthouse was built where two trails crossed, or halfway between two important plantations. In this manner there came into existence one of the most picturesque and charming features of the Virginia landscape: the isolated courthouse, often a handsome brick structure with white trim, standing by itself, surrounded by trees and lawn, far out in the countryside. In time, of course, a small settlement usually grew up around it: a tavern, a general store, a building to house the offices of the lawyers. The settlement in most cases took the name of the county and called itself Prince Edward Courthouse, or Appomattox Courthouse, but to complicate matters there were villages called James City County Courthouse and Elizabeth City County Courthouse. The South has strange ways of naming places; in Baltimore there is a Charles Street Avenue Boulevard, and I believe Atlanta is doing much the same with Peachtree Street.

For most of the year the courthouses were empty and lifeless, and sometimes families moved in and made themselves at home. But there were monthly sessions of the court and there were election days and there were days

when people paid their taxes, and at these times the courthouse and its surroundings came to life. Men and women and children, tired of home or of the
woods or of hoeing tobacco, gathered from all around the county to have a
holiday and see their friends. They came in wagons or on horseback or afoot
—hunters, backwoodsmen, small farmers, rich plantation owners. They paid
their debts, sold and bought anything from shovels to pieces of land, and,
when there was an election under way, listened to the stump speeches.

Generally speaking, the courthouse people must have been a rowdy lot.
Colonial travelers referred to them as "poor whites" or "mean whites," or as
"Buckskins" because of their dress. The men were rough and loud, given to
hard drinking, vile language, and always ready for a fight or an eye gouging;
reluctant to work, willing at all hours of the night or day to dance, wrestle,
play on the fiddle; great lovers of gambling and horse racing; but (in the
words of an early traveler) "generous, friendly, and hospitable in the extreme."
Even in colonial times most of them were poor; they lived as many of their descendants in Appalachia still live: on a hundred acres or so of exhausted land,
raising a little tobacco, a little corn, having a few cows and hogs in the nearby
woods, living in a frame house raised on piles and overgrown with honey-
suckle.

So it is no wonder that the common people of colonial Virginia loved
the courthouse. Just as New Englanders were proud of their church and made
it the center of their public life, the courthouse in the South symbolized the
community, for in those days the church and its control were identified with
the rich plantation owners and aristocratic families. That is why, when the region west of the Appalachians began to be settled in the latter years of the
eighteenth century, the landscape of Kentucky and Tennessee was promptly
organized into counties, even though at first the courthouse was little more
than a log cabin.

But in this new, postrevolutionary landscape, the courthouse was located
in a town. The world had changed, and towns had become necessary. Farmers
were raising different kinds of crops, and they needed markets which were not
too far away. The sale of new land and coming of many new settlers called for
lawyers and surveyors and the offices of the land bureau. There was need for
supplies and for craftsmen, and for teachers and clergymen and merchants.
And the courthouse became an element in these new towns.

It was only a matter of time before real estate operators and speculators
laid out towns to be county seats, setting aside a piece of land in the center of
the town where the courthouse would be built. Eventually there evolved a

JBJ, photo, Texas courthouse

typical southern courthouse town. A wonderfully complete study of such towns was made some ten years ago by the geographer E. T. Price. There are more than three thousand counties in the United States, each with its own county seat and its courthouse, and Professor Price visited most of them. That was how he was able to establish the existence of a southern type of courthouse layout.

There are in fact several kinds of courthouse squares. In Pennsylvania and Ohio and even parts of Kentucky, there are courthouses located at the intersection of two streets; these are known as Philadelphia or Lancaster courthouse squares, after the two earliest examples. But the southern-type square is much simpler: it is merely one block in the center of a town composed of similar rectangular blocks. This was thought to be the logical place for a public building, the very center of the town. But it took time to formulate this plan, and the first county seat where the courthouse was deliberately located on a block by itself, in or near the center of town, was a small town in southwestern Tennessee called Shelbyville, and this was in 1810.

How the Shelbyville plan spread we have no way of knowing; but it spread as far north as Iowa and Missouri, and into Alabama and South Carolina, and even into Texas as early as 1836. Anyone who has traveled through rural Tennessee and Arkansas, and of course eastern Texas—and not on in-terstate highways—will be familiar with these courthouse towns. The build-ing itself dominates its surroundings with a tower or dome and an elaborate facade. These courthouses are often extraordinary specimens of nineteenth-century architecture and a book about them, called *Court House,* has recently appeared. At one time I regretted the destruction of these monuments and their replacement by courthouses of a more modern style. But I have come to accept these, too. Even those dating from the 1960s and 1970s try to achieve monumentality, and in a generation or so they will be studied by architectural historians. Generally speaking, the smaller the town, the more effective the courthouse. It is almost always an important element in downtown activities. It is surrounded by retail stores, and even sometimes by vendors. Old men sit on its steps or in the shade of the trees; there are monuments on the lawn sur-rounding it. No matter how shabby it may be, it dominates its surroundings, and I know of no other urban composition anywhere in the United States that is so picturesque, so dignified, and in general so satisfactory.

The great importance of a courthouse to a town was that it brought peo-ple in from the surrounding countryside on legal or tax matters, and this in turn meant that the stores and offices and establishments designed to serve the out-of-town visitors were as near the courthouse as possible. If there was a weekly or monthly market, if there was a parade or a Fourth of July celebra-tion, or if there was any election activity, the courthouse was likely to be the center of it. Customarily the best restaurant, the only hotel, the movie theater, and the one department store were all on the surrounding streets. That was in the old days; now, I am afraid, the merchants and officials have deserted the local restaurant with its hot bread and ice tea and fried chicken and beans and cole slaw and pie for the fast-food establishments which have come to the edge of town. The hotel is either closed or the residence of so-called senior citizens. The barber shop has closed, the pool hall has closed, and the courthouse square is no longer prosperous.

But there was always a great difference between the people who lived in the town and those who lived in the surrounding country. The townspeople were usually in business or in the professions, or they held political office; they prided themselves on their greater sophistication and looked down on the country people who were in fact often poor and old-fashioned, and whose way of life was comparatively primitive. One of the peculiarities of our landscape, particularly that part of it settled later than, say, 1750, is that towns were often older than the countryside; located and laid out before there was any rural

JBJ, sketch, courthouse, 1982

population to support them—nothing but wilderness. It was only later that farmers and landowners moved in. This, of course, is the opposite of the European tradition: there, all towns and villages were first settled and inhabited by herdsmen and farmers, and as a result the ties between townsmen and countrymen are usually closer than they are in America. They share the same history, the same local lord or ruler, and the same religious traditions.

In America, on the contrary, there was for long a certain amount of antagonism between the two elements. The consequence was that in the nineteenth century rural America duplicated many of the institutions found in town, so that the landscape had a variety of small centers for country existence. In the forested hills and mountains of Kentucky and Tennessee and Alabama and Mississippi, in the wide and fertile valleys of their great rivers, settlers from the Old South, Scotch-Irish and Germans from Pennsylvania and the Carolinas, and many others cleared land for homesteads and farms. They raised cotton or tobacco, or raised livestock—horses, cattle, mules. Some of the settlers prospered and became slave-owning planters with hundreds of acres of farm land. But most of them made their living on small farms in the back country, raising a few cows, plowing a few acres for a cash crop, hunting, hauling lumber to market, practicing domestic crafts, and finding help and sociability in a nearby hamlet. Such a place would probably contain a tavern, a church, a general store, a mill, and perhaps a blacksmith's shop; it was usually little more than a cluster of a dozen houses, inhabited more often than not by families who were related or who came from the same place.

In some of these remote hamlets there was a one-room school, built by the neighbors for their children. Southerners were particularly opposed to the northern idea that the town should control education, and the one-room schoolhouse, operated by the local community, was an early feature of the midwestern and southern landscape. It survived in many parts of rural America until a half-century ago, and served as a social center at a time when town was not easy to reach over muddy, hilly roads.

But I think it could be said that the local church was the most important of those rural institutions. The small, plain churches, erected by the people of the countryside, were in part the product of the evangelistic ferment which originated after the Revolution among the Scotch-Irish and the Baptists, Methodists, and Presbyterians of the back country of Virginia and the Carolinas. They differed from the more conservative churches not only in doctrine but also in the kind of service they held. One reason why country people distrusted the people in towns was what seemed to them the artificiality of church services among the well-to-do: paid preachers, instrumental music, the practice of renting pews, and of dressing formally for Sunday—all these customs were seen as worldly and un-Christian. So the rural church emphasized simplicity of dress and spontaneity of behavior, and banned the church organ. What evolved was a kind of singing, accompanied often by a fiddle or a piano or a guitar, that has now become very popular under the name of bluegrass music. But they also produced a kind of church music now being revived and studied by folklorists: "fasola" singing—so called because of the notes fa, so, la—also called "Sacred Harp."

We could explore the southern landscape looking for traces of that early religious activity, and we would find many of them: a special kind of church, a special kind of graveyard, a special kind of meeting place, and even a special kind of college. "Grove" is very common in southern place names, and it usually indicates a spot where a camp meeting has taken place. I have always enjoyed driving through the piney woods of the South and coming across some little handmade sign pointing down a narrow, sandy road among the trees that says "Shady Grove Methodist Church" or "Pleasant Grove Camp Meeting," and so on. I believe that the word is most often related to the Methodist church, whose camp meetings before the Civil War were the only ones open to blacks. In any case, we are reminded of its original meaning in such place names as Pacific Grove, California, Webster Grove, Missouri, Hamilton Grove, Massachusetts, and Ocean Grove, New Jersey, all of which were originally camp-meeting places.

There was one institution in the southern landscape of the nineteenth century that brought townspeople and country people together: the small college; it too was the product of religious change. The new evangelical churches felt the need of schools where preachers could be trained, and they wanted to give young people a Christian education in a healthy—that is, nonurban—atmosphere. The new colleges rarely had much money or, for that matter, much of a faculty or a plant; a tremendous number of them either burned down or went bankrupt. More than two hundred such small sectarian colleges were founded before the Civil War, and at one time the highest proportion of college graduates among whites was not, as one would guess, in Massachusetts or Connecticut, but in Virginia. Most colleges had courses in the classics, in rhetoric and mathematics, and in what was called natural philosophy. The students for the most part came on horseback from the surrounding county; they read Byron, they joined fraternities. In the 1830s there was a nationwide student movement of moral reform, of so-called moral purification societies. The students were much concerned with the pros and cons of the Mexican War and of slavery, and discussed the principles of the Graham diet. Those who had little money worked their way through school; and almost everywhere the colleges were sources of local pride.

We can still see what is left of many of them, especially when we travel through the hill country of Tennessee and Kentucky and North Carolina. Tusculum College in eastern Tennessee is now a small college and not very prosperous, but it was founded in 1794, and it has a beautiful campus of decaying brick buildings in a romantic setting in the mountains. Jefferson College outside of Natchez was where Audubon once taught, where President Jackson received an honorary degree, and where the Mississippi state constitution was drawn up. It is now deserted and overgrown. Athens College in Athens, Alabama, founded in 1822, has closed for good, for lack of money. It has a campus of fine Greek Revival buildings, painted white. At the small sectarian college at Brookhaven, Mississippi, I asked a seventeen-year-old student what he intended to do when he got out of college. "Go back to preaching," he said.

These small colleges are gradually either disappearing or being assimilated into the state system; the ones which have had the hardest time are the black colleges. There are reasons for regretting their closing. They often have charming, old-fashioned, not very well cared for campuses, with magnolias and azaleas and laurel. We sometimes find that over the years loyal alumni have contributed trees so that the campus can boast of owning a specimen of every kind of tree in the country. Many small contributions at one time kept them alive: a load of firewood, a hundred acres of farmland, a side of beef. Upstairs in the oldest building (called Old Main) there is a golden oak showcase with a collection of arrowheads, given by a "Friend of the College," and in the small library a collection of hymnals, likewise given by a "Friend of the College."

In their day, which I am afraid is long past, these small colleges not only served to give boys and girls from the back country a glimpse of the world and the pride and excitement of belonging to a group; they were also centers of culture and learning for the countryside. All we can do, I fear, is recognize this neglected aspect of southern culture and enjoy a last look at it.

There are of course other institutions inspired by religious fervor that still flourish. I am thinking of the camp meeting, the revival, and the small country church. Let me mention another, much more modest southern landscape feature which was by way of being a substitute for the town: the country store. We think of the country store as a national phenomenon, but it is not: outside the South a country store means a store in a country town, but in the South a country store is a rural establishment originating in colonial Virginia, and it is located on a country road. Even in the 1600s such stores, or trading posts, were so prosperous and popular in Virginia that it was widely believed that unless they were suppressed no town could possibly flourish. The contemporary version often dates from after the Civil War, when blacks were at last free to buy and establish credit in the nearby crossroads hamlet; and country stores got a new lease on life in the South when lumbering moved into the back-country forests. They are far from imposing in appearance: a one-story, frame house with a dilapidated porch and perhaps a pump dispensing an off-brand gasoline. Its outside walls are covered with advertisements and signs and notices. There is a flimsy screen door, and inside there is everything you could possibly want: overalls, patent medicines, cokes, frozen foods, fly paper, tobacco, and often a post office. Some of them even have facilities for prayer meetings.

One final southern landscape feature deserves much more study than it has so far received: the watering place or spa or mineral springs. These also got their start in colonial Virginia and seem to have spread at an early date into Tennessee and North Carolina and Arkansas, and even as far west as New Mexico. What is noteworthy about these places is not that they are so popular with Southerners but that they are not popular with *all* Americans. Eureka, Arkansas, is well known, largely because of its traditional relationship with New Orleans; but Hot Springs, Arkansas, was the first national park to be established in this country. Mineral Wells, Texas, is where the water is supposed to be good for mental disorders. Truth or Consequences, New Mexico, is a resort for Texas farmers and ranchers suffering from arthritis and rheumatism. There is a Lone Star Motel there, and Texas newspapers and Texas flags. It is strange how the rest of America has totally neglected this form of therapy—which Europe of course takes very seriously. I am tempted to ascribe its survival in the South to that classical, sensory approach to the environment that was so much a part of the seventeenth century and which Virginia kept alive. It is, I suspect, the most valuable but at the same time the least recognized of southern landscape attitudes. It is significant that one of the first explorers to visit the South came in search of its healing waters: it was the legend of the Fountain of Youth that brought Ponce de León to Florida more than four hundred years ago.

"The Nineteenth-Century Rural Landscape: The Courthouse, the Small College, the Mineral Springs, and the Country Store," from *The Southern Landscape Tradition in Texas* (Fort Worth: Amon Carter Museum, 1980), 13–21.

# Excerpt from *American Space: The Centennial Years*

## Expansion

In the decade after the Civil War there could not have been many persons left to remember the early years of the Republic. They would have belonged to that fortunate generation which rediscovered and first celebrated the wonders of the still half-wild landscape of America. Niagara Falls, the valley of the Hudson, the White Mountains, the North Forest had moved and inspired them all when they were young. Yet sometimes it had been as if they were strangers admiring alien works of art; neither history nor daily association had as yet had time to create a bond between them and the surrounding splendor; they did not yet belong together. If as Americans they speculated about the relationship, it was to hope that the natural scenery would have an edifying effect on the people living in its midst.

The younger generation saw the national environment in a different light. Perhaps they knew it better, for they had traveled more. Though they inherited without questioning their parents' belief in the superiority of America over all other nations, they had a belief of their own that the country belonged to them by right of conquest as well as by right of inheritance: it was theirs to do with as they pleased. Unlike their fathers, they saw themselves not merely as inhabitants but as owners, and with an owner's instinct they sought to find out the value of the patrimony.

That is why, during the postwar years, the relationship between Americans and their environment began to change. The relationship had no less of love and pride, but it had less emotion and more of calculation. We had acquired new needs, and we looked to the landscape to satisfy them. Reverence for the past and for the beauties of unblemished nature was certainly a virtue; but there were practical matters to take into account. Simply to admire the richness of the land was no longer enough.

In terms of everyday work, the generation of the postwar years undertook to reorganize the national landscape and bring it up to date. With what objective in mind? Growth: but growth of an unheard-of sort, geometric and without discernible limits. It was clear to all and welcome to most that the United States was about to embark on a period of extraordinary expansion, and George Berkeley's lines on the course of empire were quoted as a prophecy soon to be fulfilled. Who could doubt that in the half-century to come the nation would outgrow its present boundaries? One statistician confidently foretold a population in 1960 of three billion; others, more cautious, calculated that by 1900 there would be three hundred million Americans, the majority west of the Mississippi; F. A. Walker suspected that even ninety million was an optimistic figure. More room, in any event, would be needed. Cuba, alternating between periods of ominous discontent and even more ominous quiet, was to be had for the taking; it was only a matter of time before Canada became part of the Union. Mexico would inevitably become an American charge, though not (so it was widely hoped) until its people had learned better civic behavior. California, in the seventies still a frontier community but already foreseeing the time when it would be the most heavily populated state in the Union, made friendly gestures toward the Sandwich Islands, as Hawaii was then called. The purchase of Alaska in 1867 was thus a sensible precaution. Worthless for the time being, it belonged to the Western Empire of the future.

State after western state estimated its future growth: Kansas with a little more than three hundred thousand inhabitants in 1870 saw itself with thirty million a half-century later. Fortunately, the new states and territories had generous dimensions; textbooks and editorials tirelessly repeated the familiar comparisons between the New West and the Old East: Colorado was twelve times the size of Massachusetts, Arizona was the size of all New England, with New York and New Jersey added for good measure; every mountain cascade was shown to be somehow superior to Niagara, every plain exceeded Mt. Washington in height. "These are marvelous boundaries," exclaimed one writer on the lands beyond the Mississippi, "and they represent the grand scale upon which our new Western countryside is laid out. . . . Nothing is done there in a small way. Human plans are as large as the states."

But the East felt the need for expansion too; dissatisfaction with existing boundaries, whether of the farm, the village, or the city, was general, and there was scarcely a large center that had not, to its own gratified amazement, expanded during the previous decade well beyond its established political boundaries. Although Manhattan island still contained patches of wilderness, New York City had started to invade the mainland in Westchester County, and Brooklyn was reaching out into rural Long Island. Along the lines of the horse-drawn streetcars, and in the seventies along the lines of the cable cars and elevated railways, cities stretched tentacles into the neighboring farmlands. Small-time contractors built rows of detached dwellings on speculation, encouraged by the eagerness of city officials to extend roads and water lines out beyond the built-up areas. "New York and Philadelphia," observed an architectural journal in 1870, "have been the scene of extensive operations in real estate within the last few years. In the neighborhood of both these cities, farms without number have been purchased by speculators and divided up into lots, which have been sold to another class of buyers, also spectators." The density of the city population—save in the oldest and poorest sections—declined, but the city itself spread wider and wider. "We are confronted with the appalling prospect of a place of business ten miles long," a New York editor complained, "with twenty-five or thirty miles of wharfage and shipping on three sides. What must be the scale of expenses when such monstrous distances must be traveled in the transactions of business?"

A flurry of speculation about the city of the future appeared in magazines and newspapers after the Chicago Fire of 1871; all agreed that more space, more spaciousness was urgently needed: but upward or outward— which way was the city to expand? The *New York World* offered "the ideal city of the nineteenth century" to its readers: a city of a downtown business section of broad streets and ample public transportation. Surrounding it was to be "a broad area . . . where every house could have a goodly expanse of ground about it filled with trees and shrubs. . . . There is no reason why a man should not spend his days in the din and turmoil of the wharves and exchanges, and walk in the close of the evening amid the trees and vines of a rural home." Alluring though the vision was, it had its detractors: flight to the suburbs meant the evisceration of the city. Already in the early seventies there were lamentations that New York was increasingly the home of the very poor and the very rich; the substantial middle class was fleeing it in increasing numbers. "A rich, specific, and magnificent life arises from the compactness of settlement in cities," the editor of a monthly magazine declared, "which diffusion and distribution would more or less impair. . . . The 'ideal city' would be prone to divide the interest, weaken the intercourse, and abridge the pleasures of the people." The writer then proposed his own solution: the expansion of the American city upward into the air space. The development of the steam-powered elevator justified thinking of great residential towers, ten stories high or higher. Roof gardens would substitute for suburban greenery.

More space was always the answer; less space, or space confined within irrational limits, was seen as the source of many environmental evils. Every attempt to design larger and more humane tenements in the seventies seemed to founder on the obsolete dimensions of the average city lot. What could be built on a piece of land with a street frontage of twenty-five feet and a depth of one hundred? This was not the only reason tenement design showed little improvement, certainly; but more and more architects clamored for some reorganization of urban space and dreamt of limitless room as the only true solution of urban problems.

Horizontal growth—swift, unplanned expansion over the countryside—was what prevailed in the smaller cities and towns, whether factory towns in the East or new railroad towns in the West. No longer limited in size by dependence on a finite source of power—falling water—the steam-powered factories which began to multiply in the seventies stretched their brick lengths parallel to the railroad tracks, mile after mile: inexhaustible supplies of coal meant limitless growth. Whereas in former times the workers had lived in a cluster near the factory, now they moved away (when they could) into the newer, more spacious flats and duplex houses provided by speculative builders on the outskirts of town, leaving their former dwellings to the poorer, more recently arrived immigrants. If at first it was the factory which promoted the sprawling growth of towns, the railroad, particularly in the metropolitan East, contributed its share. "It is curious to observe," wrote an architect in the seventies of the new towns growing up around Philadelphia, "that as they hug the railroads they almost invariably succeed." In the Midwest and in the Plains States, the landscape architect Horace Cleveland in the seventies noted how every whistle-stop confidently looked forward to becoming, at no very distant date, an important city. Its unpaved, untraveled streets were appropriately broad, the rows of stakes marking the still unsold lots extended for miles. It was another landscape architect, Morris Copeland, who in the same years advised the small towns in the East to think and plan for future expansion. "New towns," he said, "may grow to be a Chicago or St. Louis, and each should have its maturity foreseen and provided for in its infancy." He advised farmers living near towns to plant their hedges and lay out their roads with future residential developments in mind.

As always, the city dweller fancied that the rural landscape was a place of unchanging harmony, to be cherished and protected, but in fact no part of the environment was less wedded to the established spatial order. "The country is full of rural improvements," the editor of a farm journal announced in the late sixties—and then went on to suggest many more for the future.

The size of farms was increasing, and the further west one traveled, the larger they became. In the forties a farm of 80 acres had been held to be of manageable size for the new farmer in a new region, but the homestead of 1862, of 160 acres, was none too large in the Midwest, and the farmer venturing into the Great Plains soon wanted another quarter-section. Expansion of the farm not being everywhere possible, next best was expansion in the size of the fields. A generation earlier the policy had been to have many small fields— fields of ten acres, square in shape, each surrounded by a stout fence; but in the sixties, fields four times as extensive were becoming general, and a farming expert in Illinois urged the planting of hedges or the building of fences around every 80 acres of a farm. The reasons for the expansion in the size of fields were obvious: mechanized farming equipment called for more space for maneuvering, and the tendency to raise one or two commercial crops—wheat or corn or hay—instead of a variety of crops for home consumption made the former fragmentation unnecessary and highly inconvenient. Moreover, the increasing cost of fencing irritated many farmers. To the vexatious problem of how to provide space with effective boundaries, a number of solutions were proposed: hedges of various kinds, portable fences, trenches and walls of sod, strands of wire. The invention in 1874 of an effective barbed wire provided the perfect answer: fences became flexible and easy to erect, and inexpensive. They also became all but invisible, to the dismay of the first generation of livestock to brush against them.

The final effect of all these changes—increase in the size of farms, consolidation of fields, introduction of the barbed-wire fence—was to give the rural landscape of America, beginning in the seventies, a new spaciousness, a larger scale. Nowhere was the search for a more efficient organization of space more noticeable than in the new type of barn that became common throughout the United States in the years after the war. "It was a former practice," wrote the editor of the *Country Gentleman* in 1876, "to place barn buildings in the form of a hollow square, surrounding and sheltering the cattle and manure yard. The practice is now becoming more common and approved to group all the accommodations in one building, as it is more compact, less expensive in erection, is warmer in winter, and saves much labor in attendance by placing everything near at hand."

Like many other contemporaneous developments, the new barn represented the solution of a number of distinct problems, economic, social, and technological, all requiring a new organization of space. The invention of the balloon frame in the 1830s and its immediate popularity in the Midwest permitted the rapid construction of houses by relatively unskilled persons, using light, milled members of standard sizes, nailed together rather than joined. The balloon frame possessed other advantages over the traditional type of timber construction: it allowed of greater interior spaces without interruption, and it was relatively easy to modify or add to. It was therefore ideally suited to the building of barns for storing large amounts of hay and cumbersome machinery, and for indoor work calling for room. Such in fact were the needs of an increasing number of American farmers: those who raised dairy cattle or fed beef cattle found that the storage of hay and the preparation of feed called for ample storage and work space; and the new farm machinery had to be kept indoors. Balloon frame construction did little more than suggest possibilities; but the possibilities were thoroughly exploited: every farmer became an innovator in the designing and building of large, free interior spaces; ingenious and frequently daring experiments in planning and construction became commonplace on the farms of America for the next half-century.

Whatever may be the accepted theory in such matters, vernacular architecture in the United States of a century ago showed itself to be no less resourceful than architecture of a more formal kind. Unpretentious dwellings, utilitarian structures on the farm or in town, factories and warehouses designed by contractors, engineers, carpenters, and gifted amateurs often incorporated on an appropriate scale the open plan, the centralized utilities, the concern for light and flexibility that more celebrated architects were introducing into their projects. And in every instance the measure of success was the creation of a new spaciousness. If Goethe's "more light" epitomized the ideal of his generation, "more space" was what America a century ago was demanding in a score of different ways.

## Environments

The tendency of certain forms and spaces to increase in size, either by expansion or by consolidation, accounted for many of the changes in the American landscape in the postwar years. Another tendency, closely related to it but distinct in origin, was also at work: the defining (or redefining) of spaces in terms of "natural" boundaries. It manifested itself in two widely separated fields of spatial organization: in the design of parks and gardens and suburbs; and in the layout of farms and ranches in the West.

The preference for "natural" boundaries ran counter to the well-established American tradition of artificial or man-made boundaries. West of the Appalachians almost every boundary had been determined by the grid, the pattern of sections, townships, and ranges imposed by the Land Survey of 1785. The great majority of the states, territories, counties, and townships—to say nothing of individual holdings—were defined by survey lines running due north and south, east and west. A map of any large section of the United States, even today, resembles an immense composition of squares and rectangles, regardless of the nature of the terrain or the type of exploitation.

The grid system of land subdivision is unpopular with many contemporary Americans, chiefly for esthetic reasons; yet it possessed and still possesses important virtues, political as well as economic, and in the early years of western (and midwestern) settlement it served the nation well; it expressed very clearly the general belief in equality of opportunity, and in the possession of land as one of the bases of citizenship. But that was in the day of the independent, more or less self-sufficient farm; as settlement after the Civil War pushed into the Great Plains and beyond, and as farming became more of a commercial enterprise, the disregard of topography, the assumption that all pieces of land of the same size had the same value, became totally unrealistic.

This was especially true when farming invaded the relatively dry and treeless region west of the hundredth meridian, which cuts through the western half of the Dakotas, Nebraska, and Kansas. Beyond that fateful line the climate changes radically; land without the presence or availability of surface water to supplement rainfall is unfit for agriculture, and the possession of a homestead as such means nothing. The square of 160 acres, so reassuring in the more humid East, has no fixed value on the Plains; often it does not suffice to feed a half-dozen cows.

So it was water in one form or another that determined the size and location of a viable unit, whatever Washington supposed; it was topography that made land profitable or worthless. In the seventies a number of "colonies," of which Greeley was the largest and most successful, established themselves in eastern Colorado. The location which each of them chose was in a valley with a river, where irrigation could be practiced. The communities adapted themselves to the terrain, leaving the higher surrounding plains, in Horace Greeley's words, "to the half-savage herdsmen who rear cattle and sheep." They were defining their holdings in terms of physical characteristics, that is to say; and where those characteristics ceased, there they fixed their line of demarcation. Instead of all spaces being potentially equal, they fell into classifications based on natural features and natural boundaries.

Cattlemen defined their holdings in the same manner. A writer on Colorado as a prospective home for settlers in the 1870s explained the word *ranch* as "a term for a spring of water and some rude buildings, and an indefinite amount of grazing land."

So obvious was it that the old system of land subdivision did not suit the West that even the government began to see the need for classifying land in a different, more topographical way. It no longer served any useful purpose to lump all (or most) of the public domain under the heading of agricultural land, to be divided into rectangular holdings of 160 acres. Tentatively, and even reluctantly, Washington, beginning in 1866, undertook to classify lands according to physical characteristics, in terms of suitability for mining, grazing, and so on.

It was not until 1909 that a Land Classification Board was established, with the Geological Survey doing the fieldwork. But the intervening steps, ineffectual though they may have been, serve to illustrate the growth of what was then a new concept of how to organize space. First the mining lands were officially recognized as possessing distinct characteristics of their own, then land suited to irrigation, then forests, until much of the American landscape became a composition not only of political units but of natural environments. And was it not this new kind of definition of land that inspired the creation in 1872 of Yellowstone National Park? It was an environment with spectacular natural characteristics, and for that reason Congress set it aside as "a public park or pleasuring ground for the benefit and enjoyment of the people."

The man who most clearly formulated the new doctrine was Major John Wesley Powell. The first white man to descend the Colorado River, he was recognized as an authority on the geography of the desert Southwest and the culture of its Indian inhabitants. In 1870 he was commissioned by the Department of the Interior to undertake a geographical and geological survey of the Rocky Mountain region, and for the next seven years he and his small party explored and mapped the little-known plateau region surrounding the Grand Canyon. In 1878 he finally submitted his report. Despite the fact that all the recommendations it contained were rejected by Congress and that many of his judgments were bitterly resented by western publishers and politicians, Powell's *Report on the Arid Region of the United States* remains a document of exceptional importance, and it has been called "one of the most significant and seminal books ever written about the West."

It is neither long nor impressively erudite; it is a straightforward discussion of the climatic peculiarities of the desert Southwest and of the possibilities for agriculture in the region. Nowhere does Powell express any interest in its natural beauties or their preservation. Agriculture would be possible, he declared, under certain very restricted conditions: that the inhabitants practice a combination of ranching and irrigation farming on a limited scale, that they establish irrigation districts and form small communities or neighborhoods, and that they organize for communal use of the range. He further stipulated that every rancher-farmer possess at least 2,560 acres—or four square miles—most of which would be part of the community pasturelands.

The details of Powell's proposal—how the irrigation and "pasturage" districts would be organized, how the rangeland would be chosen from the public domain—need not detain us. What matters is the nature of the land units he suggested. He rejected not only the traditional homestead of 160 acres but the rectilinear survey as well. The holdings were to be defined by the physical characteristics of the land: by the availability of water and range. Two points were repeatedly made: "the division of these lands should be controlled by topographic features," and "the people settling on these lands . . . should not be hampered with the present arbitrary system of dividing lands into rectangular tracts."

A minor but interesting point in Powell's proposals was his aversion to fencing the communal pastureland, on the somewhat implausible ground that it cost too much. Powell after all belonged to his generation, and along with many contemporaries he undoubtedly objected to the artificial boundary, the man-made definition of space. Across the continent, among the farmers of the Midwest and East, the same desire for innovation in the layout of fields was already apparent: mechanization had not only eliminated many walls and fences, it was also demanding its own special terrain. "The general use of the mowing machine," observed a contributor to *Rural Affairs* in 1865, "will, we trust, make for a great improvement in the external appearance of farms. Stumps, bushes, stone heaps, and obtruding rocks must disappear." And so they did in the course of time, setting the smooth mowed fields apart from the hillsides with their rocks and stumps. With the planting of trees on the rough terrain, the contrast between the physical characteristics of the various sections of the farm became all the greater.

The effect of a landscape of fields all conforming to the topography of the farm, none of them rigidly confined within straight lines, struck many as a great improvement over the former system of rectangular divisions. Somewhat diffidently, a landscape architect suggested to the readers of a rural magazine that farms be laid out in an ornamental, not to say picturesque, manner: fields of an irregular shape, bounded by hedges or rows of trees, with gently curving carriage roads leading to the house and its neighboring barn. But the farm had to evolve in its own way, without benefit of advice from landscape architects. A countryside far more hospitable to their ideas was the new suburb. The challenge here was unmistakable: the average developer laid out the land in rectangular, more or less uniform lots with a grid pattern of streets. To transform this depressing spatial artificiality into a series of "natural" environments called for art and ingenuity. The first traditional element to be eliminated from the plan of the suburban property was the fence or wall; both had fallen into great disfavor among landscape architects and their prosperous clients. In the 1840s Emerson had quoted with approval the old New England dictum that good fences made good neighbors. A generation later the wall was seen as not only distinctly *un*neighborly but even un-Christian. The most cherished feature of the suburban domain was not (as with the farm) its crops but its privacy, its integrity as a domestic environment. Fences therefore played a different role: as polite indications that a property line existed and was not to be casually crossed. "That kind of fence," said one landscape architect, "is best which is least seen and best seen though"—but which still suggested exclusion.

Frank Scott, who described himself as a friend and student of A. J. Downing, in 1870 wrote a book entitled *Suburban Home Grounds*, in which he discussed the landscaping problems of the commuter, "the man who must leave his home after an early breakfast to attend to his office or store business," and who had built a home on a suburban lot. Urging the suburbanite to eschew all pretensions of having a parklike estate with a vegetable garden, Scott offered as the ideal a composition of trees and lawn—trees as a tactful and natural-appearing boundary, lawn as a private and sheltered environment. Jacob Weidenmann, a one-time associate of Olmsted, who achieved a national reputation in the seventies as a designer of "picturesque" lawns, and Eugene

Baumann, a New Jersey landscape architect of the period, also tackled the problem of converting the small, rectilinear suburban holding into a natural, esthetically self-contained environment. All expressed the growing dissatisfaction with the conventional-size lot: "The speculative habit of cutting up suburban lands into narrow city lots 25 × 100 feet," Scott declared, "or but little more, destroys all chance of making true suburban improvements. Such lots will only sell to citizens who are either too poor, too cockneyish, or too ignorant of their own needs to insist on something more."

The spatial reorganization under way on the farms and ranches of America, and proposed by Powell, was impressive because of the vast dimensions involved and the struggle for survival on the part of the hard-pressed men who urged it. By contrast, the contribution of landscape architects, fussily detailed and inevitably influenced by fashion, seemed trivial. Nevertheless, the new American landscape was the creation of many elements in society: farmers, ranchers, engineers; architects and landscape architects; and innumerable men and women working for urban and rural improvement. The spirit behind the new kind of space—expansive, free of the past, more and more involved with the transformation of the natural environment—derived from workaday America, but it was the artist who gave it form and meaning.

From *American Space: The Centennial Years,* (New York: Norton, 1972), 18–30.

## High Plains

We have in the last decades become well informed about the major events of American history. We have still a great deal to learn, however, concerning minor or local episodes which throw light on how we have matured as a nation, such as the invasion by agriculture of the great rangelands of the High Plains.

By 1904, the invasion was at an end. The tide of dry-farming had already conquered much of eastern Colorado and New Mexico, western Oklahoma, and the Texas Panhandle, and in certain areas it had even begun to recede. But however short its period, it left its mark, a mark clearly visible today. No one can hope to understand the western landscape, particularly that of the High Plains region of the Southwest, who does not understand this impressive and saddening chapter in our history.

What brought about this wholesale migration of eastern farmers and recent immigrants from eastern Europe into a region which until 1890 had been entirely devoted to ranching and which was held to be little better than a desert? There seem to have been a variety of late nineteenth-century causes: a serious drop in the price of cattle, affecting the High Plains ranchers; generous homestead laws; the growing use by farmers of barbed wire fences and steel plows and drilled wells; the spread of the railroad system; the increased efficiency of dry-farming techniques—these were some of the reasons why the High Plains and other areas in the West became attractive to easterners. In any case, beginning in the last decade of the nineteenth century and continuing for more than ten years, wide expanses of hitherto virgin grassland were divided into holdings of 640 acres or smaller, fenced in, plowed up, and transformed almost overnight from open range into something resembling the less attractive landscape of the Midwest.

It was a triumph of American energy and vision; and then in a few years things began to go wrong. Ranchers (who naturally did not welcome these intruders) maintain that the homesteaders failed because they were incompetent and knew nothing about the country. The dry-farmers themselves ascribe their difficulties to a change in the climate. They had come west during a series of miraculously wet years that lasted until the turn of the century, and all that time there was scarcely a crop which they could not grow on their new farms. In the early twentieth century the wet years were followed by years less wet, and eventually by years of drought; and these, together with the Depression, sufficed to ruin even the hardest-working and most experienced farmer in the 1930s. So in a sense both ranchers and farmers were correct: climatic cycles have had much to do with the failure of many High Plains farmers, and the newcomers' unfamiliarity with western conditions contributed to their downfall. In any case, by the end, hostility between rancher and farmer largely vanished; both learned that they were at the mercy of the weather and national markets. They prosper and suffer together, and for much the same reasons.

The fascination of this entire landscape and its history lies in the spectacle of modern American farmers, technologically experienced and well equipped for the job confronting them, meeting and coming to terms with an unfamiliar environment. At first, victory seemed inevitable before the year was over; and then it seemed to be a matter of luck; and finally after two or three dry years the whole undertaking hung in the balance; it became a question of whether to stay on, adapting techniques and ways of life and even standards of living, or to pull out and call off the fight.

Both solutions were tried by the High Plains farmer, and his experiences and those of the rancher have combined to produce something unusual in America: a fresh and realistic approach to the ancient problem of who is in control, environment or man. The people of the High Plains have no reason to believe in a bounteous Mother Nature, but neither are they inclined to talk about the conquest of nature by man. Too many weeks and months they

JBJ, photo, mail-order house on the High Plains

prayed for rain, and no rain came. Great social and economic forces, as remote in origin and as irresistible as the wind that blows incessantly from the west, helped form the human landscape of the region.

There is much that is bleak about the High Plains and much that is melancholy, but there is nothing small, and the countryside is not without beauty, even of a man-made sort. From the Nebraska line almost to the Rio Grande, there are thousands of abandoned homesteads, gaunt and poor, weathered the grey of heaped tumbleweed; they stand alone in the treeless expanse of drifting dust and sand where plowed fields used to be. Each of them claims the sort of respect we accord a place where a battle, with much at stake, has been fought and lost.

"High Plains" (Notes and Comments), *Landscape* 3, no. 3 (Spring 1954): 1–3.

## From Monument to Place

We live separate from one another, each in his own private realm, but we crowd the dead together on a small piece of land. They share congested towns and cities, all over the Western world.

Yet there are large regions where this is not the case. Even here in America, the Pueblo Indians do not have communal burial grounds; in parts of Africa, the dead are buried in the house or garden. In his *Géographie et religions,* Pierre Deffontaines speculates about the relationship between the settlements of the living and those of the dead. "We note that the Mediterranean zone, which is one of the regions where concentrated population is most abundant, is also a zone which knew the earliest and largest cemeteries; on the other hand China, a country of concentrated villages, is a region of dispersed graves. . . . In France, the dead are almost always gathered in cemeteries, whether the living population is dispersed or concentrated. In truth," he concludes, "the living and the dead are geographically speaking two very different kinds of population."

A complete understanding of these variations and what they signify will never be easy to acquire. We can come closer to doing it if we interpret them not simply as settlement patterns but also as different forms of devotion to the dead. It is the survivor, after all, who decides where the grave is to be, and he does so to insure a wished-for relationship with the departed.

The traditional graveyard as we know it in America was by way of being a statement that this relationship was a collective one. The living and the dead each belonged to a community. The message of the grave—or of the grave-yard—was thus addressed to everyone. Far from being confined to the family, it could be read and pondered by every passerby. The solitary or hidden grave is perhaps symbolic of an obligation finally discharged; the public graveyard is a reminder of duties constantly recurring; in the true meaning of the word, it is a monument, a "bringing to mind."

We should ask ourselves whether the modern cemetery is in fact the equivalent of the traditional graveyard or whether it is not a totally different kind of space.

We carried with us from Europe, especially from Great Britain, the cer-emonies surrounding the burial of the dead, including the making of a church-yard. The Pilgrims had not been in Plymouth a year before they had to estab-lish one; an epidemic had carried off more than half their number. The dead were buried in a bank not far from Plymouth Rock, and in the words of a his-torian, "lest the Indians should learn of the weakened condition of the com-munity, the graves were leveled and sown with grass."

In their study of colonial headstones in Massachusetts, James Deetz and Edwin S. Dethlefsen suggest that by as early as the middle of the eighteenth century local developments in church doctrine had inspired a distinctly New England type of tombstone art. It is reasonable to assume that there were other changes in the aspect of the New England graveyard. Yet from what we can now see, the colonial burial ground and the colonial concept of it were much like those of contemporaneous England, except that the clergyman played a less important role in America.

Though there no doubt existed many solitary graves and family burial grounds far from any village, particularly in the South, the commonest form of burial was in the churchyard, or graveyard next to the church. Such a bur-ial was the right of every church member, and even outsiders were sometimes admitted. There is no evidence of any kind of preconceived plan. The graves were in rows, head to foot. There were no family plots, though often a widow would be buried in the grave of her husband. When the last row was filled, subsequent graves were crowded in wherever there was room. It is unlikely that the graveyards of prerevolutionary America had any of their present well-cared-for beauty. The frequent cutting of grass to produce a lawn was a nine-teenth-century innovation; floral decorations were rare, and the custom of vis-iting the grave to tend it was still not general. Ornamental planting was unheard of. The well-to-do and prominent members of the community were often buried inside the church, so that a sort of equality prevailed in the churchyard itself. The array of headstones and markers, though by no means uniform in design or size, had none of the motley of the nineteenth-century cemetery. And this was not only because there was little money to spend ostentatiously; it was also because the function of the markers was less ornamental than instructive.

Each had a message to convey, a message contained in the epitaph which identified the dead and frequently commented on his or her career. "The principal intention of epitaphs," says Johnson, "is to perpetuate the examples of virtue, that the tomb of a good man may supply the want of his presence, and veneration for his memory produce the same effect as the observation of his life." The headstone in the colonial graveyard was thus a monument to remind us of the virtues of the deceased; name, origin, dates of birth and death; and then, more often than not, the moral, the scriptural quotation, the admonition: such is the traditional form of the epitaph.

The graveyard itself served the same didactic purpose. Located in the center of the village, concealed by no planting, plainly visible to all, familiar to all, it was a group monument, a constant reminder to emulate the virtues of the dead and to follow the precepts of the faith. All those buried there were now equal; family did not matter—and neither did wealth. It was the community of the dead, the army of the saints, admonishing the community of the living.

The first sign of another and newer concept of the graveyard appeared in 1796, when the New Burying Ground was established in New Haven. The Old Burying Ground, dating from the seventeenth century, had been located in the yard of the Congregational Church on the Green. With the growth of the town it had become greatly overcrowded, and when in the last decade of the eighteenth century it was decided to beautify and improve the Green, the town authorities considered moving the Old Burying Ground to another location.

Theological objections were soon disposed of. "When the Romish apprehension concerning consecrated burial places," Timothy Dwight remarked in 1821, "and concerning the peculiar advantages supposed at the resurrection to attend those who are interred in them, remained, this location [in the churchyard on the Green] seems to have been not unnatural. But since this apprehension has been perceived by common sense to be groundless and ridiculous, the impropriety of such a location forces itself upon every mind."

Dwight was possibly referring to a growing disbelief in bodily resurrection. In any case, the town fathers resolved that the Old Burying Ground would have to be moved.

At this juncture a prominent New Haven citizen, James Hillhouse, came forward and offered to remove the graves, suitably reinter the remains, and erect a memorial to them elsewhere, if in return the city would grant him a charter to lay out a new cemetery on a field of ten acres not far from the center of town. The offer was promptly accepted.

Hillhouse deserves to be better remembered than he is, for he was one of the fathers of urban design in the United States, as well as a benefactor of New Haven. One of the first to lay out whole new sections of a city, Hillhouse also started the program of street-tree planting that gave New Haven the nickname of the "Elm City" and made it famous for its beauty in the early nineteenth century. It was he who designed Hillhouse Avenue, for long the handsomest residential street in America, and it was he who created the New Burying Ground, the first cemetery of its kind in the world.

It was unique, first of all, in that it was carefully planned, and this was the feature which most impressed the public. In his *Travels through the Northern Parts of the United States,* Edward Augustus Kendall in 1809 commented:

> In describing New Haven it would be unpardonable not to mention the New Burying Ground. This is a square plot of large extent, divided by smooth walks into small squares. These squares are again divided into squares so minute as to be reasonably occupied by families. For the square, not being lost sight of for a moment and the smallest square being too large for the generality of families, no choice is left but to divide this smallest square into half squares. This last division, however, must be so effected as to not destroy the uniform appearance of the squares. The squares are bordered by trees which unfortunately are not square also, but which, being Lombardy poplars, have promised to grow with the least irregularity possible. There are, however, in the center of some of the squares, a few weeping willows from which quite so much cannot be hoped. Meanwhile every grave is dug in the same direction and every square is of the same dimensions. The ground is level, the walks rolled, the grass smooth, and the rails duly painted white and black.

According to Timothy Dwight (who probably knew what he was talking about, since for many years he was president of Yale College), the New Burying Ground was divided not into squares but into parallelograms and the paths were actually roads wide enough for two carriages to pass. He noted that the name of every proprietor was marked on the railing around the plot, and that the markers were located exactly in the middle of each plot "and thus stand in line through the parallelogram." He concludes: "It is believed that this cemetery is altogether a singularity in the world."

This symmetry, so admirable to Dwight, so much a source of condescending amusement to Kendall, was inspired by two things: the enthusiasm in America at the turn of the century for the grid street pattern, and the need to subdivide the land into rectangular lots, all uniform, all equally accessible and equally desirable to prospective buyers. For the New Burying Ground was a private money-making corporation. It was not until twenty-five years later that England adopted the private incorporated cemetery.

The layout devised by Hillhouse became standard in most American cemeteries. How many of the grid-pattern cemeteries were direct copies of the New Burying Ground it is not easy to say. Undoubtedly, many of those in New England were, though any corporation wishing to sell as many lots as it could would naturally divide its land into rectangles. At all events, Hillhouse's design was more significant as an innovation in cemetery layout than was the far better-known Mt. Auburn cemetery of three decades later. Mt. Auburn, in Cambridge, Massachusetts, was the first of perhaps a hundred cemeteries in the romantic style; the New Burying Ground was the first of literally thousands of graveyards in small towns scattered across the country.

Yet the really radical aspect of the New Burying Ground was something other than its design. The novelty was the nonpublic, almost domestic quality of the cemetery. That it should cost money to be buried within its precincts was in itself an important factor; but the clearest evidence of a change in the whole concept of the graveyard was the tacit recognition of the family, the division into family plots. And with this recognition of the biological group came a new kind of marker: larger, more imposing, more individual in design: obelisk, draped urn, column, statue, shaft, often imported from Italy. These were symbols of wealth and taste, to be admired and envied. The message came from the living, not the dead. The epitaph likewise began to change. The largest and most conspicuous feature in the inscription was the family name, baronial in its lapidary simplicity: "PERKINS." Around the base of the shaft or on small individual headstones were inscribed the names and dates of the individual deceased members. In the case of the single headstone, the in-

scription became briefer: name and date, often followed by a short biblical citation. And in time this citation was either dispensed with or ceased to point
a moral. Instead, it referred to the individual death as a sleep or a rest or a returning to the fold. By the end of the nineteenth century, the hortatory quality of the epitaph had all but vanished from the American cemetery. The
graveyard was no longer a monument, a public reminder; it was a place where
wealth and family piety could assert themselves.

Not only a place but, whenever possible, a *secluded* place. Hillhouse built a
wall around his New Burying Ground to insure privacy for the "proprietors,"
but he might also have built it to protect the sensibilities of the public. If Timothy Dwight is a reliable witness, there was already a new attitude toward the
spectacle of the graveyard. In Puritan times it had been accepted—perhaps
not willingly—as an edifying monument and essential feature of the public
landscape; but by the first years of the nineteenth century there existed a general distaste for this reminder of mortality. "When placed in the center of the
town," Dwight observed, "and in the current of daily intercourse, it is rendered too familiar to the eye to have any beneficial effect on the heart. . . . It
speedily loses all its connection with the invisible world in a gross and vulgar
union with the ordinary business of life." To be sure, such had been the purpose and justification of the classic monument: to remind citizens in "the ordinary business of life" of certain examples and precepts. But death and the
commemoration of death had insensibly become a private, family matter, and
the graveyard accordingly was relegated to an out-of-the-way spot. What reen-
forced this desire to move all cemeteries out of the center of town was a growing awareness of public health: it was this concern in England which eventually led to the establishing of municipal or private cemeteries to replace the old
overcrowded churchyards. But the emotional rejection of the graveyard seems
to have come before the rejection on the grounds of hygiene.

    Mt. Auburn Cemetery is familiar to all landscape architects as the first
large-scale example of romantic landscape design in this country. It is of no
less importance in the evolution of the cemetery.

    When in 1825 the Massachusetts Horticultural Society decided to create
a botanical garden, somewhere in the neighborhood of Boston, to accommodate its large collection of Massachusetts flora, it was thought desirable that
the land include several types of terrain—marsh, forest, rock and hill, valley
and meadow. Some seventy acres were finally bought, overlooking the Charles
River near Cambridge—a farm then known as Sweet Auburn.

The president of the Horticultural Society was Jacob Bigelow, a distinguished doctor and a botanist whose scientific work was only superseded many years later by that of Asa Gray. In his old age he translated Mother Goose into Latin, and until his death he maintained a lively interest in Mt. Auburn and the botanical garden. Nearly blind, he was led out to the cemetery to feel with his hands the sphinx which he had insisted be installed as a Civil War memorial.

It was soon evident that the botanical garden did not need and could not afford all seventy acres. Bigelow then proposed that fifty acres be laid out as a cemetery. The society agreed; Bigelow drew up the plans, and in 1831 Mt. Auburn Cemetery was inaugurated.

The plan took full advantage of the picturesque location and varied terrain. Paths and roads wound among the trees, the artificial bodies of water, and the planting of shrubbery. Long before it was occupied by graves, the cemetery was popular among Bostonians as the goal of excursions, and the road to Mt. Auburn was crowded with carriages on Sundays and holidays. Andrew Jackson Downing, then starting his career as a landscape architect, was much impressed by this popularity and in the *New York Horticulturist* suggested that every large city have this kind of resort—not as a cemetery but as a place for the enjoyment of nature. William Cullen Bryant, then editor of the *New York Tribune,* endorsed the idea and started agitating for a landscaped park in New York. The first proposals for Central Park were the result.

It was not long before Mt. Auburn proved popular as a cemetery as well. Its remote location, like that of the New Burying Ground in New Haven, was generally applauded, and for the same reasons: it removed from the city a menace to health, and it did not affront the public with a constant reminder of death. But whereas the appeal of Hillhouse's cemetery had been its order and almost urban symmetry, the appeal of Mt. Auburn was its picturesque woodland setting, secluded and unspoiled. As a consequence, sentiment developed in many quarters against tombs or even tombstones in the area. At the inauguration of the cemetery, a Boston clergyman declared: "To the lover of nature in its simplicity, the grave is more interesting than the tomb. The grave, when visited thoughtfully and alone, cannot but exert a favorable moral influence. . . . The child of nature is clasped again to the sweet bosom of its mother, to be again incorporated in her substance." He then criticized the public graveyard: "It is better thus than that it should lie and moulder away in darkness and silence, a cause of offense to strangers and a source of terror to those by whom it is still loved."

As a matter of fact, this ideal of the cemetery without monuments was not widely accepted for another hundred years, and imposing tombs were soon so numerous in Mt. Auburn that in 1839 an illustrated guide was issued, including an appropriately necrophilic short story by Hawthorne, one of his first works. Nor were any of the other romantic landscaped cemeteries which quickly materialized in Brooklyn, Philadelphia, New York, and elsewhere any more restrained. One of the largest and perhaps the most beautiful was Spring Grove Cemetery in Cincinnati, laid out in the late 1840s by a German land-scape gardener whose inspiration, he said, had been Alexander von Hum-boldt's description of a Chinese graveyard.

Mt. Auburn thus marks a further step in the repudiation of the monu-ment. It is now the setting, not the grave itself, which inspires emotion, and the custom of spending time at the grave (for which special furniture was de-signed) can be interpreted, at least in part, as a kind of luxuriating in a solemn and picturesque environment.

It is well to remember that the example of Mt. Auburn was never widely followed in cemetery planning. Like other design aspects of the romantic movement, it was the reflection of a relatively sophisticated and expensive taste. Comparatively few families could afford the cost of these lots carved out of a rolling or precipitous landscape, and no municipal or church graveyard was tempted to follow the new fashion. Nevertheless, Mt. Auburn and its sis-ter cemeteries undoubtedly exerted a powerful if indirect influence. The geo-metrical rigidity of many rectangular layouts was softened by the informal planting of trees, and funeral art acquired a rustic quality, not only in the grave furniture, but in the design of the headstones, and of the fences which surrounded many graves.

Perhaps the most conspicuous example of the transformation of a cemetery from monument into environment is Gettysburg. The original dedication in 1863 by President Lincoln and Edward Everett was of a small burial ground for those who had died in the battle. The speeches of both men are classic defin-itions of the cemetery as a monument. We are familiar with Lincoln's address; but Everett's lengthy description of the ancient battle of Marathon and the monument erected to its heroes was even more in the tradition. As early as 1867, land was acquired outside the original cemetery, and beginning in 1878 markers were erected to show the location of units in the battle. In 1896 the

JBJ, photo, Civil War memorial

area included 600 acres and 320 monuments. The action itself is suitably commemorated in the central buildings, but it is safe to say that when we visit Gettysburg it is usually the setting of the action, the environment that we explore. One is tempted to see in this monumentalizing of an entire landscape a peculiarly American trait, a peculiarly American way of interpreting events in terms of their environment. The evolution of American civic monumental art is another topic; we may merely mention the tendency, strong throughout the last hundred years, to dedicate whole environments—not merely civic centers and school campuses but also parks, playgrounds, beaches and forests. The traditional monument or statue, intended to commemorate a specific person or event, has correspondingly declined in popularity.

In a sense, Mt. Auburn anticipated this development, at least in its desire to do away with tombs in order to preserve the quality of a somantic environment. But it remained for a later generation of landscape architects, led by a park administrator and one-time associate of Frederick Law Olmsted, to carry through the campaign for a less cluttered landscape. Jacob Weidenmann, a Swiss by birth, was an indefatigable writer and lecturer on the subject during the last quarter of the nineteenth century. His experience as an administrator made him aware of the problems of maintenance; he had practical as well as esthetic reasons for urging the removal of the fences and hedges which still surrounded many graves. It was he who preached the beauties of the so-called lawn cemetery, the cemetery of simple landscape forms: lawn, clusters of trees, winding roads—and graves as inconspicuous as possible. The parklike environment was Weidenmann's ideal, and it may be said that his crusade was unusually successful. The cemetery environment is no longer the glen and woodland of the romantic period, it is the English park as interpreted by Olmsted.

The latest (though not necessarily the last) phase in the metamorphosis of the graveyard into an environment is the so-called memorial park or memory garden. Like many of its nineteenth-century predecessors, this is usually a private money-making venture, entirely nonsectarian. It is, generally speaking, less expensive than the conventional cemetery—partly because upkeep is reduced to a minimum, partly because it is likely to occupy relatively cheap land along the highway on the outskirts of town. Although the memory garden seems to have originated in California before the last war, there are now many examples throughout the country. Those who expect to find in them suggestions of Evelyn Waugh's *The Loved One,* or even of Jessica Mitford's *The American Way of Death,* are likely to be disappointed. Aside from disconcerting salesmanship, they are for the most part respectable and well-intentioned establishments, catering to those who cannot afford the conventional cemetery or who are far from home and family.

Their outstanding feature is the total elimination of headstones or monuments. All that marks a grave is a small bronze marker and a container for cut flowers, sunk below the level of the turf. This makes maintenance (the cutting of the grass) extremely simple, and all but does away with any individual care. The entire cemetery resembles a vast monotonous lawn, except for the occasional decorations of flowers—natural or plastic, depending on the season. That is the effect striven for: a great open green environment, restful, even cheerful. The family plot is not allowed, and in fact there seems to be little call for it among the clients of the memorial park. Some of these cemeteries, primarily for psychological reasons, no doubt, contain smaller hedged-in areas, variously called the Apostle's Garden, the Chapel Garden, the Christus Garden, and so on. The names appear to have no special significance, and the areas themselves are merely devices for introducing a certain spatial variety.

Often such memory gardens provide all the necessary funeral services in a central building—embalming, cremating, a funeral chapel; a supply of ar-

JBJ, photo, private grave

tificial flowers is always on hand, and there is someone to conduct the service; everything is taken care of.

Only one innovation is lacking, and it will not be long delayed: the use of this expanse of quiet greenery for some recreational, healthy purpose. Already one can glimpse young couples in sports dress, transistor radio in hand, quietly relaxing in the remoter sections of memorial gardens; and conduct which would seem sacrilegious in a conventional cemetery does not seem so here.

Whatever one may think of the memorial garden and its omnipresent commercialism, it is clearly the logical outcome of certain tendencies in American cemetery design. It is not the locus of a cult; it does not pretend to be. It is a place where one aspect of death — the disposal of the corpse — is promptly and efficiently taken care of. It is, to use Max Sorre's elegant phrase, a place of elimination. It exists not simply because it has been promoted by real estate agents in cahoots with morticians, but because there is obviously a widespread need for such an establishment, just as there was for Hillhouse's family plots and the romantic setting of Mt. Auburn. The memorial park is particularly valuable to transients who will soon move on and perhaps never see the grave again.

It is possible that the transformation of the cemetery from a solemn and impressive monument into a smiling expanse of lawn is a sign that we have all become or are becoming pantheists who choose to see death as a kind of returning to nature; the more "natural" the place of burial, the easier the transition. It is equally possible that it is another sign of our American fear of death and its symbols. In itself, however, the modern cemetery is not sufficient evidence for either of these conclusions, however well founded they may be. What we are dealing with in the cemetery is the death of others, not our own. In one way or another, a painful reality is being faced. Perhaps the most that we are justified in saying about this radical and relatively speedy transformation of the American graveyard is that it suggests a change in our way of accepting loss. It was once a public experience, to be shared with the world, an aspect of our common humanity, and the epitaph and monument were ways of including society. For many reasons, the death of others has become a private experience, no matter how universal. How we grieve and how we keep a memory alive are not matters of public show. The cemetery in consequence has lost its meaning both to the individual and to the community, and what has taken its place it would be hard to say.

"From Monument to Place," *Landscape* 17, no. 2 (Winter 1967–68): 22–26.

## Jefferson, Thoreau, and After

In the long chronicle of our American distrust of the city, two names stand out above the rest: Jefferson and Thoreau. One sought to destroy the city by political means; the other, fleeing it for the wilderness, wrote and preached to alert others to the city's danger. Each established a distinct anti-urban tradition, still honored by many who know nothing of its origin.

By background and vocation a countryman, Jefferson expressed throughout his life a strong aversion to the city and a preference for a rural way of living. "Those who labor in the earth," he wrote, "are the chosen people of God, if ever He had a chosen people; whose breasts He has made His peculiar deposit for substantial and genuine virtue." He never ceased to work for an order where "as few as possible shall be without a small portion of land. The small landowners are the most precious portion of the state."

Along with this partiality for an agrarian society went a vigorous dislike of "cities as sores on the body politic," places of useless luxury, corrupt wealth, and political exploitation. Cheap land and hostility to centralized urban control were two of the basic tenets of Jefferson's political philosophy.

Thoreau, as the product of a small New England village and of the urban atmosphere of Cambridge and Harvard, protested in a more personal, more emotional manner. Although the most explicit formulation of his anti-urbanism is *Walden,* the narrative of two years' withdrawal from the world of

JBJ, sketch, New York City, 1945 (courtesy F. Douglas Adams)

men, there is scarcely a page of his writings that does not express his opinion of city life, or his devotion to the landscape of nature. In the essay "Walking," his final literary testament, he voices the conviction in a passage often quoted by partisans of the wilderness experience: "I wish to speak a word for nature, for absolute freedom and wildness, as contrasted with a freedom and culture merely civil—to regard man as an inhabitant, or a part and parcel of nature, rather than as a member of society."

The influence of these two men has been to confirm a tendency marked among American intellectuals, to decry almost every aspect of life in the modern city and to praise the rural or suburban alternative. But how much does the anti-urbanism of Jefferson resemble that of Thoreau? Does it in fact resemble it at all? In *The Intellectual and the City*, Morton and Lucia White caution us that anti-urban sentiment in America had many different sources, and that the city has been found wanting as either too civilized or not civilized enough. The distinction applies to Jefferson and Thoreau; and it still separates the critics of the city into two groups.

The key passage in Jefferson's denunciation of the city and praise of the country is undoubtedly the phrase: "The country produces more virtuous citizens." What he prefers to urban society is not rural solitude but rural society; the type of man he wishes to encourage as opposed to the urban citizen, oppressed by wealth and corruption, is not simply the rural inhabitant, it is the rural citizen, an active and effective participant in the political life of his community. It is true that Jefferson held that man is more "natural" when in a rural setting, but "natural," as he used the word, had little to do with "nature"—at least in its wilderness state; a "natural" man was inevitably a social or, more precisely, a political creature. The significant relationship, the relationship which fostered better men, was that between man and man. If the rural setting was to be preferred, this was chiefly because it made the relationship easier.

To Thoreau, on the other hand, the essential distinction between town and country—or, better yet, between town and wilderness—was that between society and nature; between man as a member of society and man as an inhabitant of the earth. Far from discovering virtues in the agrarian way of life, Thoreau was scarcely more tolerant of farmers than he was of city dwellers. "There is something vulgar and foul in [the gardener's] closeness to his mistress," he remarked. In *Walden* he wrote: "By avarice and selfishness, and a groveling habit, from which none of us is free, of regarding the soil as property or the means of acquiring property chiefly, the landscape is deformed, husbandry is degraded with us, and the farmer leads the meanest of lives. He knows Nature but as a robber."

The farmer, in short, is guilty of a serious offense: of failing to see himself as part and parcel of nature. For to Thoreau the significant relationship is not that between man and man; it is the relationship between man and his environment.

If the distinction now appears academic, it was doubtless equally academic to those Americans of more than a century and a half ago who were looking westward to the virgin landscape where, they believed, the future of our country lay. The pioneer farmer settling the recently surveyed lands of the Northwest Territory, and the trapper and woodsman pushing out beyond Kentucky to cross the Mississippi, both relished their freedom from the city. Nevertheless, each stood for a different kind of revolt, each stood for a different kind of nonurban America, the one agrarian, the other romantic; and each attitude in time made its own characteristic imprint on the national landscape.

Agrarianism was the first of the two philosophies to produce its own environment. The National Survey of 1785 was not merely inspired by Jefferson, it was a clear expression of the Jeffersonian dislike of a powerful government, centralized in cities, and his emphasis on the small rural landowner. The survey permitted and even encouraged the forming of townships with the school section in the center, townships with their own local government; but it made no provision for cities. Jefferson had tried his hand at helping design the national capital. His sketches, proposing an extensive grid with the land divided into uniform lots, were scornfully rejected by Pierre L'Enfant, who had something more monumental in mind. But with the notable exceptions of Detroit, Baton Rouge, and Indianapolis, the cities built in the United States until late in the nineteenth century all conformed to the grid system; all were Jeffersonian.

In his remarkable study of nineteenth-century city planning in America, John Reps says that "the overwhelming majority of American towns were begun and extended on the grid plan." He ascribes the popularity of the arrangement to "its intrinsic ease in surveying, its adaptability to speculative activities and its simple appeal to unsophisticated minds." These were indeed striking advantages; it is impossible to separate the planning and growth of most towns and cities in nineteenth-century America from land speculation. Yet the almost universal use of the grid for towns cannot be entirely understood without some reference to the wider regional grid of the National Survey—which automatically prescribed at least the main axes of any town—nor without some reference to the American ideal. If, in terms of design, our cities are little more than extensions of a village grid, the village itself—except in the older parts of the country—is in turn little more than a fragment of the regional grid: an orderly arrangement of uniform lots frequently focused on a public square with no particular function and unvarying dimensions. The block, whether in Chicago or New Paris, Iowa, remains the basic unit, and the block is nothing more than a specific number of independent small holdings. For all its monotony, the Jeffersonian design has unmistakable utopian traits: it is in fact the blueprint for an agrarian equalitarian society, and it is based on the assumption that the landowner will be active in the democratic process. The grid system, as originally conceived, was thus a device for the promotion of "virtuous citizens." Its survival is a testimony to the belief, once so common among Americans, in the possibility of human perfectibility. So it was not only logical but appropriate that the grid, despite its obvious shortcomings and its abuse by speculators, should have remained the characteristic national design for the environment. It is, to repeat, the symbol of an agrarian utopia composed of a democratic society of small landowners.

Thoreau had no direct role in the formulation of the romantic environment. He was, however, the most eloquent American spokesman of an attitude toward the environment first expressed many years earlier by Rousseau

JBJ, watercolor, New Canaan, Connecticut, 1963

and his followers. No other American succeeded as well as he in translating the romantic point of view into native terms; none put it into practice with such consistency and fervor. Emerson's love of nature, genuine enough, always seems to derive from a pleasant afternoon's walk in the country. Thoreau's derives from a total commitment to a natural, solitary way of life.

What undoubtedly heightened his appeal was the fact that mid-nine-teenth-century America was the one modern state where the romantic attitude toward the environment still had free play; where there was still room for the frontiersman and also for the designer of large-scale landscapes.

It is one of the ironies of our history that the romantic environment remained an urban and suburban phenomenon. Whereas the Jeffersonian concern for man as a social being determined the character of our whole rural landscape, the romantic feeling for solitude and for closeness to unspoiled nature was confined to the middle-class urban citizen on the eastern seaboard. Of the thousands of square miles settled during the first half of the nineteenth century, few if any were modified or treated according to popular romantic ideas. Only in the 1870s did it become possible to interest the American public in the wisdom of preserving the scenic wonders of the wilderness West.

This exclusion of romantic environmental design from the workaday countryside has had a fateful effect on the profession of landscape architecture. In England, and to a lesser degree in France and Germany, nineteenth-century environmental design concerned itself with the country estate and with the rural scene, and it is still part of the English landscape architectural tradition to be versed in farm matters. But the American landscape architect, as if taking his cue from Thoreau, can see the wider landscape only in terms of conservation or recreation.

In its detailed description of the nineteenth-century romantic landscape in America, Reps's book is as full a compendium of so-called picturesque designs as we have ever had, though his leaving out of the American college campus is an unfortunate omission. They all seem to be there. Mt. Auburn Cemetery in Cambridge, Massachusetts, dating from as early as 1831; Alexander Davis's Llewellyn Park, New Jersey, of 1853; Lake Forest, Illinois; Frederick Law Olmsted's plans for Central Park in New York and for Riverside, Illinois. Towns, as distinguished from suburbs, are astonishingly rare in the romantic tradition. Not included, of course, are Andrew Jackson Downing's Hudson Valley estates, nor the gothic and Italianate cottages that by the thousands bordered the tree-lined streets of mid-nineteenth-century America.

Despite the variety of forms they took—cemeteries, city parks, suburbs—and despite the differences in size and in purpose, all of these designs can easily be interpreted in terms of Thoreau's convictions. The significant relationship is never that between the buildings, or between the layout and the surrounding city; it is always that between design and terrain; hence the contoured streets, the ingenious and often sensitive exploitation of every topographical feature; hence the "irregular" architecture—gothic, Swiss, romanesque—which, in its attempts to blend with its setting, anticipated Frank Lloyd Wright's by a good half-century. Man seen as "part and parcel of nature rather than as a member of society" had to have a dwelling as isolated as possible from his neighbors, and profusely planted. The assumption that man is always striving for freedom from society, always pining for closer contact with nature, produced the romantic suburb—and produced no towns at all. It is interesting to note that not one of the nineteenth-century utopian or religious communities in America had any trace of romanticism in its layout.

Yet for all its inability to understand the political side of man, despite its flirtations with primitivism, the planned environment of the romantics represented, no less than did the agrarian environment, a utopian ideal. Like the Jeffersonian landscape, it assumed that in favorable surroundings man could become better, could at last be true to his real self, given a new freedom from the city. The agrarian landscape was vast, monolithic, and without charm; the romantic landscape was fragmented, highly self-conscious, and from the beginning identified with an urban middle-class point of view. But both were ideal landscapes, and we are not likely to see anything of the sort again. The ability, as well as the desire, to create utopian landscapes seem to have disappeared with their demise.

It is easy to say that those earlier utopian landscapes were rendered obsolete by changes in American society. But utopias are not supposed to be subject to the vicissitudes of history. When one of them dies, it is for an internal reason; and our two utopias, the agrarian and the romantic, died because there were no longer utopian men to inhabit them. What justified the grid and kept it valid for almost a century was the firm belief among Americans that it was possible to produce an ideal known as the Virtuous Citizen; what justified the elaborate landscaping of the romantics was the no less firmly held belief that it was possible to produce an ideal known as Man the Inhabitant of the Earth. Thoreau and Jefferson were poles apart in their definitions of human nature, but they agreed completely as to the possibility of defining it; and, having once defined it, of creating a suitable environment for it.

What we have lost in the last generation is this assurance, and with it the capacity—or the temerity—to contrive utopias. It is of no use trying to resurrect the vanished forms, beautiful though they may have been; their philosophical justification has gone. All we can now do is to produce landscapes for unpredictable men, where the free and democratic intercourse of the Jeffersonian landscape can somehow be combined with the intense self-awareness of the solitary romantic. The existential landscape, without absolutes, without prototypes, devoted to change and mobility and the free confrontation of men, is already taking form around us. It has vitality, but it is neither physically beautiful nor socially just. Our American past has an invaluable lesson to teach us: a coherent, workable landscape evolves where there is a coherent definition not of man but of man's relation to the world and to his fellow men.

"Jefferson, Thoreau, and After," *Landscape* 15, no. 2 (Winter 1965–66): 25–27.

# 4 The Emerging American Present

JBJ, drawing, "Other-Directed Houses," *Landscape* 6, no. 2 (Winter 1956–57): 35

## Other-Directed Houses

Writing in *Harper's Magazine* almost for the last time before his death a year ago [in 1955], Bernard De Voto expressed himself on a subject close to the heart of many Americans: the increasing untidiness and ugliness of much of the landscape. He described what had happened to the New England countryside as a result of the invasion of tourists and vacation seekers, and was incensed by the roadside developments in places which a few years ago had still been unspoiled. U.S. Highway 1 in Maine came in for harsh words. "As far as Bucksport it has become what it has been from Newburyport on: a longitudinal slum. It is an intermittent eyesore of drive-ins, diners, souvenir stands, purulent amusement parks, cheapjack restaurants and the kind of cabins my companion describes as mailboxes."

I suspect this last phrase of having a lewd connotation, though what it is I cannot discover. Otherwise, Mr. De Voto's sentiments are impeccable and have been applauded and echoed by many thousands who travel the country by car for either business or pleasure; by planning and landscape experts, civic improvement groups, highway engineers; and by foreigners now seeing America for the first time. This mounting public indignation, together with the new Federal Highway Program, clearly suggest that we have reached the point of attempting some sort of reform in the treatment of our highway margins.

U.S. Highway 1 is in fact one of the most sensationally ugly roads in

America, and there is a particular stretch of it, somewhere between Washington and Baltimore, if I'm not mistaken, which when photographed through a telescopic lens seems to epitomize the degradation which in the last few years has overwhelmed our highways. Two sluggish streams of traffic, cars bumper to bumper, move as best they can over a hopelessly inadequate roadbed between jungles of billboards and roadside stands, each sprouting a dozen signs of its own, and each with its own swarm of parked cars in front. This extends out of sight for miles and miles, varied here and there by a set of traffic lights.

To a lesser degree, these conditions exist intermittently throughout the heavily populated East and Midwest. Even here in the West things can be pretty bad near any large city or along any heavily traveled highway. But by and large congestion is not one of our troubles, and I do not believe it is one of the troubles of the greater part of the country; it is the phenomenal growth of roadside establishments that most of America has to worry about. The West is tourist country, which means that our roadside businesses have their own special public, a generous and numerous one in the summer season; but at the same time the region is slowly becoming self-conscious about its man-made appearance and is wondering what it can do to control its highway margins. As it is, I suppose there are highway stretches here as hideous as anywhere in the United States. Highway 66, for instance, which traverses some of the finest scenery in New Mexico and Arizona, would be a disgrace (as far as mutilation of the landscape is concerned) to the Jersey Meadows. Its horrors end by fascinating the traveler, so that he pays little or no attention to the wider view; but there are plenty of tourists who try to find an alternate route.

It would be hard (though not impossible) to exaggerate the extent of this blight. But still we must give these roadside establishments their due. They are entitled to their day in court, and so far they have not had it. I keep remembering the times when I have driven for hour after hour across an emptiness—desert or prairie—which was *not* blemished by highway stands, and how relieved and delighted I always was to finally see somewhere in the distance the jumble of billboards and gas pumps and jerry-built houses. Tourist traps or not, these were very welcome sights, and even the commands to eat, come as you are, gas up, get free ice water and stickers had a comforting effect. Common report has it that the people get as much of your money as they can. I have rarely found that to be the case; they usually had a friendliness and a willingness to help which somehow came with their job. The gaudier the layout, the nicer it seemed, and its impact on the surrounding landscape bothered me not at all.

Nor can I forget another kind of encounter with Mr. De Voto's longitudinal slums, and that was when I have flown West. Somewhere (over western Kansas, perhaps) it begins to grow dark and at first all I can see is a dark mottled brown world under an immaculate sky of deep-blue steel; and then we fly over some small rectangular pattern of scattered lights—a farm town—and out of it, like the tail of a comet, stretches a long, sinuous line of lights of every color and intensity, a stream of concentrated, multicolored brilliance, some of it moving, some of it winking and sparkling, and every infinitesimal point of color distinct in the clear night air. The stream pours itself into the black farmlands, into the prairie, and vanishes. This, of course, is the roadside development seen from an altitude of several thousand feet; the most beautiful and in a way the most moving spectacle the western flight can offer, because for the first time you see that man's work can be an adornment to the face of the earth.

Fleeting beauty, then, and occasional usefulness; how much more can be said of many other of our products? So when I hear high-minded groups vying with each other in bitter condemnation of the highway developments and devising legal and moral means of destroying them, I find I cannot go along with them. Those two glimpses come to mind and I ask myself if it would not be better—fairer, that is to say, and more intelligent—to see if the potentialities of these roadside slums cannot somehow be realized for the greater profit and pleasure of all.

I do not mean to say that a liking such as mine for this feature of the human landscape of America should blind anyone to its frequent depravity and confusion and dirt. Its potentialities for trouble—esthetic, social, economic—are as great as its potentialities for good, and indeed it is this ambidexterity which gives the highway and its margins so much significance and fascination. But how are we to tame this force unless we understand it and even develop a kind of love for it? And I do not believe that we have really tried to understand it as yet. For one thing, we know little or nothing about how the roadside development, the strip, came into being, nor about how it grows. We know (and seem to care) far too little about the variety of businesses which comprise it. Why is it that certain enterprises proliferate in certain areas and not in others? Why are some of them clustered together, and others are far apart? Which of them are dependent on the nearby town and city, which of them depend on transients? The modern highway is of course the origin and sustainer of them all, but what a complex thing the modern highway has become; how varied its functions and how varied the public which makes use of it! To the factory or warehouse on its margin, it is essentially the equivalent of the railroad; to the garage or service station, it means direct accessibility to the passing public. The local businessman thinks of it as a way to reach and exploit the outlying suburban and rural areas, the farmer thinks of it as a way to reach town; the tourist thinks of it as an amenity, and the transcontinental bus or trucking company thinks of it as the shortest distance between two widely separated points. Each of these interests not only has its own idea of how the highway is to be designed and traced, it brings its own special highway service establishment into being. Which of the lot are we to eliminate?

Or perhaps it is more a question of which of them we are to save, for more than one program of highway reform calls for the almost complete suppression of them all. If I were asked to make a distinction among them with a view to finding out which were to survive and in what proportion, I would say that they roughly fell into two classes: those establishments serving the working economy, and those serving our leisure.

In the first I would naturally put all the factories, warehouses, truck depots, service stations, used car lots, shopping centers, and so on—the rollcall is endless; and in the second I would put restaurants, cafes, nightclubs, amusement parks, drive-in movies, souvenir stands, motels (for motels are primarily associated with vacation travel and with leisure)—in brief all those enterprises which Mr. De Voto listed and denounced, and then some. What is more, I would give them two classes—the workaday and the leisure—almost equal value, though keeping them well apart, at least when we were considering which businesses would be allowed along the highway outside of built-up areas.

My reason for so doing can be easily given: one of the unique aspects of the modern American highway (an aspect often overlooked) is that it has become the place where we spend more and more of our leisure. It plays the role which Main Street or the Park or the Courthouse Square used to play in the free time of our pedestrian predecessors: the place where we go to enjoy ourselves and spend our leisure hours. Never was the lure of the open road so powerful, so irresistible as now; for merely to *be* on a highway, entirely without a destination in view, is to many of every class and age a source of unending pleasure. Is this an exaggeration? Eliminate from any stretch of highway—always outside the largest cities and the great industrial areas—the motorists who are driving purely for enjoyment, either on vacation or for a breath of fresh air or to show off the new paint job or in search of a good time, and I believe you would eliminate more than a third of the normal traffic. This mass movement onto the highways is in no manner mysterious: given more and more leisure—not merely in terms of holidays and vacations but shorter daily working hours—and given more and more cars, what is the inevitable result? The highways leading out of our towns and cities are alive with cars, with people driving when work is over and before the evening meal to see how the new subdivision is getting on; out to the Dairy Queen five miles east to have a giant malt; to the drive-in movie still further away; cars with couples necking, souped-up cars racing down the measured mile, cars playing chicken; cars, pickups, motorcycles, scooters, all filled with people driving merely for the sake of driving. "Gliding up and down for no purpose that I could see—not to eat, not for love, but only gliding." And this leisure traffic is multiplied many times over on Sundays and holidays. Foolish or not, dangerous, unprofitable, unhealthy or otherwise, these are the ways we spend many of our carefree hours, and the highway is an essential adjunct of them all. Thus any highway reform program which has at the back of its mind the old-fashioned notion that our roads are really nothing but means for fast and efficient long-distance transportation, to the neglect of the leisurely pleasure seeker and the establishments which exist to serve him, will run head on into a flourishing American institution. And I like to think that the collision will end in the defeat of the reformers.

But the driving habits of the American public are not what I want to defend; they are in any case better than those of any other people. I am concerned with pointing out the importance of that portion of the longitudinal slum associated with our free-time motorized activities, and the need to understand it. I think it very likely that the present mood of highway reform will expend itself chiefly on those establishments least organized, least equipped economically to protect themselves, and I have a strong conviction that this highway development (or, more accurately, this whole aspect of American life) holds enormous promise of future growth, esthetic as well as social. This promise, I admit, is not always very evident. Our highway margins are littered not only with the decaying refuse of what might be called the premotorized leisure age—shanties, one-pump filling stations, rows of empty overnight cabins, miserable bars; they are also growing a second jungle crop of ill-planned, ill-designed, uneconomic enterprises. These still far outnumber the good ones. One American town and city after another is finding to its shame that its highway approaches are becoming intolerably ugly and unwholesome. And the aftermath of this discovery is more often than not a wholesale condemnation, especially on the part of the right-thinking, of the local highway strip.

I am inclined to believe, however, that we have become entirely too fastidious, too conformist, in architectural matters. In our recently acquired awareness of architectural values, we have somehow lost sight of the fact that there is still such a thing as a popular taste in art quite distinct from the educated taste, and that popular taste often evolves in its own way. Not that a recognition of such a distinction would automatically lead to an acceptance of roadside architecture; most of it, by any standards, is bad. But it would perhaps allow us to see that highway architecture is changing and improving very rapidly all around us, and allow us to find certain virtues—or at least certain qualities—in it worth respecting and fostering. In all those streamlined facades, in all those flamboyant entrances and deliberately bizarre decorative effects, those cheerfully self-assertive masses of color and light and movement that clash so roughly with the old and traditional, there are, I believe, certain underlying characteristics which suggest that we are confronted not by a debased and cheapened art but by a kind of folk art in mid-twentieth-century garb.

We must accustom ourselves to the fact that the basic motive in the design of these establishments—whether motels or drive-in movies or nightclubs—is a desire to please and attract the passerby. The austere ambitions of the contemporary architect to create a self-justifying work of art have no place in this other part of town. Here every business has to woo the public—a public, moreover, which passes by at forty miles or more an hour—if it is to survive. The result is an *other-directed architecture,* and the only possible criterion of its success is whether or not it is liked; the consumer, not the artist or the critic, is the final court of appeal.

This, to be sure, is true of almost every retail business: they all have eye appeal. But a downtown business catering to pedestrians can concentrate on relatively modest display, whereas a highway leisure-time enterprise not only has to catch the eye of the motorist, it has to offer a special attraction of its own: it has to suggest pleasure and good times. I doubt if this is always easy to do: an appearance of hospitality or inexpensiveness or reliability is not enough. What there has to be is the absence of any hint of the workaday world which presumably is being left behind: any hint of the domestic, the institutional, the severely practical, the economical; any hint of the common or plain. On the contrary, what is essential, both inside and out, is an atmosphere of luxury, gaiety, of the unusual and unreal. Imitation is quite as good as the genuine thing if the effect is convincing and the customer is happy. Go into a roadside dine-and-dance in a nonholiday mood (as happens when you stop to make a phone call) and you are affronted by the shoddy decorations, the crude indirect lighting, the menu, and the music. But go in when you are looking for a good time and for an escape from the everyday, and at once the place seems steeped in magic. It is a glimpse of another world.

The effectiveness of this architecture is finally a matter of what that other world is: whether it is one that you have been dreaming about or not. And it is here, it seems to me, that you begin to discover the real vitality of this new other-directed architecture along our highways: it is creating a dream environment for our leisure that is totally unlike the dream environment of a generation ago. It is creating and at the same time reflecting a new public taste.

Most of us can recall a time when our leisure and holiday activities were essentially imitations of the everyday activities of a superior social group—the so-called leisure class. If we dressed up on formal occasions, it was because these enviable people dressed that way all the time, and our dress was an imitation of theirs. We went to hotels which resembled at a dozen removes the palace of a prince, to movie houses which resembled court operas, to restaurants and bars adorned with mahogany and crystal and gold. All places associated with group good times—football stadiums, circuses, theaters, transatlantic steamers, even train stations and parlor cars, were designed and decorated to suggest a way of life more sumptuous than our own. Such was the other-directed architecture of the period: in the Victorian phrase, our good times were largely spent in aping our betters.

It is hard to say when this class imitation lost its appeal. Undoubtedly the Depression, by reducing the number and wealth of the leisure class as well as its prestige, had much to do with it. Still, its architectural manifestations lasted until the end of the last war. The older and more traditional regions of the country continued until a few years ago (although with decreasing enthusiasm) to design many of their places of public entertainment to look colonial or Olde Englishe—for the antique also had its snob appeal. What actually speeded the revolution in taste was something quite outside the field of art: it was the fact that the wage-earning class began to acquire more leisure than the executive or professional class had, and began to have more money than before. It was at last in a position to set its own pace in leisure activities and attitude.

If we bear in mind that along with this increased leisure came a renewed flood of automobiles, we should have no trouble understanding what happened: the new leisure ideal became a hankering after what advertising copy writers call "vacationland." We wanted to spend our free time not in a superior social world but in a world remote in terms of space. Yet vacationland is still only attainable once or twice a year; for the rest of the time we have to find a substitute, and it was in response to that need that every place of popular entertainment, and in particular every roadside place, rose up and transformed itself. At once the white tablecloth, the waiter in dinner jacket, the potted palm, the Louis XVI decorations were banished. Names like Astor and Ritz and Ambassador dropped out of the popular world, to be replaced by Casa Mañana, Bali, Sirocco, Shangri-La. The new drive-in movies built along every highway and outside every town ignored the old prestige names of Rivoli and Criterion and Excelsior to call themselves the Lariat, the Rocket, the Cornhusker. Motels designed to look like New England villages or California missions or southern plantations (depending on their location) were all but crowded out of business by brand-new establishments inspired by the Futurama of the 1939 World's Fair or by Hawaii, Hollywood, the Caribbean. Swimming pools and exotic planting made them even more inviting.

A sudden increase in holiday and free-time travel, faster and more comfortable cars, more money to spend, all helped precipitate the change. Across the country at strategic intervals of 100 to 150 miles (the average distance covered between meals), one new and expensive highway strip after another burst into activity. Sometimes they rose outside of large cities; more often they rose next to some small town remote from any neighbor. In every case, their presence affected the local pattern of leisure activities even while it served the traveling public. Never before had there been so total and dramatic a transformation of a portion of the American landscape, so sudden an evolution in habits, nor such a flowering of popular architecture.

Is it necessary to add that along with this development came a rash of billboards and a totally unrelated growth of highway-based industries? That chaos overtook countless communities and that much of the old landscape was damaged beyond repair? Those are the features we are not allowed to forget, the ones we lament. But they cannot entirely hide from us the fact that a new kind of architecture, popular in the truest sense, was for the first time given an opportunity to evolve.

Well it has not yet finished its evolution by any means, but some of its more salient characteristics are already becoming evident. At the moment flashiness seems to be the chief of these: a flashiness of color and design that overshoots its mark. In time we will learn how to astonish and attract, how to suggest exotic vacationland without resorting to shock treatment. Walls canted out for no good reason, facades placed at an angle to the highway and over-dramatized (while the other sides are left in their native cement-block naked-ness)—these are more or less clumsy attempts to capture the passerby's atten-tion, something which could be done by other means.

Actually, the style already possesses two other characteristics ideally suited to this purpose: I mean its use of lights and its use of signs. Neon lights, floodlights, fluorescent lights, spotlights, moving and changing lights of every strength and color—these constitute one of the most original and potentially creative elements in the other-directed style. It would be hard to find a better formula for obliterating the workaday world and substituting that of the hol-iday than this: nighttime and a garden of moving colored lights. It is perhaps too much to say that the neon light is one of the great artistic innovations of our age, but I cannot help wondering what a gothic or a baroque architect would have done to exploit its theatrical and illusionist possibilities, its capac-ity to transform not only a building but its immediate environment. The con-temporary architect will have none of it, and while he makes much of his syn-thesizing of all art forms, the ones he chooses are usually the traditional fresco and mural and mosaic. Matisse and Dufy might have designed in neon with great success, and so for that matter could any imaginative sculptor. A preju-dice against any taint of commercialism in decoration is so strong in a seg-ment of the public that one of the chief targets of civic reform groups is usu-ally the local display of neon lights. And yet one would have to be blind indeed not to respond to the fantastic beauty of any neon-lighted strip after dark.

The second basic characteristic of the other-directed architecture is the liberal use of signs. Their purpose is obvious: to identify and promote busi-ness. But they also serve to help establish the mood at hand, and even to com-plete the artistic composition. The tendency seems to be for all signs con-nected with roadside establishments to grow larger, more conspicuous, and more elaborate. One reason for this is well explained by Mobilgas in a bulletin telling its dealers why the Mobil sign outside service stations is to be changed: "Today's motorist drives 50 or 60 miles an hour in the open country. He is often miles from home and doesn't know where the next Mobil service station is. So he must have plenty of advance notice. . . . The problem of long range visibility becomes extremely important. . . . The old Mobilgas shield was de-signed to go with Colonial type service stations which once dotted New Eng-land and New York. But as the company expanded its marketing area and functional streamlined stations replaced the Colonial design, the shield took on a somewhat out-of-date and out-of-place appearance."

The new sign, fittingly enough, is the work of an industrial designer formerly connected with Futurama.

But aside from this very practical reason, the signs are large because they are held to be ornamental. Great pilons, masts, walls thrusting out toward the passerby serve very often to balance the architectural composition and are part of its fantastic and unreal charm. And since modesty has no place along the highway, there seems to be nothing to prevent an even further increase in size. Eventually, let us hope, the sign will concentrate in itself most of the distant eye appeal, and allow the building to assume a more restful and conventional appearance.

These, then, are some of the peculiarities of the new architecture lining our highways and catering to our leisure hours: conspicuous facades, exotic decoration and landscaping, a lavish use of lights and colors and signs, and an indiscriminate borrowing and imitating to produce certain pleasing effects. They are by no means the ingredients of a serious or lasting style, but the idiom is still only about ten years old. At present it already manages on occasion to achieve very attractive and gay effects, ideally suited to its festive purpose.

The trouble is, these successes are few and far between. They often suffer, moreover, from being located in the midst of confusion. One remedy for this (and also a partial remedy for the whole condition of the highway margin) would be the elimination of billboards. They serve no constructive purpose, they are unsightly, and they blight their immediate surroundings; no one likes them and they have many powerful enemies; if they were to go, the highway jungle would be reduced to manageable proportions and many unsuspected architectural and urbanist qualities would for the first time become visible. I would, however, allow local firms and services to advertise. Their signs often provide information not to be found elsewhere and which the stranger approaching a town has to have; and here again it must be pointed out that limitations on size are increasingly unrealistic. Even state highway departments are awakening to the fact that a public traveling at sixty miles an hour cannot be served by signs designed to be read at half that speed.

With some justice, we complain of the shoddy construction and poor design of our highway establishments, the total lack of any comprehensive scheme or of any harmony between the several parts of a strip development. But the wonder is that they are as good as they frequently are. I know of no architecture school in the country which acknowledges the existence and the importance of a popular, other-directed architecture meant for pleasure and popular mass entertainment. We have forgotten, it seems, that architecture can sometimes smile and be lighthearted, and that leisure, no less than study or work, calls for an appropriate setting. Yet the few roadside establishments designed by imaginative and skillful architects are so immensely superior to the rest that they have almost at once been imitated. At present the average highway resort—motel, drive-in movie, restaurant, or nightclub—has been put up by the owner with no sort of guidance but his own limited experience and taste, or at best by a building contractor. The display signs are usually the product of an industrial firm knowing nothing of the location or the public. The lighting itself is the work of the local electrician, relying on catalogs for inspiration. The landscaping is done by the local nurseryman, and the planning, the location, the relationship to the neighbors and to the highway is little more than an adjustment to local zoning restrictions or to the edicts of the highway department. We need not be astonished at the results.

Both of those hallmarks of an other-directed architecture, lighting and display, cry out for intelligent and artistic handling. In these fields I suspect we could learn much from Europe, for architects and decorators abroad have not been handicapped by the notion that the architect should have nothing to do with the promotional phases of his project. In Europe, neon lighting often betrays a feeling for color and design and mood. A rollerskating rink demands different treatment, different colors, than a restaurant or a motel; yet we see many of all three trimmed in the same bright green and harsh red. We also suffer in this country from that malady which Victor Hugo, a little-appreciated writer on architecture, said had killed architecture in the Western world: the tyranny of the printed word. The printed (or painted or illuminated) word has not killed architecture in America or anywhere else, but it threatens at times to overpower it, to thwart it. Our neon lights, capable of expressing a genuine poetry, have so far only been taught to shout PEPSI COLA, CAFE, STOP, and the tyranny of the word in other forms, its poverty and monotony, is nowhere more in evidence than in the clutter of letters outside every town and city, where a few universally recognized symbols would suffice to communicate the same messages more rapidly and with less fatigue to the eye. Once more, the European highway signs are clearer and neater and better understood than our own inscriptions—not to mention those traditional trade emblems—the barber's dish, the tobacconist's cigar, the butcher's flag, the locksmith's key—which enliven the European street without destroying its unity.

Here is where the advertising expert could well do us a valuable service: by devising a set of symbols for roadside use to replace the present nightmare of words.

Has the planner no contribution to make? Is it not possible to introduce order and harmony even in the midst of a collection of heterogeneous enterprises? Shopping centers show us something which we would not have believed possible a decade or more ago: that diverse businesses can willingly come together in one location, subject themselves to certain controls, learn to think in terms of a small community, and still prosper as never before. Their location off the highway with their own ample parking space likewise makes them models for other groupings. Most highway pleasure spots are hopelessly scattered; some wedged in between truck depots and service stations, others far out among the empty lots. They belong in each other's company, they are meant to share the same atmosphere of good times. If they were grouped together in clusters of, say, six at frequent intervals, traffic confusion would be reduced and the establishments themselves would be protected. Some of them appear to belong logically together: restaurants, drive-in movies, motels, and souvenir stands; and for a different (and perhaps a younger) public: sports arenas, drive-in refreshment stands, and dance halls.

For any such systematic and orderly strip development, a new kind of zone, a Zone of Amusements, would have to be recognized and created, and then protected from intrusion on the part of workaday businesses or residences. It is in the organizing and rehabilitating of this neglected and misunderstood part of the community that the planner and architect and industrial designer and advertising expert could work together.

Will they have a chance to do it? I like to believe so. I like to believe that the merits and charm of the highway strip are not so obscure but that they will be accepted by the wider public; that our professed and frequently genuine regard for the small business will protect these smallest of small businessmen from extinction, and in some manner give them a firmer footing in the community. And I would like to believe that all those architectural and planning skills, the advertiser's knowledge of public taste and custom would welcome the opportunities to broaden their scope and to work together. We can be sure of none of these things. A tide of urban improvement is beginning to rise all over the country, and it is reinforced by public money and a kind of impatience with nonconformity, as noticeable on the left as on the right. What local zeal cannot achieve may well be achieved by the Federal Highway Program: the sterilizing of our roadsides.

It is finally, I suppose, a question of which force proves the stronger: the demand for an efficient and expensive highway system designed primarily to serve the working economy of the country, or a new and happy concept of leisure with its own economic structure, its own art forms, and its own claim on a share of the highway. At present we are indifferent to this promise for our culture, and to the extinction which threatens it; is it not time that we included this new part of America in our concern? It is true that we can no longer enter our towns and cities on avenues leading among meadows and lawns and trees, and that we often enter them instead through roadside slums. But we can, if we choose, transform these approaches into avenues of gaiety and brilliance, as beautiful as any in the world; and it is not yet too late.

"Other-Directed Houses," *Landscape* 6, no. 2 (Winter 1956–57): 29–35.

JBJ, drawing, "The Abstract World of the Hot-Rodder," *Landscape* 7, no. 2 (Winter 1957–58): 25

# The Abstract World of the Hot-Rodder

The long holiday weekend approaches, and at quarter-hour intervals the radio broadcasts the words of Mr. Ned Dearborn of the National Safety Council predicting the total of highway deaths. Average Citizen listens with a vague alarm. "Gosh!" he says, "436 deaths in a seventy-two-hour period! *Gosh!*" And in the back of his mind he goes on planning the family's weekend trip. By leaving a half-hour earlier (he thinks) and by taking lunch with them, they ought to be able to make a good 350 miles by dark; then they can use the truck cutoff, where there is less traffic on Sundays.

So when the holiday begins they set out, wife, husband, children, dog, and all, heedless of warnings and prophecies, heedless of previous experiences with holiday traffic. Knowingly they plunge into the heavy stream of cars, struggle with it hour after hour, dodge from highway to country road and back again, sometimes going fast, sometimes slow, but rarely stopping, and glancing only briefly at the scenery. When the holiday is over, they come home tired, out of temper, and with little or nothing to show for their journey. Nevertheless, they are somehow glad that they have gone, and they will go soon again. Commonsense urged them to stay home and take care of many long postponed household chores; the bloody prognostications of the National Safety Council should have frightened them. But instead they chose to yield to a deep-seated urge to escape from the city and everyday surroundings into the open country, and, as I say, they were not sorry they did so.

Why the Sunday motorist likes driving even under these conditions is a puzzle worth exploring; but as to the instinct which takes him away from home, it is too universal, too elementary, I should think, to call for much analysis. We all have it, whether we indulge it or not. Far from being a product of the motor age, it is probably as old as urban existence itself, and many of us can remember a time when this weekend and holiday exodus had a different, less deadly, but no less popular form.

I find myself recalling the days when the streetcar was the chief means of Sunday transportation out of the city. In America, to be sure, we have all but forgotten what the streetcar meant; its heyday is now a good forty years behind us. In Europe it still plays a very useful role, even though it is beginning to surrender its monopoly to the private automobile, the scooter and motorcycle and chartered bus. The finest flowering of the streetcar-borne Sunday exodus in Europe occurred, I think, sometime between the two world wars. It was then that city people began to have a little more weekend leisure (and a great deal of unwanted leisure during the Depression years) for excursions but did not yet have money enough for cars or even motorcycles. In those days, almost every city family of modest means spent its Sunday in that countryside which lay within walking distance of the last stop of a streetcar line. That, in fact, was the late nineteenth-, early twentieth-century equivalent of our contemporary two-hundred-mile drive in the country. It was a very important institution in its time.

### The Pedestrian Sunday

Is it too early to look back with affection on those streetcar excursions and the country (or suburban) holidays which went with them? They were certainly not exciting by modern standards; they were repetitious and quiet, but I recall them as having the comfortable sameness of a long established tradition, without surprises, perhaps, but without disappointments. Early on Sunday morning in the silent residential streets (entirely empty of parked cars) you saw small family groups bearing hampers, knapsacks, footballs, tennis rackets, waterwings, walking sticks, folding stools, sometimes a rake or a shovel, standing at every streetcar stop. A half-hour later, out where the paved street came to an end among isolated tenements and factory yards and carbarns and cemeteries, you saw them emerge from the streetcar and set off into the open. They had a choice of roads: some went to their own well-fenced-in vegetable plot where they had a minute house with a trellis; others took off for a favorite patch of forest or a river bank or a hillside, or a rustic beer garden with a view. They all vanished in no time. Throughout the day you met them strolling at a child's pace on grass-margined lanes or playing games in a clearing, or picnicking or making love or snoozing with the newspaper over their heads, or gathering wildflowers in the woods. They clustered like flies around public swimming pools or beaches, and toward evening they tended to gather in village cafes and restaurant gardens, where they ate the food they brought with them and listened to a small band play popular music. Late into the night the streetcars were once again crowded on their journey into the center of town with drowsy men and women and sleeping children. Their knapsacks and hampers were as full as when they set out, for now they contained flowers, berries, mushrooms, herbs, bundles of twigs from the woods for kindling, and sometimes lard and eggs and butter from farmers. As usual, the outing had been rewarding.

Not merely in the material sense, of course, though I have often thought that what the Sunday holiday makers brought back with them illustrated very neatly what the city ought to derive from its green surroundings. The real benefits were of a different kind: the holiday makers were relaxed after healthy exercise and healthy rest; they had enjoyed an easy sociability with strangers, they had heard music, they had revived their awareness of natural beauty, and their ancestral ties with the land. Above all, they had known an emotion, vaguely religious in character, best expressed in the old-fashioned phrase of "being close to Mother Nature." I do not mean to imply that this experience of the outdoors was necessarily varied enough or intense enough or even long enough; I merely mean that what these families got from their Sundays included almost everything (in a small degree) that we want, or used to want, from rural nature—everything from food to esthetic pleasure to spiritual sustenance. When the time comes for us to draw up the inventory of all the contributions the old suburban Sunday made to our culture, we will be astonished by its richness. It has directly inspired schools of painting and writing and music—from the popular Viennese song, which evolved in Grinzing, to Seurat's *Summer Sunday at La Grande Jatte.* Untold minor scientific and artistic accomplishments came from the same abundant source; local botanical and geographical and historical descriptions, small books of nature verse, amateur sketches and compositions, now relegated to storerooms and second-hand shops, testify to what this custom meant. And the most wholesome benefit of all, I think, was the love of nature it instilled among city dwellers of every class from childhood on.

All this, it must be remembered, was drawn from a very small area around the city; the range of the excursionist in premotorized days rarely exceeded twenty miles. And yet, once we have duly appreciated the splendid results and the poverty of means, once we have compared the old Sunday excursion with its frenzied, unfulfilled contemporary equivalent, we have to ask ourselves in all honesty whether it is possible or even desirable for us to revert to that old order. Much more has happened to us than the advent of the automobile; we have learned to see the world differently even on our holidays; we confront the familiar setting in a new manner. Broadly speaking, the former experience of nature was contemplative and static. It came while we strolled (at three miles an hour or less) through country paths with frequent halts for picking flowers, observing wildlife, and admiring the view. Repose and reflection in the midst of undisturbed natural beauty and a glimpse of something remote were what we chiefly prized. I do not wish to decry the worth of these pleasures; none were ever more fruitful in their time; but the layman's former relationship to nature—at least as part of his recreation—was largely determined by a kind of classic perspective and by awe. A genuine sense of worship precluded any desecration, but it also precluded any desire for participation, any intuition that man also belonged. The experience was genuine enough, but it was filtered and humanized; it was rarely immediate.

## Contemplation without Participation

We need to bear these qualities in mind if we are to understand why the Sunday excursion (and the experience of nature that went with it) began to pall about thirty years ago. For even while the tradition seemed to be flourishing with unabated vigor—in the decades between the wars, that is to say—a new attitude toward the environment, a new way of feeling, began to emerge on both sides of the Atlantic. The prevalence of the automobile in America helped confuse the process, but in Europe it was easier to follow. In both parts of the world it resulted in the rejection of conventional pleasures.

What happened was that people—mostly young people—began to tire of the Sunday-streetcar-excursion relationship to nature and to go off on their own. In the process they discovered or adapted a variety of new ways of entertaining themselves and of exploring the world. Skiing, long established as a means of winter travel in Scandinavia and among a few eccentrics in America and England, first became really popular when city holiday makers took possession of it and transformed it. Rivers, once admired for their romantic turbulence, were suddenly alive with *faltboots* for white-water rafting. Mountain climbing had formerly been a highly professional (and highly expensive) sport involving several trained guides for every Russian grand duke or English milord; it now became a favorite lone-wolf pastime for amateurs. Small sailing boats, even during the Depression, multiplied on the lakes of northern and central Europe. Less popular but no less esteemed was the sport of gliding. Bicycling and hiking, neither of them novelties, of course, began to involve greater and greater distances, with youth hostels and camping sites to accommodate the traveler. Last, in the eyes of many young city dwellers the motorcycle came to be a symbol not only of cheap transportation to work but of freedom and adventure on holidays.

Since the last war the number of new sports has increased enormously, with America taking the lead in devising them: skin diving, parachute jumping, surf riding, outboard motorboating, hot-rod racing, spelunking—and a variety of outlandish combinations like water skiing and hot-rod racing on ice. Some are so new that there is no telling yet how significant they are; others are too expensive or complicated to be widely popular. In the sense of being "character-building" or "body-building," few of them can qualify as conventional sports; some of them even lack the competitive or spectacular element altogether. Nevertheless, according to the etymological definition of a sport as "a turning away from serious occupations," they certainly belong. To the question of why they should have risen when they did, sociologists are ready with answers. They represent (so it appears) rebellion against parental authority or a compensation for the monotony and security of modern industrial society. Reuel Denney, for instance, describes hot-rodding as an attempt to escape from the conformity in automobile design imposed by Detroit and its "status car." These explanations are good enough as far as they go, but I still do not see how we can interpret any human activity without some reference to its chosen setting; I do not see how we can discuss purely in sociological terms any sport which is obviously designed as a form of psychological exploitation of the environment. To put it more simply, when people choose to practice a certain activity out of doors, we ought to assume that the outdoors is somehow important to that activity. As I see it, those who adopted those sports did so because they had had enough of contemplation, and of the old sublimities which a century of poets and painters and musicians had interpreted over and over again. They may have resented the persistent loyalty of their parents to these things, but subconsciously what they wanted was a con-

tact with nature less familiar and less pedestrian in both senses of those words
—a chance to experience nature freshly and directly.

Yes, but how to achieve this freedom? One way was by acquiring mobility, mobility not only for going to new places but for seeing them in a new,
nonpedestrian manner. Mobility does not necessarily mean speed. By the end
of the nineteenth century, speed was hardly a novelty to the Western world,
and we were already boasting of the Age of Speed that lay ahead. But the sensation of speed that a previous generation enjoyed when it traveled by fast
train must have been strangely akin to its enjoyment of nature: it was passive,
detached, and I daresay respectful, for when you sat inert in an upholstered
railroad carriage and were swiftly borne along a pair of rails to an entirely predictable destination, you could not flatter yourself that you were taking a very
active part in the proceedings. It was quite a different sensation, however, infinitely more exhilarating, when you could actually manipulate the controls
yourself, choose your own course and destination and rate of progress. That
is why I would put the dawn of the new era at a time when we began to devise individual means of locomotion. The airplane and automobile, of course!
But until a very few years ago, outside of America and perhaps England
and France, how many men had ever driven a car or flown a plane? The pre-
cursors of those inventions, if not in time at least in popularity, were those
simple, easily controlled devices: skis, sailboats, faltboots, gliders, bicycles, and
motorcycles.

### The Discovery of Mobility

In any case, the holiday makers who adopted these contrivances soon found
that their weekend contact with nature had become new and exciting. Why?
Well, for one thing, skis, faltboots, and the rest were ideally suited for traveling in uncharted and hitherto inaccessible landscapes. The faltboot avoided
navigable streams in favor of "white" water; the skier found himself moving
down mountain slopes where there was no trace of man to be seen. The glider
explored a new element, and so in a sense did the sailor. The motorcyclist went
farthest afield of all and sought out rough terrain and paths impassable for
four-wheeled vehicles. Each of these sportsmen saw aspects of the countryside
that he had never seen before. To a generation which had never strayed very far
from home, particularly to the urban European, this topographical freedom
was a revelation; to be able to desert the well-marked, well-traveled path, to
leave rails and highways behind and to move swiftly at one's own free will
across remote hills and valleys and rivers and lakes, was a fundamental depar-

ture from the old Sunday walk; and when to this was added a series of physical sensations without counterpart in the traditional contact with nature, then
I think we are justified in calling this experience of the environment revolutionary.

For in the new, more or less solitary sports, there is usually a latent, not
entirely unpleasant, sense of danger, or at least of uncertainty, producing a
heightened alertness to surrounding conditions. Without much experience,
without the presence of others to help and advise, without a stock of traditional skill, the sportsman, whether on skis or aloft or in a boat or on wheels,
has to develop (or revive) an intuitive feeling for his immediate natural environment. Air currents, shifts of wind and temperature, the texture of snow,
the firmness of the track—these and many other previously unimportant aspects of the outdoors become once more part of his consciousness, and that
is why mountaineering, even though it entails a very deliberate kind of progress, has to be included among these new sports. None of them, for one reason or another, allows much leisure for observing the more familiar features of
the surroundings; the skier or faltbooter or motorcyclist moves too fast (the
mountaineer with too great concentration on technique) to study the plants
and creatures which his father loved to contemplate by the hour. A considerable loss, no doubt; nevertheless, the new style sportsman is reestablishing a
responsiveness—almost an intimacy—with a more spacious, a less tangible
aspect of nature.

An abstract nature, as it were; a nature shorn of its gentler, more human
traits, of all memory and sentiment. The new landscape, seen at a rapid, sometimes even a terrifying pace, is composed of rushing air, shifting lights,
clouds, waves, a constantly moving, changing horizon, a constantly changing
surface beneath the ski, the wheel, the rudder, the wing. The view is no
longer static; it is a revolving, uninterrupted panorama of 360 degrees. In
short, the traditional perspective, the traditional way of seeing and experiencing the world is abandoned; in its stead we become active participants, the
shifting focus of a moving, abstract world; our nerves and muscles are all of
them brought into play. To the perceptive individual, there can be an almost
mystical quality to the experience; his identity seems for the moment to be
transmuted.

The discoveries of science, and in particular the insights of artists and
architects, have made us familiar with changing concepts of space and matter
and motion; without always understanding the theories, we accept them as
best we can. But what is our reaction when the man in the street tries in his

own way to explore the same realm? We profess sympathy with the uncertainty, the inability to communicate, of the contemporary artist; why do we express little or none for the hot-rodder and his colleagues? Because his unconventionality comes too close to home; the artist and the physicist can be left to themselves (or so we think), whereas the more modest variety space explorer lives next door, and what we notice in particular about his activities is the rubbish-strewn landscape, the disregard of time-honored esthetic values, the reckless driving. Still, even these things should not blind us to the fact that the world around us, for the first time in many generations, is being rediscovered by the young, and being enjoyed. What will eventually come out of this headlong flight into space we cannot as yet predict; for my part, I see no reason why it should not in time mark the beginning of a very rich and stimulating development in our culture.

**Farewell to Mother Nature**

Certainly, here in America there can be no denying that the new attitude is evolving with bewildering speed and producing fascinating forms worth studying for their own sake. The search for some contact with abstract nature is if anything more strenuous here than anywhere else. The European sportsman-excursionist still derives a great deal of inspiration from traditional landscape features: the picturesque village, the prosperous countryside, the glimpse of an older way of life. His American counterpart, on the other hand, seems increasingly bored by such pleasures. What he wants is the sensation without preliminaries or any diversion; what he wants is, in a word, abstract travel. Even the road is replaced by an abstraction, starting and ending nowhere in particular in space—a drag-strip in the desert or on a beach, a marked course on a snowy mountain slope, a watery path between flags and buoys. And just as the contemporary artist or architect tends to simplify his medium to its essentials, to reduce the masonry elements in order to increase the flow of space, the hot-rodder strips his car to a nubbin, the diver divests himself of his heavy suit, the boat becomes little more than a shell. For the more drastically we simplify the vehicle (or the medium), the more directly we ourselves participate in the experience of motion and space. One feature of the familiar world is left behind after another, and the sportsman enters a world of his own, new and at the same time intensely personal; a world of flowing movement, blurred light, rushing wind or water; he feels the surface beneath him, hears the sound of his progress, and has a tense rapport with his vehicle. With this comes a sensation of at last being part of the visible world, and its center.

How general is this sort of experience? The answer, I suspect, is that it is not general at all, that it is confined to a very small minority. But this does not mean that there is not a very widespread interest in it, nor an equally wide-spread desire to participate. "The universal activity of racing sports cars is growing rapidly" (I quote from a letter which recently appeared in the *Christian Science Monitor*).

> This growth is no doubt attributable to the fact that the winding, sometimes hilly, often beautiful road-courses offer a challenge to many of us automobile drivers who must do 99 percent of our driving on relatively uninteresting highways and at restricted speeds. . . . The sports pages go on valiantly devoting half their space to trying to bol-ster attendance at the old sports instead of playing up contemporary interest in competitive automobiles (hot-rod, drag and sport car), skin-diving, water skiing, swimming, outboard-motorboating and racing, yachting, motorboat cruising, and flying. . . . One reason for favoring these newer sports lies in the element of participation. . . . It may require some new reporting talent and some editorial policy changes to modernize our sports pages, but I believe the time for this advance-ment has long since arrived.

In other words, the change in sports has caught the sports editors nap-ping. It could very well be that it has also caught some of our sociologists and recreationists napping just as soundly.

But to return to Average Citizen and his Sunday or holiday excursion. How, it will be asked, can he even remotely share in this new experience? In-deed, how can he know that such an experience exists? His free time is in-creasingly circumscribed by mechanized civilization and massed humanity. Each year his new car isolates him a little more completely from his surround-ings, no matter where he goes. As Paul Shepard wrote in an earlier number of *Landscape,* "The day is here when the air-conditioned automobile carries us across Death Valley without discomfort, without disturbance to our heat per-ceptors, and without any experience worth mentioning." Nor does the design of our foolproof, sleep-inducing highways, or of our cars allow us to sense the surface under the wheels or to feel the exhilaration of a steep climb, a sharp curve, or a sudden view. We are compelled to move at a uniform speed, and we no longer even have that earlier, Model T sense of participating in the functioning of the automobile—one obvious reason for the popularity of European sports cars. Like our grandparents, we are passively conveyed through a complex, well-ordered, admirable world—only now technology substitutes for Mother Nature in distributing the bounty.

Even so, from time to time, Average Citizen catches a glimpse of a different kind of environment; brief, but enough to make him want to see more of it. From the idiotically small window of a plane, he manages to see the wondrous, free, nonhuman, abstract landscape of clouds and limitless sky; on a clear stretch of road, provided no state trooper is lurking, he can step on the throttle and know the thrill of speed produced by his own will; sun baths in the back yard give him a direct bodily contact with air and light and sun, and on his vacation he sees the desert and the open sea. Furthermore, his consciousness is constantly assaulted by new ideas of space and movement whenever he opens the morning paper or looks at a specimen of modern art. His children wear space helmets and addle their brains with science fiction and interplanetary comics. The new world impinges on the old in even the best regulated of American homes. These are all fragments of a much wider experience, to be sure, but in the long run they make him discontented with the familiar, and drive him out onto the crowded Sunday highway in search of some kind of release.

**Participation through Movement**

And that is where Average Citizen is still to be found: out on the crowded highway. How is he to be freed, I wonder, to discover for himself the new reactions to nature, the new nature that awaits him? More highways? Faster highways? Newer, simpler means of locomotion, newer and more spacious sports areas, more remote vacation sites? Certainly, no more pretty parks or carefully preserved rural landscapes or classical perspectives; limited though his choice is, he still has to be on the move one way or another, and he has to be made to feel that he is part of the world, not merely a spectator.

I confess, however, that this is a problem I am content to leave to others. The man who interests me is the excursionist or sportsman or part-time adventurer who has already found his way to the other world, and is already at home in that abstract, preternatural landscape of wind and sun and motion. Because it is he, I think, who will eventually enrich our understanding of ourselves with a new poetry and a new nature mysticism. I would not go so far as to say that the Wordsworth of the second half of the twentieth century must be a graduate of the drag-strip, or that a motorcycle is a necessary adjunct to any modern "excursion"; but I earnestly believe that whoever he is and whenever he appears, he will have to express some of the uncommunicated but intensely felt joys of that part of American culture if he is to interpret completely our relationship to the world around us.

"The Abstract World of the Hot-Rodder," *Landscape* 7, no. 2 (Winter 1957–58): 22–27.

## The Movable Dwelling and How It Came to America

The origin of a word often throws a new light on the way we use it. Take the word *dwelling*. If we are using it as a noun—if we are speaking of the dwelling as a house—we should really say, "dwelling place." The verb *to dwell* has a distinct meaning. At one time it meant to hesitate, to linger, to delay, as when we say, "He is dwelling too long on this insignificant matter." *To dwell*, like the verb *to abide* (from which we derive *abode*), simply means to pause, to stay put for a length of time; it implies that we will eventually move on. So the dwelling place should perhaps be seen as temporary. Our being in it is contingent on many external factors.

How long do we have to stay in a place for it to become a dwelling? That may seem an unimportant question, yet I think we should try to answer it. I would say we stay long enough for our presence to become customary. A place becomes a dwelling when it is part of our customary behavior. To stay there overnight or even two or three nights will not do. But when we stay there because we have a steady job or are a student, then it becomes an element in a customary or habitual way of life.

This way of defining the word is borne out by the usage of the verb *to dwell* in other languages. In English (it is hard to see why) we say "live" in a place. Both French and German retain the equivalent of *to dwell* and find it very serviceable. In French you do not say, "Où vivez-vous?" you say "Où habitez-vous?" Just as in German you do not say, "Wo leben Sie?" but "Wo wohnen Sie?" Both expressions imply an habitual action, and indeed both of them are closely related to the words for custom or habit: *habitude* and *Gewohnheit.*

This usage suggests a certain detachment from the dwelling. Habits and customs are of course important and often very pleasant, but we do not think of them as really basic elements of our existence. They are adapted, they are acquired, but they are also discarded when we tire of them. And this is true also of the contemporary dwelling. No matter how comfortable or convenient it may be, we know that the time may well come when we find it wise to change: this is perhaps the best moment to sell. Perhaps a new job demands that we move or the neighborhood threatens to deteriorate or the children have grown up and left home. So we look for another dwelling; and since other people feel the same, another suitable dwelling is not usually hard to find.

What I am suggesting is that the home and the dwelling are two separate things, though they usually coincide. This truth is obvious to all modern Americans, but I believe that there was a time when people did not make this distinction.

This brings me to a second word. *Chattel,* an article of personal, movable property, is related to *cattle* and to *capital,* but the relationship with *cattle* is the older of the two. At a remote time in Roman history, all land and all power belonged to the family or clan or tribe. The only thing corresponding to individual private property was the few head of cattle (or sheep) which the man of the household grazed on common land. What made this property desirable was that it could be disposed of without consulting the larger group. The cattle could be accumulated and bought and sold and given to any son or daughter the man chose. Cattle were negotiable and could be translated into cash, and one reason they were negotiable was that they were mobile, they could be moved. So they represented two very important freedoms: freedom from the authority of the community and freedom from territorial or environmental constraints.

In the course of centuries many more things were defined as chattels, and in the Middle Ages the dwelling was likewise defined as chattel under certain conditions. This meant that it could be disposed of independently of the land to which it was often closely tied. If according to established laws of inheritance a man was legally obliged to leave his land to his eldest son, he could, if he wanted to, leave his dwelling to his widow or to his daughter or to the church. As the word *movable* implied, he could also move it to another site. But this did not hold true of all dwellings: usually only the more modest kind, those built of wood, could be separated from the operation of the farm. The farm or the estate itself could not be alienated—that is to say, disposed of—for it was to descend to his children.

This notion that the dwelling was independent of the land and was legally (and even literally) mobile naturally produced a distinctive kind of dwelling, particularly in towns and cities: houses which were built to be rented or used for a variety of profitable purposes. They tended to be simple in construction and uniform. We can think of those early rental units as the medieval equivalent of the contemporary trailer—not only in their mobility but in their standardization and construction and in their appeal to working-class families with a job somewhere nearby.

But there were from the earliest times two types of houses. The dwelling was, of course, much more numerous, but the other kind is the kind which architectural historians usually know more about. To greatly oversimplify, we can say that this second kind was in many ways the complete opposite of the first. It was identified with a family over generations—so much so that another term for a dynasty is *house*—like the house of Windsor or the house of Rothschild. It was as large and as permanent as possible because it was a symbol of power and status in the community. It was not uncommon for town and city authorities to prescribe the size and design of the houses of the rich and powerful and to insist on a certain grandeur in appearance. Furthermore, there were features to these houses which clearly indicated the rank of the occupying family: the presence of a tower or dungeon meant that the occupant was a judge of a certain type of court of justice. I need not say much more about these houses except to repeat that they were built of stone. Both *manor* and *mansion* derive from a root meaning lasting, enduring, and in Wales the word for such a house—whether a manor or a prosperous homestead—included the word *stone*. Architectural history naturally has more to say about these houses than about the peasant or worker dweller. For one thing, the so-called mansion has usually been protected by the family, and its history is a matter of record. For another, the various symbolic features—tower, dungeon, moat, courtyard, ceremonial entrance—eventually become elements in an architectural style. But the most striking difference is this: whereas the dwelling by its very poverty has few ways of preserving and providing for the long-range future, the mansion is deeply involved in both concerns. It is at once a monument to the history of the family and its power and wealth and a legacy for future generations to honor and preserve.

Much of the story of domestic architecture in the Western world, and especially in America, can be written in terms of the contrast between these two kinds of houses. Clearly, there is a class distinction between the point of view of the family of wealth and position and that of the family of job seekers and job holders perpetually on the move. There is also an obvious distinction, transcending class, between two ways of honoring the past and the future, of thinking of history. But the distinction which I find most interesting in America is a much simpler one: the distinction between the house built to last, built as a permanent part of the environment, and the house with a life expectancy of a generation or less, the house which serves a limited purpose in the lives of its occupants.

In other words, what I think worth exploring is the fluctuating fortunes of stone and wood as building materials; specifically, the low standing of wood in medieval Europe, its almost total rejection during the Renaissance, and its triumphant reemergence in America. We should explore the development of the dwelling and how we made it the standard house, part of the standard way of life, of the United States.

Our American housing tradition derives from seventeenth- and eighteenth-century England, but ultimately from what is sometimes called Atlantic Europe—that forested region of Europe north of the Alps and north of the Loire. Atlantic Europe thus includes Scandinavia, Germany, England, the Lowlands, and northern France. A thousand years ago, despite the influence of the Roman Empire, this was still a rural landscape, largely covered by forests and moor. It was therefore a region of wooden houses and a region where there was a flourishing culture of wood. This culture persists in many different forms in contemporary America, and in one way or another most Americans take part in it.

We enjoy being part-time carpenter and repairman, patching up a structure we secretly know will eventually collapse or go up in flames. Perhaps we really enjoy wood's temporary quality; that is what makes it seem alive and responsive.

I suspect this has always been the case; we seem always to have built our wooden dwellings rapidly and with the idea that we can eventually change and improve—or abandon them. Archaeologists tell us that though medieval carpentry techniques were highly developed in the building of boats and bridges and churches, the construction of the average peasant dwelling was slipshod and entirely without art. Few dwellings were expected to last more than a dozen years, and it was not unheard of for men to set fire to their own houses by way of holiday celebration. They could easily be replaced. All that was worth salvaging were the four cornerposts, beams, and rafters. The mud and brush walls, the thatch roof, and the few items of furniture were quickly reproduced. Americans lament that their houses are not allowed to grow old, and in fact the age of the average American is greater than that of the house he lives in. But even so our houses last much longer than did those of our medieval ancestors.

Impermanence was thus the chief characteristic of those early wooden constructions. A second characteristic was mobility. It was simple to disassemble a dwelling which was little more than a crude frame of a half-dozen posts and beams and which had no foundation, no floor, and no ceiling. Many medieval accounts tell of dwellings being moved to where the next job was or onto a patch of vacant land. Whole villages moved when the soil was exhausted or when they were threatened by enemy attack. The image of the peasant family rooted for generations in the same spot is being modified by modern historians. As we will see, it is better suited to the peasant of the Renaissance or even of the nineteenth century than to the peasant of the Middle Ages.

The peasant of Atlantic Europe appears to have been very loyal to the tradition of the wooden dwelling, even in regions where wood was scarce and stone or clay was plentiful, and something of that loyalty was carried over to America in the seventeenth century. Jefferson complained that ignorant Virginians objected to brick houses for reasons of health, and as late as 1795 the Salem diarist William Bentley noted that the house of a certain Mr. Lee "was demolished from the prejudice against brick houses."

But the preference for wood was not shared by the more prosperous classes. The medieval clergy and the medieval aristocracy were outspoken in their admiration of stone. The theological doctrines which endorsed stone and masonry were extremely learned, and in their time no doubt very convincing.

The schism in architectural design lasted throughout the Middle Ages, with neither point of view getting the upper hand. But beginning in the sixteenth century, masonry somewhat abruptly became much more general. The two most obvious reasons for the shift were the renewed interest in classical architecture inspired by travel to Italy, and then a serious shortage of wood throughout Atlantic Europe. Many forests had been destroyed by a growing population, the increase in the size of cities demanded more and more timber, and so did the building of fleets of naval and commercial ships. Finally, there was a great demand for wood as fuel in manufacturing.

The response to these developments was a great change in building methods. There came a wave of conservation legislation: a limitation on the amount of wood peasants could use in construction, the use of different kinds of wood, and, most important of all, a movement to replace wooden structures by structures of stone or brick. Though it started with the building of handsome houses in the city, it soon extended to include village dwellings and even whole villages and towns. This housing revolution of the sixteenth and seventeenth centuries—which the English call the Great Rebuilding and the French call the Victory of Stone over Wood—had a drastic influence on attitudes toward the dwelling. Simone Roux, in her recent historical survey of housing, says,

> It was the triumph of the heavy stone house, the Mediterranean solution imposed on the rest of Europe. . . . Here we were, reconstructing in stone that which we had originally built of wood and mud. A house weighing from four hundred to five hundred tons, meant to last for centuries without expensive upkeep, was hereafter to serve as a symbol of permanence, of solidity, of reassuring protection. It stood for the complete shelter, the perfect hearth or home, the guardian of generations of accumulated memories. The [masonry] house tied the family to the land; the heavy construction called for a large outlay of money, it represented a large investment in permanent prestige. The stone house, ideally adapted to the needs of a static society, became the center of innumerable small investments.[1]

No one can doubt that this reform in housing was by and large a benefit. The architectural revolution of the sixteenth and seventeenth centuries not only produced handsome cities and towns and palaces and mansions, it also replaced dark and unsanitary cottages with stone dwellings which were larger, better designed, and more sightly. Still, we must not lose sight of the virtues which were thereby outlawed. For all their squalor, medieval peasant dwellings had a remarkable flexibility and mobility—not only in that they could be taken down and reassembled elsewhere, but also in that they could easily change function and change tenants. If their life span was brief, it allowed for frequent replacement. When the old dwelling collapsed, the new one was apt to be better and was certain to be cleaner. Finally, the temporary nature of the dwelling, its negligible material value, meant that it could be lightheartedly abandoned when the crops failed, when war threatened, or when the local lord proved too demanding. Its flimsiness protected the family from the dangers of staying put. If people could not fight misfortune, they could at least escape it by leaving house and environment behind.

The more we learn about that victory of stone over wood, the more one question seems to demand an answer: was colonial America likewise engulfed in the Mediterranean architectural tide? There was of course no great rebuilding in North America, for there was no building, no architectural tradition to begin with. But it is certainly true, as most histories of American architecture insist on telling us, that once the first harsh pioneer days were over, the well-to-do and ambitious colonists from Virginia to Maine started to build substantial urban and suburban houses in the fashionable style of the period. Tidewater Virginia came nearest to being overwhelmed by the new design philosophy. The eighteenth-century planters delighted in massive brick construction, and in fact the authorities in London in the middle of the seventeenth century ordained that every Virginia planter who owned a hundred acres had to build a brick house—with brick foundations—of specified dimensions. If he owned more than one hundred acres, his house had to be proportionately larger. What makes the history of the Tidewater area especially interesting is that it became the favorite target of the design innovators—much more than New England did. The strange constitution which John Locke drew up for South Carolina in the last years of the seventeenth century called for a baroque organization of space, and the design of Williamsburg was a model of Mediterranean order and would-be permanence.

But these attempts to produce a Renaissance landscape in colonial America came to nothing. In Virginia as in New England, the vast majority of dwellings were wood, built by amateurs, and few of them were destined to last for many years. Of all the architectural historians, Alan Gowans is the one who has most eloquently described the medieval—or late medieval—quality of early American architecture.[2] I think most of us now agree with his verdict. The social and economic conditions in the colonies were totally different from those in Europe. Abundant land meant that every settler looked forward to a substantial allotment of ground and that dissatisfied settlers could move to new and more promising places after a few years. The immense forests provided wood for building; the absence of stone suitable for masonry (notably in Tidewater Virginia), the cost of making or importing brick, and above all the scarcity of skilled carpenters and joiners combined to foster the production of wooden houses that were often hastily put together, lacking in solid foundations, storage space, and weathered lumber. The result was a stock of small, cheaply built, short-lived wooden houses easily taken down or moved, easily modified, and designed to meet the pressing need for shelter in a pioneer landscape. But the real novelty of these dwellings was not that they were cheaply built and quickly moved or disassembled—those, after all, were the characteristics of the medieval cottage. The real novelty was that these dwellings were built, occupied, and eventually disposed of as *commodities,* merchandise designed and produced to satisfy a definite market.

What kind of market was that? In the seventeenth and eighteenth centuries it was a market composed of young, blue-collar families needing a place to live in a new environment. In those days this was assumed to be a farm, though in America it was a different kind of farm: not necessarily a permanent home, but rather merely a place of land which a family could exploit profitably for a number of years before moving on to where prospects seemed brighter: better soil, better returns, better neighbors.

For example, in his *Economic History of Virginia in the Seventeenth Century,* P. A. Bruce discusses the kind of house the first settlers built: a small, crude shelter with walls of vertical boards or slabs nailed to a horizontal board, and a pitched roof on top of the completed rectangle. The houses usually had two rooms, as well as a number of outhouses and barns and sheds. The farmer or planter at once started to raise tobacco. After two or three years he had exhausted the soil and there was nothing to do but move. Bruce comments:

> The inclination to abandon old plantations and to take up new ones
> . . . encouraged a more active destruction of the woods but at the same
> time it fostered a spirit of indifference as to the manner in which they
> used it. The [settlers] neglected the fencing of their grounds, they
> failed to establish pastures for their cattle, or to lay off orchards and
> gardens, and even to plant corn. So frail were many of the dwelling
> houses in consequence of the purpose of its occupants to desert their
> estates as soon as exhausted . . . that special instructions were sent to
> the Governor to discourage by every means in his power the erection of
> such temporary habitations.[3]

What we glimpse in this passage is the typical ramshackle frame house in the midst of abandoned fields that we find throughout contemporary America; and when we know America well, we find nothing really sad in the spectacle. The deserted house, nine times out of ten, is a chrysalis from which its inhabitants have happily escaped to some brighter or more alluring prospect. Only in the Old World, with its dream of permanence, does the deserted house or the deserted field invariably speak of human tragedy.

Several of the essential traits of the American dwelling appear in Bruce's description of early Virginia: the frailty, not to say the flimsiness, of its construction; the temporary quality, the indifference to the immediate environment, the loneliness—and of course the lavish, almost exclusive use of wood. I would add two further characteristics: the absence of storage space in the dwelling itself and the absence of a solid foundation. Finally, there is a trait which we all take for granted but which few foreign observers can begin to understand: the remoteness of many farms and dwellings from any community.

Let us repeat the familiar story of the structural evolution of the classic American dwelling: not the architect-designed house or mansion (or whatever), but the type of shelter that most Americans live in. The first step was the makeshift slab house without foundation of the colonial South. The second step, dating from the early eighteenth century in Pennsylvania and, like the slab house, identified with the pioneer frontier community, was the log cabin. It flourished in western Virginia and throughout the frontier South. Jefferson, whose architectural philosophy was definitely aristocratic and promasonry, described both types in his *Notes on the State of Virginia.* "The greatest proportion of the private buildings of Virginia are of scantling and boards, plastered with lime. It is impossible to devise things more ugly, uncomfortable, and happily more perishable." He adds: "The poorest people build huts of logs, laid horizontally in pens, stopping the interstices with mud. These are warmer in winter and cooler in summer than the more expensive construction of scantling and plank."[4]

Both types seem to have been generally temporary and were succeeded in a matter of years by a more substantial house. In both cases the plan was simplicity itself, with no provision for storage within the building, no foundation, no use of traditional carpentry skills, and no concern for appearances. Eventually, the log cabin or slab house became a barn or was allowed to fall down. The third step was of course the balloon frame—another frontier invention. It represented a radical change in construction techniques, and yet at the same time it was a logical development: like its predecessors, it was quick and simple to build, it was indifferent to local or folk architectural traditions, and it was seen as temporary; not that it would collapse, but that it would soon be sold and passed on to newcomers. Solon Robinson and other writers on western pioneering thus advised families to build their balloon-frame houses as impersonally as possible so that they would be acceptable to any prospective purchaser. In the course of a few decades the balloon frame achieved architectural respectability, but even as late as 1870 a writer telling of his journey through Arkansas and Texas noted that there was scarcely any real architecture in that region since most of the buildings were balloon-frame.

The acceptance of the balloon frame by serious architects can perhaps be explained by the development of two even simpler types of dwellings: the ready-cut or mail-order house, which flourished from the 1860s until the present and which has been studied by many architectural historians in recent years, and the simultaneous development of an even simpler type of dwelling —the box house.

Superficially—that is to say, from the outside—the box house resembles the board-and-batten house. But whereas the board-and-batten house usually has an insulating wall of brick under the exterior and a plastered interior wall, the true box house has no frame, no interior insulation, and of course no foundation. I have the feeling that it first developed in the Chesapeake Bay region. Long before the Civil War it had spread along the Gulf of Mexico and even as far as California. Horace Bushnell, a native of Hartford, Connecticut, was astonished to see box houses being built in San Francisco in the 1850s. Charles Dwyer, who wrote a book about low-cost housing in 1855, noted that workers on railroads and canals lived in settlements of box houses.

This is how the box house is described by Dianne Tebbetts in *Pioneer America*:

> Box construction is similar to plank construction that developed in
> medieval England. . . . In box construction . . . wide boards are nailed
> vertically [to sills laid on the ground] and a 2 × 4 is nailed horizontally
> along the top of these vertical boards. Additional vertical boards are
> attached to form a single thickness wall with *no framing at all.* Ceiling
> joists tie it together, and doors and windows sit in holes cut in the walls
> for them. . . . Inside the walls are usually heavily papered to keep out
> winter winds. What this manner of construction lacks in durability it
> makes up in economy, for it is the least expensive way to enclose a
> given volume. Box construction is fairly common throughout the
> Ozarks. . . . It is preferred as a evidence of some prosperity over the
> sturdier log house. Accordingly the "hillman" who has money to
> spend prefers a box house of sawed native lumber with a cheap
> tarpaper roof.[5]

JBJ, photo, pre-cut railroad workers' houses, Wyoming

The New Mexico mining community of Madrid has a great many specimens of box houses. They were brought there in 1920s from Tucumcari, two
hundred miles away, where they had provided housing for workers on the
Rock Island Railroad. I have yet to see a box house which is solid in appearance. The absence of any kind of frame saves money, but it allows the building to sag and bulge and reduces its overall strength. That is why the average
box house is only one room wide and one story high. Inevitably, it is associated
with the poorest and most transient element in the population. Even today in
much of the South it is usually called a rent house or a tenant house, and occasionally it is called a former slave cabin—even though few now standing are
old enough to have accommodated slaves. I have a strong suspicion that many
of the so-called frame buildings we see in pictures of the nineteenth-century
boom mining towns were actually box houses. There was a time when the box
house was one of the commonest types in the United States—far more common, I imagine, than the balloon frame. In the post–Civil War South the box
house proliferated in lumber company towns, plantations, and railroad camps.

JBJ, photo, mobile home park

The lumber towns, as might be imagined, produced them in great numbers, for the towns moved from place to place wherever the forest was exhausted, and they needed a mobile dwelling type.

An article on these towns and their architecture appeared in the *Geographical Review* for September 1957.[6] The writer identified at least three distinct types: the so-called bungalow (with a wide, encircling porch), the shotgun, and the log-pen house. The author suggested that the box house was popular in lumber towns because it was cheap and easy to build, suited to any size family, and easy to move by rail. The shotgun house, because of its narrowness (one room wide and two or more rooms deep), was well suited to small city lots and became very popular when moved to industrial cities.

The last chapter in the history of the box house tells of its use in remote company towns during World War I, and then of its use for migrant farm workers in the South, the Southwest, and California. We know far less about its spread and its development than we should, because it is very much part of the new American landscape.

The growth of large-scale truck gardening in the Sunbelt states fostered the growth of a very mobile work force. In the years before World War I, the average farm worker was a single man, variously called a tramp, a blanketman, or a bindlestiff. He slept wherever he could. But in the 1920s secondhand cars became relatively cheap, and instead of traveling under freightcars, the farm worker was more and more apt to travel in a car, accompanied by his family. And this of course created a demand for cheap, temporary housing: in other words, for box houses.

Most of these were probably built by small-time developers or speculators; the only reliable information we have about them is in the contemporary publications of the Department of Labor. Inevitably, these box houses for transients were overcrowded, poorly maintained, and dangerous, and one of the programs of the New Deal was to replace them. The problem of course is still with us, but by the 1950s a new form of dwelling, a dwelling strikingly similar in one respect to its medieval forebears, came on the scene: the trailer or mobile home, and even more recently the camper on the back of a pickup.

We are only beginning to recognize the impact of this new kind of dwelling on planning, on the community, and on work. I am convinced that the trailer or an improved version of it is, for better or worse, the low-cost dwelling of the future—lacking in solidity, lacking in permanence, lacking in charm, but inexpensive, convenient, and mobile.

Most of us, I suspect, find it easier to accept and even romanticize the box house and its American predecessors, at least those in rural areas, that have developed individuality and have been assimilated into the landscape. And yet I persist in seeing an underlying similarity among all those flimsy, short-lived American dwellings, each of which was denounced in its day as crude and disruptive and socially undesirable. All of them have served as dwellings for people who have to move to where the job is: migrant farm laborers, highway and construction crews, lumbermen, soldiers, and airmen. Whatever their form of construction, they have served as dwellings of old people, of young couples getting started in life; and almost always they have been seen by their occupants as temporary: something better and more lasting is to be that next step.

It is very tempting to analyze the dwelling entirely in socioeconomic terms; certainly, dwellings do not lend themselves to analysis in terms of architecture or folk art. But the real significance of the temporary dwelling, of the box house, to take one example out of many, lies elsewhere. I think it has always offered, though for a brief time only, a kind of freedom we often undervalue: the freedom from burdensome emotional ties with the environment, freedom from communal responsibilities, freedom from the tyranny of the traditional home and its possessions; the freedom from belonging to a tight-knit social order; and above all, the freedom to move on to somewhere else.

Now that environmentalism has become accepted establishment philosophy, the values we stress are stability and permanence and the putting down of roots and holding on to our architectural heritage; and no doubt this is as it should be. Still, we cannot help but be reminded, whenever we look at our rapidly changing landscape and study our changing attitudes toward the home, that we have a second architectural tradition, a tradition of mobility and short-term occupancy that is stronger and more visible than ever. Not everyone can sympathize with this other, more popular tradition, with its rejection of environmental loyalties and constraints, but all of us who think about architecture and its many bewildering manifestations are in a sense duty bound to try to understand the new kind of home we are all making in America.

"The Movable Dwelling and How It Came to America," from *Discovering the Vernacular Landscape* (New Haven: Yale University Press, 1984), 91–101.

JBJ, sketch, iron containers, Pueblo, Colorado, 1979

## An Engineered Environment

By now [1966] most of us have grown used to the idea that the urban world we live in is going on changing, and not necessarily for the better. We know what is in store: more tall buildings, more vacant downtown lots, more expressways and subdivisions and neon signs. Nurtured on science fiction, World's Fair Futuramas, Sunday spreads of the visions of real estate developers, and what the French call the literature of anticipation, we recognize behind the reality which rises to obstruct our view or intensify a traffic jam the architect's or engineer's dream.

Endurance as well as courage are needed if we are to keep on riding the wave of the future: where do they come from? From many sources, among them the firm belief, passed on from generation to generation, that there is and always will be a part of the world remote from the city where we can retreat and find ourselves. Here is where the ancient relationship between man and nature survives intact. The weekend trip, the summer vacation, the retirement years are set aside for the renewing of this bond—except that some distraction usually interferes.

The more the city expands and absorbs us, the firmer the belief in a rural paradise becomes. Our ties with the countryside no further than twenty miles from our door grow fewer; even the annual return to the family farm, a tradition still alive a generation ago, has now all but vanished. Without personal involvement, we are in the dark as to what is happening on the farm—any farm. And the result is a popular image of rural America which bears a decreasing resemblance to reality. We see it as a pleasant, drowsy region where old-fashioned people are engaged in a kind of work less essential and less profitable with every passing year, but where life has an elemental simplicity and truth. On a more sophisticated (though no better-informed) level, the countryside is seen as a vast wildlife preserve resounding with birdsong, threaded by sparkling streams—ideal for recreation and something environmental designers like to label "open space." However we look at it, this hinterland is held to be the great antidote, spiritual as well as physical, to the evils of the city. As long as it survives unchanged, we ourselves can hope to survive; urban existence is a kind of purgatory.

It so happens that the American rural landscape is composed not only of forests and lakes and mountains but of farms and feedlots and irrigation ditches and orchards and tractor agencies and rangeland. It is a place of work, and because it *is* a place of work, hard and not always rewarding, it is at present undergoing a revolution as radical in its way as the revolution in the urban environment. Moreover, this revolution is taking place entirely without help from environmental designers. No one, outside of a handful of government agencies from the Departments of Agriculture and the Interior, is trying to direct it and give it form. Thus, while we keep on counting the days until we can return to the family homestead, the homestead itself has vanished and along with it much of the nineteenth-century landscape. Quite a different rural America is emerging, and while there are still great changes in store, it is not too soon to discern its rough outline. What does it look like? How does it differ from the one we used to know and still dream about?

It can be briefly described: it has far fewer people living in it, its work is largely mechanized, and it is evolving its own attitude toward the environment.

Half a century ago there were thirty-two million Americans living on farms. Today there are less than thirteen million, and in another twenty years there will probably be not many more than ten million. An obvious result of this decline is an increase in the number of abandoned farms. In the last fifteen years, more than half of these have been in the East—particularly in the Southeast. Americans have long been familiar with the sight of deserted farmsteads on country roads: barns and houses sagging, fields choked by a second growth of trees, lanes overgrown. These have become part of our rural picturesqueness. Abandonment of this sort is on the increase; all that prevents the complete desertion of many older countrysides is the wave of exurbanites and vacationists and retired people who are willing to restore old houses in places which have either esthetic appeal or the appeal of proximity to some city.

Well, it is pleasant to have the woods back again, even though it usually means that some unlucky farmer has had to give up the fight to make a living on his own. But it is a grievous mistake to assume that every abandoned farm automatically increases the area of forest and wildland. That is an illusion common in the East, where the cult of the tree reaches almost pagan proportions. West of Missouri, roughly speaking, abandoned farmland does not revert to forest; it reverts to rangeland, "open space," or even desert, a prey to erosion. If the thousands of acres withdrawn from cultivation and scheduled for withdrawal in the middle regions of America are ever to serve any future use—whether as wildlands or recreation tracts or even farm fields—they will have to have expensive care. Furthermore (to nip any arbolatry in the bud), the few trees which grow around the abandoned places in the Great Plains will die. We should not expect the abandoned farms to produce everywhere the romantic landscape of "pleasing decay" that John Piper has defined. This will remain the exclusive property of the northeastern states; elsewhere the environmental designer will have to create it out of very scanty material.

The earliest victim of a declining farm population is the country town, and in fact the stagnating town is already typical of much of the new American landscape, especially in the High Plains. And here again we would do well not to expect any of the traditional eastern graces. There will be few if any tree-lined, lawn-bordered streets with white mansions taking in summer guests, no handsome common surrounded by nineteenth-century brick buildings, still sound and trim. The ailment affecting the average small rural center (when it has no industry) is the same one affecting our cities: a moribund downtown area. In rural terms, this means that Main Street is losing its vitality. The hotel is empty, many stores are empty, the depot is empty. The decline in the number of customers is one reason; another reason, which holds good in prosperous regions, too, is that modern farm equipment and its servicing takes up a great deal of space, and consequently that important aspect of small town business has often moved out to the highway, where there is plenty of cheap land. The chain-store supermarket has followed suit, and so has the new restaurant, and the new motel has been built out there as well. If and when the environmental designer concerns himself with small-town problems, this one ought to have priority.

Perhaps it can be solved in conjunction with another problem: the growth and persistence of small-town slums. Across the railroad tracks, near the river with its occasional floods, out by the municipal dump there are shanty towns and tent cities and hopelessly immobile mobile homes where a racial minority group lives. This is all that is left of a much larger group which once supported itself after a fashion as stoop labor on the surrounding farms. Mechanization has thrown them out of work for good; but they stay on for lack of a better place to go, living more and more miserably. It is ironic that small-town slums are typical of the most prosperous (because most highly mechanized) areas. The rich Delta cotton lands of Mississippi boast the highest percentage of unemployment in the South: more than 20 percent. This new feature of the American countryside threatens to proliferate throughout the South, the irrigated Southwest, and California.

It will undoubtedly take us time to get used to these and other indications of a population decline; we think of America as forever booming and expanding. It is true that we are no longer disturbed by the abandoned one-room school or the crossroads General Merchandise; but how will we take the abandoned, more or less modern high school with monster gymnasium? The abandoned drive-in movie theater with rows of empty stanchions emerging from the weeds? The abandoned shopping center? We will see them not only in North Dakota but in Texas and Florida and Kansas and elsewhere.

Fewer people, fewer workers brings on mechanization, or is it mechanization which means fewer people because of fewer jobs? Whichever is the case, mechanization of farm work is the most conspicuous hallmark of the new rural landscape. This dawns on us long before we reach the farms themselves. I mentioned that the farm equipment dealers have all moved out to the more spacious highway strip. Actually, this is no new development, but in the years to come, it is safe to say, it will assume spectacular proportions. We will have to develop an appreciative eye for this double row of immense, gleaming, bright-colored machines—tractors, combines, harvesters, pickers of all sorts, bulldozers, landplanes, wheel scrapers, self-propelled irrigation and spraying systems, balers, trailers, trucks, not to mention stacks of aluminum pipe and gas storage tanks—all of them more magnificent than their current versions, and more expensive. Some of them will be for sale, but more and more of them will be for rent, or owned and operated by what are called package farming outfits. California already has such enterprises which contract with farmers to do the fumigating and fertilizing of the soil, the preparing of the seed bed and the planting of the seed, the insecticide spraying, and finally the harvesting. For tomatoes the service costs ninety-five dollars an acre. Since the price of equipment is steadily increasing, and the techniques of farming are becoming steadily more complex, services of this sort are bound to become popular.

The rural highway strip lined with new farm machinery is already an impressive spectacle. It would be even more impressive and more efficient if it were properly and imaginatively laid out. This is the sort of improvement which the highway designer or the landscape architect is quite capable of undertaking. The urbanist problems of small towns are on a small scale, perhaps, but agricultural mechanization, potentially the source of local employment in servicing and repairs, has brought serious traffic and parking hardships with it.

Farther out along the strip, beyond the motels and the giant truck stop and the last rusty used car lot, lies the local landing field. Once a neglected facility, used chiefly by city sportsmen and a few well-to-do amateur flyers, it has become a vital element in the new landscape. There are planes here for spraying and dusting and seeding; in some places there are helicopters whose function it is to hover over fruit trees and shake down the ripe fruit. And it is only a matter of time before we see government planes for what is now called "remote sensing." By means of infrared photography, it is possible to check from the air the condition of crops and forest and rangeland, and spot plant diseases long before they are visible to the naked eye, especially in the vast fields which cannot be inspected from the ground.

What about the appearance of the farms themselves? That depends on where they are. It should go without saying that a northeastern dairy landscape will not resemble a Montana wheat landscape or an Arizona citrus landscape or an Alabama cotton landscape in 1986 any more than it does in 1966. But it is possible to predict that all farms in the future—commercial farms at least—will have certain traits in common, traits which are not yet widespread.

They will (for one thing) be larger. One result of a diminishing farm population is that many small holdings are consolidated into a few sizable ones, though not necessarily by outright purchase. Averages mean very little in a country as diversified as ours; just the same, it is worth noting that whereas only twenty years ago the average holding was 190 acres, it is now 357 acres. The increase has actually been proportionally much greater in the Midwest and the Far West. Generally speaking, the smaller the farm, the greater the probability of its being either abandoned or absorbed. In one relatively prosperous Illinois county, fifty farmers are going out of business each year. Most of them were working 100 acres or less, and their land has quickly been taken up by larger operators. One thing which has contributed to this expansion is the increased mobility of farm machinery. With faster-moving tractors, farmers no longer hesitate to acquire land several miles away from their headquarters. TRACTORS WITH LUGS PROHIBITED is a once common highway sign you no longer see; that is because they now have pneumatic tires.

A landscape composed of large farms or farm complexes will mean a considerable change in many ways: fewer fences and hedgerows; less variety in the vegetation; more abandoned barns and out-of-date equipment in the midst of intensively cultivated fields; bales of alfalfa bulging out of deserted farmhouse windows. If we were suddenly to come upon this new landscape for the first time in our lives, our reactions would be not unlike Gulliver's when he first glimpsed Brobdingnag: marveling at the immense fields, the great rows of trees, the giant stands of grass and wheat; but also noting the coarseness of detail: the lack of men, of animals, of small woodlots, of isolated barns and sheds.

Nevertheless, what we are more likely to notice is the artificial topography of the landscape, the manner in which the cultivated land has been remodeled.

Every American farmer in the past has sought to change the topography and vegetation of his land to suit his needs: he has cut down stands of trees, dammed and regulated streams, drained marshes, cleared the fields of stones and stumps. But his intent was usually to "assist" nature, to encourage its more productive aspects. Whether this reflected a kind of piety or merely a lack of ability to do more in the way of modification is a point which could usefully be debated; but in former times the natural order, slightly altered by man, was held to be the basis of successful agriculture. To express this in contemporary language, the traditional farmer "studied natural systems and focused his attention on discovering and applying natural laws to the behavior of these systems and on explaining the relationships and interaction of separate parts."

The kind of modification which the modern farmer undertakes is entirely different; different not only in scale but in purpose, for its purpose is to create an entirely new and artificial setting for his work. The ultimate aim is a man-made topography, a man-made soil, a man-made crop, all part of a new production process.

More and more, this is what is being achieved. The development of powerful and versatile earth-moving equipment both during the war and in subsequent highway and reclamation programs has enabled any farmer who can afford it to remake his farm. To the right-thinking suburbanite, the bulldozer is the very embodiment of ruthless destruction. To the irrigation farmer or the farmer trying to consolidate a variety of uneconomical holdings or the farmer cramped for space—and they exist—the bulldozer is a godsend. Thanks to it he can level land to be put under the ditch, suppress washes and gullies, root out unwanted vegetation, terrace slopes which are too steep for profitable cultivation. Furthermore, earth-moving equipment can regenerate the soil by means of deep plowing, it can conserve moisture and prevent erosion. The danger of abusing this tremendous power is easy to illustrate, so much so that the layman is likely to forget its beneficial capacity. The farmer is no longer strictly confined to one type of terrain, or one area. Within reasonable limits, he is free to exploit good soil wherever he finds it. So a little less vehemence, please, about urban sprawl gobbling up all the farm land—particularly when the vehemence is not entirely sincere.

The chief value of land remodeling is, however, neither soil and water conservation nor the creation of more cultivable land: it is the creation of large, flat, uniform surfaces for modern farm equipment. The larger the farm, the more economic justification for mechanization; this is the best—indeed, the only—way of saving time and labor. The tractor is perhaps the basic piece of mechanical field equipment; there are about five million of them in the United States. It is a capable and willing servant, but it is inclined to be exacting. Once it crept about the fields at five miles per hour; now it works at three times that rate. But in return it requires large fields of uniform level and texture, rectangular in layout. Thus, in addition to encouraging larger farms, mechanical equipment encourages an increasingly artificial topography. Nor is this the last of its demands; as it begins to take over more and more of the work once done by hired help—the planting of the seeds, weed control, fertilizing, cultivating, and harvesting—it insists on further changes. The human hand, however much it may cost per hour or per bushel, knows how to cope with unexpected irregularities: unevenness in the ground, plants not ripened or out of alignment. The harvesting machine is less tolerant and less adaptable: the seed has to be accurately planted and so spaced that the machine can deal with it. So with the advent of the newer, more complex processing machines there come into the landscape new kinds of rows, new spaces and intervals, and new locations for roads and irrigation apparatus.

The latest demand of the machine is the most revolutionary of all: it wants nothing less than new varieties of plants that are more uniform, easier to pick, and less perishable. The demand is being met with great dispatch; the University of California at Davis, concerned by the abrupt end of migratory labor, is undertaking to develop some twenty new varieties of commercially produced fruits and vegetables for harvesting machines. The assembled experts on soils, agricultural engineering, plant pathology, genetics, and dietetics hope to come up within the next two years with more amenable cantaloupes, lemon trees which grow to a prescribed height, grape bunches and strawberries with longer, more convenient stems. These varieties will in turn require new field layouts for irrigation and access, and new fertilizing and weed-killing techniques.

Once considered an unchanging element, the soil is now subject to drastic modification. The chemical fertilizers, which have only begun to come into their own, have made more intensive cultivation possible, and rotation of crops is much less significant in the maintenance of fertility. The ultimate in soil manipulation is probably the procedure followed in the Monrovia Nursery in California. All topsoil has been removed from the 250-acre tract, deposited in piles and chemically treated, then put in cans. Completely terraced and scraped, the land is merely a platform on which to set the plants and operate the nursery. To many commercial farmers, the soil has become one item in the production process—as much subject to improvement as is the machine or the crop itself.

In a much less familiar guise, the machine dominates another part of the farm: the headquarters. Swept clean of all the usual farmyard clutter of broken and obsolete equipment, chickens, haystacks, and manure, the area looks much like an industrial plant, with its long metal sheds and barns and its neatly parked farm equipment. But the machines which actually dominate the headquarters are not those on wheels; they are the working structures themselves.

The barn is not a shelter any more, it is a machine closely involved in the productive process. If we are prepared to accept that interpretation, then we are well on the way to understanding the nature of the revolution in the rural landscape. For much of this revolution is a matter of new definitions. A current writer on farm engineering makes two important points: "The escape of the tractor from its identity with the horse occurred when its design and use were related to the inherent utility it offered and not to replacement or substitution. . . . Structures today are evolving as units that contribute to the dynamics of farming. Many will become increasingly difficult to classify uniquely as structures or machines, and their function will range far beyond housing and storage." Viewed in this light, many new barns are machines which process their contents: provide animals with the correct amount of light and heat and air and space; preserve, prepare, and distribute feed. The best of them are designed by animal physiologists working with engineers and systems experts. In the future, they and their specialized equipment will be produced in factories and assembled on the farm; no doubt they will eventually be turned in for a newer model. What seems to be evolving in our new rural landscape is a form and concept of utilitarian architecture which the city as yet knows little about.

The structure ceases to be a shelter or a container and becomes the totally engineered artificial environment; the term could also be applied to the cultivated field. "The engineer and the farmer," the *Farm Quarterly* recently wrote, "have joined forces to control more completely the environment in which plants and animals are produced. The nutrient needs of animals and plants, the moisture requirements of plants and how to control them, have become valuable facets of farming. In the world of plants, the race has been to create through landforming, irrigation techniques, knowledge of weather patterns, the use of nutrients, spacing and environment which will permit each plant to approach its maximum potential. So too do animals respond to environment. Buildings are designed to allow concentration of animals, leading to increased production volume with less labor. . . . While facilities in many cases are designed to the requirements of plants and animals, in others the plant or animal is adapted to the facility." And the trend seems clearly to be in the latter direction: the modification of the animal or plant to suit the engineered environment. A professor in a midwestern agricultural college predicts that we will ultimately raise all our livestock in buildings, just the way we do chickens. When that day comes, there will be no more fences on the landscape.

Does all this sound like an up-to-date version of the factory in the fields? Is the landscape we have been describing really anything more than the impress of new food processing and distributing methods on agriculture, an essentially alien element in the rural scene? It is impossible to deny that the contemporary farmer is very much part of the world of chain stores, credit, government controls, technology. The hideous word *agribusiness* enjoys a wide popularity as the farmer seeks to identify himself with this other community, and he often seems proud of his new economic status; nothing irritates him more than wistful references to farming as a way of life. In current agricultural literature, there is a notable absence of any cult of agrarianism, any reference to those beliefs which only a century ago were so widely and proudly held: that the farmer, because of his hardy independence, his closeness to nature, his love of the land, was a superior type of American. Now the overriding theme is always the way the farmer can make both ends meet and plan for expansion. "How I Turned My Old Brood Sows into Dollars"—variations on this theme recur in every issue of every farm journal.

It is easy, therefore, for the outsider to pass severe judgment on the modern landscape and the men who are bringing it into being; the farmer has unwittingly created a very unattractive image of himself. It is likewise easy to dismiss this landscape as a violent modification of the natural environment entirely for the sake of more money, and with no thought of the long-range consequences. If this were indeed the basic motive of the American farmer, we would have good cause to fear for the future. Despite vastly increased agricultural yields and greatly improved techniques, there is a widespread conviction that the farmer's faith in chemical fertilizers, insecticides, growth stimulants, and genetic experimentation will eventually lead to disaster. And such easily observable practices as irrigation in regions of adequate rainfall, clean farming, continuous cultivation of one crop, increasingly narrow rows, convince casual observers that farmers are inspired entirely by eagerness for profits.

But even if all these procedures fail, we are not likely to see a return to traditional methods. And that is because the farmer, despite his bad public relations, is not entirely a businessman. He still is, and always will be, a designer of environments. His forebears were the same: they sought to design them according to what they conceived to be an order prescribed by nature or divine law; as a product of this century, the modern farmer is designing by means of constant experimentation. If present techniques backfire, he will not hesitate to drop them in favor of others. Dollars are what he is after, of course; but he is also after something like an insight into the truth.

Meanwhile, he appears to be formulating a highly intellectual, impersonal man-environment relationship which repels many because it is so at variance with the nature philosophy formulated by two centuries of urban culture. That is why it is dangerous to assume that the American countryside can continue to play its traditional role in the lives of city dwellers. When we take a second look, we are bound to recognize that the rural landscape now coming into existence has little to offer us in the way of pleasure or recreation.

It has nothing to offer the lover of romantic beauty or the seeker after undisturbed nature; it has nothing in the way of pleasure to offer the inhabitant of small country towns, or for that matter the farmer himself. Yet all of these need what the country used to provide. There are two solutions. One, advocated by the beautificationists, calls for introducing esthetic amenities throughout the landscape, a cosmetic treatment to disguise or at least adorn the workaday features of the country (tree planting, as might be expected, plays an important role). The other solution is to design and create on a large scale the appropriate settings for recreation and locate them near the engineered environment but not in it. It is essential that the two be kept distinct and separate; they should not overlap or blend.

There is plenty of room in our countryside for both kinds of landscape—the farmer's landscape of work, the city dweller's landscape of play, and there is plenty of talent among environmental designers to produce them. So far we have been singularly timid in America in creating artificial landscapes for recreation: the so-called English park is about as far as we have dared to go. But there is one lesson we can learn from the modern farmer: how comparatively easy it is to engineer the environment. There are few technological limits to our capacity to transform the land to suit our needs; all that is lacking are imagination and a sense of purpose.

"An Engineered Environment," *Landscape* 16, no. 1 (Autumn 1966): 16–20.

JBJ, photo, Main Street parade

# The Vernacular City

I live down three miles of dirt road, twelve miles from the nearest town, and that town is Santa Fe, New Mexico, with a population of less than fifty thousand. A very rural way of life, it has always seemed to me, yet going back over my activities during the last year I find that I have spent two days in each of the following American cities: Seattle, Miami, Atlanta, New York, Milwaukee, Minneapolis, Albuquerque, Chicago, and Berkeley, to say nothing of Winnipeg, a week in Paris, two months in Rome, and four days recently in London.

This represents a sizable amount of urban living, but I doubt if it is unusual. We all depend on cities now, even if we prefer not to live in them. We go to them for business or professional or health reasons; we go to conventions and trade exhibits, to hospitals and clinics, to universities and museums, and libraries and art galleries. Over the last generation, our cities have learned how to take care of our visits very well. We rent a car at the airport, go directly to the medical center or convention headquarters or campus or the downtown office. And nine times out of ten we find ourselves in a small, well-defined neighborhood with its own population, its own shops and restaurants, its own parking privileges, its own exclusiveness.

But that's the trouble. When we go to the city with one specific end in view, we see very little of it. This fragmentation of the American city is convenient, but it prevents us from exploring the place and discovering something of its character. And I'm afraid most of us dismiss American cities—always excepting San Francisco and New York and perhaps New Orleans—as very much alike. This is not how we experience a foreign city. When we spend a day or two in Paris or Rome or Munich or London, we come home with a variety of impressions as to how the city is put together and what makes it unique as an environment. But when we return from a two-day conference in St. Louis or Denver, what do we have to say of interest?

Yet what makes most modern American cities interesting in spite of their similarity is that they are not like cities in Europe or like American cities in the past: they are not pedestrian cities; they are not to be explored on foot. They have to be explored in a car, and even that takes time, because they stretch for miles and miles—street after street of one-story single-family houses. They are not for the casual nineteenth-century wanderer looking for picturesque architectural glimpses, but they are wonderfully impressive when you are traveling at a moderate thirty-five miles per hour.

My own conclusion, for what it is worth, is that almost all up-to-date American cities west of the Mississippi are variations on a basic prototype, and that prototype is Lubbock, Texas. I am not about to criticize Lubbock. Who can fail to like a city whose leading newspaper is named the *Daily Avalanche?* It is a city that a generation ago had a population of fifteen thousand; now it has a population of more than two hundred thousand. There is a new kind of city evolving in America, chiefly in the Sunbelt, and on a small scale Lubbock tells us what those new cities look like. In particular, it tells us about how the street, the road, the highway has taken the place of architecture as the basic visual element, the infrastructure of the city.

It is hard to say when this shift in emphasis first started. There are hints in the plan of Philadelphia drawn up in the late seventeenth century that the streets were to serve a new purpose: to allow for through traffic between the waterfronts of two rivers; and the grid system of Manhattan was supposed to do the same. On the other hand, all the other towns and cities in America well into the nineteenth century treated the street as a strictly local convenience. Visually speaking, the town was a compact composition of pitched roofs with brick chimneys, and here and there a white steeple or a belfry. It clustered around some feature of the landscape that could provide it with work—a good harbor, a navigable river, a waterfall. It was small but crowded, for people lived as near as they could to their place of work, and often on the floor above their workshop or office or store. Traffic, mostly pedestrian, was slow

and short-range. The town was still admired in terms of its houses and facades, its churches and other public buildings; streets merely provided access
to the individual holdings and had no character of their own. The city, in
other words, was seen as a kind of collective architectural monument.

Something of this point of view seems to linger in our universities: we
often have what we call a School of Architecture and City Planning, as if the
two were much the same. It seems to me we ought to have a School of Architecture and Landscape Architecture to take care of the design of buildings
in public spaces, and then another school—a School of City Planning and
Communications—to take care of the layout of streets and their change in
function. But most of us still like to visualize the city in terms of architecture—in terms of massive blocks of solid, well-designed buildings that we can
admire on foot.

We know what happened to that old-fashioned American city in the
years after the Civil War. The streetcar and railroad came; coal and gas and
electricity came. And the city found that it was free from the constraints that
geography and a primitive technology had imposed. It could abandon its traditional forms and relationships and expand in almost every direction. Mass
transportation gave people the freedom to live at some distance from their
place of work, and this was a freedom few of us had ever had before. In practice it was limited by the schedules and routes and fares of mass transportation
facilities, and limited by the accessibility of the workplace, but it destroyed the
homogeneity of the city and produced an ever-increasing number of specialized areas and neighborhoods based on income, on ethnic or religious background, on type of industry or type of business. It produced the streetcar suburbs that Sam Bass Warner has described.

The decay of the center of the city worried us most; every other change
represented progress and growth. One attempt to revive the center and restore
its prestige was the City Beautiful Movement. We could interpret those monumental plazas and the public buildings surrounding them as belated expressions of the belief that architecture, particularly classical architecture, is the
essence of the city. A much more significant phase of the movement was its
concern for enlarging the street for through traffic. Around the turn of the
century—well before the proliferation of automobiles—one American city
after another built handsome boulevards and parkways and formal avenues,
not only to make the downtown accessible but to reach out and attract the
new suburbs. It was as if the streets were at last being recognized as an element
in the city equal to the buildings. In fact, the street already had achieved a new

importance, partly because of the streetcar lines, but chiefly because the street (or the earth beneath its paved surface) contained all those utilities that had been introduced during the previous half-century: water and sewage disposal, gas lines, telephone, and electricity. These made the street more permanent than the houses flanking it.

Looking back on the American city of half a century ago, we can see how it was striving to overcome its old heritage and rebuild itself for mobility and greater accessibility for the automobile. One of the most vivid descriptions of the nineteenth-century city evolving in the direction of the Lubbock model is Sinclair Lewis' novel *Babbitt*. Babbitt was presumably a typical small businessman, a real estate operator, concerned with the development of Zenith, the city where he lived.

In 1923, the date of the writing of *Babbitt,* Zenith was a city of more than a hundred thousand, situated on a river somewhere in the Midwest. It was founded in 1797 and still liked to boast of its eastern or New England background, though it contained a sizable population of Italians and Slavs and blacks. Its background was agricultural, but it contained a steel mill, several dairy plants, lumber mills, and a variety of unspecified smaller industries. It already had become a financial center and boasted of the second-highest office building west of the Ohio. The railroad passed through the heart of the city, the mills and industrial plants were near the tracks, and block after block of small frame houses for the workers surrounded the factories. The whole area constituted a special part of Zenith: uninviting, dirty, smoky, inhabited by foreigners, and vaguely out of bounds to Babbitt.

Babbitt lived in a pleasant middle-class district known as Floral Heights —not a suburb in the modern sense, for it was only a ten-minute drive from the office, but a district of predominantly Dutch colonial houses with lawns and tree-lined streets and a wide view over the city with its dramatic skyline. Farther away there was an upper-class suburb called Royal Ridge, inhabited by bankers and important executives who lived in large architect-designed mansions and who were driven to work by chauffeurs. Royal Ridge had an expensive and exclusive country club, but the center of Floral Heights, socially speaking, was the church. Finally, along the streetcar lines that stretched out in every direction from the city, there were long strung-out suburbs of more modest dwellings, interspersed with empty lots, cemeteries, an occasional store or garage. One gathers that in the heart of Zenith there were the remains of an older residential section: a collection of ornate Victorian houses, all of which had fallen on evil days and had become boarding houses or funeral homes.

The Zenith of sixty years ago had certain peculiar traits. Though it had five newspapers, it had no radio station, no television, no airport. Streetcars circulated on Main Street. There were two large hotels: the Grand (which dated from the 1880s and was patronized by cattle dealers who spent the day in the overstuffed chairs in the lobby) and the Thornleigh. The Thornleigh was new and elegant: it had an oak-paneled grill, and in its ballroom were held all the fashionable events of Zenith society. Near the station in the center of town was a flourishing skid row, largely inhabited by that vagabond population Lewis described as "shabby young men who prowl ceaselessly from state to state, in the power of the wanderlust. They wear sateen shirts and carry bundles. . . . They crowd the smoking cars at night; they sit silent on benches in filthy stations . . . in a hundred cities they see only the employment agencies, the all-night lunches, the blind pigs, the scabrous lodging houses."

At the other end of the social scale in Zenith are the fortunate inhabitants of Royal Ridge—people who attend concerts and theatrical performances of New York companies; people who travel east for the summer, go to Europe, and send their sons east to college. Babbitt himself went to the State University located fifteen miles south of Zenith at the end of the streetcar line—a university of about fifteen thousand students. Most of the students lived in boarding houses. For good times the students took the streetcar to Zenith and ate in the German beer restaurants.

Babbitt's son, Theodore Roosevelt Babbitt, was destined to go to the State University. At the age of sixteen, all he was interested in was auto mechanics, and he dreamt of the day when he would own a twin-six Packard. His sister (with whom he disputed the use of the one bathroom every morning) was interested in yoga and in Kahlil Gibran.

It is hard to reconstruct certain aspects of the Zenith of sixty years ago, largely because Lewis was so determined to make Babbitt a loud-mouthed real estate operator interested only in being one of the boys at the Downtown Athletic Club. But I have researched Zenith in those years, and I can say that the city and its citizens were by no means as complacent as Sinclair Lewis implies. I have in fact been reading issues of several nationally circulated magazines for the year 1923, with an occasional glance at the years before and after.

Briefly, Zenith was concerned about the growth of the city. This was the time—no doubt because of the rapid growth in the population of every

American city—when real estate activity was assuming a new and much more powerful role. A writer on *City Growth and Values* noted in 1923:

> Fifty years ago, in the larger cities subdivisions were marketed by individuals who seldom platted more than a few acres at a time, lots which were sold in a leisurely and prosaic manner. Lot buyers contracted directly with carpenter contractors to build their homes. . . . For the past decade or two [in other words, since World War I] real estate development has expanded from a small one man affair to expert operators and great corporations which function on a large scale. . . . Hundreds of acres are sometimes included in modern allotments. Building operations often are conducted by the same company, not so much for the profit from building but rather for the purpose of establishing the character of the subdivision.

And this new scale and new attitude toward community character accounted for the type of suburb or housing subdivision that was beginning to crop up all around Zenith. It also accounted for Babbitt's displeasure with the so-called traction gang—the street railway company. They were refusing, because of the expense, to build new lines that would open up new suburban territories for development. They preferred the long, thin kind of development; and since most of the new home owners did not own cars, they were dependent on the streetcar lines.

In the meantime, the big real estate developers were building whole new communities for the well-to-do. The most sensational example was the Kansas City Country Club development, a prize specimen of large-scale suburban planning, built by J. C. Nichols. Nichols, seeing the success of his Country Club addition, announced in that same year of 1923 that he was going to build what he called a "shopping center" for his clients—a collection of shops and stores and parking facilities to serve the somewhat isolated inhabitants of his upper-class utopia, to spare them the necessity of having to go downtown.

All real estate dealers and developers and planners were also interested in such developments as John Nolan's model suburban village of Mariemont, outside of Cincinnati, an experiment which was to pay for itself, since it was to cater to the upper-middle-class family. And there was the thirty-five-million-dollar project of Palos Verdes near Los Angeles designed by F. L. Olmsted, Jr., which promised to be one of the most beautiful, most completely planned and controlled of all suburbs.

These developments produced a more respectful attitude toward city planning, and more than one agency, public or private, tried to forecast and control future growth. The highway and street departments believed that traffic counts were the answer. All attempts to understand and regulate the city were helped immensely by a new device—the aerial photograph. This use was first suggested in 1923 at a town planning conference in Paris, and it was soon in wide use. In the same year there appeared a book of two thousand air views of the best country homes in California and the East, a publication enthusiastically received by landscape architects and architects alike; the world was revealed in a totally new and objective way.

It was in 1916 that the automobile was recognized by planners as a factor in city growth. In that year the New York planner Nelson Lewis first suggested that the automobile would have a profound and probably beneficial effect on the American city. It would, he said, produce better-lighted, better-paved, broader streets; land values would be more diffused and there would be less centralization. People would know their city better. The only two dangers he foresaw were too great an emphasis on speed, and traffic jams where various types of vehicles tried to use the same street. So it was all the more important to segregate work and office and residential areas to prevent a confusion of trucks and horse-drawn wagons and streetcars.

The visible result of this interest in planning, in Zenith and elsewhere, was a concern for better streets and roads. Zenith removed objectionable overhead wires and objectionable poles. The widening of Woodward Boulevard in Detroit to make a divided artery, sixteen miles long, with a streetcar line in the median, was seen as the greatest triumph of planning for the year 1923. Streetlights were redesigned so that they illumined the street rather than the sidewalk. Curb gas pumps, common throughout America, were gradually outlawed, not only as fire hazards but as traffic hazards. In Zenith, as in hundreds of American town and cities, there were new restrictions on the inappropriate use of the street. Pushcarts were outlawed, even though in the poorer sections of town they served as grocery stores; jitney stands and taxi stands were prohibited, and so was parking.

Even small country towns around Zenith painted slots along the streets where cars could park. Highway departments, always eager to expand their territory, suggested that the surface of the streets be used for directional information—painted large on the black asphalt. And one indication of the growing dignity of the road or street was the gesture of an Ohio banker who gave thirty thousand dollars to buy bricks for a four-mile stretch of country highway. He said he considered this a more fitting kind of generosity than giving the money to a college or a library or a hospital; and the town duly erected a marker with a bronze plaque at the beginning of the new highway.

The difference between the fictitious Zenith and the Lubbock of my dreams is obvious, but not always easy to explain. Many of us have lived in Zenith, or what remains of it after half a century. It has been the background of our younger years and inevitably has affected our definition of the city. The prototypical Lubbock—elements of which we find in Phoenix and Wichita and Denver and Albuquerque and Houston and many other western cities— is still evolving. And what it will eventually become is a mystery to most of us.

But one difference between the two kinds of cities is in the way they start out. Zenith, with its vaunted New England background, slowly expanded from a village center, an area of carefully measured plots of land where every resident had a permanent place. The newer kind of city comes into existence simultaneously over a wide area—a scatteration of structures with no real focal point. The difference, as I see it, is largely a matter of the function of roads. In the old town, roads followed property lines and were vaguely connected with *one* artery to the outside world. The outlying suburbs evolved only when roads or streets were extended. But the new city grows a web of streets long before houses appear. In the beginning, there is nothing more than the interstate. Suddenly there comes an interchange, like a break in a dam or in a river bank. In no time a flood of artifacts submerges the hitherto flat and empty countryside: swarms of trailers and bulldozers and power poles and storage facilities; the rows of small, identical dwellings; gas stations, churches, used car lots, and a Holiday Inn; and a broad main street with one high-rise; more houses, more high-rises, more storage buildings; and in a year or two, more interchanges. Suddenly there is a city which no one, even a hundred miles away, had ever heard of before. It is in reality a loose constellation of developments and subdivisions and shopping centers connected by streets or thoroughfares. As Gurney Brackenfeld says in his essay in the book entitled *The Rise of the Sunbelt Cities,* "With the great shift to moving goods and people by truck and automobiles . . . the population of the new urban form created by the super shopping centers—an intricate and compact orchestration of *mixed* land uses—is precisely what used to make downtowns lively and attractive. . . . They were not conceived and constructed in order to transform the structure of our metropolitan centers. But that has been the result. And now that billions of dollars of investment have hardened the new urban form into steel, glass, and concrete, we will have to live with the result for decades whether we like it or not."

But whether we do like the Lubbock-style city depends on whether we enjoy seeing it, visiting it briefly, and remembering it. Frontier crudity is a thing of the past. Every self-respecting and prosperous new city in the West has its tree-embowered suburbs, its branch of Nieman Marcus, its ballet. There is a restaurant, slowly revolving on top of the tallest building, from which you can see the brilliantly lighted strip developments reaching out in every direction.

Yet to me (and I imagine to many others) the really interesting attraction is the priority of the thoroughfare—street or boulevard or limited-access highway—over the architectural elements in the city. Zenith vaguely recognized the potential importance of the thoroughfare. Babbitt waited for the trolley car to open up new areas for development. Now the highway department waits for developments to catch up with the latest divided highway built into the hinterland. It does not have to wait for long. The street has always brought certain essential services and utilities with it, but over the past generation it has evolved into an extremely efficient instrument for continual change and development.

Many of us still think of the origin of the street—when we think of it at all—as a process in which a space slowly evolves out of the path or roadway, a utility is adjusted to the needs of its users. But the contemporary street, especially the new street, is more like an environmental force, a river or torrent, that has to be controlled with a definite policy in view. And to many municipal authorities it represents the most effective way of handling the city and its growth. Such apparently minor changes in its functioning as the installation of traffic lights, the outlawing of parking, the change to one-way traffic, the building of a median, can strangle a whole business section, cause a residential neighborhood to blossom, and send a score of drive-in businesses into bankruptcy. The source of this power is obvious: since almost everyone now has a car, we are free to travel in the city when and where we please. Mass transportation (and before that, pedestrian travel) made for urban predictability and stability. Our allegiance was something which the parish church, the corner grocery, the neighborhood could count on, and the morphology of the city changed very slowly. But now that we have our own private transportation and are called "mobile consumers," we think nothing of traveling to a supermarket that has better parking rather than to one located two miles nearer. Retail establishments along the thoroughfares must learn to attract our business in a way they never had to do when customers were confined to a certain familiar area.

The pursuit of profits, and even survival, in a retail business firm cater-ing to the mobile consumer—the consumer who arrives in a car and is some-times served in the car—has transformed the design and relationship of streetside business establishments in a remarkable manner. The continuous fa-cade of the traditional retail street has been fragmented by parking lots, drive-in facilities, conspicuous signage, and in many cases remodeling to provide open space in the front—either for better visibility or for more convenient ac-cess. Visual competition with neighboring establishments has replaced a re-spect for architectural conformity, and we can even say that the architecture of the strip has invaded many downtown areas aspiring to woo the mobile con-sumer. The adaptations are based on traffic counts, traffic speed, type of pub-lic, placement on the street or road, and above all on visibility, accessibility, and parking.

I find this kind of building worth studying, first because it is spreading throughout highway-oriented America—not only in the West, with its new, highly mobile cities, but also in vacation areas and along the interstate at in-terchanges. I also find it interesting because I believe it represents a new and valid form of what can be called commercial vernacular. My own definition of vernacular architecture describes it as a form of building that is temporary, utilitarian, unorthodox in style, and often unorthodox in construction. Ver-nacular, as I understand it, does not aspire to express universal principles of design; it is contingent; it responds to environmental influences—social as well as natural—and alters as those influences alter. Its attachment to place is strictly pragmatic.

But we should bear in mind that the vernacular is only one response, ar-chitecturally speaking, to the thoroughfare. Lubbock, along with its sister cities, contains a growing amount of architecture that responds to the power and menace of the street by *turning away* from it. This kind of architecture, usually corporate or public and occasionally residential, strives to free itself from a subordinate role to the street. The large building—office or hotel or bank—has often declared its independence of the uninterrupted flow of traf-fic and joined with other similar buildings to form a self-contained complex with its own surrounding buffer zone, its own orientation, its own patterns of movement: office complexes, shopping complexes, sports and convention complexes, and campuses. A prestigious business address is no longer, say, 111 Lincoln Street; it is American Insurance Square or First National Plaza. Texas seems to favor "Tower" as a desirable address, but the principle is the same: the building is liberated from the tyranny of the street and begins to assert itself as architecture, as an autonomous environment within the city. This is most evident in the new downtown areas, with their groupings of high-rise buildings and pedestrian facilities. It is no less evident, though much less spectacular, in our more modest residential areas, with rows of small houses, each with its own way of protecting itself against the stream of traffic. But we seldom have time to dwell on these elements in the contemporary city: the street and its traffic call for all of our attention.

"The Vernacular City," *Center* 1 (1985): 27–43.

JBJ, watercolor, road, 1979

## Roads Belong in the Landscape

Which came first, the house or the road leading to the house? Medieval scholars with their love for origins and symbols may well have long wrestled with the question, eventually coming up with a theological counterquestion: Which of the two objects had been divinely ordained to *be* first? It could have been reasoned that if God had meant us to stay home, to be sedentary, to put down roots as farmers or husbands (a word which once signified house-dwellers), he would have first commanded us to build a house. But if he had intended us to be forever on the move—hunters or herders or pilgrims in search of an elusive goal—he would have ordered us to beat a path, to make a road and follow it.

In medieval times, the past was seen as a series of migrations and invasions, of endless wanderings over the face of the earth. But in later, more settled centuries, the above question was interpreted in more mundane terms: the one coming first would not necessarily have been the earliest but the one conferring power and prestige; and from that point of view "house" was the right answer. House is much more than shelter. It implies a territory, a small sovereignty with its own laws and customs, its own history, its own jealously guarded boundaries. House stands for family, for dynasty. However modest it may be, it still has its place in the elaborate spatial hierarchy of the European world: kingdoms, principalities, domains—then the house.

Compared with these attributes—still venerated—what could the road offer by way of qualifications for first place? Certainly it played an important role in our daily comings and goings: it might even be said that it was the road which first brought us together in a group or society. Yet the purpose of every road or lane or path is to lead to a destination, and the question itself presupposes a house. So the true function of the road is to serve us by taking us home. Without a specific destination, a road has no reason for existing. Left to its own devices it tends to wander into the wider environment and disappear. It has another tendency, much more dangerous: to introduce unwanted outsiders into the self-sufficient community or house. Finally, theology again enters the picture. The first man to hit the road was Cain, the murderer of his brother, and cursed to be a fugitive and a vagabond; Cain, the first man to build a city.

Disqualified by its own genealogy, outclassed by the prestige of private space, the road has long suffered from neglect by historians and students of the landscape: dismissed as an unsightly, elongated, crooked space used by merchants and ravaging armies and highway robbers, whereas the house (as we learn from Joseph Rykwert's essay *Adam's House in Paradise*[1]) has become the symbol of arcadian simplicity and innocence.

That simple question, at least in its cryptic form, is one we no longer bother to answer. We are now less interested in origins than in what comes after: specifically, the relationship over time between these two familiar features of the landscape. The relationship has never been easy. We are just emerging from a centuries-long period when the road was subservient to place and given little respect. Today, a hundred years after the invention of the automobile, the question would be answered in favor of the road—or its modern version, the highway—which continues to weave a tight, intricate web over every landscape in the Western world and has spawned a whole breed of roadlike spaces—railroad lines, pipelines, power lines, flight lines, assembly lines. Now the question demands a very different sort of answer: Which do we value more, a sense of place or a sense of freedom? What clouds the debate is the insistence by both parties on defining the road as a disturber of the peace, an instigator of radical change: welcome change in the eyes of the land developer and traffic engineer and urban reformer; in the eyes of the environmentalist and history buff, change as the destroyer of privacy and the acceptable status quo.

The answer will come when we define or redefine the road as it exists in

JBJ, photo, road

the contemporary world; when we recognize that roads and streets and alleys and trails can no longer be identified solely with movement from one place to another. Increasingly they are the scene of work and leisure and social intercourse and excitement. Indeed, they have often become for many the last resort for privacy and solitude and contact with nature. Roads no longer merely lead to places; they *are* places. And as always they serve two important roles: as promoters of growth and dispersion, and as magnets around which new kinds of development can cluster. In the modern landscape, no other space has been so versatile.

Odology is the science or study of roads or journeys and, by extension, the study of streets and superhighways and trails and paths, how they are used, where they lead, and how they come into existence. Odology is part geography, part planning, and part engineering—engineering as in construction, and unhappily as in social engineering as well. That is why the discipline has a brilliant future. When archaeologists uncover a pre-Columbian road system in a Central American jungle and speculate about its economic or military origin, when geographers study the environmental impact of a new highway in an isolated region, and when a city council decides to change a two-way street into a one-way street, they are all thinking in odological terms: in terms of the function of the road in question, in terms of its impact on the landscape, and in terms of traffic.

They are thus thinking in a strictly modern manner. It is only within the last two centuries that we have recognized the wisdom of building roads to last and of building them to serve a specific type of traffic. It was when commercial vehicular traffic increased (as a consequence of industrialization) that we gave thought to their location and subsequent maintenance. In the eighteenth century something like a science of road and highway engineering finally emerged.

But a further stage in the evolution of odological techniques came after World War II, when an immense increase in heavy automobile traffic took place throughout the world. The old nineteenth-century definition of road— "a passage between two places, wide and level enough to accommodate vehicles as well as horses and persons traveling on foot"—proved inadequate. We now see the highway as an essential element in the national or regional infrastructure, and the solution to problems of congestion and surface deterioration is no longer the building of more (increasingly costly) highways but the controlled and efficient use of those we have.

Consequently, contemporary odology involves much more than improved methods of construction and maintenance; it devises new traffic control systems, separate networks for different kinds of traffic, greater control over roadside and road-oriented development, and higher user fees; and we may soon reach the point in metropolitan areas of giving priority in the design and location of roads to odological rather than environmental factors.

We do not always give credit to how the motorized American—commuter, tourist, truck driver—has accepted the new odology, how docile we have been in complying with the scientific definition of the highway as a managed authoritarian system of steady, uninterrupted flow for economic benefits. Within a few decades we have learned to abandon our traditional attitudes toward the road and to adopt new driving skills, new ways of coping with traffic, a whole new code of highway conduct and highway law; learned to accept without questioning a vast and growing assortment of edicts indicated by signs and lights and symbols and inscriptions on the surface of the road itself. We have learned to drive defensively and to outwit traffic jams and lurking policemen. We have also learned to take advantage of the proliferation of high-

JBJ, sketch, freeway overpass, 1993

way-oriented businesses and diversions and to discover the joys of speeding, of seeing the landscape flash by at an inhuman rate. We have become so submissive that radical odologists are encouraged to propose further electronic controls within our own vehicles, further restrictions on our use of the highway, further tolls and fees.

That is the price we pay for uninterrupted steady flow, and no doubt the price is reasonable. But odologists seem to forget—and we ourselves sometimes forget—that the road serves other needs. For untold thousands of years we traveled on foot over rough paths and dangerously unpredictable roads, not simply as peddlers or commuters or tourists, but as men and women for whom the path and road stood for some intense experience: freedom, new human relationships, a new awareness of the landscape. The road offered a journey into the unknown that could end up allowing us to discover who we were and where we belonged. . . .

"Two roads diverged in a yellow wood / And sorry I could not travel both / And be one traveler. . . ." Robert Frost's poem "The Road Not Taken" has implications transcending the individual experience. It tells us of the dilemma of living in a world where there is no longer the one right way, the

JBJ, photo, bridge construction

royal road to happiness and success, a path to the Heavenly City. Whichever road we take ultimately leads us to the agonizing moment of private decision. As with Saul of Tarsus, the road to Damascus may lie straight ahead, but it is only in the course of the journey that we discover our true destination.

"Roads Belong in the Landscape," from *A Sense of Place, a Sense of Time* (New Haven: Yale University Press, 1994), excerpt, 189–92, 205.

## Truck City

Today there are more than 180 million cars in the United States. In 1908 there were fewer than 200,000. Two years later there were close to half a million. For the next few years the number increased annually by more than a third.

From the beginning Americans were fascinated by the automobile, though few families could afford to buy one; when the average worker earned a dollar a day, a medium-priced automobile, costing more than a thousand dollars, was clearly only for the rich. Yet the thought of how the automobile was going to transform and enrich American life was stimulating, and we followed every step in its evolution. We discussed speed records, endurance records; we applauded improvements in the motor, and the daredevil feats of drivers and racers. We were especially interested in elegance of design, and what we most admired was the passenger car, also known as the touring or pleasure car. The rich and sporting element in American society adopted the automobile because of the mobile and adventurous way of life it fostered. The social pages gave details of the groups of fans, the meets and rallies of exclusive automobile clubs, and told of who had attended the *concours d'élégance*. Academics and admirers of the traditional rural culture sought to turn us away from the automobile: in 1906 Woodrow Wilson declared that the automobile represented an ostentatious display of wealth, threatening to incite envy and class feeling; but the opposite proved true: we loved the passenger car and dreamt of when we too could own one.

So much favorable publicity had the effect of rousing general interest in the manufacture and sale of automobiles. Investors and manufacturers and engineers soon took the new invention seriously and promoted research and experimentation. Yet the greatest appeal lay in the kind of lifestyle it promised: the dawning century was to see a new culture, emancipated, healthy, infinitely mobile, and promising hitherto unknown pleasures and experiences—all because of the automobile.

The commercial automobile, however—the bus, the taxi, and especially the truck—were all excluded from this cordial welcome. In 1910 there were only eight thousand trucks in the country, and most were so uncouth in appearance, so disappointing in performance, that they belonged in a special category. In the years before World War I, it was the custom among the drivers of passenger cars to show their solidarity by tipping their hats to one another. (A similar custom prevailed until recently among motorcyclists.) But the drivers of trucks and vans were never included in this exchange of high signs. Given the social implications of the passenger car, it is easy to understand the discrimination, for the passenger car stood for a leisurely suburban or rural existence, based on family togetherness, love of nature, and a good income. The truck, on the other hand, stood for work, and work of a menial kind.

The word *truck* had been used in colonial times to describe a heavy wagon capable of carrying a load. With the coming of the automobile, we redefined the word to describe an *automotive* vehicle designed to carry a load, and that is still the accepted definition. It is a poor one, nevertheless, for it is used to include the pickup, the van, the minivan, and even the jeep; these are all supposed to be trucks. But in fact, in everyday parlance we almost always use the word *truck* to mean a large vehicle which can haul heavy loads for some distance, and does so *for pay*. Vernacular usage often defines an object— whether a house or a car or a piece of furniture—not by how it is *made* but by how it is *used*, and most trucks are used to make money. To be sure, there are marginal cases: the pickup, like the jeep, is now undergoing a process of suburban gentrification: both are popular in leisure activities and in certain off-beat sports. At one time the station wagon was a modest passenger car equipped with extra seats and was called a depot van. It was a money-making vehicle then, but look at it now!

Many of those eight thousand trucks in 1910 were small electric delivery trucks, used by such businesses as laundries and bakeries and dairies, and by the U. S. Post Office, for making daily deliveries along established city routes. They were a great improvement over the horse-drawn wagons or surreys or buggies previously used. They made no noise, they did not smell, they were easy to drive, and very sturdy. In appearance they resembled the horse-drawn wagon, and in passenger cars this last feature appealed (so we are told) to that die-hard element which was still pro-horse and anti-automobile.

But the electric van or truck had a serious shortcoming: it ran on batteries (large and heavy, slung under the chassis) which had to be frequently recharged. At best they could go eighty miles without having to turn in at one of the infrequent recharge stations, and the operation took time and cost fifteen dollars. Largely because of the weight of the batteries, the electric truck had trouble climbing hills. Finally, it was expensive. No working man could think of buying one and going into the delivery business on his own. But would he have wanted to? Driving an electric delivery van for pay, even if only a dollar a day, probably had its appeal. It was safe, relaxing, and without surprises. But Americans even in those days had a distinct impression that the automobile represented freedom and personal responsibility. A vehicle like the electric van which had to stay in the city and abide by a fixed routine was in a class with the railroad train or the streetcar: confined to a track and a timetable. In any case, as gas trucks and passenger cars became cheaper and more efficient, the electric car dropped out of favor. It lingered until 1925 as a sedan, small and elegant and eminently suited to lady drivers. Then it too vanished.

There remained that other contingent out of the original eight thousand trucks. They were gasoline-powered, and in fact the gasoline truck had been around as long as the gasoline passenger car. But it had failed to show early promise. For one thing, it had been given none of that encouragement lavished on the passenger car by social and financial leaders. No one attended the strenuous truck endurance runs, and the press had little to say about the experimental models being produced by amateurs: inventors, mechanics, retired bicycle makers, dedicated tinkerers working in stables and blacksmith shops, or on the road. A few manufacturers of trucks produced a dozen or more examples, then went bankrupt or were bought out. There were no standard parts, only parts taken from carriages or pieces of machinery. Trucks often unhappily resembled in appearance the conventional wagon—wheels, dashboard, and all—nor did they always perform much better, for they were slow and heavy, far heavier than the load they carried. Steel-rimmed wheels gave little traction on the smooth city streets, and motors deficient in power prevented them from traveling on rough and muddy country roads. It was generally agreed that all these hybrid vehicles could be used for was hauling freight from the railroad station to the factory or the warehouse, or making routine deliveries, like the electric van, within the city.

Trucks in those early years were usually owned by shipping or distributing firms, or by such public agencies as police and fire departments. They were too expensive, too unreliable for the average small business. They operated in fleets: each morning, would-be truck drivers went to the yard where the motley collection of trucks was parked and waited to be given a job for the day. At that period most drivers knew nothing about maintaining and repairing a truck, especially if it was one they had never driven before, and often they returned their vehicles at the end of the day in bad condition. Strictly speaking, the truck driver was an unskilled day laborer, easily replaced. He was assigned a clumsy, unfamiliar tool to do a job which for him had no future, and his status was not much higher than that of the factory hand or field hand. He was paid two dollars for a twelve-hour day.

The trucking industry might well have continued in that manner: with fleets of trucks operating like the old fleets of taxis. But two surprising developments occurred. First, the truck became a versatile and adaptable piece of mechanical equipment, capable of doing much more than simply hauling heavy loads and coming back empty. Second, it broke away from centralized control and in time provided many men with small businesses of their own. It thus became an important part of an American vernacular way of life, and remains so to this day.

In these transformations the manufacturers at first played a minor role. Most of the experimentation came from small-time mechanics and engineers, and it was they who in effect created a whole new industry—not a cottage industry but a garage industry; it was largely they who produced the modern truck.

Many were farmers, for farmers were acquainted with stationary engines long before they had seen automobiles. They were part-time mechanics, electricians, tinsmiths, blacksmiths, and had already automated much of their work. It was natural for them to experiment and find out how this new machine could be used for other purposes. One problem was getting their vegetables and dairy products promptly to city markets. Railroad schedules were often inconvenient and involved time-consuming transfers and delays. It was a master blacksmith in a small Wisconsin farm town who first produced the four-wheel drive, which enabled trucks to negotiate bad roads and cut across fields, pick up the produce, and take it directly to the distributor. It was another small-town mechanic who built the first auto trailer, which often doubled the truck's capacity. In 1915 pneumatic tires were introduced, and another now forgotten innovator gave the truck headlights, enabling it to travel by night; others devised the dump truck and the truck with a low bed for loading heavy loads and for dockside loading. None of these were technological breakthroughs, but they contributed to a redefinition of the truck, and eventually to its being used for more than simply transportation. Its increasing versatility made it essential in heavy construction, in road building, and in the extraction of hitherto inaccessible natural resources—in oil fields and forests located in rough terrain where the railroad could not go.

The Ford Model T, introduced in 1908, proved to be particularly useful on the farm. Though strictly speaking it was a small passenger car, any ingenious owner could transform it into a pickup truck for carrying produce or even transporting livestock. Once a pulley was attached to the crankshaft or rear axle, the Model T provided power for sawing wood, pumping water, grinding feed, or furnishing electric light in emergencies. In the 1920s several farm equipment firms offered attachments designed to turn the Model T into a cultivator or tractor; but these proved impractical.

There is undoubtedly an axiom to the effect that any tool which has proved efficient in accomplishing its original function is to be used for some other, totally unrelated job—and used successfully. That would account for the truck, even before it was twenty years old, being used as a snow plow, as a digger of post holes, as a road grader, as a temporary platform for derricks, and as a source of emergency power. More important, it was also used not simply to *carry* a load but to *process* or modify the load, even as it traveled on the highway. The mobile cement mixer, familiar to us all, appeared as early as 1916, and the refrigerator truck (controlling the temperature of its load) appeared in 1920. The modern ambulance is actually a truck equipped to give medical aid to its passenger. The evolution of the truck has not come to an end; and while the passenger car, no matter how luxurious, remains faithful to its original function of carrying passengers, the truck has in many instances become a part-time office, or a part-time workshop, part-time operations center, and part-time sleeping quarters. The introduction of the two-way radio and car phone has given the truck and its driver a greater freedom of movement and of decision making; so much so that it can be said of certain trucks that they are actually small mobile business or service establishments; and a large element in urban traffic consists of such mobile workplaces.

By the 1930s the truck had become a much more sophisticated vehicle: larger, more reliable, more powerful, and more sightly. Even though trucks constituted only a minority of automobiles, they had become increasingly essential in many types of business enterprises, largely because they could accommodate small loads at short notice and could go directly to the customer. Their final acceptance as a form of commercial transportation—for short distances in partnership with railroads—came in the late 1930s.

At that period the typical American factory was likely to be a multistoried brick building with many windows located in the built-up downtown section, as near as possible to the railroad. At that time that was the best place to be; for transportation for both raw materials and the finished product, access to local supplies of coal. The labor force, living nearby, often came to work on foot. Multistory construction, caused by lack of space, allowed for gravity flow in the manufacturing process, and usually allowed for the use of natural light—hence the many windows.

But by the 1920s there were reasons for changing the layout. The automobiles of commuting office workers crowded the narrow downtown streets and made shipping and receiving a nightmare for factories. New machinery called for sturdier construction; yet there was no room for expansion. No doubt the most compelling reason for wanting change were the new theories of industrial organization propounded by F. W. Taylor and his followers. Though primarily meant to introduce more efficient work methods, Taylor's "scientific management" involved a radical reorganization of the industrial plant itself. It proposed a factory layout emphasizing continuous, uninterrupted *horizontal* flow in the whole production process, a speedy in-and-out of raw materials and finished products, and a great reduction in storage and space for storage. The assembly line, introduced by Ford in 1913, was the logical product of Taylor's management methods.

Scientific management proved to be a popular idea, and it was not long before new industries and the older and larger ones started to move out of the congested city into the outskirts, where space was available.

Remote from the built-up city streets and from the railroad lines, there soon emerged many examples of the kind of factory and warehouse we are now familiar with: one-story constructions, often windowless, with vast interior spaces interrupted by a few reinforced-concrete or steel columns or uprights—where a variety of mobile conveyors and forklifts and miniature industrial tractors can circulate freely. The light, whether from skylights or artificial, is diffused and the pattern of movement is everywhere horizontal.

JBJ, photo, "Truck Plaza"

Unlike the situation in the center of the city, here in the open landscape the factories are not close together. Surrounded by their own spacious territory, they sit some distance from one another, many with well-kept lawns and trees. With no water tower, no smoking chimneys, only a discreet sign next to an imposing entrance driveway, they often have an institutional appearance, as if they were centers of research.

Here the truck comes into the picture: not one truck, but trucks by the dozens—in some cases large trailer-tractor units capable of hauling thirty tons or more—immaculate, identical, are backed up in a row against the long loading dock.

The loading dock is a feature of the modern factory not much discussed in architectural circles, but it is not only an essential part of the building, it has to be designed and built with great precision. Its level and the level of the truck waiting to be loaded (or unloaded) have to be the same; the continuous horizontal movement of the interior has to be extended by means of forklifts into the truck itself. The loading dock in turn relates to the vast space surrounding the plant devoted to the parking and maneuvering of the trucks, as well as to the parking of the employees' cars. Finally, the whole complex leads out to the highway. Loading docks, along with extensive parking areas, are

something new in factory layouts, and what has evolved is an industrial structure with two facades: one for the offices and the formal entrance, the other
for shipping and unloading. This obvious arrangement has now become general in all establishments depending on commercial vehicle traffic: the dark
and rubbish-littered rear area in the factory complex is a thing of the past.

The road which the flow of trucks follows until it reaches the interstate
passes through an empty and spacious landscape of isolated factories, truck
terminals, warehouses with a scattering of road-oriented service stations,
trailers, landfills, and what were once fields: a landscape waiting not to be
lived in but to be built on; deserted after work hours and dominated by the
curving pattern of roads and projected roads, power lines, and billboards saying 12.75 ACRES AVAILABLE, ZONED C; with not a pedestrian in sight. We have
all passed through this landscape on our way to the airport or to the interstate.

Have we forgotten how we responded to that landscape when it was only
beginning to take form a half-century ago? In those years after World War II,
we were on the lookout for a new world of peace and prosperity and leisure,
and that new landscape contained many elements which we thought held
promise. That was when the general public first became aware of what we
then called "modernistic architecture"—the International Style; and those
one-story factories stripped of ornament, functional in layout, helped us understand and accept the new idiom. Commenting on the modern horizontal
industrial factory, John B. Rae wrote that "the modern warehouse is no longer
a store house but a 'transit shed' for continuous inventory replenishment.
More space is devoted to processing orders, docks, and aisles for self-propelled
vehicles than to actual storage."[1] That absence of storage space and the emphasis on flow was typical of the factory as well, but the average American was
already familiar with other versions of the transit shed: the supermarket, the
drive-in restaurant, the great variety of businesses from the liquor store to the
bank where customers as well as goods and services were part of the environment organized for flow and the elimination of storage or time-consuming
transactions. Instinctively, we discerned in the new landscape and its buildings
aspects of a bright future.

We marveled at the new roads and highways, anti-urban in their green,
semipastoral margins and in their rejection of the grid. The large-scale sweep
of the new interstates, with their cloverleafs and overpasses and their steady,
uninterrupted flow, reminded us of the visionary displays of the road of the
future in the Futurama of the 1939 World's Fair: bypassing the city, heading

out into the green countryside, where housing developments and trailer courts spoke of young families starting out in life.

What gave the new industrialized landscape style was the presence—in parking lots, lined up at loading docks, barreling along the new white highways—of trucks: enormous and sleek and shiny. Since we ourselves had cars and went to work in cars, we felt an affinity with the burgeoning truck culture of truck stops identified with home-style southern food and truckers' songs in the juke box; for the trucker was replacing the cowboy as folk hero. Watching the evolution of the drive-in, driving through the highway-dominated landscape with its new spaces, its brightly colored signs and structures, seemed a good way of observing our progress toward a new social order.

It cannot be said that this response represented a conscious rejection of the traditional landscape order; but it is not totally remote from the visions of the future propagated by the design professions. In the popular vision of the new city, there were elements—distorted and oversimplified—of Ebenezer Howard's Garden City, of Le Corbusier, even of Lewis Mumford; expanses of greenery, small clusters of dwellings, landscaped highways, and a feeling for new architectural forms, for clarity and accessibility and freedom to move.

But that was a half-century ago, and neither the discovery of the new landscape nor the landscape itself has survived. The elegance of its new architectural forms is now concealed or modified, the open land of the earlier years has been subdivided, and even the splendid space of the new highway becomes increasingly congested; uninterrupted flow means more often than not uninterrupted traffic jams. The old factories and warehouses are rediscovered, remodeled, gentrified, while the new-style factories hide as best they can behind a miniature wilderness. The truck, finally, is identified with noise and pollution.

What is left? A vernacular, blue-collar version of the truck-oriented landscape of the urban fringe has moved into the city and is destroying the traditional urban culture. When we venture beyond the traditional center of town into the less prosperous neighborhoods, we see that the transit shed in several versions is by way of becoming the standard commercial building, and even the standard institutional building. It is a form suited to enterprises operating with small inventories—chain stores, gas stations, discount houses, art galleries, even museums and libraries: all depend on services and supplies brought in at regular intervals. Even the prestigious streets of the city, with their hotels, restaurants, department stores, and office buildings, operate on the same Taylor-inspired principles of steady in-and-out flow, horizontality, and the elimination of storage. Main Street, which not so many years ago was still lined by impressive, more or less uniform facades of conventional architecture, and still retained an atmosphere of permanence and limited accessibility, is now perforated by drive-in entrances, parking lots, underground garages, service alleys, and the brief appearance of transient business enterprises.

For the generation which still remembers the traditional street and its monumentality, this transformation is a depressing spectacle, and it does not help us to be told that in the past cities have frequently suffered the same decay of the central area. In many cases they have survived by moving the central city to another location. In Europe popular wisdom says that cities move to the west, that the center of power and prestige always shifts in that direction.

Were those cities the victims of a new kind of traffic in their streets? By traffic we mean not simply the vehicles which take over the street and threaten to eliminate existing forms of transportation, but also people and loads: those are the elements which bring about change. The Trojan horse was welcomed by the inhabitants of Troy; it was when that wooden horse disgorged its passengers that there was dismay.

In the case of the American town or city, the automobile—especially the commercial automobile, the truck, the pickup, the van and minivan and jeep—has been most effective in introducing a different spacial order. For what those vehicles contain (and distribute) is not only new attitudes toward work, new uses of time and space, new and more direct contacts with customers and consumers, but new techniques of problem solving. One reason factories and other industrial enterprises have tended to congregate in special areas is that they locate where they can make use of what are called "external economies"—specialists and subcontractors who can take on short-term jobs. The mobile specialist can in many cases provide that help, no matter where the client is located, and in consequence the traditional concentration in the downtown area of specialized crafts is no longer essential: even the shopping center and the mall can serve as go-betweens uniting consumer and specialist, thanks to mobile collecting and delivery and service operations.

But aside from its impact on the central city, the current small-scale commercial vehicle is introducing into the newer and low-income sections of the city a kind of vitality and movement which seemed to have vanished. The working-class dwelling, already reduced in size, is fast losing its self-sufficiency and depends more and more on mobile services. The commercial street, bordered by one transit shed after another—supermarkets, used-car lots, fast-food outlets—is in itself an elongated transit shed devoted to steady flow automatically controlled by traffic lights; and the traffic is largely composed of mobile enterprises—delivering, collecting, hauling, and distributing within the neighborhood. Social interaction moves into the street and takes the form of cruising or gathering in parking lots or around gas stations.

As of now the proportion of trucks—vans, pickups, jeeps, and medium-size trucks for city use—to passenger cars is approaching one in two. The operation and servicing of the growing number of trucks constitutes a respectable sector of our economy. Nor are these vehicles confined to the business sector. If the old establishment residential streets seek to exclude commercial traffic, there are vast areas of the city where small-scale commercial and service traffic is welcome. What keeps those trucks and vans and pickups and converted passenger cars constantly on the move? They are hauling small loads, sometimes hauling passengers, but they are also making repairs, installing and removing and replacing and servicing small businesses. Before the proliferation of these vehicles, remoter areas of the city suffered from neglect and social isolation. Now they are once more related to the city, and even the poorest of households is, at least in theory, within reach of help. Ascribe that not to a zealous welfare department or an efficient public transit system or a new clustering to foster a sense of community, but to the presence of a highly mobile sector of artisans and craftsmen, mechanics, maintenance personnel, and small-time franchise holders who will come to any customer and bring reassurance that he or she has not been forgotten.

The small commercial or service vehicle is helping weave together the city which an earlier generation of automobiles tore apart. Both kinds of vehicles, the passenger car and the truck, share responsibility for decentralization, but each has begun to mitigate the effect of the other. The passenger car has relocated many experiences and pleasures (once identified with private life) back in the public realm and the neighborhood; the truck has reintroduced small-scale services and skills into the private realm and new communities. Both responses are helping create a vernacular type of city; loosely structured, fluid, and expansive.

"Truck City," from *A Sense of Place, a Sense of Time* (New Haven: Yale University Press, 1994), 173–85.

5  Taking on the Modern Movement

JBJ, sketch, Düsseldorf, Germany, 1959 (courtesy F. Douglas Adams)

## Editor's Introduction

Beginning in 1952, J. B. Jackson published critiques of the international style in book reviews and articles in *Landscape*. The pieces anticipate by over a decade Robert Venturi's *Complexity and Contradiction in Architecture*, published in 1966, the book that many writers cite as the opening volley of architectural postmodernism.

Jackson's writings opposing the modern movement appear under his own name and under several pseudonyms. Initially, Jackson's pseudonyms disguise the fact that the journal began with a single author. As *Landscape* proceeds, Jackson's pseudonyms find an additional purpose: they allow him to review books outside his announced interests and to express himself on a wide range of subjects. Of particular significance are the reviews by "H. G. West" and "P. G. Anson," in which he questions the modern movement in architecture and celebrates the baroque. Jackson's experience as a writer of fiction gave him the literary skills to use pseudonyms successfully. His trenchant analysis, pointed wit, and good sense enable his critiques to hit the mark.

In 1994, I asked Jackson about his early encounters with modern architecture. He recalled that he saw his first modern building as a schoolboy of sixteen at the Paris Exposition of Modern Art in the summer of 1926. He was visiting his mother, who had spent the year in Paris. In the middle of the art deco buildings of the exhibition was the house designed by Le Corbusier.

Jackson remembered simply, "I didn't like it." He saw his reaction to Le Corbusier as characteristic of the time. "Everybody was kind of making fun of his houses on stilts and saying it was for chickens. . . . You had to be really intelligent to see that it was novel."[1]

As he continued his schooling, Jackson did not revise his opinion of modern architecture. His classes and reading at Harvard seemed to confirm his youthful judgment and gave him language to resist modernism's pull. In the course of his wanderjahr after college graduation, he went to the 1934 Stuttgart exhibit. There he took a second look at a Le Corbusier structure and had a more wide-ranging view of the work of the Bauhaus. In a section of the exhibit focusing on dwellings, each modern architect had built a house. In 1994 Jackson recalled his reaction: "I hated it." He saw the houses then as "ridiculous, intellectual architecture."

In this period, when his interests were largely focused on observing the rise of nazism, Jackson was aware of the many approaches to building vying for attention. Although never sympathetic to fascism, he responded to elements of German nationalism. He was aware of German efforts to build in a national style that did not rely on fake gothic or half-timbered houses.[2] At this point, Jackson was exploring in print the relation of monuments to place.[3] Thus he had some respect for the popular German reaction that the Bauhaus was anti-German.

For more than a decade, Jackson chose to leave the world in which architecture was discussed and criticized, ranching in New Mexico and serving in North Africa and Europe during World War II. *Landscape* magazine, launched in the spring of 1951, gave him a forum to present his opposition to modern architecture.

Jackson lays the groundwork for his critique in spring 1952, in a review of a book on the baroque in Latin America. Jackson writes under the initials H. G. W., standing for H. G. West, a pseudonym he had taken once previously. The review is both a praise of the baroque and a statement about what constitutes an effective understanding of architecture. Jackson/West criticizes the book's illustrations of buildings that show only their facades. He writes that architecture exists "not merely in terms of façade treatment: but in terms of plan and location, of the organization of space, of perspective and drama." It is "a three dimensional art, and no collection of photographs of façades can replace the plan, or in the case of a whole city, the map."[4]

Jackson addresses modernism in a subsequent 1952 issue of *Landscape*. Writing again under the pseudonym H. G. West, he reviews *A Decade of New*

*Architecture,* edited by Siegfried Giedion, the important Zurich writer on modern architecture, and *Early American Architecture* by Hugh Morrison. Jackson/West lambastes modernism for its emphasis on houses of the rich and its overly intellectual and antiseptic public buildings. It is not that buildings in the international style are not beautiful; they are. Jackson/West's criticism is that they spring from an aim not "to improve the lot of Man but a desire to create pure geometrical forms, an autonomous art of cubes and cylinders and two dimensional planes; independent of the past, independent of the earth and of life."

As Jackson/West looks toward the future of architecture, he reflects that those within an architectural movement cannot perceive the enemy. He pairs his review of Giedion's book with Morrison's discussion of American buildings because the latter is a narrative appropriate to the present. Just when the American classicists of the eighteenth century had established clear standards, an enemy appeared from an unanticipated quarter—"eclecticism and functionalism"—and "in the matter of a few decades swept the field." Was this about to happen to the international style? While its aging advocates restate their principles and simplify the design of the house, "all the while there enters through the back door of the modern dwelling a troop of interior decorators, landscape architects, home consultants, psychologists, appliance and television salesmen, each of them bent on making the modern home as complex and irrational and individual as possible."[5]

Modernism, Jackson/West asserts, holds strongly to the tenet "that the architect knows better than the client." In Europe, modern architects thus look to the state as builder. In the United States, however, building is in the hands of business. "One need not admire flimsy construction, the short-sighted planning, the over-dramatized, over-colored, pseudo-modern ranch houses which are rising all over the country; but one ought to be able to recognize them for what they are: the first grass-roots indication of the dwelling of the future."

Jackson continues his critique in the summer of 1953, again under the pseudonym of H. G. West, with a harsh review of *Built in U.S.A.,* edited by Henry-Russell Hitchcock and Arthur Drexler and published by the Museum of Modern Art. In his view, this book renews the tradition of the museum's involvement in and "patronage" of the modern movement in architecture. He compares the book to the pre–World War II landmark publication by the Museum of Modern Art, *Built in U.S.A., 1932–44.* The new book narrows its presentation of the international style and limits itself "to those architects who continue to profess allegiance to the teachings of Gropius, Mies van der Rohe and Le Corbusier." The result, according to Jackson/West, is a deeply flawed endeavor. The book misses the vital vernacular building of the postwar period, with its profusion of architectural forms: the tract house, the factory, and the drive-ins and businesses lining the highway.

Instead, the book focuses on suburban private houses, office buildings, and apartment houses, all sharing one salient characteristic: they are expensive. As a result, they are either large, dominant structures or they are located in the country. Thus they do not have to adapt to a neighborhood or the street. They are free to be "works of art." They are undeniably beautiful; but they are not architecture. They cannot be thought of as "true expressions of domestic or communal life. They have been inspired less by a desire to accommodate existence as we know it than by an almost fanatic rationalism."[6]

Jackson was hardly the only critic of modern architecture in the 1950s. What sets his judgment apart was its grounds. He was not arguing, as Henry Hope Reed did, for a return to a specific historic style or, as Carroll Meeks did, for a return to a "creative eclecticism," or to any notion of "style," for that matter.[7] Although he loved seventeenth-century structures, he had been schooled by Oswald Spengler to understand that each era has its own spirit and that a person living in the twentieth century must look to engineering and technology rather than to art. What Jackson wanted was not a return to the past but an architecture responsive to the needs of the present. He accepted critical tenets of modernism: the need to break with academic Beaux Arts principles and the importance of adapting to new materials and methods. What he opposed was an architecture devoted to the beauty of pure geometric forms.

Jackson saw architecture as unlike other art forms, such as painting or sculpture. Architecture's true purpose was to organize space to enhance human existence in structures expressive of domestic and social life. Architects should not limit themselves to buildings that only the rich or the state could afford, structures so large and expensive that no consideration need be given to the neighborhood, the street, or traffic patterns. Jackson protested against an architecture blind to actual construction of the present—housing developments, factories, and drive-ins—and that ignored the dwellings and structures that ordinary people were choosing for themselves.

One way to challenge modernism is to state the case for its opposite. If discussions of contemporary architecture were ignoring "new vernacular forms," such as the current dwelling, then Jackson himself would write about them. Having proclaimed the primacy of the house, he began to explore the building concerns of ordinary people. This purpose adds an additional dimension to "The Westward-Moving House." To look at the extended essay as a historical piece places the focus on its first two sections: "Nehemiah's Ark," a study of the house of Nehemiah Tinkham, the imagined Puritan settler in Massachusetts, and "Pliny's Homestead," describing that of Nehemiah's fictional mid-nineteenth-century descendant who established a farm in Illinois. To see the essay as a critique of modern architecture, however, emphasizes "Ray's Transformer," the third section dealing with the present scene.

"The Westward-Moving House" was Jackson's second attempt to describe the historic evolution of the contemporary house. His first, an H. G. West piece entitled "A Change in Plans: Is the Modern House a Victorian Invention?" appeared in the first volume of *Landscape* and discussed the postwar American dwelling as an outgrowth of modern architecture: "It has broken with every tradition, social and esthetic; it recognizes the authority of no other period or class or place. More than any other specimen of the Modern style it has repudiated ancient conventions, and comes close to being what its designers wanted it to be: a shelter, informal and free and hospitable; youthful and capable of taking on any character given it."[8] By the time of "The Westward-Moving House," however, it was clear to Jackson that the current dwelling did not really belong in the modern movement.

In "Ray's Transformer," as Jackson imagines a house being built in Bonniview, Texas, in the 1950s by Ray Tinkham, a descendent of Nehemiah and Pliny, he sees it built of cement in no architectural style. Its planning is in the hands of Shirley Tinkham, Ray's wife, a reader of home decorating magazines, who has decided that her goals are informality and efficiency. She does without ceremonial spaces in order to acquire the labor-saving devices that will make her life easier. Her design decisions are best understood as springing from the changing uses of the house. Although Ray works the soil, the family will live twelve miles from the farm, and the house no longer needs to have spaces to process farm products for family use. Nor in the modern age is the house a place to educate children or to care for the sick. It is not even a primary source of social status. The kind of family life that Ray's father had enjoyed in Illinois—"reading out loud together, Bible instruction, games, large holiday dinners, winter evenings in the sitting room, and so forth"—has disappeared, much to Shirley's satisfaction. The house does not serve as a basis of broader culture or family religion.

Although on one level Jackson indicts American postwar culture, on another he attempts to step back and understand the positive functions the present-day house serves: it remains a place of renewal and is, in this sense, a transformer. Jackson is describing the kind of house being built in countless subdivisions in the 1950s, the kind of house that surveys of modern architecture completely ignore.

The house that architectural critics admire is the house that Jackson wickedly mocks in "Living Outdoors with Mrs. Panther." Using the pseudonym Ajax, the voice of his playful satires, he pretends to be a reporter visiting Babs Panther, the chic wife of a New York publisher in her expensive suburban dwelling in Connecticut. He plays with the meaning of "natural," an artifice if there ever was one. Setting down Mrs. Panther's various formulations, Jackson/Ajax lets them speak for themselves, revealing social snobbery, dislike of the real out-of-doors, and pretense. He uses the voice of the 1950s shelter magazines to summarize ironically: "The artificialities of city existence are far, far removed from the quiet little eight-room house out here on stilts in the Connecticut woods."[9]

Jackson understands that the American vernacular does not just mean functionalism; it also means extravagance. In "Notes and Comments," his editorial forum, he speaks boldly and humorously in his own voice against the international style. In "Hail and Farewell" (Winter 1953–54), he writes about the commemoration of Walter Gropius's seventieth birthday and irreverently suggests that it is time for the Bauhaus proponents of modernism to depart from the scene. Real American buildings have a purpose different than that suggested by the theories of modern architects: "They are required to sell goods, to establish social position, to inspire confidence, to impress or elevate or excite. The result is a carnival of extravagant taste, an architectural idiom partaking more of advertising or theater or landscaping than of 'pure space arrangements and the balance of tense contrary forces.'"[10]

This is the notion upon which Jackson elaborates in 1956 in "Other-Directed Houses," his celebration of the highway strip.[11] "In all those streamlined facades, in all those flamboyant entrances and deliberately bizarre decorative effects, those cheerfully self-assertive masses of color and light and movement that clash so roughly with the old and traditional, there are, I believe, certain underlying characteristics which suggest that we are confronted not by a debased and cheapened art but by a kind of folk art in mid-twentieth-century garb." On both experiential and aesthetic grounds, Jackson questions criticism of the American highway and the buildings that line its path. He analyzes the strip, separating out its leisure functions and those of work, and validates the pleasures of going out for a drive.

Jackson thinks about the appeal that a highway establishment must offer to attract patrons, noting changes in American notions of pleasure. As automobiles have flooded the roads since World War II, a new idea of leisure has emerged: dreams of the future or the West or the South Pacific along the highways have taken the place of the older urban pleasure palaces. Facades and lights are designed to please those speeding by in a car at forty or more miles an hour. Lights and signs erase the workaday world and create in their place one of festivity.

As he considers the strip, Jackson develops more fully the planning ideas about which he has been writing in *Landscape* since 1953. Under the pseudonym P. G. Anson, he explicitly opposes a number of modern architects in Le Corbusier's circle in a review of their book on urban planning, *The Heart of the City*, edited by J. Tyrwhitt, J. L. Sert, and E. N. Rogers for the Congrès Internationaux d'Architecture Moderne.[12] In a signed review of Garrett Eckbo's *Landscape for Living*, also of 1953, Jackson addresses other concerns about planning, questioning both practitioners' faith in a central planning authority and their belief that nature can be completely mastered.[13]

"Southeast to Turkey" gives Jackson's fullest response to modern planning principles. This 1958 essay, in the guise of a travel piece, allows Jackson to explore European urbanism as well as landscape and history, national cultures, and the impact of the Soviet Union on Eastern Europe. The examination of Old World cities also gives him an opportunity to critique modern notions of planning. Jackson elaborates what it is that is so marvelous about Istanbul, a city with every conceivable flaw from a planner's standpoint: narrow streets, filth, dangerous buildings, and rats. "And yet what marvelous color and variety, what a superabundance of life! . . . We can study the anatomy of the city, its physical structure until the cows come home; we can design on paper cities which are models of efficiency, comfort, hygiene, even beauty of a sort; but until we learn to study its physiology, to listen to its heartbeat, as it were, to watch its regular breathing, every such project will be dead at birth. For all its sordidness, Istanbul is a city where urban life has created its own forms, and not the other way around."[14]

By 1958, readers of *Landscape* have at hand a fundamental critique of the modern movement in architecture and planning and a set of new guiding principles, some of which anticipate, in important ways, architectural postmodernism. J. B. Jackson—and H. G. West and P. G. Anson—write that buildings are not to be understood as freestanding works of art like pieces of sculpture, created by a romantic artistic genius. They are not to be judged, via photographs of beautiful facades, as expressions of pure geometry. Buildings are structures designed for human use. They are three-dimensional compositions, and their interior spaces are as important as their exterior masses. Buildings are intended for actual clients who hold clear notions of what they want. Architects may be creating dwellings in the international style for the wealthy, but American housing developments reflect the average homeowner's desire for convenience and individuality. Americans are choosing houses that accommodate their families' needs as they define them, rather than reflecting a utopian modern vision.

Commercial buildings in present-day America have a new purpose, given the universality of automobile travel. Those that line the strip promise to satisfy contemporary notions of pleasure to those driving by at high speeds. Thus their extravagant shapes and neon signs must attract attention and offer the delights of places far removed from home and work.

Planners, including landscape architects, can learn nothing from practitioners of the international style, Jackson argues. Houses and corporate structures in the modern mode have failed to respond and interact with their neighbors. Buildings need to be planned in the context of the street. Jackson cautions his readers to be wary of any work coming from a centralized, bureaucratic planning authority that tends to favor a sanitized social order. He asks for a reevaluation of the Old World city in all its messiness as an organism overflowing with complexity, intricacy, and abundance of life.

In the last two decades of his life, Jackson came to reconsider modern buildings, especially those erected since the 1950s, in the light of use rather than beauty. In 1982, in a collective article entitled "Whither Architecture? Some Outside Views" in the *AIA Journal,* he expressed a warm appreciation of contemporary office buildings, surrounded by parking and open plazas, as self-contained environments serving the broad American public.

## Review of *Built in U.S.A.*

The New York Museum of Modern Art has probably been more influential than any other institution in the country in introducing Modern architecture to the American public. Since its first important exhibit of contemporary European building more than a generation ago, it has not slackened in its interest and patronage, although it has become increasingly selective.

Its prewar publication, *Built in U.S.A. 1932–44,* was a very comprehensive survey of what was formerly called the International Style. This new version covers one aspect of contemporary architecture in America since 1944 in much the same manner as did the earlier book. One aspect; because as this collection of photographs (and accompanying essays by Henry-Russell Hitchcock and Arthur Drexler) makes abundantly clear, the Museum of Modern Art now limits its interest and approval to those architects who continue to profess allegiance to the teachings of Gropius, Mies van der Rohe, and Le Corbusier.

The result is inevitably a one-sided and incomplete survey. Few periods have seen more building in this country than the last eight years; no period has seen the development of more new architectural forms: forms of dwellings, of commercial and public buildings, and of collective planning. The mass-produced community of one-family residences, the monotype windowless factory, the whole series of drive-in and highway enterprises—these have all be-

Emblematic figure, man bent over book

come part of the modern American landscape, and their efficient design taxes the ingenuity of the vast majority of younger architects. *Built in U.S.A.* contains not one specimen of these new vernacular forms. Out of more than fifty examples considered worthy of inclusion by the editors, almost a third are expensive suburban private houses. There are expensive office buildings (Lever Brothers and the United Nations Secretariat), expensive laboratories (Johnson Wax and General Motors), and expensive apartment houses. By far the greatest number of these buildings have not been obliged to adapt themselves to their immediate surroundings, either because they are located in the country or because they are so large and important that they dwarf the houses around them; they are not concerned with street alignment, traffic flow, or the existing character of a neighborhood. Thus emancipated from all worries relating to expense or new and perplexing functions or social conformity, they have been conceived of primarily as works of art—symbols of a freedom that the workaday architect can only envy.

What is the quality which they have in common? They are all of them specimens of an architectural doctrine carried to its logical conclusion. This is a development rarely seen in architectural history before the very end of a style; in a sense these buildings are the contemporary equivalent of the Flamboyant and the Rococo—not that they share any of the exuberance of these two idioms. On the contrary; it is impossible not to admire the sober elegance, the harmony, and even in some cases the monumentality of these houses and office buildings and laboratories. Whatever the long-range future of this kind of Modernism may be, it will have set a standard of beauty for all subsequent American architects. But it is equally impossible to think of them in terms of architecture in its broadest sense, to think of them, that is to say, as true expressions of domestic or communal life. They have been inspired less by a desire to accommodate existence as we know it than by an almost fanatic rationalism.

An unworthy appeal to intellectual snobbery (of which the Museum of Modern Art is not entirely guiltless) has assured the acceptance of this version of the Modern style among a large segment of the public. Nevertheless, the fact that it is evidently unwilling (or unable) to deal with the more prosaic architectural problems of the present indicates that its days of influence are numbered. The idiom developed by Gropius, Mies van der Rohe, Neutra, and Le Corbusier belongs to a much simpler society and a much simpler view of the world. It represents the last flowering of the nineteenth century—the era of the important freestanding house which bore little or no relation to its surroundings. And a comparison between this book and its predecessor of 1944 makes one thing obvious: the practitioners of this type of Modernism are fast losing their interest in interior plan; it is as if the task of organizing life within the home or the place of work—a task which once inspired the best efforts of the architect—had ceased to have any meaning for them.

In his introductory survey, Mr. Drexler defines architecture as "conspicuous space," and as far as this collection goes it is a very adequate definition. That no doubt is why the book includes so few legible floor plans. Those offered appear to have been chosen with very little thought of their use—the ground-floor plan of a house on stilts is surely of small value—and in some cases they are omitted altogether. But this is quite in line with the architects' indifference to spatial subdivisions; the creation of uninterrupted space, regardless of the requirements of everyday life, has become their obsession, and whatever limits its extension—even the wall and the ceiling—is viewed with increasing impatience. Thanks to such surveys as this—and it is very much to be hoped that there will be subsequent ones—it is possible for the public to watch the dissolution of what was once a vigorous architectural style; to watch it literally dissolve into thin air. Just as certain very advanced developments in music produce compositions which cannot be played, this rationalistic Modernism will doubtless eventually produce designs too ethereal, too space-conscious, to leave the drafting board.

H. G. West, review of Henry-Russell Hitchcock and Arthur Drexler, eds., *Built in U.S.A.*, *Landscape* 3, no. 1 (Summer 1953): 29–30.

## Living Outdoors with Mrs. Panther

"The immediate experience of nature": How many of us really know what that means? Well, plenty of Young Moderns do, and Mr. and Mrs. Jeffrey Panther—he's the New York publisher, of course—have gone about proving it in a smart, typically Young American way.

Quite simply, quite casually, entirely without fanfare, the Panthers have decided to live out of doors. Not in a tent like their pioneer ancestors—Mrs. Panther, incidentally, is a direct descendant of Clara Peabody Newell—No; in a house specially designed by famed Modernist Mies van der Rohe. On a small ten-acre lot in Connecticut's Fairfield County there has recently been built a gay little $100,000 home for the enterprising young family of four.

"Jeff and I call the whole thing an experiment in Modern Living," Mrs. Panther laughingly explained when we telephoned her one day last summer. "But do come and see what fun we're having."

So we did, and because we found the Panther home so excitingly modern (in the wholesome American sense of the word), we want to tell the readers of *Landscape* all about it.

### Art Belongs in the Modern Home!
Enchantingly sleek and simple in appearance—a long white box perched on stilts—the Panthers' house is situated in a grove of wonderfully natural-look-

ing trees. Mrs. Panther—"Babs" to her many friends in the World Federalists and on the Community Forum Committee—meets us at the door. She is wearing black velvet toreador tights, ballet slippers, and a divine yellow linen shirt. With her blonde hair in a horsetail, she looks for all the world like a little girl. "This is my year-round costume," she explains later; "I never wear anything different. You see, the house is temperatrolled."

We glance, fascinated, into the enormous living room—or, as the Panthers call it, the play space. We are speechless with delight: one entire wall is occupied by a vast window (of Sanilite glass, of course, which lets in only the health-giving rays) reaching fifteen feet from brick floor to ceiling. Outside is a charmingly unspoilt view of trees and rocks and underbrush. "Here we sit, like Hansl and Gretl, Jeff and I, right in the heart of the woods! We even have a tree here in the middle of the play space!" And so they have: the slender trunk of a maple rises out of the floor and then disappears through the ceiling. "We love our tree," she says softly, laying her hand on the trunk. "The texture of the bark is so exciting. Mies van der Rohe was a lamb and let us have it." And how wonderfully *right* it is! It lends just that simple sophisticated touch to the décor of the room. The natural form is repeated by a small but important piece of Henry Moore sculpture on the floor; a witty Calder mobile twinkles overhead. "Don't you adore our tiny little art collection? These two," Mrs. Panther says, "and a sweet little Braque are all we could afford; we saved and saved and *saved* to buy them." A gay little smile admits us to her confidence. "But we simply *had* to have them," she continues, "because if you love plants and animals and birds the way Jeff and I do, you just have to have that kind of art—like nature."

### The American Home at Its Simple Best

Despite the summer heat out of doors and the bright clean light streaming through the uncurtained windows, the play space (living room) is wonderfully cool and fresh. And that, of course, is because of the temperatroll. Pointing to an instrument panel, Mrs. Panther explains this modern miracle, this triumph of the American will to live beautifully and wholesomely—and with simplicity. "Oh, we scraped pennies in order to have our own special climate. Jeff and I are essentially outdoor people—like all our younger and more stimulating friends," she adds. "We simply couldn't *stand* living in an old-fashioned Victorian house with all that absurd closing and opening of doors and windows. We want to live indoors just the way we would live outdoors: freely and informally and spaciously. If you know what I mean."

So there is no need to open any of the windows in the Panther house. Not that it's complicated to do so; a telephone call to the local ventilating engineer, and out he comes at once with his special equipment, and in no time the great windows are opened outwards.

"We spend hours in the outdoor play space." Mrs Panther remarks. "That's where we have our swimming pool and the squash court. Of course we had to cut down on the cost of the house in order to have them. But Mies was a darling about it."

For a moment she disappears to spread a special insect-repellant suntan oil on herself, and to get her special sunglasses and a shade hat, before taking us out into the garden. What a fabulous spot it is! Small, but so natural and so modern in feeling! No prim flowerbeds and tiresome hedges; a stretch of that chic Brazilian gravel which is so popular in California this season; a few potted jub-jub trees ("They were flown in from Hawaii") and a casual array of Chinese ivy in pots. That's all. Italian beach furniture and gaily striped parasols are grouped in front of a wall of the stylish split-beech French fence. We catch a glimpse of the pool beyond: a spot of turquoise in a free-form basin. "Of course," she confesses, "the color is artificial. But the water has been thoroughly tested; it is chlorinated and filtered and kept at the correct temperature. The children splash about in it like savages! I *do* dislike old-fashioned restrictions, don't you? Ronny and Jody" (those are the two Panther children) "can do anything they like, provided they take their multivitamin shots and never eat anything except what comes out of the kitchen or pick wild plants or fondle stray animals or play with children who might be dirty or socially maladjusted.

"That's why Jeff and I won't have pets around." (The squash court building contains a shower and an air-conditioned exercise room with a marvelous family-size sunlamp.) "We don't believe in interfering with nature. We spray the trees, disinfect the soil, and change the potted plants every two months— and then we let things take their course."

We find this admirable; we like this forthright rejection of pruning and clipping and transplanting. Do the Panthers have a vegetable garden?

"No; but we're trying hydroponics in the guest bathroom so that the children will have a feel for growing things."

### Science Plus Amusing Informality Is the Watchword

Nor do the Panthers sleep or eat out of doors. "Jeff, poor darling, is allergic to practically everything that grows in Connecticut—or anywhere else, for that matter. He has to have an air-conditioned room all of his own." As for eating outside: "Well," Mrs. Panther says with a delightful smile, "I think I prefer to keep the outdoors for the very simplest kind of pleasure. And I adore my work area" (kitchen, in old-fashioned parlance) "and spend a great deal of time there. When we have company I open some cans and toss a salad; we have a bottle of French wine, some cheese, and then sit around on cushions and discuss McCarthyism and how we dislike it. I've become quite a cook," she adds proudly.

The children? They have their own rooms—sound-proof and out of the way. "Besides, they spend most of their time at the Play Clinic in town, where there's a marvelous psychiatric guidance expert."

Yes, we reflect, as Mrs. Panther leads us back into the house, this typical American family leads a *natural* life for young Moderns. The artificialities of city existence are far, far removed from the quiet little eight-room house out there on stilts in the Connecticut woods. Nightclubs, traffic jams, dirt, and confusion are no part of their life. Excitement? A casual little concert on recorders, or a new wine-and-shallot sauce Babs discovers, or waking up on a winter's morning to see the Japanese-printlike effect of snow on the black branches—these comprise the Panthers' happiest moments. The Panthers, by the way, have an automatic snow-melting system from the garage door to the road a hundred yards distant, so that Jeff need not shovel snow like his Victorian forebears. What's more, it disposes of the melted snow so that no ice is ever formed on the driveway. "Let it snow," says Babs in the words of the once popular song. She turns up the thermostat, adjusts the temperatroll to suit her toreador tights and yellow shirt and little-girl hairdo; and once the children have been called for by the school bus, she settles down with a volume of her favorite author, André Gide, to enjoy a winter's day in the country. "I'm afraid," she laughingly tells us, "that I wouldn't know how to behave in the city any more. But we young Moderns are like that: we want to live abundantly, the way Jeff and I do: in a simple kind of house with this immediate kind of experience of Nature." She thoughtfully caresses the Henry Moore composition. "Or do you think I'm utterly barbaric?"

Well, frankly, Mrs. Panther, since you ask . . . .

Ajax, "Living Outdoors with Mrs. Panther," *Landscape* 4, no. 2 (Winter 1954–55): 24–25.

## Hail and Farewell

It is appropriate that the seventieth birthday of Walter Gropius should have been the occasion for honoring the architect and his work. The larger part of his life has been spent in Central Europe, and it was there that his theories were formulated; but the two decades during which he has worked in America represent perhaps the most fruitful period in his career. Ever since his appointment to Harvard in 1934, Gropius has been the most important and often the healthiest influence in American architecture. If his present following is numerous and devoted, it is because he has not only excelled as an architect and teacher but has known how to use his prestige with moderation.

Having said this much, we must add that we are among those who believe that the undisputed authority of Gropius and his disciples is fast approaching its end. The virtues of that philosophy of architecture usually identified with the Bauhaus, so novel and so unwelcome a generation ago, are by now almost universally accepted. We have learned to discard meaningless ornament and academic design, we have learned to use new techniques and materials. Our eyes have been opened to a new (or at least a neglected) kind of beauty, and a new kind of architecture as well as a new kind of architect have evolved, both well suited to the problems of our times. We have much to be grateful for to the Bauhaus and its leader.

But as we have grown adept at using the new idiom, we have become aware of its shortcomings. Many current esthetic tendencies the Bauhaus style expresses with unrivaled clarity and ease; others—and the number is increasing—it cannot express at all. The collaboration of several arts, painting and sculpture and stagecraft and landscaping, that has marked previous architectural styles has never been entirely successful with the Bauhaus movement, even though the importance of the collaboration was recognized at the start. The style is undoubtedly seen at its best when movement and color and monumentality are absent and when its effects are achieved solely by architectural means. That is a perfectly legitimate trait; and yet we do not have to look very far to see that there exists in America a kind of architecture which seeks to attract attention to itself—shops, factories, institutions, roadside enterprises—and that this architecture uses every artistic device to this end: colors, lights, monumental facades, landscaping, and so on. Moreover, these techniques are having an effect on all other types of building in America. By Bauhaus standards this is an unwarranted development, but is it likely that the designers of such buildings will be much influenced by the autonomy of the Bauhaus style? That they will sacrifice a popular flamboyance in order to conform to uncongenial standards of sobriety?

The same autonomy, the same self-imposed isolation is typical of the Bauhaus in its relation to environment, whether architectural or natural. Not only does the style see little virtue in using local materials and forms, it sees little virtue in trying to "blend" with its surroundings. We have ceased to be shocked by the spectacle of an elegant Gropius or Mies van der Rohe house of gleaming plate glass and smooth white wall rising in the midst of a New England woodlot or among nineteenth-century city residences; we have learned that the success of a Bauhaus design is to be judged independent of its setting. But again we discover a strong national tendency in the opposite direction. The average American house makes much of the merging of indoors and outdoors, and of the use of materials whose color and texture harmonize with the surroundings. It is worth remembering that neither city planning nor landscaping were part of the original Bauhaus curriculum; the house was all that mattered then. But contemporary American architecture, influenced as it has been by public housing and private real estate developments, would be unthinkable without some attempt at coordination between the various structures and between the structures and the site.

Perhaps the basic characteristic of the Bauhaus style is this: It evolved out of a new concept of the relation between the artist and his medium. If the style developed, it did so as the result of the use of new materials and new techniques; public taste was an unimportant factor. And this is also true of the function of the house as the Bauhaus interprets it. Function is thought of almost entirely in terms of interior organization—in terms of the occupants and immediate users—not in terms of its effect on the passing public. This means, of course, that exterior decoration, facade treatment, adaptation to the surroundings are held to be of minor importance.

In contrast, modern run-of-the-mill American architecture has remained essentially traditional and unintellectual in its outlook. The average American architect sees his art as developing out of the relationship between artist and public—or client, whichever you prefer. He sees style evolving not from the use of new materials and techniques but from new requirements on the part of the public. His art, therefore, like that of all artists who think in terms of public demand, is representational. It seeks to communicate some message or emotion. That is why the American architect unconsciously defines function in a much broader sense than the Bauhaus architect does. He defines it not simply in terms of the house occupant but in terms of impact on the public. The exterior appearance of a church is of no consequence to the Bauhaus, but to the average American architect it suggests the mystery and solemnity of religious experience, just as the exterior of the public building suggests the power of the state and the exterior of the dwelling suggests the privacy and individuality of domestic life. The architect designs accordingly.

From the point of view of theory, the Bauhaus is coherent and on sure ground. We are not dealing with theory, however, but with the fact that American architecture is going its own way. It is idle to argue whether architecture is an art of communication or of form when it is apparent that our buildings are being called upon to say something to the public. They are required to sell goods, to establish social position, to inspire confidence, to impress or elevate or excite. The result is a carnival of extravagant taste, an architectural idiom partaking more of advertising or theater or landscaping than of "pure space arrangements and the balance of tense contrary forces."

Yet in spite of that we welcome the current development as a release, a promise of greater freedom and creativity. The fact that the flag-waving Philistines are opposed to the Bauhaus and that many of the best architects in the country are still enthusiastic about it gives us pause, but it cannot in the long run deter us from hoping that the days of the Bauhaus are numbered.

"Hail and Farewell" (Notes and Comments), *Landscape* 3, no. 2 (Winter 1953–54): 5–6.

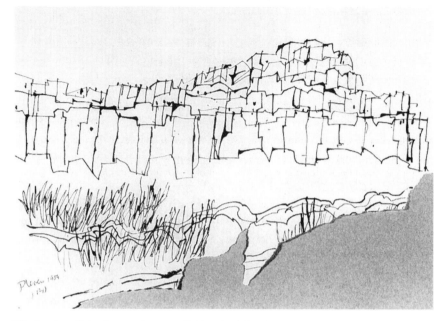

JBJ, drawing, Bulgaria, 1959 (courtesy F. Douglas Adams)

## Southeast to Turkey

ISTANBUL. If I were the Ford Foundation, I would give lavish fellowships to students of city planning on the following conditions: that for a year they would look at no picture-books of Brave New Sweden, attend no lectures entitled "Planning for a More Abundant Democracy" (or "Housing at the Crossroads"), cease all speculating about the City of the Future, and spend the time instead deep in the heart of some chaotic, unredeemed, ancient city. Preferably Istanbul.

To be sure, there are changes under way even here; broad, straight boulevards are being cut through the oldest section, and the city is expanding north—out where the new Hilton stands in self-conscious elegance and where a new European quarter is rapidly coming into being, a quarter Bucharest might well boast of. But most of the city is being allowed to survive: squalid, smelly, disorderly, exciting, and magnificent. The streets are narrow, crooked, dirty, and without system; almost every building is a jerrybuilt firetrap. For every man, woman, and child in Istanbul there must be a thousand rats. The countless architectural and archeological wonders are for the most part hidden away in rubbish-strewn courtyards or unrecognizable behind a parasitic growth of shanties: an urbanist's nightmare; a reformer's dream.

And yet what marvelous color and variety, what a superabundance of life! Crowds that you have to edge your way through, crowds not on their way

JBJ, drawing, Bursa, Turkey, *Landscape* 7, no. 3 (Spring 1958): 4

to some place but already there: buying, selling, arguing, gesticulating, working. Everything is shamelessly open to view, and at the same time there is glimpse after glimpse of an almost domestic intimacy: a mother nursing her child on the edge of the pavement, someone thoughtfully dictating a letter to a public scribe, someone asleep. This is the kind of life Samuel Johnson must have observed at Charing Cross and which he called the "full tide of human existence"; this is what the city used to be when it still preserved the human scale: not streams of fast-moving traffic between rows of multistoried buildings but a succession of alleys, streets, squares, each with its own characteristic light and rhythm and sound, its own special trade and nationality and faith. And always in the background looms a monument to give continuity and meaning to this life. We can study the anatomy of the city, its physical structure, until the cows come home; we can design on paper cities which are models of efficiency, comfort, hygiene, even beauty of a sort; but until we learn to study its physiology, to listen to its heartbeat, as it were, to watch its regular breathing, every such project will be dead at birth. For all its sordidness, Istanbul is a city where urban life has created its own forms, and not the other way around.

There are two directions, it seems to me, in which we can turn for guidance in planning the cities of the future: to the synthetic creations of doctrinaire urbanists, or to the living, pulsating, infinitely complicated organisms which man has made over and over again for thousands of years, and out of which has come all civilization. It is finally a choice of Istanbul or Caracas; and even Istanbul we had better study before it is too late.

"Southeast to Turkey," *Landscape* 7, no. 3 (Spring 1958): 17–22, excerpt.

## Statement in "Whither Architecture? Some Outside Views"

Americans have had more than fifty years in which to get used to what we call the modern style in architecture. At first it bothered and sometimes shocked us, but that was long ago. We have learned to accept it as part of our workaday world and even to associate it with certain contemporary values. The school we go to, the office or plant where we work, the museum, the library, the shopping center we visit, even the hospital where we were born, are probably all examples—good or bad—of the modern style.

It is true that familiarity in itself does not necessarily mean that we have any real understanding of the modern esthetic canon, but in the long run I think it produces a sense of what to look for in the way of forms and spaces and surfaces and relationships, and above all it produces expectations of a special kind of environment. The layman does not accept modernism because he finds it beautiful but because he finds that it works, and so he is sometimes more sensitive to change than the architect is.

Writing as a layman who has watched the style evolve in the smaller cities of America over half a century, let me suggest a few of the ways in which it seems to have matured and come of age.

The most conspicuous change that I have noticed is in the relationship between architecture and the urban plan. We have always thought of them as inseparable. The Renaissance, perhaps because of the importance it attached to the facades of buildings, did much to make urban architecture a decorative feature of the street. The row upon row of similar facades contributed to the glorification of the baroque *Prunkstrasse*, or representational avenue. One of the basic objectives of modernism in its early days was to free architecture from this subordinate role.

Le Corbusier surrounded his high-rise buildings with green parks and sited them far from the street. But it remained for a later generation, especially here in America, to see that motorized traffic was destroying streetside architecture, and to establish a new and more balanced relationship between building and street. We eventually, and largely by accident, gave the building its independence and allowed it to join with other buildings to form a self-contained complex with its own surrounding spaces, its own orientation, its own patterns of movement. Withdrawn at a safe distance from the rapid, all but uninterrupted flow of traffic, these complexes assume many new forms: office complexes, shopping complexes, sports and convention complexes. Small specialty shops, the first victims of the motorized street, become boutiques and take refuge in back alleys and converted warehouses.

So now the modern building has its protective buffer zone of drive-in facilities, parking lots, and carefully landscaped open spaces or plazas. A prestigious business address is no longer, say, "111 Lincoln Street," it is "American Insurance Square" or "First National Plaza." Texas modernism seems to favor "tower" as a desirable address, but the principle is the same: The building is liberated from the tyranny of the street and begins to emerge as an autonomous environment.

By this I mean that the modern building—school or office high-rise or shopping center or whatever—is rapidly evolving as the container of a self-sufficient, man-made environment. I would say that the first step in this redefining of the building was the wholesale installation, in the 1950s, of air-conditioning in places of work. It was soon followed by sophisticated lighting systems designed not only to produce better lighting but to differentiate various kinds of space and to foster moods of one sort or another. Both air-conditioning and new lighting enlarged work areas and changed office and factory layouts.

Sensory response to the building as a self-contained environment was further enriched by the introduction of acoustical walls and ceilings and piped-in music. Perhaps we should include wall-to-wall carpeting as still another environmental improvement. But who can enumerate the many devices meant to establish the environmental self-sufficiency of the contemporary consumer-oriented building—shopping center, hotel, hospital, or office: the resplendent tropical landscaping—replaced every six weeks—in lobbies and malls and waiting rooms, the carefully engineered color codes, the reassuring textures of walls and upholstery, the artful shifts in floor levels and ceiling heights? Not one of these innovations, it is safe to say, was ever dreamt of by the early masters of the modern style, but they are now essential. What is more, they are all justified by developers and promoters and designers as expressions of unimpeachably progressive ideas: energy conservation, efficiency, health and safety, and the dignity of the common man.

A third change has been this: Modernism has become the idiom of the public sector; it is more and more identified with buildings intended to serve a very heterogeneous public. Those who lived in the years when modernism (or, as we called it then, the international style) was introduced to this country will remember how little it was noticed outside of a small group of art and architecture critics, how it was appraised almost entirely in esthetic terms, and how strongly its democratization was resisted. I am inclined to think we overlook the popularization and commercialization of what we now call art deco as a factor in the public acceptance of modernism. Art deco was never a true style, it was an attempt to soften and "humanize" the radical new forms of the modern style. By and large it succeeded. It replaced traditional styles—burdened as they were with history and class distinctions and symbolism—by a style which was novel and ingratiating, easy to understand and adapt, with an essentially meaningless ornamentation, useful in all large, impersonal spaces.

This was the influence that changed modernism in America and made it what it now is: the appropriate style for buildings used by a wide public. This was the influence that in the eyes of the more severe critics destroyed the purity of true modernism and led to its downfall. But critics overlook the difference between the way the bureaucracy, the establishment, handled the public in the past—and still does in much of the Old World—and how we try to handle the public in America. By law as well as by general consensus, the American public means *everyone*, regardless of class or age or physical condition or degree of schooling, and for such a public we have sought to devise an architecture accessible to all.

We have paid a high price, esthetically speaking. We have been obliged to eliminate all subtleties and refinements in design, all experimentation and surprise in favor of easily interpreted forms and space; we have eliminated all solemnity and disturbing symbolism in favor of friendly, easily understood signs and topical references. Exteriors and interiors in the modern public-oriented building abound in what are called redundant clues: messages that are both visible and audible and even bodily designed to inform and protect and reassure the public. Our buildings aspire to be accidentproof, fireproof, vandalproof, and foolproof. We are less concerned with art than with producing a man-made environment that contributes to the physical and psychological well-being of every man, woman, and child who enters.

Are we succeeding? Not altogether, but give us time. I think there are innumerable changes of this pragmatic sort waiting for us in the years ahead. We need not expect them to produce a new style in the sense of new forms, but perhaps we are the victims of a faulty reading of recent architectural history. The modernism that we see being built in contemporary America, and that the architectural critic easily dismisses as without significance, does not derive from the principles enunciated in the first decades of this century. It derives from the discovery or invention of the building as a planned, self-contained environment. The first phase of modernism was the structural-mechanical phase, and it lasted until the 1950s. The second phase, the phase we are in, is the biological-environmental phase. The third, when it comes, will be the phase that discovers the religious ingredient in our efforts to build better houses and a better world.

Statement in "Whither Architecture? Some Outside Views," *AIA Journal* 71 (Mid-May 1982): 205–6.

# 6 Thinking about Landscape

## The Word Itself

Why is it, I wonder, that we have trouble agreeing on the meaning of *land-scape?* The word is simple enough, and it refers to something which we think we understand; and yet to each of us it seems to mean something different.

What we need is a new definition. The one we find in most dictionaries is more than three hundred years old and was drawn up for artists. It tells us that a landscape is a "portion of land which the eye can comprehend at a glance." Actually, when it was first introduced (or reintroduced) into English it did not mean the view itself, it meant a *picture* of it, an artist's interpretation. It was his task to take the forms and colors and spaces in front of him—mountains, river, forest, fields, and so on—and compose them so that they made a work of art.

There is no need to tell in detail how the word gradually changed in meaning. First it meant a picture of a view; then the view itself. We went into the country and discovered beautiful views, always remembering the criteria of landscape beauty as established by critics and artists. Finally, on a modest scale, we undertook to make over a piece of ground so that it resembled a pastoral landscape in the shape of a garden or park. Just as the painter used his judgment as to what to include or omit in his composition, the landscape gardener (as he was known in the eighteenth century) took pains to produce a stylized "picturesque" landscape, leaving out the muddy roads, the plowed fields, the squalid villages of the real countryside and including certain agreeable natural features: brooks and groves of trees and smooth expanses of grass. The results were often extremely beautiful, but they were still pictures, though in three dimensions.

The reliance on the artist's point of view and his definition of landscape beauty persisted throughout the nineteenth century. Olmsted and his followers designed their parks and gardens in "painterly" terms. "Although three-dimensional composition in landscape materials differs from two-dimensional landscape painting, because a garden or park design contains a *series* of pictorial compositions," the *Encyclopedia Britannica* (thirteenth edition) informs us, "nevertheless in each of these pictures we find the familiar basic principles of unity, of repetition, of sequence and balance, of harmony and contrast." But within the last half-century a revolution has taken place: landscape design and landscape painting have gone their separate ways. Landscape architects no longer turn to Poussin or Salvator Rosa or Gilpin for inspiration; they may not even have heard of their work. Knowledge of ecology and conservation and environmental psychology are now part of the landscape architect's professional background, and protecting and "managing" the natural environment are seen as more important than the designing of picturesque parks. Environmental designers, I have noticed, avoid the word *landscape* and prefer *land* or *terrain* or *environment* or even *space* when they have a specific site in mind. *Landscape* is used for suggesting the esthetic quality of the wider countryside.

As for painters, they have long since lost interest in producing conventional landscapes. Kenneth Clark, in his book *Landscape into Painting,* comments on this fact. "The microscope and telescope have so greatly enlarged the range of our vision," he writes, "that the snug, sensible nature which we can see with our own eyes has ceased to satisfy our imaginations. We know that by our new standards of measurement the most extensive landscape is practically the same as the hole through which the burrowing ant escapes from our sight."[1]

This does not strike me as a very satisfactory explanation of the demise of traditional landscape painting. More than a change in scale was responsible. Painters have learned to see the environment in a new and more subjective manner: as a different kind of experience. But that is not the point. The point is, the two disciplines which once had a monopoly on the word—landscape architecture and landscape painting—have ceased to use it the way they did a few decades ago, and it has now reverted, as it were, to the public domain.

What has happened to the word in the meantime? For one thing we are

using it with much more freedom. We no longer bother with its literal meaning—which I will come to later—and we have coined a number of words
similar to it: roadscape, townscape, cityscape, as if the syllable *scape* meant a
space, which it does not; and we speak of the wilderness landscape, the lunar
landscape, even of the landscape at the bottom of the ocean. Furthermore, the
word is frequently used in critical writings as a kind of metaphor. Thus we
find mention of the "landscape of a poet's images," the "landscape of dreams,"
or "landscape as antagonist" or "the landscape of thought," or, on quite a different level, the "political landscape of the NATO conference," the "patronage
landscape." Our first reaction to these usages is that they are far-fetched and
pretentious. Yet they remind us of an important truth: that we always need a
word or phrase to indicate a kind of environment or setting which can give
vividness to a thought or event or relationship; a background placing it in the
world. In this sense, *landscape* serves the same useful purpose as do the words
*climate* or *atmosphere,* used metaphorically. In fact, *landscape* when used as a
painter's term often meant "all that part of a picture which is not of the body
or argument"—like the stormy array of clouds in a battle scene or the glimpse
of the Capitol in a presidential portrait.

   In the eighteenth century, *landscape* indicated scenery in the theater and
had the function of discreetly suggesting the location of the action or perhaps
the time of day. As I have suggested elsewhere, there is no better indication of
how our relation to the environment can change over the centuries than in the
role of stage scenery. Three hundred years ago Corneille could write a five-act
tragedy with a single indication of the setting: "The action takes place in the
palace of the king." If we glance at the work of a modern playwright, we will
probably find one detailed description of a scene after another, and the ultimate in this kind of landscape, I suppose, is the contemporary movie. Here
the set does much more than merely identify the time and place and establish
the mood. By means of shifts in lighting and sound and perspective, the set
actually creates the players, identifies them, and tells them what to do: a good
example of environmental determinism.

   But these scenic devices and theater landscapes are mere imitations of
real ones: easily understood by almost everyone, and shared. What I object to
is the fallacy in the metaphorical use of the word. No one denies that as our
thoughts become complex and abstract, we need metaphors to give them a degree of reality. No one denies that as we become uncertain of our status, we
need more and more reinforcement from our environment. But we should not
use the word *landscape* to describe our private world, our private microcosm,

and for a simple reason: a landscape is a concrete, three-dimensional, shared reality.

## Lands and Shapes

Landscape is a space on the surface of the earth; intuitively we know that it is a space with a degree of permanence, with its own distinct character, either topographical or cultural, and above all a space shared by a group of people; and when we go beyond the dictionary definition of landscape and examine the word itself, we find that our intuition is correct.

*Landscape* is a compound, and its components hark back to that ancient Indo-European idiom, brought out of Asia by migrating peoples thousands of years ago, that became the basis of almost all modern European languages— Latin and Celtic and Germanic and Slavic and Greek. The word was introduced into Britain sometime after the fifth century A.D. by the Angles and Saxons and Jutes and Danes and other groups of Germanic speech. In addition to its Old English variations—*landskipe, landscaef,* and others—there is the German *landschaft,* the Dutch *landscap,* as well as Danish and Swedish equivalents. They all come from the same roots, but they are not always used in the English sense. A German *landschaft,* for instance, can sometimes be a small administrative unit, corresponding in size to our ward. I have the feeling that there is evolving a slight but noticeable difference between the way we Americans use the word and the way the English do. We tend to think that *landscape* can mean natural scenery only, whereas in England a landscape almost always contains a human element.

The equivalent word in Latin languages derives in almost every case from the Latin *pagus*—meaning a defined rural district. The French, in fact, have several words for *landscape,* each with shades of meaning: *terroir, pays, paysage, campagne.* In England the distinction was once made between two kinds of landscape: woodland and champion—the latter deriving from the French *champagne,* meaning a countryside of fields.

That first syllable, *land,* has had a varied career. By the time it reached England it signified *earth* and *soil* as well as a portion of the surface of the globe. But a much earlier Gothic meaning was *plowed field.* Grimm's monumental dictionary of the German language says that "*land* originally signified the plot of ground or the furrows in a field that were annually rotated" or redistributed. We can assume that in the Dark Ages the most common use of the word indicated any well-defined portion of the earth's surface. A small farm plot was a land, and so was a sovereign territory like England or Scotland; any area with recognized boundaries was a land. Despite almost two thousand years of reinterpretation by geographers and poets and ecologists, *land* in American law remains stubbornly true to that ancient meaning: "any *definite* site regarded as a portion of the earth's surface, and extending in both vertical directions as defined by law" (italics added).

Perhaps because of this definition, farmers think of land not only in terms of soil and topography but in terms of spatial measurements, as a defined portion of a wider area. In the American South, and in England too, a "land" is a subdivision of a field, a broad row made by plowing or mowing, and horse-drawn mowers were once advertised as "making a land of so-and-so many feet." In Yorkshire the reapers of wheat take a "land" (generally six feet wide) and go down the length of the field. "A woman," says the *English Dialect Dictionary,* "would thus reap half an acre a day and a man an acre." In his book on English field systems, H. L. Gray mentions a typical medieval village where the two large, open fields "consisted of about two thousand long narrow 'lands' or selions [furrows] each containing usually from one fourth of an acre to an acre."[2]

This is very confusing, and even more confusing is the fact that to this day in Scotland a *land* means a building divided into houses or flats. I confess that I find this particular use of the word hard to decipher, except that in Gaelic the word *lann* means a building divided into houses or flats. Finally, here is an example—if it can be called that—of *land* meaning both a fraction of a larger space and an enclosed space: infantrymen know that a land is an interval between the grooves of a rifle bore.

I need not press the point. As far back as we can trace the word, *land* meant a defined space, one with boundaries, though not necessarily one with fences or walls. The word has so many derivative meanings that it rivals in ambiguity the word *landscape.* Three centuries ago it was still being used in everyday speech to signify a fraction of plowed ground no larger than a quarter-acre, then to signify an expanse of village holdings, as in grassland or woodland, and then finally to signify England itself—the largest space any Englishman of those days could imagine; in short, a remarkably versatile word, but always implying a space defined by people, and one that could be described in legal terms.

This brings us to that second syllable: *scape.* It is essentially the same as *shape,* except that it once meant a composition of *similar* objects, as when we speak of a fellowship or a membership. The meaning is clearer in a related word: *sheaf*—a bundle or collection of similar stalks or plants. Old

English, or Anglo-Saxon, seems to have contained several compound words using the second syllable—*scape* or its equivalent—to indicate collective aspects of the environment. It is much as if the words had been coined when people began to see the complexities of the man-made world. Thus *housescape* meant what we would now call a household, and a word of the same sort which we still use—*township*—once meant a collection of "tuns" or farmsteads.

Taken apart in this manner, *landscape* appears to be an easily understood word: a collection of lands. But both syllables once had several distinct, now forgotten meanings, and this should alert us to the fact that familiar monosyllables in English—house, town, land, field, home—can be very shifty despite their countrified sound. *Scape* is an instance. An English document of the tenth century mentions the destruction of what it called a "waterscape." What could that have been? We might logically suppose that it was the liquid equivalent of landscape, an ornamental arrangement, perhaps, of ponds and brooks and waterfalls, the creation of some Anglo-Saxon predecessor of Olmsted. But it was actually something entirely different. The waterscape in question was a system of pipes and drains and aqueducts serving a residence and a mill.

From this piece of information we can learn two things. First, that our Dark Age forebears possessed skills which we probably did not credit them with, and second, that the word *scape* could also indicate something like an organization or a system. And why not? If *housescape* meant the organization of the personnel of a house, if *township* eventually came to mean an administrative unit, then *landscape* could well have meant something like an organization, a system of rural farm spaces. At all events, it is clear that a thousand years ago the word had nothing to do with scenery or the depiction of scenery.

We pull up the word *landscape* by its Indo-European roots in an attempt to gain some insight into its basic meaning, and at first glance the results seem disappointing. Aside from the fact that, as originally used, the word dealt only with a small fraction of the rural environment, it seems to contain not a hint of the esthetic and emotional associations which the word still has for us. Little is to be gained by searching for some etymological line between our own rich landscape and the small cluster of plowed fields of more than a thousand years ago.

Nevertheless, the formula *landscape as a composition of man-made spaces on the land* is more significant than it first appears, for if it does not provide us with a definition, it throws a revealing light on the origin of the concept. For it says that a landscape is not a natural feature of the environment but a *synthetic* space, a man-made system of spaces superimposed on the face of the land, functioning and evolving not according to natural laws but to serve a community—for the collective character of the landscape is one thing that all generations and all points of view have agreed upon. A landscape is thus a space deliberately created to speed up or slow down the process of nature. As Eliade expresses it, it represents man taking upon himself the role of time.

A very successful undertaking on the whole, and the proof, paradoxically enough, is that many if not most of these synthetic organizations of space have been so well assimilated into the natural environment that they are indistinguishable and unrecognized for what they are. The reclamation of Holland, of the Fens in England, of large portions of the Po Valley are familiar examples of a topographical intervention producing new landscapes. Less well known are the synthetic landscapes produced simply by spatial reorganization. Historians are said to be blind to the spatial dimension of history, which is probably why we hear so little about the wholesale making of agricultural landscapes throughout seventeenth-century Europe.

It is not a coincidence that much of this landscape creation took place during a period when the greatest gardens and parks and the most magnificent of city complexes were being designed. A narrow and pedantic taxonomy has persuaded us that there is little or nothing in common between what used to be called civil engineering and garden or landscape architecture, but in fact from a historical perspective their more successful accomplishments are identical in result. The two professions may work for different patrons, but they both reorganize space for human needs, both produce works or art in the truest sense of the term. In the contemporary world, it is by recognizing this similarity of purpose that we will eventually formulate a new definition of *landscape:* a composition of man-made or man-modified spaces to serve as infrastructure or background for our collective existence; and if *background* seems inappropriately modest, we should remember that in our modern use of the word it means that which underscores not only our identity and presence but also our history.

It is not for me to attempt to elaborate on this new definition. My contribution would in any event be peripheral, for my interest in the topic is confined to trying to see how certain organizations of space can be identified with certain social and religious attitudes, especially here in America. This is not a new approach, for it has long been common among architectural and landscape architectural historians; and it leaves many important aspects of the contemporary landscape and contemporary city entirely unexplored. But it has the virtue of including the visual experience of our everyday world and of allowing me to remain loyal to that old-fashioned but surprisingly persistent definition of *landscape:* "A portion of the earth's surface that can be comprehended at a glance."

"The Word Itself," from *Discovering the Vernacular Landscape* (New Haven: Yale University Press, 1984), 3–8.

## By Way of Conclusion
## How to Study the Landscape

For a number of years I taught an undergraduate course at Harvard and at Berkeley that was called "The History of the American Cultural Landscape." It dealt with such commonplace things as fences and roads and barns, the design of factories and office buildings, the layout of towns and farms and graveyards and parks and houses, and toward the end of the course I talked about the superhighway and the strip and certain new kinds of sports which I referred to as psychedelic. Throughout the course I showed a good many slides, and each student had to write a term paper on some aspect of the contemporary American landscape.

Slide shows are popular in the classroom, and though my slides were poor in quality, they were of familiar, everyday objects and places, and that, I suspect, was the principal reason for the success of the course. Of necessity, much college education deals with ideas and theories and is based on reading and study, and so an undergraduate course which required no preliminary experience, which discussed the contemporary world and how it had evolved over the past two centuries, and which was not overly critical of American culture—such a course was probably welcome as a relief, or at least a change.

It is the accepted European procedure, as I understand it, to start exposing a line of thought by first enunciating a few guiding principles and then providing examples, and this is the method followed by many American pro-

JBJ, photo, New England common

fessors. But the traditional Anglo-Saxon procedure is the opposite: it states the facts, provides examples, and only at the end presumes to draw conclusions. This was my approach and I found it satisfactory, if for no other reason than that I had no clear-cut conclusions or generalizations to offer. I had traveled enough in the United States to know the country well, and I had tried to familiarize myself with what can be called its vernacular history; and it was this experience which I undertook to pass on to the students. I confined my introductory remarks to such obvious statements as that a landscape (whether urban or rural) gradually took form when people moved into a place, did what they could to survive and prosper with the resources at hand, and that they soon organized themselves into a group for mutual help and protection and for celebration of one kind or another. I added that landscapes grew and changed and that they had a chronology that was often interesting to explore. This was followed by the display of a few slides illustrating change in certain familiar places.

So, the logical beginning of the course on the history of the American landscape, as I saw it, was a brief account of the arrival of the first settlers in a region—whether Virginia, New England, or North Dakota. The settlers appeared on the scene, explored their surroundings, and then proceeded to make themselves at home. This is also how conventional history books begin. They give a description of the way the new community sets up certain basic institutions; for government, for defense, for communication with the outside world; the way it establishes a school and a church, and builds places to live and work in.

But the student of landscapes has another interest: how space is organized by the community. This means the drawing of a boundary, the efficient dividing up of the land among the several families, the providing of roads and a place of public assembly, and the setting aside of land for communal use. So, while the conventional historian prefers to date the birth of the community as a political entity from that moment when all gather together in a tent or under a tree and pass a number of solemn resolutions, the landscape student likes to call attention to another, equally significant moment—when the first line is scratched in the soil or the first blaze is cut in a tree or the first stone marker is erected. These are the "traces on the Rhodian shore" that Clarence Glacken has described in his wonderful book of that title. The event is no doubt trifling and soon forgotten, but how is a society, even a small pioneer society, to function, how is it to have form and a degree of permanence unless it has its own territory, unless it creates and occupies its own space?

No one has written with greater authority and insight on the subject of space than Professor Yi-Fu Tuan, and his book *Space and Place* continues to be the inspiration and guide of every landscape student. For the significance of space in landscape terms, the allotment of land for private or public use, is that it makes the social order visible. Space, even a small plot of ground, identifies the occupant and gives him status, and, most important of all, it establishes lasting relationships. As the word itself suggests, a boundary is what binds us all together in a group, that which excludes the outsider or stranger. The boundary creates neighbors; it is the symbol of law and order and permanence. The network of boundaries, private as well as public, transforms an amorphous environment into a human landscape, and nothing more clearly shows some of the cherished values of a group than the manner in which they fix those boundaries, the manner in which they organize space. And because these values change in the course of time, the organization of space also undergoes a change. That is one reason why the contemporary landscape is so different from that of even a hundred years ago.

The original layout of spaces is well worth studying, it seems to me, if only because it unconsciously reveals so much about the ideas of the men and women who devised it. If I had to reconstruct my course, or if I were asked what I thought should be emphasized, I think I would say that the significance of boundaries and spatial divisions could hardly be overstressed. Few Americans, I discovered, have any notion of what the national grid system signifies in terms of political philosophy. We either criticize its monotony and its disregard of the lay of the land, or else we assume it was the product of real estate speculators. But as we should know, the grid system is, in fact, one of the most ambitious schemes in history for the orderly creation of landscapes, of small communities. When its scope and purpose are explained, I find that students are quick to respond, and from then on they are alert to other kinds of spatial organization—the careful distribution of land according to the merits of the family in colonial New England, or the laissez-faire procedure followed in the Oklahoma land rush. And what I find most satisfying is that some students even learn to appreciate the grandeur and beauty of the grid.

To talk about the grid means talking about fields and fences and roads and crossroads and schoolhouses, and eventually it means talking about the grid in towns and cities. We have to backtrack and discuss the Philadelphia version of the grid and the Philadelphia way of naming streets versus the southern grid and the southern way of naming streets, and even the Mormon grid—more familiar in the West, of course, than elsewhere. And then there are several kinds of courthouse squares, as Professor Edward T. Price has told us; and while we are on the subject of the spatial organization of the early American town, it is easy to discuss the unique qualities of the American addition or subdivision—which in the old days meant simply the selling of land, the house being built by the purchaser; whereas in Europe, the original landowner also built the houses and thereby created a distinct community or neighborhood. The grid system, at least during its early days, allowed for a wonderful flexibility in the use of space, and even a degree of interchangeability, for all lots, all blocks, all streets were of uniform dimensions and you could build what you liked, *where* you liked. A good illustration of how interchangeability was characteristic of the early, preindustrial landscape was the popularity until about 1850 of the Greek revival style. It was considered equally appropriate for banks, courthouses, mansions, post offices, college buildings, and churches. Using slides, I showed how versatile the style could be.

It was the preindustrial town that we discussed, the town which flourished before the factory and the railroad had invaded every part of the landscape, even through there was a water-powered mill in the average town, and often there were steamboats on the river. But a preindustrial town can be a very complicated element in any landscape, and I long hesitated to discuss the

JBJ, photo, grid from the air

urban scene before discussing the rural scene. There were several reasons, however, why I eventually thought the time had come. First of all, it is one of the
peculiarities of the United States, as Richard Wade has pointed out, that in
many regions towns came before farms; towns as trading posts, as defense installations, as transfer points in river navigation, were often in existence long
before the surrounding forest had been invaded by pioneer farmers. So it was
the town that set the pace in the development of the landscape, that established forms and spaces. But another reason for discussing the preindustrial
town was that it still represents for most Americans the most picturesque and
appealing aspect of our past. The small town of that period is familiar in our
popular art and literature and folklore: the town with its central square or
marketplace, with its fairground and local academy or college, its so-called
block of offices on the main street, the First Church with its graveyard where
the first settlers are buried, and the Greek revival facades along the tree-lined
streets leading out to the open country. There is always the danger, in dealing
with that remote period, of lapsing into sentimental antiquarianism, a glorification of the simpler ways of the early republic that many young people are
very susceptible to. On the other hand, since most students have an urban
background, they have an instinctive understanding of how to interpret the

town's spaces, and are often expert at discovering its style and its search for order.

My final reason for discussing the town instead of the country was this: the town, particularly the preindustrial town, offers the best material for studying the house or dwelling.

There is a school of cultural geographers which believes that the dwelling is not only the most important element in the landscape but is the key to understanding all other elements in the landscape: the social order, the economy, the natural resources, the history, and culture. It so happens that the dwelling which these geographers usually have in mind is the European farmhouse or farmstead—a combination under one roof of residence, storage, and work areas. In use and in design and in materials, this farmhouse is closely attuned to the surrounding land, and is, in fact, a product of it. Few American farmhouses, however, resemble the farmhouses of the Old World. Most of them are designed and used as residences, pure and simple, and are essentially like the dwellings in the nearby town, inhabited by lawyers and merchants and clergymen. Indeed, our farmhouses are often copies of these urban counterparts. We ought to be cautious, then, in accepting some of the European theories about the relationship between dwelling and landscape. A house in Juneau, Alaska, is much more likely to resemble a house in Shreveport, Louisiana, than an Eskimo dwelling a few hundred miles away. Perhaps we deplore this circumstance, but it is essential that we learn to live with it; and I can think of no better way for landscape studies to achieve academic respectability than for it to formulate a new and American way of defining house types based not on the nineteenth-century concern for regionalism, use of local materials, local craftsmanship, and local agriculture, but on thoroughly contemporary notions: the dwelling defined in terms of its longevity, of its relationship to work, to the family, to the community, and of its psychological relationship to the natural environment.

What makes an enterprise of this sort easier and at the same time more appropriate is that all students—and indeed all people—have an innate interest in houses. Whether they come from the city or the country, whether they live in a trailer or an apartment or a bungalow or a mansion, students, I have found, immediately respond to any discussion of the dwelling, its construction, its layout, its appearance, its many functions, and its evolution over the centuries. Like every other instructor, I have read many hundreds of term papers. In my case, they discussed some aspect of the contemporary landscape—usually the landscape of the small town or the farm countryside. Those which I found most enjoyable and most perceptive dealt with such modest topics as the front porch or the local Civil War monument, or with barns and roads. I enjoyed them not only for their content—they often revealed obscure historical information—but because they seemed to be based on childhood memories and family traditions. It was from such papers that I learned about the complicated make-up of towns which to the outsider seemed entirely homogeneous: the nicknames for certain sections, certain streets and alleys, the location of all-but-invisible ethnic communities. The papers told of family customs, high school rituals, church festivities; they revealed half-forgotten farming practices and beliefs, and the existence of small gardens where plants unheard of in the region were grown, year after year. All this made for pleasant reading. But there were also papers—not many of them—that recorded everyday sensory experiences of the landscape: the sound of snow shovels after a blizzard, the smell of wet bathing suits, the sensation of walking barefoot on the hot pavement. A woman student from North Dakota wrote of her family driving each fall to the nearest town to see the autumn foliage in the streets and yards; out where she lived there were no trees. This kind of landscape perception is something no instructor can teach. We can only be grateful when it comes our way, and encourage students to record such fleeting memories as these, and share them. They often make a whole landscape, a whole season, vivid and unforgettable.

I have already mentioned it in passing and I will say it again for emphasis: this kind of landscape study is essentially preparatory. It deals with the rural or small-town past, with an America which, except in a few isolated regions, has disappeared or changed beyond recognition. Why then, it will be asked, should we bother to study it? Why should we not follow the geographer's precedent, and simply acquaint ourselves with the current scene?

I can think of three good reasons for starting by examining the landscape of the early nineteenth century and before. The studies provide the student with a better view of our vernacular history than do Disneyland and its imitations, or than the student is likely to acquire from tendentious socioeconomic texts. Second, it is an excellent and relatively painless way of learning about the purpose of landscape studies, for it deals with familiar, more or less simple archetypes. And third, we can only start to understand the contemporary landscape by knowing what we have rejected and what we have retained from the past. I doubt if there is any other part of the modern world where the contrast between the traditional landscape and the contemporary landscape is so easy to observe; where the two exist in relative harmony, untroubled by class or race identification.

So there comes a day, usually around midterm, when the students are informed that we are about to embark on the study of a landscape of a very different kind: the landscape which began to emerge around the middle of the nineteenth century and which is now approaching full flower. It is popular to say that we are in a period of transition—and it has been said, with some justification, for the past hundred years. But the phrase represents a kind of evasion, an unwillingness to recognize that in many areas of our culture the final form can be discerned. The notion of a kind of perpetual transition has the effect of making us appraise many things in terms of a familiar past instead of in terms of present-day realities. The widespread belief that ours is a transitional landscape is a case in point: we tend to see it not as it is, with its own unique character, but as a degenerate version of the traditional landscape, and to see its history as a long, drawn-out backsliding, the abandonment of old values, old techniques, old institutions, with nothing developing to take their place.

But a more sensible approach, it seems to me, is to try to discover when some of its characteristics first made their appearance, rather than to dwell on the disappearance of the old. The gradual obsolescence of the traditional multipurpose barn is not so important as the rise of a kind of farming where no barn is needed and all produce is trucked to a local processing plant.

The discussion of the contemporary American landscape should start with the transformation of a basic landscape element: the piece of land or the farm. In the traditional order of things, at least in the United States, the ideal was that the family who owned the land also lived on it and worked it; family status came from the relationship, and in fact many colonial statutes, and even the Homestead Act of 1862, stipulated that a dwelling must be built on the piece of land. But with the sudden availability after independence of immense amounts of federal land for settlement, this concept was gradually abandoned. In the new territories in the West, land was acquired purely for speculation and its distant owner neither lived on it nor worked it. Other pieces of federal land were often occupied by squatters who neither bought it or worked it, and still other land was exploited for its timber or its grazing by persons who neither lived on it nor bothered to buy it. This is how a writer on land use in America sums up the situation: after 1812, he says, "we meet for the first time on a large scale one of the significant realities to which folk myth has blinded us; independence of the three variables: transfer of land from federal title, actual settlement, and economic development."[1]

As a result of this change, land ceased to indicate the status of the owner or occupant or user. Environmentalists are fond of talking about the need of a bond between man and the land, a biological tie or a mystic relationship. But in the traditional landscape, that bond meant something very specific: it meant that a family was legally and economically and even historically identified with the land it owned and lived on and exploited. The bond was the basis of citizenship. Finally, the house itself symbolized the family attachment, and was, in a sense, the matrix of the landscape.

Thus, when that threefold bond began to lose its power in the course of the nineteenth century, the landscape *had* to change. Land was defined in a new way: as a commodity which could be bought and sold and used in a variety of money-making ways, and the house was redefined in much simpler terms: as a place of residence, to be designed and located as such. Home and place of work were no longer necessarily identical and were even sometimes far apart. Land was put to new and unpredictable uses, or left untouched for future speculation. The fabric of the traditional landscape became loose and threatened to fall apart.

It is when we try to follow this development that we discover the importance of a landscape element which we had previously paid little attention to, and that is the road or highway. It had always been there, of course, but it had been so modest, so limited in its influence that we had taken it for granted. For centuries the country road had merely been a path, a cleared space created by some local ordinance to enable people to come to town to pay taxes, go to church, go to market—a political device, as it were, never given any but the most perfunctory care. But shortly after the Revolution, the building of roads became a matter of national concern, and from then on it began to play a role in the landscape, until (as we all know) it is now the most powerful force for the destruction or creation of landscapes that we have.

There is an enormous amount of writing on roads and railways, and some of it—not all of it, by any means—makes interesting reading. But naturally enough, most of it deals with either the engineering aspect or the traffic which the highway handles, and it is full of superlatives and statistics. When I first decided to discuss the road, I was sure that it could be disposed of in two lectures, illustrated with appropriate slides contrasting old, narrow, rutted roads with the interstate. But I soon found out that from the point of view of the course, the really significant thing about the road was how it affected the landscape; how it started out as a wavering line between fields and houses and hills and then took over more and more land, influenced and changed a wider and wider environment, until the map of the United States seemed nothing but a web of roads and railroads and highways.

And to further complicate matters, I began to see how the road altered not only the way people traveled but how they perceived the world. The first turnpikes, in the early years of the nineteenth century, gave the youth of America its first taste of speed: sulky racing got its start on the turnpikes of New York State, and other turnpikes, by traveling straight across country and by-passing the small villages, revealed the wilderness aspect of the American landscape. The cult of new models and accessories and driving techniques got its start when travelers learned to admire the handsomely painted stage coaches and the shiny harness and the bells on the horses, and when stagecoach drivers competed in style and elegance. The railroad made an even more profound impression: its business methods in those days were the first glimpse most Americans had had of the efficiency of big business, and they were widely imitated. Hard as it is to believe, it was the railroad which taught Americans to be punctual and to watch the clock, and the intricate maneuvering of trains on a single track taught many manufacturers how to organize production and movement.

The automobile, especially in its early days, introduced the notion of exploration. Remote country villages, mountain trails, and the trackless regions of the West were rediscovered by adventurous drivers, and there was talk about the revival of the countryside with country inns and country food.

I suspect that each of these experiences of the road increasingly revealed the abstract joys of relatively effortless fast motion, so that in a sense we were psychologically prepared, even a century ago, for surfing and skiing and kite sailing and even skateboarding.

But the road soon began to change the landscape itself. When the railroad came into a town, it destroyed the uniformity of the grid system. Railroad Avenue, with its skid row and its hotels, and with its railside factories and warehouses, introduced an axial development and distorted the original spatial order. The streetcar had much the same effect: it extended the range of commuters and gave them a wider choice of places to live, it decentralized many small businesses, and at transfer points it fostered a cluster of stores and services. And the street itself began to assume a new role: the practice of placing utilities under the street pavement—water, gas, sewerage, light, and eventually telephone lines—gave the street a permanence which it had never previously had, so that it became more important than the property on both sides of it. As in almost every other part of the landscape, the road or street or highway became the armature, the framework of the landscape. The piece of land no longer determined its composition.

What I am saying is an old story. We know, because we see evidence of it every day, that the street or highway is like a magnet that attracts houses, factories, places of business and entertainment to its margins. We are all aware that the important streets and arteries no longer exist to serve the local population, but that they create their own community, their own architecture, their own kind of business, their own rhythm, and their own mobile population. I have found, somewhat to my embarrassment, that students are, generally speaking, far better informed about the highway and its culture than I am, and if there is any risk in discussing the topic, it is the risk of too much enthusiasm, too great a readiness to describe the drive-in, the truck stop, the advertising, and the psychology of the mobile consumer as forms of pop culture, as topics important and attractive in themselves.

That is one reason why I think the emphasis should be put not so much on the road or highway as on the broader landscape created or influenced by the highway. For the highway is merely a symbol of how we learned to organize space and movement; and our zeal to reduce every action, every undertaking to a process of steady, uninterrupted flow of energy and productivity is actually better illustrated in the organization of a factory, a farm, even a university than it is in the incessant activity of the highway. It is in that broader landscape that we can study how the dwelling partakes of the spirit of the highway, and the history of the dwelling over the last 150 years demonstrates the slow emergence of new ideas of community and of mobility. The balloon frame was not the outcome of a gradual evolution of folk building techniques; it was invented by harassed carpenters in boomtown Chicago. It rejected tradition and group collaboration in favor of speed and impermanence. The prefabricated or ready-cut house, developed in the mid-nineteenth century, was popularized by the expansion of railroad lines into the treeless High Plains and made rapid settlement possible. The latest innovation in the dwelling, the trailer, was a response to the need of the motorist for a mobile home. The time has not yet come when we can define the contemporary American home with any finality—in this instance we are indeed in a period of intellectual transition, still thinking of the traditional European dwelling. But the geographers' point is still valid: the house is in many ways a microcosm of the landscape; the landscape explains the house. So let me, in finishing, suggest how the spatial organization of the two landscapes differ—and how, in consequence, the two types of dwelling differ and could be defined.

The old spatial organization, as I mentioned earlier, laid great store on the visible and permanent divisions of space—whether on the land or in the house or city; contemporary space is no less well defined, but the divisions are seen as temporary, and communication between them is essential; the dwelling favors the open plan.

Spatial divisions often meant permanent social distinctions, and autonomous organizations of work: the farm grew and processed and stored and disposed of its own products; the household was an autonomous society responsible for the education, health, and welfare of its members. We now delegate various stages in a process to another space—or another institution: the processing plant, the packing plant, the wholesale distributor, and so on—and, of course, we delegate domestic responsibilities to the school, the hospital, the various service agencies.

The old spatial organization made much of the need for storage, for provisions for the future, for preserving elements of the past—in barns and attics and warehouses. The modern spatial organization dispenses, whenever possible, with storage space. The supermarket, the factory, the commercial farm depend on trucks either to remove stock or to replenish it. The modern dwelling, without attic or cellar, depends on the mini-storage facility or gives every old item to the local museum or to the Goodwill outlet.

And finally, I would say that the old landscape was conservative and even unimaginative in the use of energy; it saw no further than the visible horizon, and was skeptical as to the existence of sources of energy hidden in the ground or untapped within the individual. As for the modern demand for all kinds of energy in unlimited quantities, the daily paper tells us enough about that. But there are other forms of energy which the past knew nothing about—inexhaustible energy which we are seeking to tap by means of spiritual discipline, self-education, and a new experience of nature. The contemporary dwelling, for all its cultural impoverishment, for all its temporary, mobile, rootless qualities, promises to capture and utilize more and more of this invisible, inexhaustible store of strength. So we can perhaps think of it as a transformer: a structure which does more than depend on the energy provided by the power company, which transforms for each of its inhabitants some of that invisible, spiritual energy we are only now beginning to discover.

"By Way of Conclusion: How to Study Landscape:" from *The Necessity for Ruins and Other Topics* (Amherst: University of Massachusetts Press, 1980), 113–26.

# 7 Landscape Revisions

Seattle, 1983

J B Jackson

JBJ, sketch, Seattle, 1983 (courtesy F. Douglas Adams)

## The Tale of a House

There was once a landowner by the name of Jonathan who possessed a house and garden. The house was so large that many families could live in it, and from these tenants Mr. Jonathan derived a handsome income.

It occurred to him one day that he could increase the income if his house were made to accommodate even more tenants, and he accordingly went to inspect it from top to bottom—something he had never done before—to see how best to modify it with this end in view. He was much surprised to find it in an extremely bad state of repair. While some of the apartments were overcrowded, others, for lack of proper equipment, stood empty. The roof leaked, the walls needed patching, and the staircases threatened to collapse. Though the furnace gave off powerful fumes which blackened the rooms, it provided the feeblest kind of heat. There were doors which could not be opened and windows which failed to keep out the rain. As for the corridors and public rooms, they were so littered with rubbish and discarded bottles that it was as much as he could do to make his way from one story to another. Strange persons loitered in the hallways and peered from behind corners. For lack of supervision, the water ran ceaselessly from the faucets and lights burned throughout the day.

The garden, once his pride, had become a tangle of vines and weeds and waste paper. Many trees had been cut down, the flower beds were neglected, and paths had been beaten across the lawn. The ornamental pool contained stagnant water, and to his dismay the summer house now accommodated an individual who sold ice cream. Even as he surveyed this destruction, the many children of some of his tenants, the Blackmans and the Urbanskys, noisily invaded the garden and set about uprooting what flowers were left, throwing stones at the birds and fighting among themselves, desisting only in order to harass old Mr. Bumpkin, who was endeavoring to cultivate a vegetable patch. Mr. Jonathan watched their behavior with indignation. "If I am to have any house and garden left," he said to himself, "I must certainly see to their repair, and my tenants will have to mend their ways immediately."

He recalled how he had once asked one of his tenants, Mr. Croesus, to keep an eye on the mansion, and he now decided to go see him. Mr. Croesus occupied the most splendid apartment in the house, using the living room as his place of business. He greeted Mr. Jonathan as an old friend and listened attentively to his complaints.

"What you say is true," said Mr. Croesus when he had finished. "The house has indeed fallen on evil days. The explanation is simple: you have many dirty and lazy tenants. I refer especially to the Blackmans and the Urbanskys. I suggest you get rid of them and install tenants of a more desirable kind."

"And what," Mr. Jonathan inquired, "do you understand by more desirable?"

"Tenants who have more money," Mr. Croesus replied. "Even a business enterprise or two. I would be happy to furnish names of likely candidates. You could then raise the rents and undertake some of the repairs you mention. If I may say so, you would do well to think of your house as a device for making money and to organize it accordingly."

"Perhaps I should begin acting on your advice, Mr. Croesus, by raising your rent."

This pleasantry was not well received. Flying into a rage, Mr. Croesus demanded to know how much more he was to spend out of his own pocket. He reminded his visitor that he had, at some expense, installed a small library in the public room and planted several shrubs in the garden. His wealth, acquired by unremitting labor, was what enabled him to give occasional employment to Mrs. Blackman or Mrs. Urbansky. And, in a fresh burst of fury, he declared that if the house still possessed any reputation, it was because of his presence.

Alarmed by this violence, Mr. Jonathan quickly withdrew to continue his examination of the house by himself. He learned that none other than Mr.

Croesus had been responsible for cutting down the trees for firewood, and that it was he who had leased out the summerhouse without consulting anyone. Furthermore, he had taken over much of the basement for his own use and, heedless of all protests, had put a large padlock on the door of the attic, to signify that he had preempted its space.

Two things were by now clear to Mr. Jonathan. First, that the house needed a thorough cleaning and refurbishing; second, that a permanent caretaker would have to be engaged. For, if repairs were not promptly made, the house would soon collapse, to the inconvenience of those within it and to his own considerable disgrace.

### How Mr. Jonathan Looked for a Caretaker and at Length Found Two of Them

Mr. Jonathan then remembered two elderly tenants who had often shown a lively interest in the house and garden. These were Mrs. Lovetree and Mrs. Taste; they lived in a small but agreeable apartment overlooking the garden, and were reputed to be connected with persons of the highest quality.

He paid them a call and found them seated in their livingroom, surrounded by potted plants and objects of virtu. He explained the circumstances which had led him to seek their counsel, and added that he was in search of someone to act as his agent in the restoring and subsequent managing of the house.

When he had finished, they assured him that they shared his distress. "The house is a beautiful one," said Mrs. Taste, "and it has long been a source of pain to me to witness its decline."

"I, too," said Mrs. Lovetree, "have felt no less strongly about the garden and its neglect."

Mrs. Taste continued: "I am aware that Mr. Croesus is well to do, and I do not forget that he gave a small collection of books for the enjoyment of the tenants, and that he further paid for several flowering shrubs. But in his legitimate zeal to make money I fear he has failed to display a sense of responsibility for the more beautiful aspects of life. I sometimes wonder whether he really cares about the appearance of the house."

"As for his chopping down the trees and thereby depriving a family of finches of their long-established nesting place," said Mrs. Lovetree, "that is something I find difficult if not impossible to condone."

These sentiments impressed Mr. Jonathan and he lost no time in begging the two ladies to assume charge of the house. They hesitated, then consented. Their sense of duty, they said, bade them undertake the mission. "In working toward the restoration of the mansion to its true character, we will not rely on our own judgment alone," Mrs. Taste assured him. "We are fortunate in possessing many friends of discrimination and learning, and with their guidance I have no doubt that this house will soon be greatly admired for its beauty and correctness."

"Moreover," Mrs. Lovetree added, "the garden will be put back in proper order according to the accepted rules governing such operations. You may depend upon it, my dear sir, it will once again be a sacred grove, undefiled by the presence of rapacious man."

Happy at having found two such paragons to manage his property, Mr. Jonathan took his leave. He foresaw not only an end of domestic vexations but the transforming of his house into an object of beauty, the envy of his neighbors, and a source of satisfaction to himself and his descendants.

## How the Two Caretakers Fared

A few months later he once again visited the mansion. Great was his delight when he beheld it entirely changed. The facade had been freshly painted, the shutters replaced and the brick pavement restored. The improvements within the house were no less striking. The rubbish which had formerly encumbered the halls had been done away with, and the glaring overhead lights replaced by brackets holding candles. Indeed, so completely had the old excrescences been removed that it was not easy to find and read the discreet list of the tenants. The public room was locked; a notice stated that it was open to visitors on stated hours. The garden abounded in trees and flowers, and Mr. Jonathan glimpsed several peacocks on the lawn. A high iron fence enclosed the place.

He congratulated the two ladies on the success of their endeavors.

"We have done our utmost," said Mrs. Taste. "The public room has been put back into its original condition and made into a small museum, open to the public four hours a day. The garden has been fenced, and since it now contains many rare and valuable plants, as well as animals and birds, we have decided to exclude the tenants. We have ruled on the curtains and window decorations used, and have prescribed a minimum decency of dress in the public rooms and corridors. A flautist of our acquaintance gives fortnightly concerts in the public-room museum."

"Excellent," said Mr. Jonathan. "I trust the tenants appreciate all these improvements."

Mrs. Taste sighed, then spoke as follows: "At every turn we have met with hostility. All that the Blackmans and Urbanskys have to say is, 'How about the plumbing? How about parking?' Even Mr. Croesus has been less than friendly. When we removed the large and ugly sign which announced his business, he inquired, how was he supposed to make money when the house was disguised as an eighteenth-century residence?"

"Mr. Bumpkin was beside himself when his vegetable patch was removed," said Mrs. Lovetree. "It was in vain that we told him that cabbages of a better quality and at a low price could be bought in the local market. And, though I have repeatedly told the other tenants that the garden is best seen from the balcony on the first floor and that the most exalted pleasure comes from watching the behavior of birds at a distance, the Urbanskys and Blackmans persist in lying on the grass with their shoes off."

Mr. Jonathan, disturbed by these reports, asked the ladies what remedies they had to suggest.

A complete change of tenants, was the answer. "I hesitate to make the charge," said Mrs. Taste, "but I fear the Blackmans and the Urbanskys are lacking in refinement. With my own eyes I have seen them discard candy wrappers in the garden."

"It is not that we have failed to try to correct their ways," Mrs. Lovetree said. "We have given them informal talks on the history of the house and we have taken the children on nature tours of the garden. We have urged them to attend lectures and visit art galleries. Our success has been slight. To use a somewhat popular expression, we do not speak the same language."

Mr. Jonathan then inquired: "What kind of tenants would you prefer?"

"Persons of education, respectful of the house and its traditions," was the answer.

Said Mr. Jonathan after taking thought: "I fear it would be most difficult to fill a house as large as this with tenants of that somewhat specialized description. And I also fear that the present tenants cannot possibly be evicted."

"In that case," said Mrs. Taste with some coolness of manner, "Mrs. Lovetree and I must reluctantly resign our charge. We will resume our previous occupations: polite social intercourse and the cultivation of the fine arts."

To which Mrs. Lovetree added in a low voice: "And the contemplation of nature, insofar as the presence of the Blackmans and the Urbanskys permit of it."

"Alas," said Mr. Jonathan when he had left the house, "my troubles are by no means at an end. Though the house is now in an excellent state, the tenants are unhappy. Yet they too are my responsibility."

### How Mr. Jonathan Found Another Caretaker and How This One Fared

In a small apartment on the top floor there dwelt a man by the name of Dr. Wellfair. Though poor, he was a scholar of great attainments, well versed in sociology, psychology, political science, and the correct use of computers. Partly because of his wide repertory of contemporary folksongs (which he sang to his own guitar accompaniment) and partly because of his friendly disposition, he was well liked by all the other tenants.

It occurred to Mr. Jonathan that he could do worse than talk to Dr. Wellfair and see if he were suited to the post recently vacated by the ladies. He found the scholar half buried in a welter of books and papers, and explained his predicament.

"Mrs. Taste and Mrs. Lovetree are ladies of great cultivation and the highest principles," said the doctor when Mr. Jonathan had explained his problem, "but their point of view is basically that of the Anglo-Saxon Protestant bourgeoisie in its late capitalist or pseudoliberal phase. It is a question in my mind whether their stimulus-adjustive-response system isn't essentially anal aggressive in orientation. Be that as it may, their management of the house has certainly not been conducive to a state of robust mental health among the tenants."

Mr. Jonathan said he had gathered as much. "The two ladies performed miracles with the appearance of the house and garden, but I am inclined to believe that attention ought also be given to the people who live in it, though I agree that they can be very troublesome at times.

"Mr. Jonathan, this happens to be my chosen field. If you will leave the whole problem to me you will not regret it. I guarantee, if I become your caretaker, to maximize the happiness of the tenants."

"And how do you propose to accomplish this?"

The doctor assumed a mysterious air. "It is a question of group dynamics," he said, "and psycho-therapeutic environmental controls. I'll need their medical histories, their school records, and a sampling of basic personality structures. After that will come a microbioclimatological survey of the area and an analysis in depth of the psychosocial resources of the house and garden. Then I will be able to start the preliminary study. The Rockefeller Foundation will have to help with the field work."

While not entirely understanding what the doctor had said, Mr. Jonathan was encouraged. "You appear to have a remarkable grasp of the situation," he observed, "a fresh, untrammeled point of view. I am happy to leave the management of my house to one of your talents."

"From now on," said Dr. Wellfair, "let us think of it not as a house but as an exciting social laboratory."

It was not for several months that Mr. Jonathan visited the mansion again, for he wished to give Dr. Wellfair time to finish his studies. By good luck he arrived at the house on the very day when these were to be translated into action. A swarm of carpenters, electricians, plasterers, plumbers, and painters blocked the hallway, and Dr. Wellfair, a roll of blueprints in hand, was surrounded by a dozen solemn-faced men. "These," said the doctor by way of introducing them to his landlord, "are my consultants: color psychologists, recreationists, community leaders, traffic experts, sociometricians, human ecologists. Their advice is proving invaluable."

"And all the workmen?" Mr. Jonathan inquired.

"We have at last discovered why Mr. Bumpkin is antisocial: his door faces onto a blank wall, and naturally this inhibits any communication and/or interaction. So we are cutting a new door which will open directly into the Urbanskys' living room."

"How have the Urbanskys responded?"

"Very poorly. The family is status-minded and an interesting psychosis seems to be developing. I'm encouraging Mr. Urbansky to take up a new kind of employment."

"Tell me, please, what other structural changes you have in mind."

"An intercom system linking the Blackmans' apartment with that of Mrs. Taste and Mrs. Lovetree. The Blackmans don't realize it, but they are suffering terribly from big-city anomie. The traffic engineers have recommended cutting a new corridor on the second floor to stimulate movement into the rumpus room; at present it is deserted half the time. On the other hand, to foster more neighborhood feeling on the third floor, where Mr. Croesus lives, we are suppressing the staircase altogether; the fire escape will have to do."

Mr. Jonathan glanced into the public room. It was much changed since the time Mrs. Taste and Mrs. Lovetree had made it into a museum. Three persons sat silently at a large table, confronting a blackboard.

"That's the workshop on extramarital sex problems," the doctor explained; "some of its members are missing. We use the public room exclusively for adult education groups, forums, panels, round table discussions of contemporary issues."

"Why is it painted orange?"

"The color is recommended by mental health experts. It seems to stimulate cooperative attitudes." Dr. Wellfair continued: "I've not made up my mind what to do about the garden. I've ordered a shipment of avant-garde playground equipment from Denmark, but the rest of the garden will probably be set aside for recreation. The trouble is, no one is quite sure what recreation means: is it picnics, or a jazz festival, or scuba diving, or weaving? So perhaps a deep layer of gravel is the best answer. We've had several panel discussions on the subject. It was generally agreed that the phallic symbolism in trees made them somewhat undesirable—at least in large numbers."

Mr. Jonathan continued to look about him. The Blackman and Urbansky children gathered to watch the carpenters tear down a partition. "How can we have a sense of community with all these walls?" the doctor asked.

"I presume, Dr. Wellfair, that you are well on your way to achieving your goal: the maximizing of the tenants' happiness?"

"Once the house has been remodeled. Because that is what houses are for: to make over in order to produce the state of mind we decide is best. It is simply a matter of applying the approved techniques of environmental science."

"So it does not really matter what sort of tenants you have to begin with?"

"Not in the least. Given enough environmental skill on our part, enough skill in persuasion, they will all conform to desirable social attitudes."

After a pause Mr. Jonathan said: "I have no doubt that your intentions are of the best. But I have grounds for concern. In the first place, this promises to be a very costly series of alterations. In the second place, I am not sure that I like to see my tenants used in this manner."

"Used? But my dear Mr. Jonathan," the doctor exclaimed. "There is absolutely no compulsion involved. It is all entirely democratic and scientific, achieved by persuasion alone."

"Perhaps. But unremitting persuasion is almost as hard to resist as compulsion itself, especially when it is offered in the guise of philanthropy. So I must ask you to dismiss your contractors and consultants and let my tenants continue in their disorderly, antisocial ways."

"Very well," said Dr. Wellfair. "I am being asked to resign; I am a generation in advance of my times, and this is the thanks I get." As he withdrew he was heard to mutter: "Clearly a schizoid personality, identifying improvements to the house with castration."

### How Mr. Jonathan at Last Found a Caretaker to His Liking

By now Mr. Jonathan did not know which way to turn. The time was past when with an easy conscience he could neglect the house, but though he saw the shortcomings of the previous caretaker, he did not know how to find another who would satisfy him.

While wrestling with the problem, he heard a knock upon the door. It was a tenant of his who paid part of his rent by working in the garden.

"My name," said the visitor, "is Ecos, and I have come to ask for the position which Dr. Wellfair had."

Mr. Jonathan looked at him with skepticism. "And may I ask your qualifications?"

"I can so repair your house that it will be sound and weather-tight and livable for many years to come. I can care for your garden so that it will be more productive than ever."

"Worthy skills," said Mr. Jonathan, "but do you know how to take care of the tenants?"

"I can see that they have a good roof over their heads; I can see that they can move about and come together easily, or stay by themselves without fear of interference. I can see that each has a plot of ground to do as he likes with."

"Those are benefits so commonplace as to be scarcely worth mentioning," said Mr. Jonathan. "Can you make them rich as Mr. Croesus proposed? Can you give them elevated notions of beauty, as the two ladies sought to do? Can you, in the words of Dr. Wellfair, maximize their happiness?"

"That is their own business, I think," said Ecos.

"You are deficient in philanthropy," said Mr. Jonathan severely, "the prerequisite of an enlightened caretaker. Nevertheless, since the house badly needs repairs (for your predecessors overlooked them in their pursuit of higher goals) and since I have no one else in mind, I will hire you to put my property in order. But once that is done, I warn you I will look about for a caretaker who will know how to improve the lot of my tenants."

And with that he closed the door on his visitor.

Several months later he went to his house to observe what Ecos had done. He did not announce his presence but stealthily examined the house by himself and asked questions of the tenants.

When his investigations were finished, he sought out the caretaker, whom he found working in the garden. "Ecos," said he, "I have inspected the house from roof to cellar. I find it in excellent repair."

"There was much that needed doing."

"The roof has been mended, the floors and stairways are solid. The furnace has been put in shape and the water is abundant and pure. I perceive you have introduced a cat to reduce the number of rats and mice: a sensible move.

Hitherto I have always found the corridors and public rooms full of litter and frequented by importunate drunks and peddlers and worse; or else I have found them devoid of life, with the public rooms locked against the tenants. Today they were orderly and full of life, and there were more public rooms than before. I applaud the present sociable arrangement. Yet I have been dismayed," Mr. Jonathan continued, "to see that many windows and doors of every shape and size have been cut; that there are balconies and bays and alcoves where there were none before; that there are a number of small pavilions on the roof, as well as many wings or additions, some of them well constructed, others extremely flimsy, projecting into the garden. Lastly, I have observed that the garden itself, except for a sizable public area, well maintained, is now a horrid patchwork of vegetable beds, horseshoe pitches, pens for chickens and goats, interspersed with tents and arbors and fragments of amateur sculpture. How do you explain this anarchy?"

"The tenants did those things themselves."

"And you allowed them to?"

"As long as they did not damage the permanent fabric of the building or reduce its efficiency, and as long as they did not interfere with their fellow tenants, yes."

Mr. Jonathan was silent for a moment. "Despite your leniency, I must inform you, Ecos, that you are by no means well liked by my tenants. They expressed great satisfaction with their living arrangements, but I regret to say they were unanimous in their resentment of your presence. Mr. Croesus accuses you of pampering them; Dr. Wellfair on the other hand referred to you as my lackey and the preserver of the status quo. Mrs. Taste and Mrs. Lovetree declared that you were a vandal, bent on destroying the character of the house. Yet the Urbanskys and Blackmans complained that you had obliged them to help in maintaining the house and garden and had even compelled them to make decisions. Is all this true?"

"Yes," said Ecos, "it is all true."

"They have said to me," Mr. Jonathan went on, "'We no longer have need of a caretaker. We can not only manage our own apartments, we can join together if need be to take care of the house and garden. Tell Ecos that you are through with him,' they urged."

"They were mistaken," said Ecos. "No doubt they know enough to take care of their own households, but there must still be someone to think of preserving the house itself. There must be someone to see that it lasts and continues to be useful, while tenants come and go."

Emblematic figure, house

Mr. Jonathan agreed. "Nevertheless," said he, "I am at a loss to understand your philosophy. You have painstakingly restored the house so that it is as firm and convenient as when it was new, and yet you have allowed it to be covered with excrescences and protuberances which all but hide its beauty. Why is that?"

"I have made it so strong," said Ecos, "that no temporary change can possibly weaken it."

"And again, you have somehow managed to make the tenants content with their apartments and friendly with one another, and yet one and all they wish to see the last of you. How do you account for that?"

"They have become free. They have not become better or wiser or happier because I have mended the roof and done other things, but they have become free."

"I perceive you are still not a philanthropist," said Mr. Jonathan.

"It would be better to think of me as a gardener," said Ecos, "one who prepares and maintains a place where plants can grow and flourish and eventually bear fruit. A gardener sees to it that they are protected and are given healthy and suitable surroundings and that each has its own appointed spot. If he knows his business, the plants will do better in his garden than in the wilderness outside. But he does not try to prescribe the kind of fruit they will bear: indeed, he cannot always be sure that they will bear any fruit at all. That is out of his hands."

To which Mr. Jonathan responded: "From what you tell me I see that the good custodian should be likened to a gardener of men; his skill should be judged not by the ingenuity of the layout of the beds and paths, the elegance of the vistas, but by the number of free men that are produced."

He resolved to keep Ecos in his employ. He had seen his house resemble a place of business, a work of art, and a social institution dedicated to the reform of its inmates. It now resembled an incomplete dwelling inhabited by a bewildering collection of people, each with definite notions of his own which had to be expressed, yet each somehow tolerating the rest. The effect was not beautiful but it had variety. "And in any event," he said to himself, "it will continue to change."

Ajax, "The Tale of a House." *Landscape* 14, no. 2 (Winter 1964–65): 21–24.

# Notes and Comments

Jackson used the section in *Landscape* he titled "Notes and Comments" as an editorial forum for expressing his understanding of the contemporary American scene. He wrote on a wide range of topics—from supermarkets and superhighways to the relationship of man to nature—in voices that were alternately whimsical, biting, and philosophical. The following is a sampler of excerpts from "Notes and Comments" organized around four of Jackson's most enduring topics: basic principles; man and nature; the true purpose of landscapes; and principles to guide American planning and design.

## Basic Principles

Before "Notes and Comments" became his forum, Jackson wrote occasional editorials. In the second year of *Landscape*, he sets out his statement of purpose in an editorial entitled "Human, All Too Human, Geography." Surveying the field of geography, he contrasts his position with that of environmental determinists and those he calls "economic-sociologically minded." Jackson wants "to study man the inhabitant."

Not man the product of nature, nor man the product of economic forces, but man the creator of dwellings and landscapes; the creator of his own habitat, his own microcosm. Man is the only creature who deliberately makes his own habitat—his own "natural" or congenial place of abode. He destroys forests, plants fields, constructs houses and roads and towns and canals and so on. He has done these things and continues to do them not merely to satisfy his biological needs (which basically call for no such elaborate modification of the earth's surface) but to satisfy his social and spiritual needs as well. To be sure, these lend themselves to no easy definition, but one of them—and from the geographical point of view the most important— is the need to transform his environment into the image of what man conceives to be a perfect prototype. His basic motive can be stated in very simple terms: it is the recreation of heaven on earth, just as the basic motive of his self-cultivation is the recreation of a divine nature. For if we are to put the study of the relation between man and environment on an enduring basis, we must not be afraid to rediscover and reassert a neglected truth: that man is the product, the child of God and that his works must therefore always betray, even in a distorted form, that identity. Man the inhabitant reveals his origin in the habitat which he himself creates.

The relation, therefore, between man and his environment is in some respects similar to that existing between the artist-craftsman and the material which he has chosen as his medium. This may be a relationship admitting of an infinite number of variations: the attitude of the carver in wood, who considers the texture and grain of his medium part of the completed beauty, is different from that of the modeler in clay who creates something almost entirely new; and different from that of a sculptor who uses stone. In a like manner, one group of men will set about creating their habitat by radically transforming the natural environment, while another will modify it scarcely at all, and a third will seek to perfect the already existing features. The human landscapes of midwestern America, of the Pueblo Indians, and of Japan are illustrations of the three attitudes. But there are countless others, and one of the tasks of human geography is the locating and defining of the areas in which such distinct attitudes toward the environment prevail. . . .

What is the best point of departure? The basic premise of our argument suggests that if we are to study man the inhabitant, his habitat provides the most reliable indication of his essential identity. The region is but an extension and an elaboration of the province; the province, if it possesses any genuine homogeneity, is merely a countryside on a larger scale. The countryside in turn is but a magnified version of the true microcosm, the dwelling and its immediate surroundings. In short, *the primary study of the human geographer must be the dwelling* and the establishing of dwelling types corresponding to those psychological areas.

There is nothing new in the statement that the analysis of the dwelling is the first and most important task of the human geographer. The only thing that can be new is the affirmation that the dwelling is to be regarded as the microcosm, as the prime example of man the inhabitant's effort to recreate heaven on earth. It was characteristic of the environmentalists, with their belief that man was the product of nature, that they held the dwelling to be in essence nothing more than a shelter, a response to environment. It was characteristic of the economic determinists that one of them defined the rural dwelling as an agricultural tool—in other words, as something essential to the farm economy. It is enlightening to see how rapidly and how uncritically this definition has been accepted. The farmhouse has, of course, its economic function, but it has many other functions as well. It is the center of social life and of family tradition. It has often been the center for schooling and vocational training and for religious observances; and in certain primitive societies it has served as a place of defense and the administering of patriarchal law. Finally, for many generations the dwelling was the only means of permanent expression in the arts and crafts.

In many regions of the world, and not the most primitive of regions, the dwelling retains most if not all of these traditional functions. In others, such as the United States, it has lost the greater number of them. These regional differences remain to be defined. But in this variety of the functions of every dwelling—and consequent variety of dwelling types—we have a significant and practical illustration of the varied relations between man and his habitat. The modern American home, even the modern farm home, is fast becoming little more than a place where members of the family (not all of them, by any means) eat one or two meals a day, sleep, and enjoy occasional sociability. Likewise, for the vast majority of Americans the countryside is no longer a place of work but a place for occasional relaxation. A Pueblo Indian uses much the same ritual when he starts to build a house as when he plants his fields. The ancestor worship of the Chinese influences not only the design of their dwellings but their sentiment toward nature, so that they think of it as a wise parent to whom they owe filial duty. Is there not a deep connection between our attitude toward our dwelling and our attitude toward the man-made environment? Is not one microcosm the prototype of the other? Does not the ordering of man's most intimate world, the domestic scene, suggest to him how to order the larger landscape?

A solution can only come when human geography seeks it; no other discipline is equipped to deal with these relationships. But first of all must come

a change of heart; many preoccupations which now seem so vital and exhilarating must be relinquished to planners and sociologists and climatologists
and economists, and many topics once considered of minor importance must
now be fully explored. To reaffirm the unity of man and of his world, his divine origin and his ceaseless efforts to recreate here on earth a dimly perceived
divine order, is the only way to establish on a firm footing the study of man's
modification of his environment.

"Human, All Too Human, Geography," *Landscape* 2, no. 2 (Autumn 1952): 2–7, excerpt.

As Jackson inaugurates the sixth year of *Landscape,* he reflects on his original purposes
in founding a magazine devoted to the Southwest, a region rich in cultural variety and
experiencing dramatic change. His ultimate goal, stated at the close, is to offer "a publication which attempts to experience the landscape in terms of its inhabitants, so that
others may learn to do the same." In the process, he has moved outside the region and
presented the work of European writers.

One element of our southwestern interest has persisted: the conviction that
some human landscapes are better than others; not merely richer, more
densely populated, more efficient; or even more beautiful; but better from the
point of view of the people living in them. And this, we freely confess, marks
a serious deviation from the scientific approach. The true human geographer
confines himself to ascertaining and analyzing such matters as patterns of land
use and settlement, and techniques of exploitation, and economic setup, and
population distribution, and so on—a comprehensive series of scientifically
ascertainable factors. When he has finished, he has presented a complete and
factual picture which can be of the greatest use to sociologists and economists,
and to other geographers. But for better or worse we reached the conclusion
that the character of every human landscape derives from a great many more
factors than these and their like; that if we are really to understand a landscape, we must look upon it in wider human terms: as the expression of a culture, of a way of life. We must learn to see the human landscape as we have
learned to see certain cities: as a complex and moving work of art, the transcript of a significant collective experience.

   To be more specific, we were persuaded that certain landscapes (usually
the older ones) were more intensely lived in than were others. The Southwest can offer two examples of what we mean. The Hopi landscape in Ari-

zona, wretchedly poor economically speaking, and in many respects under-developed (though it has been inhabited for almost a thousand years), is nevertheless an integral part of Hopi culture. Whatever nature knowledge the Hopis possess—of what crops to grow and how, of weather lore, of edible or medicinal wild plants, of game, of soils—has been almost entirely derived from contact with this patch of desert landscape; it has not been learned elsewhere or learned from books. The local landscape provides them (or used to provide them) with every material they use in their industries, their construction, and with their food; it teaches them what tools and techniques to develop; their dwellings and construction are adapted to it, so are most of their religious observances, so are their games and sports. In short, they not only work in harmony with the landscape—which is what every farmer eventually has to do—they think and create and invent and play in harmony with it.

Obviously, the Hopi landscape is an extreme example of self-sufficiency and of an almost mystical relation between man and environment; we can hardly expect to find anything remotely like it in the modern world. But take an example of the opposite point of view: that of the so-called suitcase farmers in the wheat country of southeastern Colorado. Here we find farmland rented on a yearly or even a monthly basis to some passing farmer-speculator from elsewhere. He prepares the fields, plants them, and goes away, to return only at harvesting time. He then harvests the crop (with machinery brought in from outside) and disappears for good. He never lives in the house, has little or nothing to do with his neighbors, has no business or social contacts with the community, does not care what happens to the fields after he has left them, and in fact usually leaves them far worse than he found them. For all he cares, the house can tumble down, the trees die, the dust bowl take over. He pays no taxes, and all that he knows about the landscape is that it will (at least for one year) produce a crop he can sell. To the suitcase farmer the human landscape does not exist. All that he sees is a work area—or, more strictly speaking, a money-making area; he cannot be said to have experienced the landscape any more than he has lived in it.

Well, both of these landscapes are interesting to the human geographer, even though they represent two very different attitudes toward the environment. We can make our point briefly by saying that the great difference between them, as we see it, is in the number of functions they serve: the Hopi landscape serves just about every function imaginable—economic, cultural, spiritual—whereas that of the suitcase farmer serves only one: producing a cash crop. So we came to the opinion (which we still hold) that the more functions a landscape serves, the more productive it is in terms of human values. If this is true of a strictly rural landscape, is it also true of a city or town? Yes, within certain limits, we believe it is. A town composed entirely of work establishments is no town at all; it is a plant or a collection of plants. A town composed only of residences (usually of one class) with a few service establishments is likewise not a true community. What is needed is a diversity of age groups, income groups, of occupations and interests, and a degree of cultural and economic self-sufficiency. The Southwest, again, can provide flagrant examples of one-function towns: from Los Alamos down to the coal-mining villages now happily becoming extinct; and also of towns with a remarkable degree of self-sufficiency. This is largely the result of their isolation. For in this region cities are hundreds of miles apart; and they are obliged to be independent. In the East, where they are often almost neighbors, each one tends to specialize, to reduce its functions.

It would appear, then, that the community can be judged in much the same manner as we judge the wider countryside: by the variety of purposes it serves. And how about the smallest (but most significant) element in the human landscape, the individual dwelling? Is it, too, better for serving more than the one function of providing shelter? If we believe that domestic life has any value that life in a dormitory does not have, then the answer can only be yes. The old-fashioned western ranch house was in fact probably the most completely self-sufficient dwelling America ever evolved; and the modern trailer, already so ubiquitous a feature of the southwestern scene, is probably the least self-sufficient — though evidently none the less attractive on that account. In short, we seem several times to have run across evidence of a long-term process in the evolution of *every* element in the modern landscape: a process of increasing specialization and centralization. The study of the human landscape could therefore easily resolve itself into a study of its cultural and economic functions and their gradual shift from dwelling to town to metropolis.

This undoubtedly would be an agreeable topic for academic speculation, were it not for one fact: landscapes are neither static nor permanent, and they can be created and modified by deliberate design. What we are considering, then, is not some inevitable historic process but a collective activity which can to a great extent be controlled. There is no longer any need for putting up with anarchy and ugliness in our environment; we do not have to watch helplessly the destruction of cultural values. The human landscape of the future can in a great measure be planned; it can be made to include those features of the old and new that we like, and it can leave out the others. So two questions actually confront us: *what* is to be done to make sure that the future landscape is habitable, and *how* is this to be done?

"A Statement of Policy," *Landscape* 6, no. 1 (Autumn 1956): 2–5, excerpt.


## Man and Nature

In 1960, the tenth anniversary of *Landscape* provides Jackson an occasion to step back and review his intentions.

We have published nothing dealing with the untouched scene — the landscape which to many people is the only one which is truly natural. That is because our concern has always been with the kind of adjustment men make with their environment and the pattern which this adjustment assumes; we have never held that the mere absence of man from the scene automatically sanctified it. . . .

We are all victims, whether we know it or not, of a way of thinking that sets the city apart from any other kind of environment. At the root of this confusion is one single error: the error which proclaims that nature is something outside of us, something green which we can perhaps enjoy as a spectacle or examine for future exploitation, but which is only distantly related to us. Nature, thus defined, belongs in the country and is all but totally excluded from the city; hence the oft-repeated outcry that urban man is alienated from it. . . .

[We have reminded readers that] nature is actually omnipresent in the city: in the city's *climate, topography and vegetation,* that we are in fact surrounded by an impalpable or *invisible landscape* of spaces and color and light and sound and movement and temperature, in the city no less than in the country.

"Notes and Comments," *Landscape* 10, no. 1 (Fall 1960): 1–2, excerpt.

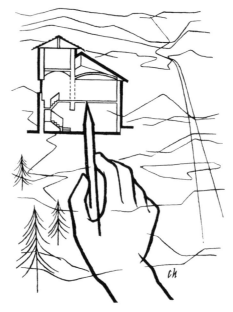

Emblematic figure, hand sketching house

**Jackson's report of a campaign in Germany to abolish ornamental garden dwarfs leads him to larger issues.**

What we think we see behind this drive, however, is another stealthy attempt on the part of the extremists among nature worshipers to quarantine still one more fragment of the green outdoors, to protect a little more of nature from the defiling presence of man and his works. We would be among the last to deny that protection of this sort is often necessary, but the garden seems to us the worst place to start. For this is precisely where men have already established a very satisfactory relationship with other forms of life, where we have manipulated and tamed nature to suit our convenience. It was in the garden that we first taught wild plants to be vegetables and to grow in rows, and taught wild animals to work for their keep. The garden is *not* a shrine; by rights it is an extension of the house, an extension of the living room and workshop and kitchen; it is even a kind of school where we learn what we can and cannot do to the outside world, and what the outside world can and cannot do for us. Bad taste in every form should be as inviolate here as on the mantelpiece. If we are to surround our workaday lives with untouchable shrubbery, unwalkable lawns, unpickable flowers, the long-range results could be disastrous. We would begin to spend our vacations reacting violently against nature worship, desecrating the green outdoors on an even more grandiose scale than now. The garden at least offers us a chance to transform nature in any way we fancy without doing great harm. A dwarf in the garden may in the long run prove to be less of an evil than a destructive monster in the wilderness.

"Expulsion from the Garden," *Landscape* 11, no. 1 (Fall 1961): 1–2, excerpt.

**Jackson's appreciation of the botanist and writer Edgar Anderson gives a sense of their shared principles.**

[Edgar Anderson] was the first to discuss for us a topic which is now uppermost in most of the articles we publish: the relation between man and his environment. Like many other contemporary nature writers, Anderson takes as his point of departure the fact that man is part of nature. But whereas most of his colleagues assume that we have somehow destroyed our original oneness and can only restore it by turning our backs on modern civilization, and somehow immersing ourselves in a wilderness order, Anderson repeatedly makes the point that man himself, just as he is . . . , is a rewarding subject for the naturalist. . . .

He does not hesitate to blame much of our present urban blight on an exaggerated enthusiasm for "undefiled nature." "The Amateur Thoreaus," he wrote in the Winter 1957–58 issue of *Landscape,* "and the professional naturalists of our culture are more fundamentally to blame than they realize. They have in the United States raised the appreciation of nature to a mass phenomenon, almost to a mass religion; yet at the same time they have refused to accept man as part of nature. For the beneficial contemplation of the world around us they would have us get as far away from man as possible. . . . They are one of the chief ultimate sources of our unwritten axiom, that cities are something to flee from, that the harmonious interaction of man and other organisms can only be achieved out in the country, that the average man is too noisy, too ugly and too vile to be accepted as a close neighbor." . . .

[Anderson] is warning us not to divide our world into two irreconcilable parts: a man-made world and a wilderness world. What he as a naturalist is saying has been said by others in different fields: that we must somehow learn to live in cities; we must somehow make our cities livable and put an end to our flight from the man-made environment. . . .

It would be hard to deny that the point of view most closely identified with the conservationists—that modern civilized man is by and large an unwelcome intruder on the natural scene—has had a very decisive influence on many environmental designers. A decisive influence and a restrictive influence; for, unfortunately, the more sensitive the designer is, the more he is likely to succumb to naturolatry. No one is more outspoken in criticism of the bulldozer and the dragline than the first-rate landscape architect; no one is more eager to have his construction "blend" with the surrounding scenery than the architect who admires F. L. Wright; no one, finally, is more determined to preserve the natural character of the landscape than the enlightened regional planner. Yet the bulldozer, directed by an artist, can and often does create magnificent forms, and no architecture in the past ever showed the slightest concern for "blending" with its environment; and all too often the conscientious preservation of the original landscape, empty of all human amenities, produces that flight from the community which Dr. Anderson has so justly condemned. One explanation for this overdone reverence for nature is easy to find: horrified by the destructive practices of highway departments, land promoters, and power company engineers, the enlightened environmental designer tends to react by coming to the rescue of what is so brutally threatened, relinquishing his role of *creator of human landscapes* for that of *defender of natural landscapes*. But he thereby only widens the gap between man and nature; to the city dweller the wild landscape becomes not a place for living but, in the tell-tale phrase of the conservationists, a "living museum."

"Once More: Man and Nature," *Landscape* 13, no. 1 (Autumn 1963): 1–3, excerpt.

### The True Purpose of Landscapes

As much as he loves viewing American scenery, Jackson sees the need for understanding it in terms of the lives lived within it.

Of all the reasons for preserving a fragment of the landscape—picturesque farm valley, village with fields and meadows, pastoral view—the esthetic is surely the poorest one. And the fact that many still think it the best reason of all derives from a point of view which should be discarded as fast as possible. . . .

We have got to find new criteria for the worth of a human landscape, existing or projected. Its place on the evolutionary ladder won't do, either will its esthetic qualities or its capacity for making money. . . . We can get nearer to an answer [to the question of what is worth preserving] by abandoning the spectator stance and seeking to identify ourselves and our desires with the landscape, by asking ourselves how any man would fare who had to live in it. What chances, for instance, does the landscape offer for making a living? What chances does it offer for freedom of choice of action? What chances for meaningful relationships with other men and with the landscape itself? What chances for individual fulfillment and for social change? Judged in these terms, many industrialized and suburban landscapes would be found wanting; but so would many picturesque rural landscapes as well.

We are, to be sure, not likely to adopt these standards as long as we prefer simply to think of the landscape as something to look at, a spectacle conducive to day-dreaming. And, if it were really nothing but that, it would be right for us to preserve it, design it, transform it according to a popular taste for the picturesque. If we did that, America would be a far more beautiful country than it is. But we are *not* spectators; the human landscape is *not* a work of art. It is the temporary product of much sweat and hardship and earnest thought; we should never look at it without remembering that, and we should never tinker with the landscape without thinking of those who live in the midst of it—whether in a trailer in an oil field or in a city tenement.

"Goodbye to Evolution," *Landscape* 13, no. 2 (Winter 1963–64): 1–2, excerpt.


In the mid-1960s, as Americans begin to explore their cities, Jackson warns them that looking is not enough.

People, the magazines tell us, are once again beginning to appreciate the city. Books of glossy photographs of graffiti, ironwork details, and abstract landscapes are financially successful despite formidable prices. The Museum of Modern Art has its walking tours; restoration of old market districts is in full swing, with the end products economically viable, if often self-consciously precious. All this is good. We will have handsome cities only if people want handsome cities. People will want handsome cities only if they see that cities can be, and indeed once were, *handsome*. But it will be too bad if the awakened interest in isolated urban examples of visual delight allows us to forget the social plight of our cities. Building watching, like bird watching, is a rewarding hobby. Both can refresh the person who practices them. Both can drive away apathy and ennui and reawaken a sense of vitality in the watcher by underscoring the beauty to be found in everyday life by one who will search for it. But building watching is a very small and isolated part of the urban experience. It bears the same relationship to living in a city as bird watching does to working a farm or ranch.

"The Building Watchers," *Landscape* 15, no. 3 (Spring 1966): 2, excerpt.

Jackson's insistence that the landscape must be appreciated as a place of work engaged in by ordinary people was, in part, a response to his own aesthetic inclinations. Immediately after reading Jane Jacobs's *The Death and Life of Great American Cities*, he writes of his love of the city as a work of art. Reacting to her argument for the city teeming with a "diversity of people and activities at all hours," Jackson recalls a different city.

Nothing of late has brought home to us so abruptly the passage of years as the sudden realizing (prompted by Mrs. Jacobs) that a whole postwar generation to whom this urban tempo is natural has now come of age. In a decade or two few will be alive who remember a quieter and more spacious kind of city. Someone had better record those memories before they are vanished: the tree-lined downtown streets that you could cross wherever and whenever you liked, the sidewalks broad and empty enough for aimless wandering, the lights that went out at ten o'clock in the evening; no standing in line at bus stops or theaters or restaurants, and residential streets stretching for block after block without a single parked car. The Depression showed us cities with vacant houses and vacant stores, a slowed-down tempo and an air of hopeless permanence. The war years—in Europe at least—revealed darkened cities devoid for hours on end of any sign of life. Those were none of them happy years, but they did allow us, perhaps for the last time in our history, to see the urban landscape without the intruding presence of people; we could still fall in love with the city as a work of art. The beauty of Paris, they say, was never so apparent as during the miserable years of the German occupation, and London, lighted only by the moving searchlights in the sky, was to its inhabitants a new and marvelous place.

It has always been this nonhuman aspect of the city that has attracted artists; all urban landscapes, from Piranesi to Kokoschka, have either reduced the human figure to insignificant proportions or eliminated it altogether. A generation which has only experienced the city knee-deep in parked cars, disguised and defaced by colored and moving lights, crawling with humanity, may well have the perspective of the neorealistic Italian movie: the moist humanitarian eye relentlessly focused on the day-by-day existence of the Little People. But it is possible to maintain that there is more than one way to see and love a city, and it was as a work of art with its own destiny and beauty, distinct from those of its inhabitants, that London was revealed more than a century and a half ago: a city which

> doth like a garment wear
> The beauty of the morning, silent, bare,
> Ships, towers, domes, theatres and temples lie
> Open unto the fields and to the sky;
> All bright and glittering in the smokeless air.

"Cities and People," *Landscape* 11, no. 2 (Winter 1961–62): 1, excerpt.

**Jackson is ever aware that the city of his imagination is not the city that others carry in their minds. Writing immediately after the urban riots of 1967, Jackson reflects on what the city might mean or not mean to the rioters in that long, hot summer.**

It will be long before we learn to understand the true nature of the disturbances which occurred in so many American cities this past summer. Their social and economic background we think we know, but why they evolved *as* they did and *when* they did are questions which will continue to bewilder us.

We are confronted by a totally new kind of mass public protest, and because protests of this sort have been rare in America, we are inclined to think of them in terms of European or Latin American revolt: in terms not only of political organization but of close involvement with the urban setting. It was the French Revolution which first established the classical form of mass public protest by a deeply rooted urban population, and we still expect to witness the classical gestures: the overturning of statues, the barricades, the gathering of crowds at certain squares and open places, and above all the reaction to certain public buildings—church, prison, palace—as universally recognized symbols of oppression or hope.

But in the recent American riots none of these gestures was evident: the urban setting, for all its guilt, seems to have aroused no desire for vengeance:

JBJ, photo, freeway clearance

it was as if the slum landscape had suddenly been seen not as a degenerate version of the city but as a senseless, featureless jungle which for a few hours could be exploited and left half destroyed.

Most of us, and almost all environmental designers, live in a world where the demolishing or erecting of public symbols is still of immense meaning, and where the design of the environment and purposeful movement through it are held to be an essential part of our culture. And yet here, to our astonishment, are millions of Americans, mostly young, who are so alienated that they see their environment as almost totally without significance or value as a means of self-expression—a squalid, obsolete stage-set having nothing to do with the drama being enacted in front of it.

Shall we ascribe this reaction to the peculiar form of the American city—its monotony, its emphasis on the street, its neglect of place and monument? Had there been more conspicuous symbols of the status quo in the slums, would there have been less looting? Or is it that the rioters, black or white, were all of them unassimilated, with none of our feeling for traditional symbols and traditional urban behavior? There is perhaps a touch of Appalachia in the figure of the random sniper, shooting at policemen for lack of squirrels.

Before we set out to improve the slums in the image of a more prosperous urban environment, we would do well to study this new widespread mentality which so despises its surroundings that the only change it attempts is pillage, and the only symbol it honors is the traffic light.

"The Non-environment," *Landscape* 17, no. 1 (Autumn 1967): 1, excerpt.

## Pleasures and Displeasures

Jackson remained a skeptic about the application of scientific research to the human condition. In the 1960s, he questioned new findings about the impact of crowding on rats and what it might mean for urban planning.

We are afflicted with a recurrent nightmare: a horrifying vision of all mankind in an endless procession, stumbling to follow and listen to a monster rat at the head of the parade. This latter-day Pied Piper (who wears the starched white garb of a laboratory technician) plays no flute; instead, he sings out from time to time in a shrill, authoritarian voice: "Recent scientific tests with rats conclusively prove that. . . ." Then follows one fearful statement after another: smoking produces cancer, untreated water produces caries, a diet of baker's bread produces every symptom of malnutrition, an environment painted red produces aggressiveness, unobtainable pleasures produce a mood of frustration, uncertainty produces collapse. And, in these nightmares, the mob desperately clamors, "More! Tell us more!"

It was the guinea pig which, in our youth, suggested what was wrong with mankind, notably our tendency to multiply. But the contemporary rat is clearly a much more sophisticated prophet, and he has recently shown a sociological awareness which must be gratifying to his followers. Thus it appears that rats, when crowded together into cages, given plenty of food and water and materials for nest building, but very little space, develop some extremely unattractive habits—ranging from irritability to sexual promiscuity and an inclination to eat their own young, and finally to produce no young at all.

As was to be expected, this sorry adventure in togetherness, the prestige of the rat being what it is, has been seized upon by the more alert social critics as irrefutable evidence that present-day slum existence will eventually spell the doom of humanity. We had a notion, even before reading the scientific account, that this might be the case; it is good to have it confirmed by an unimpeachable source, all the same. But what leaves us vaguely dissatisfied is that the account made no mention of what the rats did to try to remedy their plight—unless cannibalism can be considered a workable solution. Did they organize their existence or the available space in any manner? Did any new social order develop? Any group activities, cultural or otherwise?

Apparently not: the rats remained defiantly ratlike until the bitter end. And that is what makes rats so much better subjects than men. Men have an unscientific tendency to take just such measures under abnormally crowded conditions: in PW camps, in concentration camps, on shipboard, on desert islands, and even in slums, so that the whole scientific basis of an experiment is spoiled and a different kind of man is produced.

Our faith in the rat would, however, be entirely restored if science were to investigate the suburbanite of the species in the same thoroughgoing manner. Let a certain number of healthy rats be given plenty of room, feed, water, and masses of nest material, and let the nests be well isolated from one another. Then let the adult male rats be sent off during the daylight hours and the infant rats be put all together in a special cage until the middle of the afternoon. Then let the scientific observation start. If the female rats expire of boredom, if the male rats return to the nest exhausted—and muttering about commuting as a "man-race"—if the infant rats, once let out of their cage, immediately become unmanageable, then we will be happy to admit that parallels between suburban rat society and our own are too exact to be ignored. But if, as we suspect, the rats flourish and multiply and display remarkably glossy coats of fur, then the experiment, as far as we are concerned, would indicate that we had better find some other animal to show man the folly of his ways; something less rational, less predictable.

It's just a suggestion; but what would be wrong with the goose?

"Brother Rat," *Landscape* 13, no. 2 (Winter 1963–64): 2–3.

Many of Jackson's insights came from his reading of trade journals. In this 1964 piece, he tries to explain why supermarkets make it so difficult to find their wares.

The American supermarket is one of the noblest products of our civilization. Its architecture is above reproach, the variety of its wares and their low price are a complete and final vindication of free enterprise, and the social contacts formed at the meat counter, at the checkout stand, and in the parking lot are not only democratic but proof that the supermarket is fully the equivalent of the forum or agora as the place for the exchange of ideas and the refinement of manners.

But why is it that supermarkets cannot agree on a universally acceptable layout? Why do we find the sequence coffee–tea–canned milk in one supermarket, coffee–chocolate–spices in another, coffee–percolators–kitchenware in a third? How can these monuments to rational organization and service be so irrational and indifferent to notions of convenience in their displays? . . .

Why this shabby treatment of the American consumer? You have to be a reader of the *Progressive Grocer,* the *NARGUS* (National Association of Retail Grocers of the U.S.) *Bulletin, Chain Store Age, Rack Merchandising,* and *Supermarket Equipment* (to name but a few of our sources) before you can begin to understand this aversion to a general plan. The average progressive-minded dynamic supermarket executive does *not* want the public to know its way around his store; surprise is what he is after. "The average purchase made by customers who shop less than ten minutes is $3.67, while customers who shop over forty minutes spend on the average of $22.02," researchers have discovered. "Every minute beyond one half hour a customer can be enticed to spend shopping in the store increases her purchases roughly 50 cents. This means," *Progressive Grocer* explains, "that every possible means to detain the customer has to be used, every subtlety of department arrangement, produce location and facing, display, point of sale promotion and other merchandising devices." That is why certain fortunate shoppers have been sold "Indian bread" by nine salesgirls wearing Indian-style headbands, with an extra girl in a buckskin costume selling rolls and doughnuts. Improvised trees attract shoppers to buy birdseed and bird feeders. "As a reminder of the oldtime store," an authority on design writes in *Supermarket Equipment,* "fun type interest factors and accessories should be strategically located in the supermarket. These should include old-fashioned coffee grinders, cabbage presses, meat hooks with decorator slabs of bacon hanging on them, old muskets with decorative ducks and pheasants. Good design," he wisely adds, "pays off in happier customers who enjoy their shopping"— and who stay longer.

Placing these "fun type interest factors," or what the *NARGUS Bulletin* calls "Summer Fun Centers," from week to week calls for an extremely flexible layout. Not only does the produce have to be shifted about to catch our eye ("a cold remedy displayed in the canned goods section . . . sold almost three times normal shelf movement") but the counters and racks and gondolas (accent on the second syllable) have to be moved, because this further helps the customer to lose her way. . . .

In all this, is there a lesson for those who plan on a larger scale? Possibly those involved in reviving drooping downtown business areas can imitate the flexible layout based not on tradition or reason or convenience but on ability to astonish and surprise: garages temporarily transformed into produce markets, tents on empty lots, banks disguised as drug stores, and streets blocked off for outdoor bowling alleys. Above all, fun events and fun decorations, the more incongruous the better; for while the public may think it prefers a predictable order and the freedom to choose without pressure, it is much more amenable when it loses its way and is constantly bewildered by novelties.

"Fun Planning," *Landscape* 14, no. 1 (Autumn 1964): 1–3, excerpt.

**Often critical of those he calls "recreationists," professionals who plan leisure activities in nature, Jackson reports on a statement of their goals and hopes. As he does, he demurrs in defense of personal freedom.**

[The recreationists have set out] doubtless worthy ideals, but before we buy them it might be wise to pause and ask ourselves whether by engineering a creative concept of leisure we are not also engineering out of existence one of the last areas where the individual can be his own natural, inactive, uncooperative, moody self. It would be ungracious to remind the recreationists that many valuable things have come from introspection and solitude, but there is still something to be said for leaving a few untouched, unredeemed wilderness areas not only in the landscape but in our daily lives.

"Notes and Comments," *Landscape* 7, no. 2 (Winter 1957–58): 1, excerpt.

**In this 1954 piece, as elsewhere, Jackson gives an ironic voice to his questions about American tourists' experience of the West.**

We have just been going through some back numbers of *Holiday* and *Town and Country* and *Vogue,* and we are immensely reassured by the kind interest in the West that these people show; there is nothing condescending about it. We are now convinced that we have been doing a gross injustice to the Amer-

JBJ, sketch, trees and purple grass

ican tourist. Underneath that city veneer there beats the heart of an eager and bewildered sightseer, addicted (so *Harper's Magazine* recently told us) to juicy steaks and scenic camera shots and unobstructed highways; above all, a fervent seeker after the romantic.

In those articles on the West by regional writers, there is not a word about Le Corbusier and the pure architectonic forms of silos and grain elevators. Not a word about Mondrian and the huge rectangularities of the wheatbelt. . . .

The West which these writers recommend is the country of spectacular scenery and fine roads, but most of all it is the country of the Gold Rush and the Pioneer Days and the Santa Fe Trail; the romantic region full of what one authority in *Harper's* euphoniously terms "vestiges of yesterday's westering." . . .

How comforting it has been to learn all this! It means among other

JBJ, sketch, Hooper, Colorado, August 24, 1984

things that our fears of having no tourists in the future were quite unfounded, and that instead of trying to sell other aspects of the region we can go right on peddling the old reliable line of goods: Billy the Kid and Pioneer Day beards and Central City and Tombstone and burlesque Gay Nineties melodramas and chuck-wagon suppers sponsored by the Chamber of Commerce. We can take it from those who have studied the question: the thirst of the American tourist for Romance is insatiable, and the West is where he prefers to look for it.

But can the supply of Old Western color hold out forever? Yes, in a sense it can. We wouldn't want the tourists to know what is happening to our economy out here, but, confidentially, it is changing fast. The faster it changes, the faster things become obsolete, don't they? And the more obsolete a thing is, the more eager the public is to buy it. Why, God only knows; but the average American tourist wants anything, provided it is out of date—anything from a glass doorknob to a New England gristmill. If it's too small for a coffee table, it will be made into a lamp. True enough, the present Gay Nineties stock is pretty well exhausted; sold or worn out or simply destroyed; but westward, look, the land is bright; social changes out here are steadily producing, year after year, a whole new crop of abandoned depots, mustard yellow and maroon; abandoned one-room country schoolhouses, complete with flagpole . . . ; abandoned coal mines and country stores and marginal farms; battery radio sets and hand-operated gas pumps and horse collars. They'll all be collectors' items before long.

And even after they have disappeared, the West will still be turning out nostalgia for the tourist—by the simple process of outgrowing its past. In a sort of vision, we see the brand-new landscape of antiquities which will have evolved a generation hence. When sprinkler systems replace surface irrigation, someone will fall in love with the abandoned ditches—long and straight and deep—and somehow terribly evocative. What Piranesi did for Rome and what Charles Addams has done for Victorian America, some as yet unborn artist will do for our grain elevators and freight yards when they too become obsolete and useless. And all those marvelous ghost oil fields! . . .

Incidentally, we know of a place out west where you can pick up the entire office furniture of a small-town general practitioner for a song. How do you suppose *that* ever happened to come on the market?

"The Lure of the West," *Landscape* 4, no. 1 (Summer 1954): 3–4, excerpt.

**Jackson's enjoyment of the automobile often led him to question planning practice. In this defense of the automobile, he draws on Edward T. Hall's notions about space, that "men move through, build around them, and carry about with them, certain structured volumes of psychologically differentiated space."**

The automobile allows one to travel almost at will anywhere in the public domain while remaining in a completely private world unequivocally defined by physical boundaries. . . . It might be that the rapid and continuing changes in the American social scene over the last fifty years have produced a general uncertainty and unease that places more importance and value upon the protection and clear definition of the private, personal realm. While the traditional utopian visions have been built around a communal structure, modern Americans are attempting to build very personal or at least familial utopias—utopias structured around detached houses, television, and automobiles. . . .

This ability to move through public space without suffering impingements upon, or readjustment of, one's own personal space could explain much more than the commuter's attachment to his private automobile. [It explains the success of the auto rental company, the use of the car in wilderness areas.] Surely it explains much of the success of the motel business, for a motel is more than just convenient—it enables one to move between the personal spaces of car and bedroom without traveling through the more public and often spatially ambiguous realms of lobby, elevator, and corridor associated with the traditional hotel. . . .

The appeal of the automobile is not just a silly habit easily gotten rid of, but a means of fulfilling deeply rooted concepts of human territoriality.

"Auto Territoriality," *Landscape* 17, no. 3 (Spring 1968): 1–2, excerpt.

## To Pity the Plumage and Forget the Dying Bird

We like to think of ourselves as an urban people, but much depends on what we mean by urban. The National Planning Association informs us that by 1975, 73 percent of the American population will be living in metropolitan areas. A very impressive statistic, until we discover that among these metropolitan areas are Pittsfield, Massachusetts, Waterloo, Iowa, and Laredo, Texas, with projected populations of eighty-eight thousand.

At present, 58 percent of our population lives in towns of fifty thousand or fewer; more Americans live in towns of ten thousand or fewer than live in all of the cities of a million or more; and one of every four Americans lives in a place with fewer than twenty-five hundred inhabitants. Most of us, in brief, still live in a small city or in a semirural setting, and the chances are that even in 1975 the proportion will still be sizable.

One puzzling thing about this situation is, who is responsible for the rural/small-town/small-city environment: County? State? Federal government? What group, what profession, what department is primarily concerned with its well-being? Now that the cities have their own Department of Housing and Urban Development, they cannot complain of neglect; forests and public lands are taken care of by the Department of the Interior; the Army Corps of Engineers and the various state highway commissions have their own bailiwicks. But who is responsible for what is left of the American landscape? Who is interested in making it more livable?

More livable, not necessarily more beautiful. Scenically speaking, few parts of the world can boast of such magnificent countrysides or such attractive towns as those in the United States. A tight fitting together of all the parts, a crowded efficiency, is not so typical of this country as it is of older landscapes, and the architecture and monuments in our towns are not usually worth a second glance. But nowhere else are the works of man on such a generous scale, nowhere else do towns and cities stand out so dramatically against their setting. There are hundreds of towns with long, straight streets engulfed in shade trees, hundreds of suburbs that are models for the rest of the Western world; charming campuses unique to America, and more often than not an old-fashioned urban dignity achieved with the simplest of means. Nowhere are newly built towns so bright and full of energy; even the ugliest of Main Streets is enlivened by the occasional elegance of a shopping center, a cluster of grain elevators, a burst of greenery. The towns and small cities of Europe are fast being submerged by a flood of good taste; theirs is the fixed smile of welcome to tourists; over here we still retain a varied and exuberant beauty. It is impossible after traveling through the American landscape, from city to town to village, not to feel love for it, and finally a pride of possession.

But it is then that you begin to see the landscape with a different eye, and to see what you have not seen before.

You turn off the broad highway, leaving the panoramas behind, and follow a dirt road that humps straight ahead out of sight; no roadside landscaping here, merely a borrow pit deep enough to drown in; but the road seems little used. There is a grey, dilapidated house with a swarm of junked cars under the half-dead trees of the orchard. The barn is about to fall down, erosion is eating into the cornfield. Half a mile ahead is a crossroad (this one all but abandoned) with another decrepit house, a weed-grown cemetery, and a vacant church. There is a third house with a half-dozen trailers in the front yard. This place is littered with trash and broken toys.

The road, now grass-grown, follows a stream through a disorderly tangle of vines and trees, and you see how the water is dirtied by the overflow from a nearby feedlot. Eventually it leads to a lake, the lower end of which has been transformed into a swamp by the enormous steep embankment of a new highway. The dirt road falters, looks for its path among stumps and puddles, and finally goes through an underpass.

JBJ, photo, "American West Wood"

Ten minutes later you succeed in getting onto the new divided, limited-access highway. It cuts diagonally across the pattern of fields and roads and fences so that the right-of-way has a kind of sawtooth border of triangular pieces of land. Each sprouts a sign: FOR SALE; WILL FILL (OR LEVEL) TO SUIT TENANT; INDUSTRIAL SITE. The nearer you get to town, the thicker the signs and billboards become; then service stations, trailer courts, used car lots, supermarkets, and motels appear. On dirt roads bulldozed through alfalfa fields stand rows of identical tract houses, all perched on fill held in place by a scanty growth of grass. The climax to the whole strip development is "Towne and Country Plaza," a stylish, three-hundred-thousand-square-foot shopping center recently built by a Chicago firm, and almost entirely tenanted by chain stores.

Town itself, as approached by the new highway, has a familiar aspect: a mass of trees, a steeple or two, one tall conspicuous building. The water tower is adorned with spray-can inscriptions of high school scores. As usual, Main Street is wide and handsome, with splendid maple trees in the residential section and solid white houses, each with an immaculate lawn. The side streets display the same formal beauty, though on a smaller scale.

Getting through the business district is no easy undertaking since it has been transformed, from motives of efficiency, into a maze of one-way streets. But there are solid brick churches, solid banks which tell both the temperature and the time, and several blocks of not-so-solid-looking retail stores, some of them for rent. In an effort to promote a festive downtown atmosphere, plastic geraniums have been hung from the light poles. In the basement of the yellow brick hotel is the office of the Chamber of Commerce: BLANK TOWN, THE DASH CAPITAL OF THE WORLD. THE FRIENDLY TOWN WITH A BIG FUTURE. VISIT THE WORLD FAMOUS MYSTERY ROCKS. INDUSTRIAL SITES AVAILABLE.

All of this constitutes the conventional transient view of the town; what every tourist sees and usually likes; it is very reassuring: America is the best country in the world. But when you deliberately turn off Main Street and head for the station in the lower part of town, you see something different. Cross Third Street and Second Street and Railroad Street; the buildings are shabby, the stick-style depot is boarded up. The surface of the streets is broken and full of dusty holes; there are overhead lines and half the trees are dying. Instead of neat white houses as in the upper section there are close-packed rows of frame tenements and duplexes dating from 1893, an occasional vacant lot, garages black with grease, corner groceries with screen doors, lodging houses. Here is where the local minority lives: Negroes or Spanish Americans or Indians or unassimilated hillbillies, along with idle old men and drifters vaguely looking for a harvesting or construction job. The section merges into a wasteland of rusting tracks, cinders, flood plain. Most of the people here are on relief, but some work in the nearby factory.

It makes wire coat hangers or carburetors for power lawn mowers or plastic bookends; whatever it makes, the by-product is a black fluid which oozes down the margin of McKinley Avenue and passes through a used car lot, under some billboards, until it spills into the river. The billboards say KEEP ILLINOIS (OR ALABAMA OR COLORADO) BEAUTIFUL; BUY A FORD; SUPPORT YOUR LOCAL POLICE.

There are a fine municipal swimming pool, a fine football field, a country club with a golf course, a county fair grounds in poor shape. Fairmonte Acres is the choice suburb; it has gas lighting along its winding roads named after Indian tribes.

The street leading out of town passes several trailer courts, not very pretty ones, then it rejoins the highway; once more you are in the midst of well-cared-for fields, winding valleys full of greenery; and off on the horizon fifteen miles away is another water tower, and presumably another town like the one behind you.

What does a detour of this sort reveal? Nothing deliberately hidden, merely that much of the American landscape, even in prosperous areas, is neglected and mismanaged, constricted by long-out-of-date ideas of planning and preservation.

It reveals that widespread reform and change are in order; but what kind of reform? There is a sharp difference of opinion here as to whether it should be ecological or social. The so-called Beautificationists, together with the many groups and foundations dedicated to Quality in the Environment, and some of the old-line landscape architects and regional planners are chiefly worried about preserving and improving the natural features of the environment—*any* environment—and for several reasons theirs are the voices we hear most often. In the case of this particular landscape, they have a set of ready answers: "Hide the junked cars, turn the stream into a recreation area, turn the road into a bridle path or bicycle path, the eroded fields into a forest or a nature study preserve. As for the town itself, the former nineteenth-century appearance of Main Street should be carefully restored, more trees planted, and the factory told not to pollute the river. The billboards, the trailer courts, and all other aspects of urban sprawl should be eliminated, and tourists should be attracted by means of an Annual Pioneer Pageant. Would it be possible" (a diffident tone creeps into their voice) "to revive handicrafts? Bedspreads and homemade jam?"

Well, no; but otherwise these proposals are sensible enough. If they were put into effect, the landscape would undoubtedly be more sightly and, in ecological terms, much more healthy. Health and recreation—they have become almost obsessions with some environmental reformers; are they the only things that matter?

There exists, however, another way of approaching the neglected and mismanaged landscape, and this other way is just as much concerned with the people who live there as with the countryside or town itself. Health and recreation are essential to the people, of course, hut no less essential are the possibilities of making a good living and of being active members of society. Who belongs to this other school? Some are rural sociologists, some are officials with various government agencies—agricultural, economic, welfare. Others are the latter- day homesteaders, like those the "Green Revolution" and "Way

Out" describe . . . advocates of "intentional communities," refugees from the metropolis. Then there are members of farm reform movements, decentralists, rural priests, and school teachers. Very few come from the design professions. What they all seem to have in common is a desire to see rural/small-city America revitalized socially and economically, and they are all trying to do something to bring this to pass.

This second group of reformers sees the problems in a light entirely different from that of the ecologically minded. To them this landscape—well above the American average in livability, or health for that matter—is suffering from a very specific ailment or combination of ailments: poverty and political inertia. These can eventually ruin the most fertile countrysides in the richest among nations; likewise, prosperity and modernization can restore them and in the process restore their beauty.

The reactions of the two groups to public eyesores—especially junked cars and trailers—are typical. The Beautificationists view them quite simply as deliberate affronts to the passerby, expressions of total indifference to questions of taste. In a sense they are not so wrong. But by this time everyone ought to know that junked cars in a farmyard or a pasture have an economic explanation: they mean poverty. Poverty *and* laziness, or poverty *and* ignorance; but poverty in any case. Junked cars are where they are either to be cannibalized to produce one half-way decent car for a family which cannot afford to buy one, or else because a city junk dealer is paying a small rent in order to park his surplus stock.

The same holds true of many billboards: they represent a small income to an impoverished landowner. It is very convenient to ascribe the despoliation of our landscape to the greed of large economic interests: power companies, coal mining companies, lumber companies, ranchers and real estate developers with immense landholdings. All these certainly contribute to the mess, and they are the ones who especially threaten exurbia, where most of the Beautificationists live. So the cry goes up that if we once teach social responsibility to capitalism, all will be saved. But who is going to teach social responsibility to the poor? The sad truth of the matter is that most of the damage is done by them. Much strip mining is the work of unemployed miners who happen to own a few acres of coal-rich land. Much overgrazing and indiscriminate tree cutting is the work of needy farmers and stockmen; water is polluted by families which have no decent plumbing, by small, inefficient country operators; and a 1956 jalopy is more likely to pollute the air than a 1967 Cadillac. For every poorly designed, poorly located subdivision owned by a multimillion-dollar developer, there are a dozen small ones, no less poorly designed, owned by farmers short of cash or sick of being poor. The moment we get the courage to blame poverty for some of our environmental troubles, we will have taken the first real step to reform.

If the Soil Conservation Service is right, there are about three hundred thousand miles of stream bank in the United States that are not covered by any conservation program. Most of this is in private hands, and the average farmer or rancher does not have the money to undertake reclaiming or re-seeding land at three hundred dollars an acre. So he continues to abuse the stream even though it is of value to him. Is there really any sense in preaching a "new land ethic" to men who would promptly wind up on relief if they practiced it? Poverty, as the French say, is not a vice. Perhaps not, but it is a bad habit which interferes with good habits.

Poverty in the country, smelling of laying mash and kerosene. Poverty, public or corporate, in the towns and small cities manifest in slums, pollution, un-paved streets, and a determination not to change. Perhaps what our smaller municipalities need is a guaranteed annual income: pressed by the constant cry for new streets, new schools, higher welfare costs, the only solution they see is to attract more industry. And when they *do* manage to attract a plant, the last thing they dream of doing is protecting the air and water from pollution. What available money there is goes either into trying to keep downtown alive or into the inevitable youth facilities—athletic fields, schools, recreation pro-grams. What you find in small American factory or mining towns, and even in farm processing towns in Kansas or Texas, are not the most extensive slums but far too often the *worst* slums: dirtier, more primitive, more ghettolike, more isolated from the rest of the community than any slum in Chicago or New York. The proportion of substandard housing in rural America is four times what it is in the cities, and though this includes the shanties of the cot-ton South, the shacks, tents, chicken coops, and car bodies where some sixty thousand southwestern Indians live, it also includes the squalid trailer courts, the miserable do-it-yourself houses along unpaved streets on the edge of town, the company tenements which no large city would tolerate, if only for health reasons. The trailer and the trailer court are for hundreds of thousands of Americans the only alternative to slum living. But they have another virtue: along with the new highway, they disrupt the old pattern of the city and de-stroy established land values, and thus represent real possibilities of change.

As the Office of Economic Opportunity has discovered, poverty is not an easy thing to define, particularly in a landscape of million-dollar farms, million-dollar schools, multimillion-dollar highways, and space-age industries with their attendant thirty-thousand-dollar suburban homes. But we are learning not to confuse these installations with those which contribute to the permanent well-being of the landscape and its inhabitants. They can and often do exist in the midst of an environment which in human terms suffers from severe impoverishment.

An impoverished environment is one which can no longer help the people who live in it to become full-fledged individuals and citizens. Not all of our development comes from contact with the environment; but much of it does, and when that contact is made difficult, we are badly cheated. Each of us needs a chance to create or modify some part of our world—house or place of work or place of leisure; and an environment which is so mismanaged and disorganized that most of us are simply tenants or guests or spectators can be called impoverished. That is what has happened in many parts of America. The young American without means can sooner hope to be president of a bank than the owner of a working farm; there are millions who can never aspire to owning a house. More than one European country is actively encouraging some form of ownership of land—if no more than a vacation cottage or a garden plot. We have pretty well outgrown the nineteenth-century concept of the homestead and the family farm; but there are other forms of land tenure that we have yet to try. The real estate developer, whatever his ethical shortcomings, has broken the inflexible pattern of one kind of ownership. The highway, on the other hand, threatens to become the landscape of franchises—an area all but inaccessible to the small operator. Our countryside can become the same thing unless we pay attention. How many of our states and counties are thinking about new, more flexible, more equitable forms of land tenure?

An environment is impoverished when its internal structure is too rigid to change on its own—and when the public authorities make no real effort to change it to suit new circumstances. We are seeing landholdings getting larger and more specialized, new kinds of farm centers evolving, old centers going out of existence, and all of these developments call for new political forms and new types of administrative units. But our countryside remains entangled in a web of inefficient, arbitrary boundary lines which handicap social or economic action: obsolete townships and counties and school districts, expensive to operate; property lines based on the old grid system which paid no attention to topography; administrative frontiers which correspond to no social entity. How many enterprises, how many promising centers has this system not already strangled? But how many of our states and counties are giving serious thought to some kind of territorial and administrative reorganization? In the last twenty-five years, *eight* counties out of the thousands in existence have been consolidated.

An environment is impoverished when its inhabitants cannot come together easily and agreeably, and when there are no suitable places of public assembly. Much of our rural road network, based as it is on the old-fashioned grid, is hopelessly inadequate, costly in maintenance, little used. Larger farms mean that many farmsteads are now remote from adequate roads; faster forms of transportation mean that farmers are abandoning old centers in favor of newer, more distant ones. Yet the old network persists, leading straight to places no one wants to go to any more. Fewer but better and more direct highways are what the countryside calls for. And in the towns and cities it is much the same. There are still a disgraceful number of unpaved streets, based as usual on a grid system which has at present no justification—menaces to health, eyesores, social stigmas, and obstacles to public assembly. Political inertia and lack of imagination are again to blame: we continue to perpetuate a street system which focuses on the old downtown business section and local traffic, instead of on the new recreation and shopping centers where people would prefer to go. Main Street is no longer the civic center, it is no longer the place where citizen decisions are reached, if for no other reason than that it no longer has parking space. How many of our states and counties and smaller cities are seriously studying the need for a rational road and street system which would serve the new centers of activity?

Finally, an environment which has no conscious purpose, which is incapable of deciding its own future, which does not know how to locate highways, developments, industries, recreation areas, new areas for exploitation except on a hit or miss basis, is robbing its inhabitants of any kind of economic security and making responsible citizenship next to impossible. How many of our states and counties have a comprehensive plan for land use and future growth?

Economic poverty and political inertia are certainly not confined to the rural/small-city countryside in America, but here they are a peculiar kind of menace because they are well disguised. Yet no matter how beautiful our landscapes may appear to be, they are often inadequate as settings for a well-rounded life. The division of land, down to the smallest farm, and its tenure are frequently neither just nor efficient; the coming together of people for business or public affairs is unnecessarily handicapped; the destruction of symbols and monuments continues; and the need for a new public landscape of new boundaries, new roads, new centers, rededicated sites is still not taken seriously.

The question comes up again: who is going to devote time and energy to helping this neglected landscape? If we are at last trying to do something to make our cities more livable, we can thank the sociologists and planners and economists and political scientists who have shown us what was wrong. The problems of this other America are very similar, but they call for a different approach; we are dealing here with a different kind of economy, a different kind of society, and a different kind of environment. It would be encouraging to believe that the environmental designers, particularly the landscape architects, could in time direct this particular war against poverty. There is a long and valuable tradition in landscape architecture of involvement in the total rural/small-city landscape, dating back in this country more than a century to Andrew Jackson Downing, and reinvigorated two generations ago by L. H. Bailey: wilderness, park, and suburb to those men and their followers were little more than specialized fields in the wider province of landscape architecture, and they would have had little patience with the current exclusive enthusiasm for recreation areas. What seems to have happened is that a generation of environmental designers has allowed itself to be persuaded by the Beautificationists and their ample financial resources that the task of preserving Marin County, California, or Westchester County, New York, is somehow worthier of its talents than is the preservation of Madison County, Arkansas, or Cheyenne County, Nebraska.

How long is this illusion likely to last? First of all, until the environmental design professions take one look at Cheyenne County and *see* what ails it. But what is also essential is for every responsible American to add a new social dimension to his definition of landscape beauty. We will have to see that an inhabited landscape is neither beautiful nor sound unless it makes possible an unfolding of the individual in work and social relationships just as much as in health and recreation.

"We are dealing with a problem more complex than billboards and automobile junkyards, utility poles and telephone wires," W. A. Crook declared at the 1965 Texas conference on "Our Environmental Crisis."

"The crisis is one of human worth. Planting hedges around junkyards, banning billboards from roadsides and going underground with telephone lines will have cosmetic effects, but the nation is not just disheveled, it is sick, and it needs medicine as well as cosmetics. . . . Unless the attempts to beautify our physical environment are coordinated with even more serious efforts to meet the gut needs of society, they will prove more detrimental than helpful. They will prevent diagnosis and treatment."

"To Pity the Plumage and Forget the Dying Bird," *Landscape* 17, no. 1 (Autumn 1967): 1–4.

## "Sterile" Restorations Cannot Replace
## a Sense of the Stream of Time

I am aware that much restoration of formal gardens and parks has taken place in this country as well as in Europe. The motives for this are understandable. A formal garden, whether public or private, is by way of being a work of art in the strictest meaning of the term. It is conceived and executed by an artist in accordance with the traditional canons of his art, and its purpose is to give esthetic pleasure. The fact that he may be called a gardener or a landscape architect and that the garden, once completed, is also used as a place for sociability and games does not really change the essential nature of the formal garden as a work of art—an identity further confirmed by its symbolic, cosmological origins. It may or may not be an important specimen of the art. That is for the art—or landscape architecture—historian to decide. No educational or sociological justification has to be given for restoring it, provided the means and talent are at hand.

But whether we are to restore (or preserve) environments originally intended as settings for everyday activities—meant to serve as means to specific ends—is quite a different question. Form and function rarely coincide for very long in any environment, no matter how conscientiously it may be designed. There eventually occurs what the French term a *décalage* (literally, an unwedging)—a kind of disharmony between the two that calls for remedy. Our present tendency is to give priority to function, to use: if a structure or an environment cannot serve a new or modified purpose, then it has to go. The house, too small and too inconvenient, is torn down for a condominium; the farm, taxed too high, becomes a subdivision.

It is this tendency to destroy old forms and old environments that the landscape—and architectural—preservationists are thoroughly justified in resisting.

It is the alternative which they often propose that I find hard to accept: preserve the form, preserve the environment, even if has no discernible function, because *it is part of our history*. It is quite true that much valuable conservation—not necessarily of historically significant environments—is being brought about as a form of recycling: why destroy when a modicum of remodeling can prolong the usefulness of the environment? Yet it is safe to say that many conservation and preservation efforts, especially in small cities and towns, are actually inspired by antiquarian zeal masquerading (in this bicentennial year) as historical conscience. Age is the real criterion: an old building, an old environment, natural or man-made, *must* be saved either because it is unique or because it is typical of thousands of others.

In the United States there are scores of museum villages, museum farms, museum streets and alleys and structures, and as tourism becomes big business, more and more of them come to the surface. That the public enjoys them is beyond dispute. The public also enjoys Disneyland, and for much the same reason: a "period" disguised as American history is dramatized and illustrated in an attractive manner.

And what is wrong with that? Two things: Functional environments, environments which serve as means to an end—the farm, the factory, the dwelling, the park or recreational area—evolve and change, and the usual preserved historical environment, like Sturbridge Village, excludes not only subsequent developments but the remoter past. Whether it is a tastefully restored colonial village or a ghost mining town or a Gay Nineties downtown street, the preserved environment is no more typical of its period than a brand-new subdivision, with three model furnished homes on display, is typical of American life in 1976: all of them are essentially sterile.

My second objection is this: A collection of antiques housed in a restored dwelling with attendants in period costumes is not the best place to learn history—even material history. *Landscape Architecture* very perceptively has asked how we are to graduate from idle tourism to inquiring about how people lived and felt about their contemporary landscapes. The answer, I'm afraid, is the traditional answer: by reading history books, newspapers, novels;

looking at pictures, talking to people about the past, exploring the present-day scene so that dependence on the make-believe is overcome. Certainly, we have been brutally destructive of environments with a past; we must save what is worth saving and worth using. But to keep them alive means to give them a living function; the power which an ancient environment possesses to command our affection and respect derives from its having accepted change of function; its beauty comes from its having been part of the world, not from having been isolated and protected, but from having known various fortunes.

Kevin Lynch, in *What Time Is This Place?*, has written a wise and helpful book which all preservationists and conservationists should read. He ends by saying: "In now concentrating our historical anxieties on a few sacred places, where new construction is taboo, we encounter multiple dilemmas: everyday activities progressively decamp, leaving behind a graveyard of artifacts; tourist volume swells, making it impossible to maintain the site 'the way it was'; what is saved is so self-contained in time as to be only peculiar or quaint. A sense of the stream of time is more valuable and more poignant and engaging than a formal knowledge of remote periods. New things must be created, and others allowed to be forgotten."

Letter to the editor, *Landscape Architecture,* May 1976: 194.

JBJ, photo, "End of City Limits"

## Permissions

Reprinted by permission from *Landscape*:

"The Stranger's Path," vol. 7, #1, Autumn 1957

"The Almost Perfect Town," vol. 2, #1, Spring 1952

"Chihuahua as We Might Have Been," vol. 1, #1, Spring 1951

"The Westward-Moving House," vol. 2, #3, Spring 1953

"Ghosts at the Door," vol. 1, #2, Autumn 1951

"The Domestication of the Garage," vol. 20, #2, Winter 1976

"High Plains," vol. 3, #3, Spring 1954

"From Monument to Place," vol. 17, #2, Winter 1967–68

"Jefferson, Thoreau, and After," vol. 15, #2, Winter 1965–66

"Other-Directed Houses," vol. 6, #2, Winter 1956–57

"The Abstract World of the Hot-Rodder," vol. 7, #2, Winter 1957–58

"An Engineered Environment," vol. 16, #1, Autumn 1966

[H. G. West,] Review of *Built in U.S.A.*, vol. 3, #1, Summer 1953

[Ajax,] "Living Outdoors with Mrs. Panther," vol. 4, #2, Winter 1954–55

"Hail and Farewell," vol. 3, #2, Winter 1953–54

"Southeast to Turkey," excerpt, vol. 7, #3, Spring 1958

[Ajax,] "The Tale of a House," vol. 14, #2, Winter 1964–65

"Human, All Too Human, Geography," vol. 2, #2, Autumn 1952

"A Statement of Policy," vol. 6, #1, Autumn 1956

"10th Anniversary Issue," vol. 10, #1, Autumn 1960

"Expulsion from the Garden," vol. 11, #1, Autumn 1961

"Once More: Man and Nature," vol. 13, #1, Autumn 1963

"Goodbye to Evolution," vol. 13, #2, Winter 1963–64

"The Building Watchers," vol. 15, #3, Spring 1966

"Cities and People," vol. 11, #2, Winter 1961–62

"The Non-environment," vol. 17, #1, Autumn 1967

"Brother Rat," vol. 13, #2, Winter 1963–64

"Fun Planning," vol. 14, #1, Autumn 1964

"Notes and Comments," vol. 7, #2, Winter 1957–58

"The Lure of the West," vol. 4, #1, Summer 1954

"Auto Territoriality," vol. 17, #3, Spring 1968

"To Pity the Plumage and Forget the Dying Bird," vol. 17, #1, Autumn 1967

"Looking at New Mexico." Reprinted by permission from *The Essential Landscape: The New Mexico Photographic Survey with Essays by J. B. Jackson.*

"The Virginia Heritage: Fencing, Farming, and Cattle Raising" and "The Nineteenth-Century Rural Landscape: The Courthouse, the Small College, the Mineral Spring, and the Country Store." Reprinted by permission from *The Southern Landscape Tradition in Texas*, no. 1 in the Anne Burnett Tanday Lectures in American Civilization (Fort Worth: Amon Carter Museum, 1980).

"Expansion" and "Environments." Reprinted by permission from John Brinckerhoff Jackson, *American Space: The Centennial Years, 1865–76* (New York: W. W. Norton & Company, Inc., 1972), pp. 18–30; copyright © 1972, W. W. Norton & Company, Inc.

"The Vernacular City." Reprinted by permission from *Center: A Journal for Architecture in America*, vol. 1, with the express permission of the Center for American Architecture and Design, School of Architecture, University of Texas.

"By Way of Conclusion: How to Study the Landscape." Reprinted by permission from *The Necessity for Ruins and Other Topics* by J. B. Jackson (Amherst: The University of Massachusetts Press, 1980), copyright © 1980 by J. B. Jackson.

Statement in "Whither Architecture? Some Outside Views." Reprinted by permission from *AIA Journal.*

"'Sterile' Restorations Cannot Replace a Sense of the Stream of Time." Reprinted by permission from *Landscape Architecture*, May 1976.

# Notes

## J. B. Jackson and the Discovery of the American Landscape

1. This he ultimately stated in J. B. Jackson, "Forum 1: Landscape Reflects Culture, History," *Centre Daily Times* (State College, Penn.), Oct. 2, 1975.
2. J. B. Jackson, "Human, All Too Human, Geography," *Landscape* 2, no. 2 (Autumn 1952): 5.
3. I am grateful to Doug Adams for copies of some of Jackson's sketches, to Paul Groth for copies of Jackson's photographs.
4. D. W. Meinig gives an informative and sensitive portrait of Jackson in "Reading the Landscape: An Appreciation of W. G. Hoskins and J. B. Jackson," in D. W. Meinig, ed., *The Interpretation of Ordinary Landscapes* (New York, 1979), 210–32.
5. I interviewed Jackson on tape in successive days in January, late May, and early June 1994. Paraphrases of his ideas and quotations that are otherwise uncited come from the transcript of these interviews.
6. J. B. Jackson, "Most Influential Books," *Landscape Journal* 10, no. 2 (Fall 1991): 174.
7. Helaine Kaplan Prentice first pointed this out in her insightful essay "John Brinckerhoff Jackson" in *Landscape Architecture* 81 (November 1981): 743.
8. Harvard University Archives, Cambridge, Mass.
9. 1994 interview.
10. J. B. Jackson, speech to the graduating class in geography, University of California at Berkeley, May 1986, typescript, 4.
11. Brinckerhoff Jackson, "Our Architects Discover Rousseau," *Harvard Advocate* 117, no. 8 (May 1931): 46–57.
12. Brinckerhoff Jackson, "Prussianism or Hitlerism," *American Review* 3 (April–October 1934): 454–71; "A Führer Comes to Liechtenstein," *Harper's Magazine* 170 (February 1935): 298–310; *Saints in Summertime* (New York, 1938).

13. Review by Ralph Thompson, *New York Times,* July 21, 1938.

14. "President's Report, 1935–36," *Official Register of Harvard University* 34, no. 11 (Cambridge, Mass., 1937), 5.

15. Interview transcripts of J. B. Jackson talking with Bob Calo, c. 1988, 149, prepared for the video that Calo produced in 1989, *J. B. Jackson and the Love of Everyday Places* (transcript copy in author's possession). The video captures Jackson's maverick western spirit, in contrast to the more eastern establishment Jackson of the contemporaneous *Figure in a Landscape: A Conversation with J. B. Jackson,* produced by Janet Mendelsohn and Claire Marino. For a discussion of both video portraits, see my review in *Landscape* 30, no. 3 (1990): 44–46.

16. Ernie Pyle, *Brave Men* (New York, 1945), 280–81. I am grateful to Calo, *J. B. Jackson and the Love of Everyday Places,* for this reference.

17. The following discussion is taken from "Landscape as Seen by the Military," in *Discovering the Vernacular Landscape* (New Haven, 1984).

18. J. B. Jackson interviews, 1994. Jackson remembers especially those books that dealt with the natural environment, such as Pierre Deffontaines, *L'Homme et la fôret* (Paris, 1933) and Jules Blache, *L'Homme et la montagne* (Paris, 1934). For a discussion of the Gallimard series, see Anne Buttimer, *Society and Milieu in the French Geographic Tradition* (Chicago, 1971), 89.

19. Interview transcripts of J. B. Jackson talking with Bob Calo, c. 1988, 129.

20. J. B. Jackson, "The Spanish Pueblo Fallacy," *Southwest Review* (Winter 1950): 19–26; "The Pueblo as a Farm," *Southwest Review* (Spring 1950): 107–13.

21. Maurice le Lannou, "The Vocation of Human Geography." This is a translation, presumably by Jackson, of Maurice le Lannou, "La Vocation actuelle de la géographie humaine," *Etudes Rhodaniennes* 4 (1948)): 272–80.

22. J. B. Jackson, "The Need of Being Versed in Country Things," *Landscape* 1, no. 1 (Spring 1951).

23. Paul Groth, "Most Influential Books," in *Landscape Journal* 10, no. 2 (Fall 1991): 180.

24. Interview transcripts of J. B. Jackson talking with Bob Calo, c. 1988, 10; emphasis added.

25. Paul Groth has suggested that he also used the names H. G. West and R. B. R. When questioned in summer 1995, Jackson stated to this author that it was possible, but that he could no longer recall the many names he used. He did agree to the statement that he wrote the entire first two issues of the magazine, and that his brother, Wayne Jackson, was his first outside contributor. This would add to the list of pseudonyms the following: G. A. Feather, P. G. A., P. K., and A. M. A.; and confirm H. G. West.

26. This precise critique is the subject of the section "Taking on the Modern Movement," below.

27. See, for example, P. G. A., review of Frank Waters, *Masked Gods, Landscape* 1, no. 1 (Spring 1951): 25–28; H. G. West, review of Hugh Morrison, *Early American Architecture* and S. Giedion, *A Decade of New Architecture,* Landscape 2, no. 2 (Autumn 1952): 37–39.

28. Interview transcripts of J. B. Jackson talking with Bob Calo, c. 1988, 133–34.

29. In *Saints in Summertime,* Jackson's antihero espouses liberal and leftist views. Jackson took to calling himself a conservative; perhaps Tory-populist is a better designation.

30. Robert Venturi, Denise Scott Brown, and Steven Izenour, *Learning from Las Vegas* (Cambridge, Mass., 1972). A fuller discussion of "Other-Directed Houses" is found in "Taking on the Modern Movement," below.

31. J. B. Jackson, "Places," *Places* 1, no. 2 (1984): 3.

32. J. B. Jackson, "Once More: Man and Nature," *Landscape* 13, no. 1 (Autumn 1963): 1.

33. Paul Groth interview with J. B. Jackson, March 14, 1978. I am grateful to Professor Groth for permission to quote from this interview.

34. J. B. Jackson, unpublished speech to the graduating class in geography, University of California at Berkeley, May 1986, typescript, 6. In "Frameworks for Cultural Landscape Study," Paul Groth has suggested that Michel Foucault ought to be added the list of stimulating influences at Berkeley during this period (Paul Groth and Todd Bressi, eds., *Understanding Ordinary Landscapes* [New Haven, forthcoming]).

35. Marc Treib describes this well in "J. B. Jackson's Home Ground," *Landscape Architecture* 78 (April–May 1988): 52–57.

36. John Brinckerhoff Jackson, *American Space: The Centennial Years* (New York, 1974), 238.

37. In 1972, pointing to a phenomenon perceivable all over the United States, he considered the growing taste for horizontal spaces in countryside and city (J. B. Jackson, "Metamorphosis," *Annals of the Association of American Geographers* 62, no. 2 [1972]: 155–58).

38. Marc Treib, "Most Influential Books," *Landscape Journal* 10, no. 2 (Fall 1991): 176.

39. John Brinckerhoff Jackson, *Discovering the Vernacular Landscape* (New Haven, 1984), xii.

### The Domestication of the Garage

1. David Handlin, "Efficiency and the American Home," *Architectural Association Quarterly* 5, no. 4 (October–December 1973): 50–54.

### The Movable Dwelling and How It Came to America

1. Simone Roux, *La Maison dans l'histoire* (Paris, 1976), 171.

2. Alan Gowans, *Images of American Living* (Philadelphia, 1964), 3ff.

3. Philip Alexander Bruce, *Economic History of Virginia in the Seventeenth Century,* vol. 2 (New York, 1895), 543.

4. Thomas Jefferson, *Notes on the State of Virginia* (London, 1787), 145.

5. Dianne Tebbetts, "Traditional Houses of Independence County, Arkansas," *Pioneer America* 10 (1978).

6. George A. Stokes, "Lumbering and Western Louisana Cultural Landscape."

### Roads Belong in the Landscape

1. Joseph Rykwert, *Adam's House in Paradise* (New York: Museum of Modern Art, 1972).

### Truck City

1. John Bell Rae, *The Road and the Car in American Life* (Cambridge: MIT Press, 1971), 255.

### Taking on the Modern Movement

1. I interviewed Jackson on successive days in January, late May, and early June 1994. Quotations that are otherwise uncited come from the transcript of these taped interviews.

2. Interview with author, June 1, 1994.

3. Brinckerhoff Jackson, "A Führer Comes to Liechtenstein," *Harper's Magazine* 170 (February 1935): 298–310.

4. H. G. W., review of Pál Kelemen, *Baroque and Rococo in Latin America, Landscape* 2, no. 1 (Spring 1952): 31.

5. H. G. W., review of Hugh Morrison, *Early American Architecture* and *A Decade of New Architecture,* ed. S. Giedion, *Landscape* 2, no. 2 (Autumn 1952): 37–39.

6. H. G. West, review of *Built in U.S.A.,* ed. Henry-Russell Hitchcock and Arthur Drexler, *Landscape* 3, no. 1 (Summer 1953): 29–30.

7. This is made explicit in H. G. West, review of Henry Hope Reed, Jr., *The Golden City, Landscape* 8, no. 3 (Spring 1959): 37–38.

8. H. G. West, "A Change in Plans: Is the Modern House a Victorian Invention?" *Landscape* 1, no. 3 (Winter 1952): 18–26.

9. Ajax, "Living Outdoors with Mrs. Panther," *Landscape* 4, no. 2 (Winter 1954–55): 24–25.

10. "Hail and Farewell," *Landscape* 3, no. 2 (Winter 1953–54).

11. The date of "Other-Directed Houses"—1956—should be noted, in light of similar themes in Robert Venturi, Denise Scott Brown, and Steven Izenour, *Learning from Las Vegas* (Cambridge: MIT Press, 1972).

12. P. A. Anson, review of J. Tyrwhitt, J. L. Sert, and E. N. Rogers, eds., *The Heart of the City;* Gerald Breese and Dorothy E. Whiteman, eds., *An Approach to Urban Planning; New World Writing, Landscape* 3, no. 1 (Summer 1953): 30–31. P. A. Anson is obviously a typographical error for the constant contributor P. G. Anson. Because the pseudonym P. G. Anson does not appear until volume 2, no. 3 (Spring 1953), internal evidence makes me certain that Jackson was using the name of an eighteenth-century writer as a pseudonym. In this particular review there are two giveaways: a reference to a piece by another contributor elsewhere in the issue, something known by an editor but normally not by a reviewer; and a correction about the founding date of Harvard, clear in the mind of the editor who had worked for Harvard's tercentenary in 1936.

13. Review of Garrett Eckbo, *Landscape for Living, Landscape* 2, no. 3 (Spring 1953): 34–35.

14. "Southeast to Turkey," *Landscape* 7, no. 3 (Spring 1958): 17–22.

## The Word Itself

1. Kenneth Clark, *Landscape into Painting* (New York, 1950), 140.

2. H. L. Gray, *English Field Systems* (Cambridge, 1915), 19.

## By Way of Conclusion: How to Study the Landscape

1. Thomas Le Duc, "History and Appraisal of U.S. Land Policy to 1862," in *Land Use Policy and Problems in the U.S.,* ed. Howard W. Ottoson (Lincoln, Neb., 1963), 8.

# Bibliography

## J. B. Jackson's Writings on the Landscape

1950

"The Spanish Pueblo Fallacy." *Southwest Review* (Winter 1950): 19–26.

"The Pueblo as a Farm." *Southwest Review* (Spring 1950): 107–13.

1951

*Landscape* 1, no. 1 (Spring 1951)

"The Need of Being Versed in Country Things," 1–5.

"Chihuahua as We Might Have Been," 16–24.

Review of Dorothy L. Pillsbury, *No High Adobe*, 28–29.

*Landscape* 1, no. 2 (Autumn 1951)

"Ghosts at the Door," 3–9.

Review of Ross Calvin, *Lieutenant Emory Reports*, and Kenyon Riddle, *Records and Maps of the Old Santa Fe Trail*, 31–32.

"Notes and Comments," 37–38.

1952

*Landscape* 1, no. 3 (Winter 1952)

"What We Want," editorial, 2–5.

"Many Mansions: Introducing Three Essays on Architecture," 10.

Review of Erna Fergusson, *New Mexico*, 3736.

Review of Henry Madison Kendall, *Introduction to Geography*, 38.

"Notes and Comments," 39–40.

*Landscape* 2, no. 1 (Spring 1952)

"The Almost Perfect Town," 2–8.

Review of F. Stanley, *Socorro,* and *The Las Vegas, New Mexico, Story,* 29–30.

"Notes and Comments," 34–35.

*Landscape* 2, no. 2 (Autumn 1952)

"Notes and Comments," inside front cover.

"Human, All Too Human, Geography," 2–7.

Introduction to "State versus Nature in Soviet Russia" [distillation of Soviet periodical literature and other sources], 14–15; captions, 16–26.

Review of Jacquetta Hawkes, *A Land,* 34–35.

1953

*Landscape* 2, no. 3 (Spring 1953)

"The Westward-Moving House," 8–21.

Review of Garrett Eckbo, *Landscape for Living,* 34–35.

"Notes and Comments," 36.

*Landscape* 3, no. 1 (Summer 1953)

"Notes and Comments: The Unknown Country," 2.

"The Highways," 3.

"Green Deserts," 3–4.

"Comes the Revolution?" 4–5.

Review of E. A. Gutkind, *Our World from the Air,* and George R. Stewart, *U.S. 40,* 28–29.

1954

*Landscape* 3, no. 2 (Winter 1953–54)

"Notes and Comments: Still the Southwest," 2–3.

"Preternature," 3–4.

"Roads to Ruin," 4–5.

"Hail and Farewell," 5–6.

"Pueblo Architecture and Our Own," 20–25.

Review of Christopher Tunnard, *The City of Man,* 28–29.

*Landscape* 3, no. 3 (Spring 1954)

"Notes and Comments: High Plains," 2–3.

"The Unseeing Eye," 3–4.

"Two Street Scenes," 4–5.

"High Plains Country," 11–22.

Review of Charles Dudley Eaves and C. A. Hutchinson, *Post City, Texas,* 29–30.

*Landscape* 4, no. 1 (Summer 1954)

"Notes and Comments: Décalage," 1–2.

"Maps," 2–3.

"The Lure of the West," 3–4.

Review of T. H. Robsjohn-Gibbings, *Homes of the Brave,* 34–35.

1955

"Amerikanische und europäische Landschaft." *Der Aufbau* 10 (1955): 53–59.

*Landscape* 4, no. 2 (Winter 1954–55)

"Notes and Comments: Town and Country," 2–3.

"The Lost Leaders," 3–4.

"Helicodrome," 4.

Review of Robert B. Mitchell and Chester Rapkin, *Urban Traffic: A Function of Land Use,* and Gerald Breese, *Industrial Site Location,* 36–37.

*Landscape* 4, no. 3 (Spring 1955)

"Notes and Comments: Architecture East and West," 2–3.

"Preserving Nature," 3.

"The Other East," 3–4.

"Back to the Desert," 4.

*Landscape* 5, no. 1 (Summer 1955)

"Notes and Comments: Arid Lands," 2–3.

"Conservation," 3.

"Tourism," 3–4.

"Where to Begin," 4.

Review of Lewis Atherton, *Main Street on the Middle Border,* 39–40.

1956

*Landscape* 5, no. 2 (Winter 1955–56)

"Notes and Comments: Out of Africa," 2–3.

"The Choice of Land," 3–4.

"Pedestrian Urbanism," 4.

"The Flying House of America," 4–5.

Review of Robert Moore Fisher, ed., *The Metropolis in Modern Life,* and Christopher Tunnard and Henry Hope Reed, *American Skyline,* 39.

*Landscape* 5, no. 3 (Spring 1956)

"Notes and Comments," 2–3.

Review of Lloyd Rodwin, *The British New Towns Policy,* 38–39.

*Landscape* 6, no. 1 (Autumn 1956)

"Notes and Comments: A Statement of Policy," 2–5.

Review of G. E. Kidder Smith, *Italy Builds,* 38–39.

1957

*Landscape* 6, no. 2 (Winter 1956–57)

"Notes and Comments: Highway Robbery," 2.

"Technics and Technique," 2–3.

"Names on the Land," 3.

"Other-Directed Houses," 29–35.

*Landscape* 6, no. 3 (Spring 1957)

"Notes and Comments: Back to the Land," 2.

Review of M. R. Hodgell, *Contemporary Farmhouses,* and John C. Wooley, *Planning Farm Buildings,* 33–34.

*Landscape* 7, no. 1 (Autumn 1957)

"The Stranger's Path," 11–15.

Review of Poyntz Tyler, ed., *American Highways Today,* 39.

1958

*Landscape* 7, no. 2 (Winter 1957–58)

　　"Notes and Comments," 1.

　　"The Abstract World of the Hot-Rodder," 22–27.

*Landscape* 7, no. 3 (Spring 1958)

　　"Southeast to Turkey," 17–22.

*Landscape* 8, no. 1 (Autumn 1958)

　　"Our Unexplored Surroundings," 26–28.

1959

*Landscape* 8, no. 2 (Winter 1958–59)

　　Review of M. Borissavlievitch, *The Golden Number*, 35.

*Landscape* 8, no. 3 (Spring 1959)

　　[nothing in J. B. Jackson's name]

*Landscape* 9, no. 1 (Autumn 1959)

　　"Notes and Comments," 1–2.

　　"The Imitation of Nature," 9–12.

1960

　　"Nature's Newest Explorers or: The Coming Re-birth of Landscape Architec-
　　　ture." *Landscape Architecture* 50 (1960): 159–63.

*Landscape* 9, no. 2 (Winter 1959–60)

　　"Notes and Comments," 1.

　　"First Comes the House," 26–32.

　　Review of Walter Kohler and Wassili Luckhardt, *Lighting in Architecture*, 37–38.

*Landscape* 9, no. 3 (Spring 1960)

　　"Notes and Comments: ASLA," 1–2.

　　Review of Earle Schultz and Walter Simmons, *Offices in the Sky*, 39–40.

*Landscape* 10, no. 1 (Fall 1960)

　　"Notes and Comments," 1–2.

　　"The Four Corners Country," 20–26.

1961

　　"Precarious Balance," letter to the editor. *Landscape Architecture* 51 (1961): 182.

*Landscape* 10, no. 2 (Winter 1960–61)

　　Review of Eric Sloane, *Return to Taos*, 15.

*Landscape* 10, no. 3 (Spring 1961)

　　"Essential Architecture," 27–30.

　　Review of Verna Cook Shipway and Warren Shipway, *The Mexican House, Old
　　　and New;* Pauline Arnold and Percival White, *Homes;* and George Ordish,
　　　*The Living House*, 34–35.

*Landscape* 11, no. 1 (Fall 1961)

　　"Notes and Comments: Expulsion from the Garden," 1–2.

　　　"Food and Drink," 2–3.

　　　"Images of the City," 3–4.

1962

"The Purpose of the City." *Journal of the American Institute of Architects,*
November 1962: 99–101.

*Landscape Autoguide, Tour I: From Santa Fe to Taos by Way of the Rio Grande
Valley; from Taos to Santa Fe by Way of the Mountain Villages.* Landscape
Magazine, 1962; rev. ed., 1963.

*Landscape* 11, no. 2 (Winter 1961–62)

"Notes and Comments: Cities and People," 1.

"Half a Million Landscape Architects," 1–2.

"Explosion into the Green," 2–3.

*Landscape* 11, no. 3 (Spring 1962)

"Notes and Comments: Traveling Man," 1.

"Roadscape," 1.

"To Be a Pilgrim," 1–2.

"Conquest of the Pole," 2.

"We Are Taken for a Ride," 20–22.

*Landscape* 12, no. 1 (Autumn 1962)

"Notes and Comments: The Hazards of Uglitudinizing," 1–2.

1963

*Landscape Autoguide, Tour II: From Santa Fe to Pojoaque, San Ildefonso,
Espanola, Chamita, San Gabriel, Lyden, Alcalde, San Juan, Santa Cruz, and
Return.* Landscape Magazine, 1963.

*Landscape Autoguide, Tour III: Santa Fe to Pecos and Villanueva.* Landscape
Magazine, 1963.

*Landscape* 12, no. 2 (Winter 1962–63)

"Notes and Comments: Pretty Cities?" 1–2.

*Landscape* 12, no. 3 (Spring 1963)

"Notes and Comments: A Clutch of Gardens," 1–2.

"Cumbernauld: The Newest New Town," 17–19.

*Landscape* 13, no. 1 (Autumn 1963)

"Notes and Comments: Once More: Man and Nature," 1–3.

1964

"'The Meanings of Landscape.'" *Kulturgeografi* 16 (1964): 47–50.

*Landscape* 13, no. 2 (Winter 1963–64)

"Notes and Comments: Goodbye to Evolution," 1–2.

"Brother Rat," 2–3.

*Landscape* 13, no. 3 (Spring 1964)

"Notes and Comments: Spring: Silent or Raucous?" 1.

"In Praise of Anarchy: Urban Department," 1.

"The Pedestrian Loses a Friend," 2.

*Landscape* 14, no. 1 (Autumn 1964)

"Notes and Comments: Sorcerer's Apprenticeship," 1.

"Fun Planning," 1–3.

"Limited Access," 18–23.

1964

*Landscape* 14, no. 1

Review of Bainbridge Bunting, *Taos Adobes*, 38.

1965

*Landscape* 14, no. 2 (Winter 1964–65)

"Notes and Comments: Signs of Life," 1.

"Cities of the Plain," 1–2.

"Catherine Bauer Wurster," 2.

*Landscape* 14, no. 3 (Spring 1965)

"Notes and Comments: The Message on Natural Beauty," 1.

Review of Ian Nairn, *The American Landscape,* 35.

*Landscape* 15, no. 1 (Autumn 1965)

"Notes and Comments: Pop America," 1.

"The Heavenly Twins," 1.

1966

"Ninety-year Wonder: It Rarely Broke the Human Barrier." *Landscape Architecture* 57 (1966): 38–39.

"The Meanings of Recreation." *Landmark '66,* 5–7.

"The Purpose of the City: Changing City Landscapes as Manifestations of Cultural Values." In Marcus Whiffen, ed., *The Architect and the City.* Cambridge: MIT Press, 1966, 13–36.

*Landscape* 15, no. 2 (Winter 1965–66)

"Notes and Comments: Ah Wilderness," 1.

"The Highway as a Road," 1.

"Ethics or Esthetics," 1–2.

"Jefferson, Thoreau, and After," 25–27.

*Landscape* 15, no. 3 (Spring 1966)

"Notes and Comments: Voyage to the Interior," 1.

"Environmental Perception," 1.

"Design for Depravity," 1.

"The Onward March of Beautification," 1–2.

*Landscape* 16, no. 1 (Autumn 1966)

"Notes and Comments: Cars and Customers," 1.

"Artur Glikson," 1.

"Eternal Cities," 1–2.

"The Building Watchers," 2.

"An Engineered Environment," 16–20.

Review of Dorothy Jacobs, *A Witch's Guide to Gardening,* 35.

1967

"The American Landscape Seen in Passing: Limited Access." *Northwest Architect* 31 (1967): 36–37, 65–67.

*Landscape* 16, no. 2 (Winter 1966–67)

"Notes and Comments: Technotopia, Anthropotopia, and What Comes After," 1–2.

*Landscape* 16, no. 3 (Spring 1967)

"Notes and Comments: Where the Action Is, Is Where the Contemplation Was," 1.

"Garden History," 1.

*Landscape* 17, no. 1 (Autumn 1967)

"Notes and Comments: The Nonenvironment," 1.

"To Pity the Plumage and Forget the Dying Bird," 1–4.

Review of Historic Santa Fe Commission, *Historic Santa Fe,* 39.

1968

*Landscape* 17, no. 2 (Winter 1967–68)

"Notes and Comments: Shared Environments," 1.

"Pretensions and Delusions," 1–3.

"From Monument to Place," 22–26.

*Landscape* 17, no. 3 (Spring 1968)

"Notes and Comments: Life-Worship," 1.

"Auto Territoriality," 1–2.

Review of Roderick Nash, *Wilderness and the American Mind,* 31–32.

1969

"Ghosts at the Door." *The Subversive Science.* Edited by Paul Shepard and Daniel McKinley. Boston: Houghton Mifflin: 1969. Pp. 158–68.

*Landscape* 18, no. 1 (Winter 1969)

"1951–1968: Postscript," 1.

"A New Kind of Space," 33–35.

1970

*Landscapes: Selected Writings of J. B. Jackson.* Edited by Ervin H. Zube. Amherst: University of Massachusetts Press, 1970.

"Jefferson, Thoreau, and After"

"The Westward-Moving House"

"Several American Landscapes"

"Other-Directed Houses"

"Life-Worship"

"The Imitation of Nature"

"Images of the City"

"The Stranger's Path"

"Two Street Scenes"

"The Many Guises of Suburbia"

"The Almost Perfect Town"

"To Pity the Plumage and Forget the Dying Bird"

"The Social Landscape"

"The Public Landscape"

"Several American Landscapes"

1972

"Metamorphosis." *Annals of the Association of American Geographers* 62, no. 2 (1972): 155–58.

*American Space: The Centennial Years.* New York: W. W. Norton, 1972.

1975

"Forum 1: Landscape Reflects Culture, History." *The Centre Daily Times* (State College, Penn.), Oct. 2, 1975; "Forum 1: Grid System Provided Privacy, Order," Oct. 9, 1975; "Landscape of Work Changes in U.S.," Oct. 16, 1975; "Technology Affects Individual, Land," Oct. 23, 1975.

"The Historic American Landscape." In Ervin H. Zube et al., eds., *Landscape Assessment: Values, Perceptions, and Resources.* Stroudsburg, Pa.: Dowden, Hutchinson, and Ross, 1975. Pp. 4–9.

1976

"'Sterile' Restorations Cannot Replace a Sense of the Stream of Time," letter to the editor. *Landscape Architecture* 66 (1976): 194.

*Landscape* 20, no. 2 (Winter 1976)

"The Domestication of the Garage," 10–19.

"Prologue." *Journal of Architectural Education* 30, no. 1 (September 1976): inside cover, 1–2. J. B. Jackson, guest editor.

"The Landscape Appearance." *Monadnock* 50 (1976): 12–17.

1977

"Craftsman Style and Technostyle." *Via 3* (1977): 56–63.

*Changing Rural Landscapes.* Edited by Ervin H. Zube. Amherst: University of Massachusetts Press, 1977.

"Back to the Land"

"The New American Countryside: An Engineered Environment"

"Ghosts at the Door"

"Spring: Silent or Raucous?"

"A New Kind of Space"

"The Four Corners Country"

"Cities of the Plain"

"The Abstract World of the Hot-Rodder"

1979

"The Public Park Needs Reappraisal." In *Urban Open Spaces.* New York: Cooper-Hewitt Museum, Smithsonian Institution, 1979. P. 15

"The Order of a Landscape: Reason and Religion in Newtonian America." In D. W. Meinig, ed., *The Interpretation of Ordinary Landscapes.* New York: Oxford University Press, 1979. Pp. 153–63.

*Landscape* 23, no. 1 (1979)

"Landscape as Theater," 3–7.

1980

*The Necessity for Ruins and Other Topics.* Amherst: University of Massachusetts Press, 1980.

"Learning about Landscapes"

"Nearer than Eden"

"Gardens to Decipher and Gardens to Admire"

"The Discovery of the Street"

"Landscape as Theater"

"The Sacred Grove in America"

"The Necessity for Ruins"

"The Domestication of the Garage"

"By Way of Conclusion: How to Study the Landscape"

*The Southern Landscape Tradition in Texas.* Fort Worth: Amon Carter Museum, 1980.

"The Virginia Heritage: Fencing, Farming, and Cattle Raising"

"The Nineteenth-Century Rural Landscape: The Courthouse, the Small College, the Mineral Springs, and the Country Store"

"The Sunbelt City: The Modern City, the Strip, and the Civic Center"

1982

"The Dwelling as Chattel." *New Mexico Studies in the Fine Arts* 7 (1982): 5–9.

Statement in "Whither Architecture? Some Outside Views." *Journal of the American Institute of Architects* 71 (Mid-May 1982): 205–6.

"New Fields." *Arts and Architecture* 1, no. 4 (December 1982): 27–29.

1983

"Country Town." In Robert Craycroft and Michael Fazio, eds., *Change and Tradition in the Small Country Town.* Jackson: University of Mississippi Press, 1983, 17–30.

1984

"New Mexico Houses." *MASS* 2 (Summer 1984): 2–5.

"The American Public Space." *Public Interest* 74 (Winter 1984): 52–65.

"Places." *Places* 1, no. 2 (1984): 3–6.

*Discovering the Vernacular Landscape.* New Haven: Yale University Press, 1984.

"The Word Itself"

"A Pair of Ideal Landscapes"

"A Puritan Looks at Scenery"

"Agrophilia, or the Love of Horizontal Spaces"

"Country Towns for a New Part of the Country"

"Vernacular"

"The Movable Dwelling and How It Came to America"

"Stone and Its Substitutes"

"Craftsman Style and Technostyle"

"The Origin of Parks"

"Landscape as Seen by the Military"

"A Vision of New Fields"

"Concluding with Landscapes"

1985

"Urban Circumstances." *Design Quarterly* 128 (1985): entire issue.

"The Vernacular City." *Center* 1 (1985): 27–43.

"Vernacular Space." *Texas Architect* 35, no. 2 (March–April 1985): 58–61.

*The Essential Landscape: The New Mexico Photographic Survey, with Essays by J. B. Jackson.* Edited by Steven A. Yates. Albuquerque: University of New Mexico Press, 1985.

"Looking at New Mexico"

"First Comes the House"

"Pueblo Dwellings and Our Own"

"High Plains Country"

"The Social Landscape,"

"Two Street Scenes"

"Goodbye to Evolution"

"Chihuahua as We Might Have Been"

"Landscape as Theater"

1986

"The Vernacular Landscape" and discussion. In Edmund C. Penning-Rowsell and David Lowenthal, eds., *Landscape Meanings and Values.* London: Allen and Unwin, 1986. Pp. 65–77; discussion, 77–81.

"Fields of Play: Sport and Public Spaces." *Cite; A Publication of the Rice Design Alliance* (Fall 1986): 16.

"Vernacular" and "Introduction." In David G. De Long, Helen Searing, and Robert A. M. Stern, eds., *American Architecture: Innovation and Tradition.* New York: Rizzoli, 1986. Pp. 141–51, 155–57.

"A Sense of Place, a Sense of Time." In *Oz* [College of Architecture and Design, Kansas State University] 8 (1986): 6–9.

"Addressing the American City: Four Interviews: John B. Jackson, Jerzy Soltan, Denise Scott Brown, Francesca Dal Co." In *Crit* 17 (1986): 4–8.

1987

"After Olmsted." *MASS* 5 (Fall 1987): 2–4.

"The Popular Yard." *Places* 4, no. 3 (1987): 26–32.

1988

"The Accessible Landscape." *Whole Earth Review* 58 (March 8, 1988): 4–9.

"Images of the New Mexico Plaza." *El Palacio* 94 (Winter 1988): 2733.

Review of Edward Relph, *The Modern Urban Landscape: 1880 to the Present, Triglyph* 7 (Winter 1988–89): 3736.

1990

"The Future of the Vernacular Landscape." In Paul Groth, ed., *Vision, Culture, and Landscape.* Department of Landscape Architecture, University of California, Berkeley, 1990, 27–39.

"Of Houses and Highways." *Aperture* 120 (Late Summer 1990): 64–71.

"The House in the Vernacular Landscape." In Michael P. Conzen, ed., *The Making of the American Landscape.* New York: HarperCollins Academic, 1990, 355–69.

1991

"Our Towns: The Struggle to Survive." *New Mexico* 69, no. 2 (February 1991): 343.

"The Past and Future Park." In Stuart Wrede and William Howard Adams, eds., *Denatured Visions: Landscape and Culture in the Twentieth Century.* New York: Museum of Modern Art, 1991. Pp. 129–34.

"Afterword." In *Terra Incognita: The Recent Sculpture of Charles Fahlen.* Philadelphia: Institute of Contemporary Art, 1991. Pp. 39–43.

"Anthrophobia, Or the Death of Landscape." *Modulus* 20 (1991): 109–16.

"The Vernacular Landscape is on the Move . . . Again." *Places* 7, no. 3 (1991): 24–35.

1992

"Sulla strada: In auto o a piedi." *Casabella* 56, nos. 86–87 ( January–February 1992): 14–21, 115–16.

"Cultures and Regionalism." *MASS* 9 (Spring 1992): 12–13.

"Working at Home." *Cite: The Architecture and Design Review of Houston* 28 (Spring 1992): 13–15.

"The Timing of Towns." *Architecture California* 14, no. 2 (November 1992): 4–8.

"Foreword: Joe Deal and the Vernacular." *Joe Deal: Southern California Photographs, 1976–86.* Albuquerque: University of New Mexico Press, 1992. Pp. 3–7.

1994

*A Sense of Place, a Sense of Time.* New Haven: Yale University Press, 1994.

"The Accessible Landscape"

"Seeing New Mexico"

"Pueblo Dwellings and Our Own"

"Church or Plaza?"

"The Mobile Home on the Range"

"Beyond Wilderness"

"In Favor of Trees"

"The Past and Future Park"

"Vernacular Gardens"

"Working at Home"

"A Sense of Place, a Sense of Time"

"Looking into Automobiles"

"Truck City"

"Roads Belong in the Landscape"

1995

"In Search of the Proto-Landscape." In George F. Thompson, ed., *Landscape in America.* Austin: University of Texas Press, 1995. Pp. 43–50.

"The Past and Future Park. *Landscape Architecture* 85 (1995): 22–23.

"Cultures and Regionalism." *Designer/Builder* 3 (July 1996): 4–5.

"Der we als verbinding met het landschap: van het beslotene naar het openbare." *Architect* 27, no. 2 (1996): 31–35.

"Discovering the Vernacular Landscape." In *Human Geography: An Essential Anthology.* Edited by John Agnew et al. Cambridge: Blackwell, 1996. Pp. 316–28.

### Pseudonymous or Unsigned Articles in Landscape, Probably by J. B. Jackson

1951

*Landscape* 1, no. 1 (Spring 1951)

A. W. Conway, "Southwestern Colonial Farms," 6–9.

G. A. Feather, "Desert Harvest," 10–15.

P. G. A., review of Frank Waters, *Masked Gods*, 25–28.

A. W. C., review of Trent E. Sanford, *The Architecture of the Southwest*, 29–31.

Review of Albert N. Williams, *The Water and the Power*, and Bernard Frank and Anthony Netboy, *Water, Land, and People*, 31–35.

"Tourism," 36–40.

*Landscape* 1, no. 2 (Autumn 1951)

"Southwestern Landscapes as Seen from the Air," 10–19.

A. W. Conway, "A Northern New Mexico House-Type," 20–21.

Ajax, "Storm Brewing," 22–23.

H. G. West, "The House Is a Compass," 24–27.

P. K., review of Kenneth Clark, *Landscape Painting*, and Christopher Tunnard, *Gardens in the Modern Landscape*, 28–31.

P. G. A., review of Laura Thompson, *Culture in Crisis*, 32–35.

A. M. A., review of Marion Clawson, *Western Range Livestock Industry*, 35–36.

1952

*Landscape* 1, no. 3 (Winter 1952)

H. G. West, "A Change in Plans: Is the Modern House a Victorian Invention?" 18–26.

"A Catalog of New Mexico Farm-Building Terms," 31–32.

Ajax, "Tyger, Tyger, Burning Bright," 33–34.

P. G. A., review of Frank C. Hibben, *Treasure in the Dust*, 36–37.

R. R. F., review of B. A. Botkin, *A Treasure of Western Folklore*, 37.

P. G. A., review of Edwin Corle, *The Gila*, 37.

A. M. A., review of William A. Keleher, *Turmoil in New Mexico*, 37–38.

*Landscape* 2, no. 1 (Spring 1952)

A. W. C., "Village Types in the Southwest," 14–19.

Ajax, "A Golden Treasury of Western Prose and Song," 25–28.

H. G. W., review of Pál Kelemen, *Baroque and Rococo in Latin America*, 31.

*Landscape* 2, no. 2 (Autumn 1952)

H. G. West, review of Hugh Morrison, *Early American Architecture*, and S. Giedion, *A Decade of New Architecture*, 37–39.

A. W. Conway, review of S. E. Rasmussen, *Towns and Buildings*, 39.

1953

*Landscape* 2, no. 3 (Spring 1953)

>   Ajax, "Lepidoptera; or, The Changing World of Walter Curtis," 29–30.

>   H. G. West, review of Joseph Leach, *The Typical Texan,* 31–32.

>   P. A. Anson, review of Josué de Castro, *The Geography of Hunger,* 33–34.

*Landscape* 3, no. 1 (Summer 1953)

>   H. G. West, review of *Built in U.S.A.,* ed. Henry-Russell Hitchcock and
>   Arthur Drexler, 29–30.

>   P. A. Anson, review of *The Heart of the City,* ed. J. Tyrwhitt, J. L. Sert, and E.
>   N. Rogers; *An Approach to Urban Planning,* ed. Gerald Breese and Dorothy
>   E. Whiteman; and *New World Writing,* 30–31.

>   G. A. Feather, review of Alice Marriott, *Hell on Horses and Women,* 32.

1954

*Landscape* 3, no. 2 (Winter 1953–54)

>   P. A. Anson, review of George H. T. Kimble, *The Way of the World,* 29–31.

*Landscape* 3, no. 3 (Spring 1954)

>   Ajax, "Living Outdoors with Mrs. Panther," 24–25.

>   P. G. Anson, review of *New Mexico: A Guide to the Colorful State,* 30–31.

*Landscape* 4, no. 2 (Winter 1954–55)

>   H. G. West, "And Another Point of View . . . ," 20–24.

1955

*Landscape* 4, no. 3 (Spring 1955)

>   P. G. Anson, review of *City Planning at Yale: A Selection of Papers and Projects*
>   and *Urban Land Problems and Policies,* 40.

1956

*Landscape* 5, no. 2 (Winter 1955–56)

>   P. A. Anson, review of Virginia Madison, *The Big Bend Country,* 40.

*Landscape* 6, no. 1 (Autumn 1956)

>   P. G. Anson, review of David Dodge, *The Poor Man's Guide to Europe,* Richard
>   Joseph, *Richard Joseph's Guide to Europe and the Mediterranean,* Temple
>   Fielding, *Fielding's Travel Guide to Europe,* and *Greece* (Guides Bleus
>   Series), 39–40.

1957

*Landscape* 6, no. 2 (Winter 1956–57)

>   C. W. C., review of Olga Wright Smith, *Gold on the Desert,* 40.

*Landscape* 6, no. 3 (Spring 1957)

>   P. G. Anson, review of Harvey S. Olson, *Aboard and Abroad,* 39–40.

1958

*Landscape* 7, no. 2 (Winter 1957–58)

>   P. G. Anson, review of George R. Stewart, *N. A. I. Looking North, N. A. I.
>   Looking South,* 28–29.

>   P. G. Anson, review of *Autoguide: Switzerland* (Baedeker), 29.

1959

*Landscape* 8, no. 3 (Spring 1959)

   H. G. West, review of Henry Hope Reed, Jr., *The Golden City,* 37–38.

1960

*Landscape* 9, no. 2 (Winter 1959–60)

   "Brief Notice," 40.

*Landscape* 10, no. 1 (Fall 1960)

   P. G. Anson, review of Ernest R. Bartley and Frederick H. Bair, Jr., *Mobile Home Parks and Comprehensive Community Planning,* 25.

1961

*Landscape* 10, no. 2 (Winter 1960–61)

   "Briefly Noted," 39–40.

*Landscape* 11, no. 1 (Fall 1961)

   "The Many Guises of Suburbia," 22.

1962

*Landscape* 11, no. 2 (Winter 1961–62)

   P. G. Anson, "Rocks and Gardens," 3–4.

   "California Plans," 29–30.

*Landscape* 11, no. 3 (Spring 1962)

   J. V. Pellegrini, "Karl Baedeker in America," 3–5.

   "Design for Travel," 6–8.

   P. G. Anson, review of Eleanor B. Pierce, *Living Abroad,* 36.

*Landscape* 12, no. 1 (Autumn 1962)

   "New Farms, New Villages," 7–8.

   K. F. B., "Green Companions," 11–12.

   "A Woodland Heritage," 12.

   B. E. F., "Braziliana," 24–26.

   "Wild Blue Yonder," 29–30.

   Review of Paulhans Peters, *Atriumhaeuser,* 45–46.

1963

*Landscape* 12, no. 2 (Winter 1962–63)

   "Aspects of the City," 14.

   P. G. Anson, "Architecture without Architects," 18.

   B. E. F., "Highways as Scenery," 23–24.

   "Wind in the Trees," 27.

   "Hydrorama," 32.

*Landscape* 12, no. 3 (Spring 1963)

   "The Planned Campus," 13.

   "New Towns in Germany," 16.

   "Refresher Course," 27.

   J. V. P., "Planning Bibliographies," 35.

*Landscape* 13, no. 1 (Autumn 1963)

   "Conservation as Others See It," 3–4.

   "Uncertain Architects," 9.

"Tourism: More Give and Less Take," 27–28.

H. G. West, "Slicks and Pulps," 31–32.

1964

*Landscape* 13, no. 2 (Winter 1963–64)

"Geopathogenesis," 3–4.

"Highway Notes," 22.

B. E. F., "The Sign of Aquarius," 23–25.

*Landscape* 13, no. 3 (Spring 1964)

"The Suburban Forest," 2–3.

*Landscape* 14, no. 1 (Autumn 1964)

"Changes in the Farm Landscape," 3.

1965

*Landscape* 14, no. 2 (Winter 1964–65)

"Changes in the English Landscape," 3.

Ajax, "The Tale of a House," 21–24.

"Factory Farms," 25–27.

*Landscape* 14, no. 3 (Spring 1965)

"All about Highways," 22.

*Landscape* 15, no. 1 (Autumn 1965)

"Brief Mention," 43–44.

1966

*Landscape* 15, no. 2 (Winter 1965–66)

"The Operators," 12.

*Landscape* 15, no. 3 (Spring 1966)

"Highway Landscapes," 2.

"The Natural Landscape," 13.

*Landscape* 16, no. 1 (Autumn 1966)

"The Evolving Forest," 2.

"The Evolving Industrial Landscape," 7.

"The Evolving Strip," 14.

"Design and Behavior," 15.

1967

*Landscape* 16, no. 2 (Winter 1966–67)

"The Evolving Tourist Landscape," 2.

"The Evolving Strip," 11.

"The Evolving Highway," 14.

"The Evolving Forest," 25.

"Books on Building," 39–40.

*Landscape* 16, no. 3 (Spring 1967)

"The Evolving Strip," 2.

C. R. J., "Good Weather: Not a Privilege but a Right!" 17.

"The Evolving Highway," 24.

*Landscape* 17, no. 1 (Autumn 1967)
    "Evolving Landscapes," 5–7.
*Landscape* 17, no. 2 (Winter 1967–68)
    "Evolving Landscapes," 4–9.
*Landscape* 17, no. 3 (Spring 1968)
    "Evolving Landscapes," 17.
    "The Evolving Highway," 21.

### Selected Published Articles on J. B. Jackson

Bowden, Martyn J. "J. B. Jackson: A Foreword." *Monadnock* 50 (1976): 9–11.

Dean, Andrea Oppenheimer. "Riding in the Future." *Landscape Architecture* 86 (1996): 58–63.

Horowitz, Helen Lefkowitz. Essay review of the videos *J. B. Jackson and the Love of Everyday Places,* produced by Bob Calo, and *Figure in a Landscape: A Conversation with J. B. Jackson,* produced by Janet Mendelsohn and Claire Marino. *Landscape* 30, no. 3 (1990): 44–46.

Meinig, D. W. "Reading the Landscape: An Appreciation of W. G. Hoskins and J. B. Jackson." In D. W. Meinig, ed., *The Interpretation of Ordinary Landscapes.* New York: Oxford University Press, 1979, 210–32.

"Most Influential Books." *Landscape Journal* 10, no. 2 (Fall 1991): 173–86.

Prentice, Helaine Kaplan. "John Brinckerhoff Jackson." *Landscape Architecture* 71 (1981: 740–46.

Treib, Marc. "J. B. Jackson's Home Ground." *Landscape Architecture* 78 (1988: 52–57.

Zelinsky, Wilbur. "Essays by Jackson." *Landscape* 24, no. 3 (1980): 32–33.

Emblematic figure, man with a plow

# Index